SEEKING THE BOMB

Princeton Studies in International History and Politics

G. John Ikenberry, Marc Trachtenberg, William C. Wohlforth, and Keren Yarhi-Milo, Series Editors

For a full list of titles in the series, go to https://press.princeton.edu/series/princeton-studies-in-international-history-and-politics

Seeking the Bomb: Strategies of Nuclear Proliferation, Vipin Narang

The Spectre of War: International Communism and the Origins of World War II, Jonathan Haslam

Active Defense: China's Military Strategy since 1949, M. Taylor Fravel

Strategic Instincts: The Adaptive Advantages of Cognitive Biases in International Politics, Dominic D. P. Johnson

Divided Armies: Inequality and Battlefield Performance in Modern War, Jason Lyall

After Victory: Institutions, Strategic Restraint, and the Rebuilding of Order after Major Wars, New Edition, G. John Ikenberry

Cult of the Irrelevant: The Waning Influence of Social Science on National Security, Michael C. Desch

Secret Wars: Covert Conflict in International Politics, Austin Carson

Who Fights for Reputation: The Psychology of Leaders in International Conflict, Keren Yarhi-Milo

Aftershocks: Great Powers and Domestic Reforms in the Twentieth Century, Seva Gunitsky

Why Wilson Matters: The Origin of American Liberal Internationalism and Its Crisis Today, Tony Smith

Powerplay: The Origins of the American Alliance System in Asia, Victor D. Cha

Economic Interdependence and War, Dale C. Copeland

Knowing the Adversary: Leaders, Intelligence, and Assessment of Intentions in International Relations, Keren Yarhi-Milo

Seeking the Bomb

Strategies of Nuclear Proliferation

Vipin Narang

PRINCETON UNIVERSITY PRESS
PRINCETON AND OXFORD

Published by Princeton University Press
41 William Street, Princeton, New Jersey 08540
6 Oxford Street, Woodstock, Oxfordshire OX20 1TR

press.princeton.edu

ISBN 978-0-691- 17261-3
ISBN (pbk.) 978-0-691-17262-0
ISBN (e-book) 978-0-691-22306-3

British Library Cataloging-in-Publication Data is available

Editorial: Bridget Flannery-McCoy and Alena Chekanov
Production Editorial: Jenny Wolkowicki
Cover design: Lauren Smith
Production: Erin Suydam
Publicity: Kate Hensley and Kathryn Stevens

Cover image by Mike Wagnon. Courtesy of Eleanor Hansen

This book has been composed in Adobe Text Pro and Gotham

10 9 8 7 6 5 4 3 2 1

CONTENTS

ILLUSTRATIONS

Figures

Tables

ACKNOWLEDGMENTS

The germ for this book was planted when I was an undergraduate chemical engineer at Stanford who was broadly interested in international security affairs, and it was, perhaps fittingly, completed amid a full-blown global pandemic. In my first year of college, India and Pakistan tested nuclear weapons. As I was leaving the Bay Area several years later, the United States was preparing to invade Iraq, in part due to suspicions of a clandestine nuclear weapons program. Nuclear weapons proliferation is largely what drove me to switch careers and devote my life to studying international security, with the incredible encouragement of my two most supportive gurus at Stanford: Scott Sagan and Taylor Fravel. Scott took a chance on this curious chemical engineer and invited me into the CISAC family, which is the real Hotel California: even when you check out, you never really leave. Scott has been a source of unwavering support over almost two decades who not only has been an incredible guide and friend but has served as a role model in how to do first-rate scholarship, how to be a supportive (and sometimes necessarily tough) mentor, and how to do it with unimpeachable integrity. I can never repay Scott for all that he has done for me; I can only hope that I can pay a fraction of it forward to my own students. Taylor and I reunited at MIT after I finished my doctorate and is my partner in crime at the Security Studies Program. We have battled travel systems, fundraising, classes, administrative bureaucracy, bulk wine orders, and life together. There is no one with whom I would rather be in the trenches fighting this fight. No two people are more responsible for this book than Scott and Taylor. You can blame them. Those that wanted me to go to medical school still do.

Along the way, Yuen Foong Khong, Stephen Rosen, and Iain Johnston encouraged me to not abandon my passion for nuclear security when pretty much everyone around me was telling me it was a dying field. Steve indelibly left a line in my head that I have never forgotten: so long as nuclear weapons continue to exist, we need people to study them.

Although my first book was about strategies of nuclear deterrence, this book returns to my roots and focuses on strategies of nuclear proliferation. When I got into this business, the bulk of the literature on nuclear proliferation focused on why states such as India, Pakistan, and Iraq might want to seek nuclear weapons. By the time I finished my first book, I was struck that no one had yet asked *how* these states went about pursuing nuclear weapons and why those choices mattered. Why did India take a quarter century to decide to finally weaponize its nuclear deterrent? How did Pakistan escape American pressure to terminate its nuclear program? And of course, Iraq's (failed) clandestine pursuit of nuclear weapons in the 1980s set the stage for a seismic reordering of Middle East politics in 2003. This is a book about the various ways in which states seek nuclear weapons, why those choices are important, and how they may be managed or stopped. Many people helped along the way, and I apologize if I have inadvertently forgotten anyone.

MIT's Department of Political Science and Security Studies Program have been the ideal intellectual home for my academic career, and this book. In addition to Taylor, Dick Samuels, Roger Petersen, Steve Van Evera, and Owen Cote have been exceptionally supportive mentors and colleagues in this business. They keep me honest and push me to be a better, and smarter, scholar, though I often fall short. A special thanks to Barry Posen, who, as a leader and a role model, has done more to inspire me to want to be precise in my language, rigorous in my thinking, and honest to the data than anyone—because he expects nothing less from himself, his colleagues, and students. Frank Gavin was part of our merry band for too short a time but left an indelible mark on me and our program, pushing me to try to be fearless in challenging conventional wisdoms. Melissa Nobles, David Singer, and Andrea Campbell have provided invaluable support, and served as fantastic leaders, in the political science department. And I am especially indebted to Lynne Levine, Maria DiMauro, and Janine Sazinsky for helping me keep the trains running on time. Also, a special thanks to MIT itself, which managed the pandemic as well as can be imagined, including prioritizing reopening the campus daycare full time—with its incredible teachers and staff, without whom I would not have been able to complete this book.

My MIT PhD students have been, and will forever remain, my pride and joy. Not only am I proud of each of their own scholarly and policy achievements, but many have helped me immeasurably on this book as research assistants: Mark Bell, Nicholas Blanchette, Christopher Clary, Fiona Cunningham, Suzanne Freeman, Mayumi Fukushima, Jason Kwon, Sameer Lalwani, Nicholas Miller, Aidan Milliff, Cullen Nutt, Reid Pauly, Rachel Tecott, and Raymond Wang. It became apparent to me exceptionally early in my career that my students are far smarter than I am, and they have made me a better teacher, advisor, and scholar, and many have helped make this book stronger as a result.

Many colleagues and friends around the world have provided feedback on various parts of this manuscript and in general have been tremendous sources of support. I am grateful to James Acton, Amit Ahuja, Gary Bass, Målfrid Braut-Hegghammer, Jonathan Caverley, Toby Dalton, Alex Debs, Jennifer Erickson, Ryan Evans, Matt Fuhrmann, Charlie Glaser, Avery Goldstein, Sheena Chestnut Greitens, Mike Horowitz, Robert Jervis, Shashank Joshi, Colin Kahl, Devesh Kapur, Josh Kertzer, Ulrich Kuhn, Jeffrey Lewis, Julia MacDonald, Tanvi Madan, Rose McDermott, Steve Miller, Rohan Mukherjee, Ankit Panda, George Perkovich, Joshua Pollack, Srinath Raghavan, Jonathan Renshon, Elizabeth Saunders, Todd Sechser, Ashley Tellis, Milan Vaishnav, Jane Vaynman, Tristan Volpe, and Amy Zegart. I want to especially thank Paul Staniland and Caitlin Talmadge, who have endured and tolerated me for almost two decades and have helped me through the business, this book, and life more than they know.

I have benefited from extensive feedback at various colloquia and seminars over the years. I thank participants of these seminars at Brown University, Columbia University, Dartmouth College's Dickey Center, Harvard Kennedy School's Belfer Center, Ohio State University's Mershon Center, Stanford University's Center for International Security and Cooperation (CISAC), Princeton University, the Centre for Policy Research, and Carnegie India.

Several foundations and institutions provided generous financial support for this project. I am particularly grateful to the Carnegie Corporation, the Carnegie Endowment for International Peace, the Smith Richardson Foundation, and the Stanton Foundation for investing in me and this project over the years. It was on a Stanton Junior Faculty Fellowship back at Stanford's CISAC in 2013 where the idea for this book actually congealed. The Carnegie Endowment has been kind enough to allow me to be a nonresident scholar in the Nuclear Policy Program, and I have benefited significantly from their generosity and intellectual vibrancy. The Carnegie Corporation and Smith Richardson Foundation keep the field of security studies alive in academia and have provided valuable research support over the years that has enabled me to complete the research and writing for this book.

Eric Crahan, Bridget Flannery-McCoy, and Alena Chekanov at Princeton University Press believed in this book and have been absolutely fantastic to work with. I could not have asked for a better team—their kindness, patience, support, and sense of humor have always been refreshing through the process. Jenny Wolkowicki and Jenn Backer were an exceptional copyediting team and made the book much stronger. The reviewers for the manuscript provided incredibly valuable feedback that helped sharpen and tighten the book. I am grateful to MIT Press for granting me permission to reproduce some portions of this book that appeared in an earlier *International Security* article. All errors, of course, remain my own.

Finally, I am indebted to my friends and family who support me unconditionally—even when I do not deserve it—and helped shepherd me through this book, the challenging times of the COVID pandemic, and life with love and humor. Lifelong friends, especially during the pandemic, became extended (virtual) family and made daily life not only tolerable but entertaining: Somesh Dash, Antara Datta, Prithviraj Datta, Justine Fisher, Sujay Jaswa, Allon Klein, Aparna Krishnan, Krishna Kumar, Neil Kumar, Adam Lauridsen, Neil Malhotra, Rohan Murty, Newman Nahas, Mark Paustenbach, Amy Rogers, Roohia Sidhu, Kavita Sivaramakrishnan, Saranya Sridhar, Mike Sulmeyer, and Jason Wasfy. My parents, Inderpal and Sushil, my brother and sister-in-law, Sameer and Neha, and my extended family, notably Ricky and Anisha and Mona and Rajeev, made me the person who I am and have supported me every step of the way, forward, sideways, and sometimes backward. My in-laws, the Aiyars—Mani, Yamini, Suranya, but most especially Suneet, who, along with my mother, dropped everything to help us in our most dire moments—have enriched our lives and, when we are in Delhi or Goa, our stomachs. The people to whom I am most indebted, by far, however, are my immediate family. Sana keeps me grounded, humble, and honest. We have navigated many challenges together over the years—pandemic, doctorates, disease, broken bones, broken spirits, travels and travails, tenure, small children in a time of COVID—and every time I think I am about to fall, she is there to catch me. And the infectious energy and sparklingly mischievous eyes of our two children, Ishaan and Leela, make our adventures more numerous but invariably more fun. This book is for them, so that they may inherit a world that may be just a little less dangerous.

SEEKING THE BOMB

1

Introduction

Just after midnight on September 6, 2007, four Israeli F-15s and four F-16s screamed low over the desert and leveled a nondescript structure in the Syrian hinterland on the banks of the Euphrates River.[1] For years, American and Israeli intelligence satellites had noted the building but were not overly concerned—the "cube," as it was known, was undefended. There were no suspicious traffic patterns or activity, and the facility was littered with debris, making it appear like one of the many abandoned structures in the area. There was nothing to suggest that the Syrian government even cared about the building. Not until an Israeli intelligence operation in March 2007 copied the contents of a laptop belonging to the head of Syria's Atomic Energy Agency did the Israelis learn that the "cube"—officially called al Kibar—was in fact a replica of North Korea's Yongbyon nuclear reactor. The eponymous cube was a superstructure to conceal what lay underneath from satellites passing overhead: a nearly complete graphite-moderated nuclear reactor. With no visible evidence that it was designed to ever plug into Syria's electrical grid, American and Israeli intelligence concluded that the building had only one purpose: to produce plutonium for a Syrian nuclear weapons program.

As a junior varsity member of the Axis of Evil, Syria's president Bashar al-Assad had reasonable grounds to fear that, without nuclear weapons, he might be an easy target for mid-2000s America on a regime-change binge.

1. See Amos Harel and Aluf Benn, "No Longer a Secret: How Israel Destroyed Syria's Nuclear Reactor," *Haaretz*, March 23, 2018, https://www.haaretz.com/world-news/MAGAZINE-no-longer-a-secret-how-israel-destroyed-syria-s-nuclear-reactor-1.5914407.

Nevertheless, the United States was stunned at Assad's sheer audacity: attempting to hide an *aboveground nuclear reactor* built with North Korean assistance, in the year 2007, knowing that America and Israel were continuously watching overhead. The Israelis took no chances and decided to destroy the building on September 6, risking a war with Syria to flatten the reactor. The strike likely occurred weeks before fuel elements were to be added to the reactor core making it "hot," after which it would have been nearly impossible to destroy without significant environmental damage. Syria, a member of the Nuclear Nonproliferation Treaty (NPT) in otherwise good standing, was attempting to pursue a clandestine nuclear weapons program in the most creative and brazen way possible. Syria's nuclear program, though it was ultimately thwarted, illustrates that the way states pursue nuclear weapons rarely resembles the American Manhattan Project or China's determined state-mobilized effort to build the bomb. This is a book about these different strategies of nuclear proliferation and why they matter.

There are two core questions motivating the book. First, how do states pursue nuclear weapons and why do they select a particular strategy of proliferation over the alternatives? Second, how do their choices of strategy affect nuclear proliferation and conflict dynamics? This is the first book to systematically analyze how states seek nuclear weapons, identifying the strategies available to them, and why they choose a particular strategy to do so. It shows that nuclear aspirants' strategic choices follow a clear logic and have important consequences for nuclear proliferation and conflict. Different strategies of proliferation have different likelihoods of success and provide different vulnerabilities that can be leveraged by nonproliferation policies to try to stop states from attaining nuclear weapons. As the world finds itself in a new nuclear era now thirty years after the end of the Cold War, understanding the dynamics and consequences of the proliferation process—which strategies of proliferation are available to states, which strategy a nuclear aspirant might select and why, and what the international community can do to thwart nuclear proliferation depending on the aspirant's strategy—is critical to global security.

The proliferation literature to date has almost exclusively focused on the question of why states pursue nuclear weapons. The question of how states pursue nuclear weapons, once choosing to do so, has received less attention. To the extent that scholars considered it, they have focused on the technical choices states made rather than on political choices and strategies of proliferation. Most scholarship on nuclear proliferation further assumes that states pursuing nuclear weapons prioritize speed of development and attainment over all else—a strategy I call *sprinting*. When nuclear pursuers stop short of a functional arsenal, scholars often assume that technological barriers or external pressure impeded them.

I correct these misconceptions. I show that states choose from four discrete strategies of proliferation and that the logic that leads them to one of these strategies has little to do with resource constraints. States that seek the bomb—or develop an option to seek it in the future—approach the problem with ruthless pragmatism, weighing their domestic and international constraints and opportunities. Security considerations motivate a state to consider developing a nuclear weapons option, but I highlight the crucial role of domestic political consensus in driving a state toward an active nuclear weaponization strategy. My theory emphasizes the degree to which proliferators anticipate attempts by outsiders to frustrate their efforts. Fear of preventive action drives many of their calculations. The danger of prevention leads proliferators to seek creative alternative strategies to develop nuclear weapons: some cultivate or exploit the protection of great powers who can deter or dissuade adversaries from mounting preventive attacks on the proliferator, while others attempt to hide their proliferation from the outside world with a clandestine nuclear weapons program.

What are these different strategies of nuclear proliferation available to states? The first part of the book offers a novel typology of nuclear proliferation strategies, which I call *hedging*, *sprinting*, *sheltered pursuit*, and *hiding*. Some states, such as Japan and Sweden, choose to *hedge* on their potential path to attaining nuclear weapons, seeking not the rapid development of a nuclear weapons capability but rather to put the pieces in place to weaponize at a later date if necessary. I show that hedgers do not hedge in uniform ways or for uniform reasons. My theory offers insights into what might trigger a particular type of hedger—I differentiate between technical hedging, insurance hedging, and hard hedging—to choose to exercise its nuclear weapons option. Hedgers do not fail to develop nuclear weapons; they intentionally choose to not try, yet. Identifying hedging as a proliferation *strategy*—unpacking it into its various forms, locating it on the continuum of the proliferation process, and identifying the circumstances that will make hedgers resume their pursuit of the bomb or make a U-turn—rather than treating it as a disconnected phenomenon is an important contribution of the book.

For states seeking nuclear weapons, rather than just a future option, there are three active strategies of proliferation. The early nuclear proliferators such as the Soviet Union, France, and China were *sprinters* that sought to build nuclear weapons as quickly as possible, trying to match the first-mover, the United States. Others, like Israel and Pakistan and North

Korea, leveraged the complicity of a superpower patron to adopt a *sheltered pursuit* strategy, which exploits forbearance from a more powerful state as a shield against nonproliferation efforts. Other states, such as Iraq and Syria who cannot avail themselves of a major power shelterer, have no choice but to pursue a *hiding* strategy, prioritizing secrecy over speed and aiming to present their completed nuclear weapons as a fait accompli to the world. This book is the first effort to systematically identify the various strategies of proliferation available to nuclear aspirants, showing that states pursue nuclear weapons in distinct ways.

Why do states choose a particular proliferation strategy over the available alternatives? I develop a decision-theoretic framework, Proliferation Strategy Theory, identifying a sequence of security and domestic political variables to explain why a state selects a specific nuclear proliferation strategy. I apply this framework to explore empirical cases of each proliferation strategy, often leveraging primary documents and data to highlight novel features of states' proliferation journeys. I use the framework to generate a proliferation strategy prediction for each of the 29 states that have pursued nuclear weapons (46 total strategies including over-time shifts) and find that the framework accurately predicts over 85 percent of all nuclear proliferation strategies since 1945. Subsequent chapters provide detailed case studies on almost twenty of these nuclear aspirants, those that provide crucial variation in the independent and dependent variables showing why states select the strategies they do, and why they may shift strategies.

The chapter on varieties of hedging includes what I call *technical hedgers* such as Brazil and Argentina that most closely resemble the concept of "nuclear latency," *insurance hedgers* such as Japan and West Germany who hedged against the possibility of American abandonment, and *hard hedgers* such as India, Sweden, and Switzerland who stopped short of weaponizing due to ambivalence or a lack of domestic political consensus in favor of nuclear weapons. States typically make the decision to hedge for strategic reasons. I demonstrate, however, that domestic political consensus in favor of nuclear weapons is the crucial regulator for shifting from hedging to an active proliferation strategy, as in the case of India's stilted march to nuclear weapons. This is an important revision to recent scholarship that veers toward one extreme or the other, with some scholars arguing that it is almost exclusively regime type that drives nuclear proliferation,[2] while others argue that security

2. See Jacques E. C. Hymans, *Achieving Nuclear Ambitions: Scientists, Politicians, and Proliferation* (Cambridge: Cambridge University Press, 2012).

considerations alone explain proliferation.[3] I argue that both are important, but in a particular sequence, with security threats providing the stimulus and domestic political consensus providing the momentum for nuclear weapons.

External protection or prevention at this stage can prove critical to whether the state ultimately attains nuclear weapons. For powerful states with the luxury to openly march for nuclear weapons without fear of prevention, *sprinting* for a bomb is the optimal proliferation strategy. Most states that are powerful enough to sprint, though, already possess nuclear weapons—the Soviet Union, China, and France, for example—although some potential sprinters such as Australia, Japan, and potentially Germany remain should they ever decide to pursue nuclear weapons. The remaining nuclear weapons aspirants are forced to be more creative. A preferable option, if it is available or if it can be cultivated, is building nuclear weapons under the *shelter* of a major power that shields the pursuer from outside pressure and refrains from applying any pressure itself. The major power essentially tolerates nuclear proliferation in pursuit of higher-priority geopolitical goals, while the proliferator attempts to weaponize before the shelter disappears. This is how Israel, Pakistan, and North Korea all successfully developed the bomb. The rest of the states who seek nuclear weapons—those that fear external coercion because they are likely the states the world least wants to possess nuclear weapons—have no choice but to hide and pursue nuclear weapons clandestinely. The very threats that motivate nuclear pursuit drive the program underground. *Hiding* is a high-risk, high-reward strategy that attempts to present the world with a nuclear fait accompli before the program is detected—as South Africa succeeded in doing—but risks military strikes if it is caught before it gets there, as Syria discovered.

Why are these strategies of proliferation important? First, states adopting different strategies experience differing rates of success in attaining nuclear weapons. Hedgers do not fail to attain nuclear weapons, for example. They simply have not actively tried, yet. Among active proliferation strategies, almost *half* of those states that have attempted to develop actual nuclear weapons have succeeded in doing so, with sprinters and sheltered pursuers reaching the finish line at very high rates. Hiders may fail at high rates, but the seduction of potentially succeeding as South Africa did motivates many to keep trying. The typology offers a valuable first cut at assessing the danger that a proliferation threat might come to fruition. Second, and

3. See Alexandre Debs and Nuno P. Monteiro, *Nuclear Politics: The Strategic Causes of Proliferation* (Cambridge: Cambridge University Press, 2017).

related, the typology and my explanation of what drives nuclear aspirants' choices offer hints as to how to stop different kinds of proliferators. Notably, in states that have not generated the domestic consensus for explicit weaponization, keeping domestic political consensus fractured is key to forestalling proliferation and keeping a hedger hedging. Third, the typology offers predictions about the likely consequences for international politics as a function of proliferation strategies. Hiders, for example, are especially dangerous and disruptive to the international system since they either successfully attain a nuclear weapons capability, irrevocably altering the global power structure, or they are discovered, potentially triggering military crises as external powers try to destroy a previously unknown clandestine nuclear weapons program. Indeed, pushing active hiders, such as Iran, back to hedging is in itself an important nonproliferation success, as I show in chapter 7. Given that the pool of likely future proliferators is dominated by potential hiders, the focus on hiders is especially important to understand the looming nuclear landscape. This book is therefore the first effort to identify the variety of proliferation strategies and analyze both their sources and their profound consequences for international security.

Existing Proliferation Scholarship: Focusing on Why, Not How

Why is a focus on strategies of proliferation so novel? First, the literature on nuclear proliferation since the end of the Cold War has generally focused on the *motivations* for state pursuit of nuclear weapons. Scott Sagan's landmark article outlined "three models in search of the bomb," three canonical motivations for nuclear weapons: security, prestige, and domestic politics.[4] Subsequent literature offered additional or refined motivations such as a state's political economy, more nuanced and sophisticated security dynamics, supply side temptations, and oppositional nationalism.[5]

4. Scott D. Sagan, "Why Do States Build Nuclear Weapons? Three Models in Search of the Bomb," *International Security* 21, no. 3 (Winter 1996–97): 54–86.

5. T. V. Paul, *Power versus Prudence: Why Nations Forgo Nuclear Weapons* (Montreal: McGill-Queen's University Press, 2000); Etel Solingen, *Nuclear Logics: Contrasting Paths in East Asia and the Middle East* (Princeton: Princeton University Press, 2007); Matthew Kroenig, *Exporting the Bomb: Technology Transfer and the Spread of Nuclear Weapons* (Ithaca: Cornell University Press, 2010); Matthew Fuhrmann, *Atomic Assistance: How "Atoms for Peace" Programs Cause Nuclear Insecurity* (Ithaca: Cornell University Press, 2012); Stephen M. Meyer, *The Dynamics of Nuclear Proliferation* (Chicago: University of Chicago Press, 1984); Jacques E. C. Hymans, *The Psychology of Nuclear Proliferation: Identity, Emotions, and Foreign Policy* (Cambridge: Cambridge University Press, 2006); Nicholas

If we know why states might pursue nuclear weapons, however, do we automatically know how they might do so? No. This is the case for several reasons. First, as Sagan shows in an evaluation of the broader literature, and Mark Bell demonstrates with respect to the quantitative literature, the scholarship on why states initiate nuclear weapons pursuit has produced inconsistent and sometimes contradictory answers, yielding no generalizable theory as to which states might do so, and when or why.[6] Thus any inferences about how states might pursue nuclear weapons based on their underlying motivations may be dubious. Indeed, shifting the focus to strategies of proliferation—which endogenizes a state's level of desire for nuclear weapons (demand) and its ability to develop them (supply)—is not only important in its own right but may help integrate the presently disconnected literatures on the supply and demand for nuclear weapons.[7] Second, a review of the almost thirty cases of nuclear aspirants suggests that that there is little relationship between the motivations for nuclear pursuit and a state's ultimate choice of proliferation strategy. States that pursued nuclear weapons for security reasons might select the same strategy of proliferation as those that pursued them for status and prestige reasons. Likewise, states that have had security motivations for pursuing nuclear weapons have chosen every available strategy of proliferation. Therefore, although varying *intensity* of demand—how much a state wants nuclear weapons—is certainly important to the strategy of proliferation a state selects, with lower-intensity demand more likely to correlate with hedging strategies, the *source* of that demand—security, prestige, or domestic—matters less. That is, *why* states pursue nuclear weapons is largely independent of *how* they do so. The literature on why states want nuclear weapons—the overwhelming majority of the proliferation scholarship in the past quarter century—has little to say about how they may attempt to do so.[8]

Miller, *Stopping the Bomb: The Sources and Effectiveness of U.S. Nonproliferation Policy* (Ithaca: Cornell University Press, 2018); Alexandre Debs and Nuno Monteiro, "The Strategic Logic of Nuclear Proliferation," *International Security* 39, no. 2 (Fall 2014): 7–51. For overviews and evaluations of the literature on the causes of proliferation, see Scott D. Sagan, "The Causes of Nuclear Weapons Proliferation," *Annual Review of Political Science* 14, no. 1 (June 2011): 225–44; Jacques E. C. Hymans, "The Study of Nuclear Proliferation and Nonproliferation: Toward a New Consensus?" in *Forecasting Nuclear Proliferation in the 21st Century, Volume 1: The Role of Theory*, ed. William C. Potter and Gaukhar Mukhatzhanova (Stanford: Stanford University Press, 2010); and Mark S. Bell, "Examining Explanations for Nuclear Proliferation," *International Studies Quarterly* 60, no. 3 (September 2016): 520–29.

6. Bell, "Examining Explanations for Nuclear Proliferation"; Sagan, "The Causes of Nuclear Weapons Proliferation."

7. Sagan, "The Causes of Nuclear Weapons Proliferation," 227–36.

8. One exception is Hymans, *Achieving Nuclear Ambitions*.

Moreover, analyzing strategies of proliferation is novel because the extant literature on nuclear proliferation tends to treat nuclear pursuit as a binary, a-strategic process: states are either pursuing nuclear weapons or they are not, and those that are uniformly aim to weaponize a nuclear capability as quickly as possible. This literature assumes that all states with nuclear weapons programs invariably seek to create a functional arsenal as fast as technically possible. For example, Jacques Hymans's work on how efficiently states achieve their nuclear ambitions assumes that nuclear aspirants all try to develop a nuclear weapons capability as quickly as possible and vary only in their ability to manage the project and the process.[9]

These assumptions are not always true. For example, states including Japan, Sweden, and India at times have sought to put the pieces in place to weaponize at a later date if necessary but have consciously and strategically stopped well short of attaining nuclear weapons with a form of hedging strategy.[10] Their goal was not nuclear weapons but erecting a nuclear weapons program that could be activated and consummated at a time of their choosing if necessary. Hedgers can stall at this point for years, or indefinitely. Certainly, the early nuclear proliferators such as the United States, the Soviet Union, and China sought to weaponize as quickly as possible in a sprinting strategy. These are the stereotypical proliferators in the extant literature. But under 20 percent of the states that pursued nuclear weapons have followed their strategy. Some states may not prioritize speed but secrecy, pursuing a hiding strategy that aims to present a fait accompli before the program is discovered. Still others can leverage the complicity of a major power's knowledge of their program and adopt a sheltered pursuit strategy, which attempts to cultivate major power immunity to shield them from nonproliferation or counterproliferation efforts. Few states after the 1950s fit the archetype of the sprinters, trying to build nuclear weapons as quickly as possible. Many states seeking nuclear weapons may value considerations besides speed and outcomes besides a fully functional nuclear weapons arsenal. The existing literature has little to say about this variation.

Why does variation in strategies of proliferation matter? To begin with, a theory of how a potential nuclear aspirant goes about trying to seek nuclear weapons identifies additional opportunities and policy levers to halt nuclear weapons proliferation. How a state chooses to pursue nuclear weapons

9. Ibid.

10. E.g., Ariel E. Levite, "Never Say Never Again: Nuclear Reversal Revisited," *International Security* 27, no. 3 (Winter 2002/2003): 59–88; Avner Cohen and Benjamin Frankel, "Opaque Nuclear Proliferation," *Journal of Strategic Studies* 13, no. 3 (1990): 14–44.

matters as much as—if not more than—its underlying motivations when it comes to identifying and implementing policies to prevent nuclear proliferation. There are different *types* of nuclear proliferators, and the distinctions between them are important for scholars hoping to understand the proliferation landscape and for policymakers hoping to shape it. Understanding the different strategies of proliferation allows the international community to tailor inducements or punishment to try to dissuade or deter states from developing nuclear weapons. This book outlines these different strategies, develops a theory for why states might select one strategy over another, and demonstrates the power of the theory on a variety of cases. Three decades of scholarship on *why* states want nuclear weapons has neglected that *how* they pursue them has crucial implications for international security. This book thus opens new terrain in the proliferation literature by systematically analyzing how states pursue nuclear weapons and why strategies of proliferation matter to the nuclear landscape and international politics.

Why States Need to Think about Proliferation Strategies: Duress

Why do states have to carefully devise a strategy of proliferation? As the Syrian example demonstrates, states that pursue nuclear weapons often do so under duress. On average, nuclear proliferators, as they approach the point of weaponization, experience systematically more pressure—whether the threat of sanctions or military conflict—than they did prior to and after weaponization.[11] There are three reasons why this might be the case. First, of course, there may be some reverse causality where increased levels of duress further motivate pursuit of nuclear weapons. Second, as states approach the point of weaponization, other states might have motivations to destroy a state's nascent nuclear capabilities.[12] Third, anticipating the attainment of nuclear weapons or in the immediate aftermath of attaining them, proliferators might become emboldened, relying on ambiguous or limited capabilities to deter retaliation.[13] These are often treated as distinct mechanisms,

11. David Sobek, Dennis M. Foster, and Samuel B. Robison, "Conventional Wisdom? The Effect of Nuclear Proliferation on Armed Conflict, 1945–2001," *International Studies Quarterly* 56, no. 1 (March 2012): 149–62.

12. Matthew Fuhrmann and Sarah Kreps, "Targeting Nuclear Programs in War and Peace: A Quantitative Empirical Analysis, 1941–2000," *Journal of Conflict Resolution* 54, no. 6 (December 2010): 831–59.

13. See Mark S. Bell, "Beyond Emboldenment: How Acquiring Nuclear Weapons Can Change Foreign Policy," *International Security* 40, no. 1 (Summer 2015): 87–119.

but they are related to each other. Proliferators that others fear might be emboldened are more likely to be the potential target of greater coercive or preventive efforts. Similarly, these efforts might trigger greater emboldenment or aggression by the proliferator. This is not a new phenomenon. The historical record is dotted with conflicts where targeting nuclear weapons programs was salient: the 1967 Arab-Israeli Six Day War, episodes in 1984 and 1986–87 where India contemplated using a broader conflict to target Pakistan's uranium enrichment facility, Israeli strikes against Iraq and Syria, and the multiple wars with Iraq.[14] For potential nuclear aspirants, such as Libya and Iran, these examples can be powerful demonstrations of what may be awaiting them if they try to pursue nuclear weapons against the will of major powers.

The pursuit of nuclear weapons can therefore result in substantial international turbulence and conflict. There is a "window of volatility" for proliferators that becomes pronounced in the decade prior to weapons attainment and that seems to last until a decade after. To illustrate the extent of this duress on the most extreme indicator—military conflict—I show that a state experiences systematically more military conflict as it approaches the point of weaponization. This analysis understates the true level of duress a proliferator faces on average, because it does not include other forms of pressure a state may experience, such as economic threats or military harassment that falls below the militarized threshold. I align all non-superpower nuclear possessors by their date of nuclear possession (normalizing that date as t_0) and plot the level of conflict that they experience in the two decades prior and subsequent to achieving a nuclear capability, using militarized interstate disputes (MIDs) as a reasonable indicator for conflict.[15] This approach takes the point of nuclearization as the uniform moment to assess conflict levels for proliferators, so it normalizes China in 1964 with, for example, Pakistan in 1987 to observe conflict levels across the proliferation process.[16]

14. Also see Muhammet Bas and Andrew J. Coe, "A Dynamic Theory of Nuclear Proliferation and Preventive War," *International Organization* 70, no. 4 (Fall 2016): 655–85.

15. Dates are from Philipp C. Bleek, "Does Proliferation Beget Proliferation?: Why Nuclear Dominoes Rarely Fall" (PhD diss., Georgetown University, 2010), appendix A, http://hdl.handle.net/10822/558060. I exclude the United States and USSR here because they had wartime proliferation programs, and the number of MIDs around their programs is artificially high.

16. This approach necessarily restricts the sample to nuclear states. In theory, this bias favors the null hypothesis because these are the successful proliferators; those states whose programs were terminated by the counterproliferation efforts of others are not included but would strengthen the results.

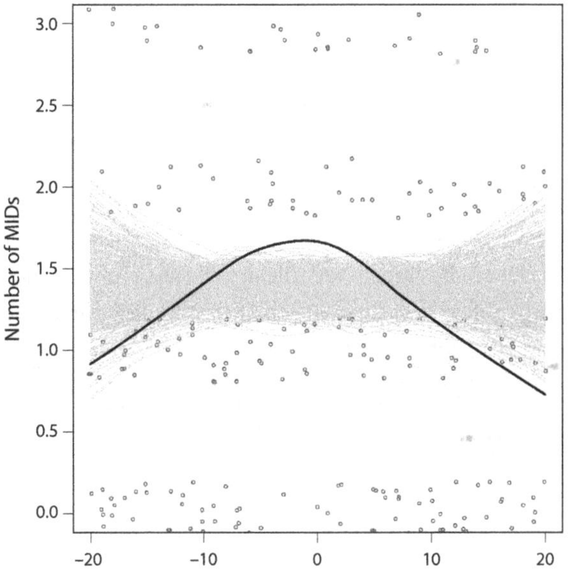

FIGURE 1.1. Window of Volatility. This illustrates the relationship between armed conflict and nuclear proliferation, where t_0 is the point of attainment (bold line). Compared to conflict levels twenty years prior to, and subsequent to, weaponization, states face an average of one additional armed dispute per year. This uses randomization inference and 500 random draws (light lines) from the reference distribution under the null hypothesis ($p < 0.001$).

I use randomization inference, which tests the sharp null hypothesis that there is no relationship between nuclearization and conflict level for any unit through many random draws. Compared to the null hypothesis, figure 1.1 shows a significant and substantively large relationship between the proliferation process and conflict levels.

States pursuing nuclear weapons thus face more average armed conflict through the *process* of nuclear proliferation.[17] Nuclear proliferation can be a rough process for the international system and the proliferator. Potential proliferators must therefore carefully decide *how* to pursue nuclear weapons and succeed in developing them under this duress. That is, they must carefully choose a strategy of proliferation that tries to minimize their exposure to pressure. This book is about how states think about their strategies of nuclear proliferation given their domestic and international constraints and opportunities, as they navigate this potential window of volatility.

17. The results in figure 1.1 are robust to different attainment dates, removing any one regional nuclear power, MIDs 4.0. Contact author for any desired robustness checks.

Plan of the Book

The book is organized as follows. Chapter 2 identifies the various strategies of proliferation available to states and develops a decision-theoretic framework to explain why a given state might select a given strategy at any point in time, based on a clear sequence of systemic and domestic political variables. The theory generates a determinate prediction for whether a state will select a variety of hedging—technical, insurance, or hard hedging—or an active nuclear proliferation strategy: sprinting, hiding, or sheltered pursuit. This chapter makes a substantial theoretical contribution by providing a testable and falsifiable theory for why states might select a particular strategy of nuclear proliferation, giving insights into future potential proliferators and which strategies they may select and which variables might be manipulated to possibly stop them.

After conducting a full analysis in tabular form in chapter 2, the empirical chapters that follow perform a medium-n analysis covering 19 of the 29 nuclear aspirants thus far, testing the theory against several alternative explanations such as technological determinism, a rigorous (realist) security model, and international nonproliferation regime explanations for state behavior. I focus on key cases in each of the empirical chapters to highlight novel mechanisms and illustrate important variation across the independent or dependent variables. The cases are not randomly selected but chosen because they are important cases of proliferation that highlight key theoretical mechanisms or offer novel historical value. These chapters demonstrate the power of the theory by identifying and establishing the crucial variables that pushed states to select a particular strategy of nuclear proliferation. These chapters provide substantial empirical value. I offer the first systematic coding of strategies of proliferation, providing an original framework to analyze the 29 states that have pursued nuclear weapons—and those that may pursue them in the future—and illuminate key and novel features of their proliferation experiences. Where possible, I present new or primary data to best understand the strategic decisions nuclear aspirants and great powers such as the United States made during the proliferation process.

Chapter 3 focuses on the varieties of hedging. As I highlighted at the outset, hedging is an important waypoint in the proliferation process. States often consciously choose variants of it for strategic reasons—seeking not the bomb but a bomb option. I present new and primary data on hard hedgers such as India, Sweden, and Switzerland, insurance hedgers such as Japan and West Germany, and technical hedgers including Brazil and Argentina. These cases show why hedging is central to the proliferation process as some, like India, opt to resume their quest for nuclear weapons, while others such as Sweden and Switzerland forswear them entirely, and still others like Japan may remain idle at the hedging stop indefinitely. Chapter 4 presents the case of the sprinters, the stylized version of proliferation in the literature: the states who openly and quickly marched to nuclear weapons without fear of prevention or reprisal. Chapter 5 centers on three important sheltered pursuers—Israel, Pakistan, and North Korea—who probably would not have been able to develop nuclear weapons if not for the shelter afforded them by the major powers that valued these countries for more important geopolitical reasons and essentially turned a blind eye to their development of nuclear weapons and shielded them from nonproliferation efforts. Chapter 6 focuses on three crucial hiders: Iraq, Taiwan, and South Africa. These cases illustrate how allied abandonment can generate proliferation pressures and, even though Taiwan was unsuccessful in eventually hiding its nuclear weapons program, it highlights the need to remain vigilant against potential hiders—both adversaries and allies alike. South Africa is a case of a successful hider, showing that it is indeed possible even against immense intelligence capabilities—both the United States and Soviet Union opposed South African nuclearization—to successfully build nuclear weapons through hiding under the right conditions. The case of Iraq shows how disruptive hiders can be to the international system as Iraq's clandestine program in the 1980s set the stage for two decades of tumult and conflict—once he was suspected of being a hider, Saddam Hussein was presumed to always be a hider.

The penultimate chapter focuses on the consequences of these choices. First, which strategies are more likely to successfully lead to nuclear weapons? This chapter highlights the variation in successful nuclear proliferation as a function of strategy, showing that although sprinting rarely fails for those who select it, sheltered pursuit is also a particularly successful strategy, with profound implications for future nuclear proliferation and the major powers that may extend shelter and tolerate additional nuclear states. Second, what are the different nonproliferation consequences of these strategies? What are the key variables that have been, and can be, manipulated to successfully halt states from attaining nuclear weapons depending on which strategy they select? Finally, what are the consequences for international conflict? In particular, hiding is a very disruptive strategy. An effective hider, such as a South Africa, can entirely bypass the so-called window of vulnerability identified earlier and substantially improve its global power position. But a hider that is caught, like Iraq or Syria, can generate very high likelihoods of preventive conflict and war. Knowing which states might be hiders, then, helps highlight future potential flashpoints for conflict and war. It also highlights why diplomatic initiatives, such as the 2015 Joint Comprehensive Plan of Action (JCPOA) between Iran and the so-called P5 + 1 that pushed Iran back from hiding to hard hedging by attempting to empower moderates in Tehran who opposed nuclear weapons, are such important nonproliferation successes.

This book is the first systematic attempt to analyze the diversity of strategies of nuclear proliferation, their sources, and their consequences. It shows that states have systematically selected *different* strategies to try to attain nuclear weapons, and that these choices matter deeply to international security. It advances scholarship on nuclear proliferation by opening new terrain, showing that although why states want nuclear weapons is undoubtedly important, how they go about pursuing nuclear weapons is fundamental to the global nuclear landscape. Understanding this dynamic is crucial for the United States as it confronts the increasing possibility that a growing number of states—friends, foes, and frenemies—may pursue nuclear weapons in the future.

2

Strategies of Nuclear Proliferation and Their Sources

This chapter outlines the four strategies of nuclear proliferation—hedging, sprinting, sheltered pursuit, and hiding—and develops a theory for which strategies are likely to be chosen by a given nuclear aspirant at a given time. I set forth how I operationalize the variables in my theory, identify competing theories, and then present the coding for each of the twenty-nine states who have pursued nuclear weapons, noting whether the theory accurately predicts the proliferation strategy each state selected. The logic I lay out entails several steps. I highlight two of the most important here. First, states that have motivations to pursue nuclear weapons do not automatically do so—some stop short of active weaponization by developing a bomb option or a nuclear hedge. A key condition must be present for a state to weaponize its nuclear hedge: strong consensus among key domestic constituencies is necessary to push states onto the path of active pursuit. Second, states select their active strategies of nuclear proliferation based on careful consideration of their international threats and opportunities. Active proliferation, I argue, is shot through with the fear of prevention. In short, this chapter shows that nuclear aspirants select proliferation strategies for coherent and strategic reasons but that domestic politics plays a powerful and predictable intervening role in the bridge between hedging and an active weaponization strategy.

The Various Strategies of Nuclear Proliferation

What are the strategies of nuclear proliferation available to states? That is, what are the various ways in which a state can try to pursue a nuclear weapons capability?[1] There are two basic questions a potential nuclear weapons aspirant asks. The first question is whether it seeks to fully weaponize its nuclear capabilities. If the state simply seeks the option to weaponize in the future, or hedge, the second question is what are the conditions under which it might break out and fully weaponize, and where does it want to stop on the spectrum of a nuclear weapons program.[2] If the aspirant does seek weapons, it must then ask how to go about developing them with the highest chance of success given its circumstances. In this section, I outline the typology of nuclear proliferation strategies that states have selected. In generating any typology, one must attempt to ensure that the categories are analytically distinct and mutually exclusive so that states can be identified as being in one category rather than others at any point in time, and at least empirically—if not conceptually—exhaustive. The following typology meets these requirements. I identify four broad strategies of proliferation—hedging, sprinting, sheltered pursuit, and hiding—that vary in terms of a state's nuclear goals, the extent of its work on nuclear weaponization, and the efficiency sacrifices that the state makes to ensure secrecy. Within hedging, there are three distinct varieties, such that the full typology has six strategies in total: three types of hedging (technical, insurance, and hard) and three active weaponization strategies (sprinting, sheltered pursuit, and hiding).

1. This is a study of the political strategies of nuclear weapons pursuit, but the technical pathways to nuclear weapons are important. To build a nuclear weapon, the key ingredient is weapons-grade fissile material. This can be either the fissile uranium isotope (^{235}U), which must be enriched from its ~0.7 percent content in natural uranium to greater than ~90 percent using enrichment technologies such as gaseous centrifuges or gaseous diffusion, or the fissile plutonium isotope (^{239}Pu), which can be isolated by reprocessing spent nuclear reactor fuel. Developing sufficient weapons-grade fissile material is often the most difficult technical challenge for states. Once a state has sufficient weapons-grade fissile material, it must machine weapons cores and develop explosive designs to compress the cores so that they go "critical" and sustain a fission reaction, yielding energy on the scale of 15–20kT for a basic fission weapon. A state must also develop a capability to deliver a nuclear weapon and have weapons designs suitable for the delivery system it chooses to use. A strategy of proliferation aims to develop the indigenous capability to produce nuclear weapons and the means to deliver them.

2. If the answer to this question is that the state explicitly forswears the option of nuclear weapons, the state is presumed to not have a strategy of proliferation.

HEDGING

Hedging is a strategy to develop a bomb *option*, laying the groundwork for weaponization in the future under some set of strategic conditions. A hedger intentionally refrains from actively developing nuclear weapons while simultaneously putting various pieces in place for a future nuclear weapons program, such that it will be easier to weaponize if it becomes necessary. The hedger's answer to the question of whether the state wants nuclear weapons is "maybe." A hedger often develops capabilities that contribute to a peaceful nuclear energy program but would also be valuable for a weapons program, reducing the state's "breakout time" and providing options if its desire for weapons shifts. Hedgers includes states with civilian energy programs that possess—or are in a position to gain—control of the fuel cycle or those that seek to develop indigenous uranium enrichment capabilities that could provide weapons-grade uranium or reprocessing capabilities for its spent reactor fuel for plutonium weapons.[3] Hedging is not simply a technological condition or so-called nuclear latency—which describes a state's enrichment and reprocessing capabilities.[4] Hedging is the result of an *intentional, political* choice to develop nuclear capabilities without commencing the development of actual nuclear weapons.[5] There are several varieties of hedging that differ in how and why they hedge, and are therefore important to disaggregate.

Technical Hedging

The first variety—the farthest from weaponization and with the least centralized intent—is "technical" hedging. Technical hedgers put the technological

3. See Scott D. Sagan, "Nuclear Latency and Nuclear Proliferation," in *Forecasting Nuclear Proliferation in the 21st Century: The Role of Theory, Volume 1*, ed. William C. Potter and Gaukhar Mukhatzhanova (Stanford: Stanford University Press, 2010), chap. 5 for an overview of the relationship between plutonium and uranium enrichment technologies and nuclear proliferation. On "nuclear ambivalence," see Itty Abraham, *The Making of the Indian Atomic Bomb: Science, Secrecy, and the Postcolonial State* (New York: St. Martin's Press, 1998).

4. For an excellent contribution in this regard, see Matthew Fuhrmann and Benjamin Tkach, "Almost Nuclear: Introducing the Nuclear Latency Dataset," *Conflict Management and Peace Science* 32, no. 4 (September 2015): 443–61; also see Tristan A. Volpe, "Bargaining in the Sweet Spot: Coercive Diplomacy with Latency," working paper.

5. What distinguishes hedging from latency, and why I use the term "hedging," is that the former is largely a technical condition while the latter is a strategy with the *intent* to preserve the option of nuclear weapons. Organizing hedging behavior politically rather than technically has the advantage of identifying certain types of hedgers that are more likely to forswear nuclear weapons pursuit, particularly technical hedgers who lack significant demand for nuclear weapons and hard hedgers if domestic political consensus congeals against, rather than for, weaponization.

pieces in place that may enable them to pursue a military program at a later date and hedge as a by-product of a civilian energy program and infrastructure. This type of hedging may be characterized by the existence of fissile material production (not weapons grade), but no work is undertaken on military applications such as weaponization or explosives research, nuclear delivery systems, or organizational routines to manage nuclear weapons. In these cases, there is no immediate demand for nuclear weapons. Technical hedging signifies a position of "explicitly not now, but implicitly not never." It may arise because access to nuclear technologies tempts certain constituencies within the state to flirt with the idea of pursuing nuclear weapons even as overall demand is weak and contained to fringe elements in politics, the military, or energy organizations.[6] Technical hedging is the type that most closely resembles pure nuclear "latency," because technical hedgers lack centralized intent for further nuclear weapons pursuit. For many years, Argentina and Brazil were quintessential technical hedgers. They established the technological basis for a nuclear weapons option, but interest in nuclear weapons was limited to fringe elements in the military. In the contemporary landscape, emerging technical hedgers could include states like the United Arab Emirates, which possesses the Gulf's first nuclear reactor—Barakah, a light water reactor complex—under stringent International Atomic Energy Agency (IAEA) safeguards, having signed the additional protocol.[7] But with Iran's potential nuclear weapons program lurking across the Gulf, it is not inconceivable that this also lays the basis, for some in the Emirati government, for a future military potential.

Insurance Hedging

The second variety of hedging is "insurance" hedging. Insurance hedging involves steps to reduce the time to the bomb should a state need to develop nuclear weapons (e.g., if a security threat intensifies or if the hedger is abandoned by an ally). Insurance hedging explicitly threatens breakout under specific conditions. Indicators of insurance hedging may include theoretical work on weaponization and nuclear explosions, movement toward indigenous control of the fuel cycle, development of the capability to produce weapons-grade fissile material, and work on dual-use delivery vehicles. Insurance hedgers should exhibit little or no thinking about organizational

6. See Fuhrmann, *Atomic Assistance*; and Kroenig, *Exporting the Bomb*.

7. Vivian Lee, "U.A.E. Becomes First Arab Nation to Open a Nuclear Power Plant," *New York Times*, August 1, 2020, https://www.nytimes.com/2020/08/01/world/middleeast/uae-nuclear-Barakah.html.

routines for the management of nuclear weapons and no physical work on weaponization. Insurance hedging signifies a position of "explicitly not now, but explicitly in the future if X happens." X is usually either a breakout threat against an adversary or an ultimatum to an ally in order to ensure continued protection. Insurance hedging lays the foundation—pays the premiums, so to speak—for the more accelerated development of an independent deterrent should the state face abandonment—the disaster, in this analogy—but it can also be leveraged to maintain an ally's commitment to the state (to get a better deal, as it were), especially since the United States, in particular, is often opposed to allied proliferation because the superpower alone wants to control nuclear use and escalation decisions.[8]

Hard Hedging

The final variety of hedging is "hard" hedging. Hard hedgers attempt to become threshold nuclear states with many of the pieces in place for a functional weapons program. They have potentially intense demand for nuclear weapons but intentionally stop short of the finish line. These states may be more or less threshold nuclear weapons states but consciously exercise restraint from taking the final steps to weaponization. Hard hedging may include theoretical work on nuclear explosives, the capability to produce weapons-grade fissile material, work on weapons designs, delivery vehicles, and the development of bureaucratic organizations to manage a nuclear weapons capability. But hard hedgers stop short of outright weaponization, adopting the position of "explicitly not now, but explicitly not never." In this strategy, a state not only puts the technological pieces in place but also intentionally undertakes organizational and theoretical weaponization work that is ultimately necessary to build nuclear weapons. Hard hedging is conceptually close to the notion of "nuclear ambivalence," where a state has all the pieces in place to become a nuclear weapons power but is undecided and ambivalent about whether it will ultimately take the final step and develop nuclear weapons.[9] Hard hedgers do not consider nuclear weapons attainment inevitable, but hard hedging brings the question of nuclear weapons

8. See Francis J. Gavin, "Strategies of Inhibition: U.S. Grand Strategy, the Nuclear Revolution, and Nonproliferation," *International Security* 40, no. 1 (Summer 2015): 9–46; and Gene Gerzhoy, "Alliance Coercion and Nuclear Restraint: How the United States Thwarted West Germany's Nuclear Ambitions," *International Security* 39, no. 4 (Spring 2015): 91–129. For an inquiry into why states might no longer engage in insurance hedging, see Tristan Volpe and Ulrich Kühn, "Uninsured Allies: When Do States Divest from Nuclear Latency?" working paper.

9. Itty Abraham, "The Ambivalence of Nuclear Histories," *Osiris* 21 (2006): 49–65.

TABLE 2.1. Indicators for the Varieties of Hedging

	Technical Hedging	Insurance Hedging	Hard Hedging
Fissile Material Production	Non–weapons grade	Non–weapons grade, potential work on capability to produce weapons grade	Capability for weapons-grade production
Weaponization Work	None	Possibly limited (secret?) theoretical work	Theoretical work, no physical work
Nuclear Delivery Vehicles	None	Possibly dual-use delivery vehicles	Development or work on dedicated nuclear delivery vehicles
Declared Interest in Weapons	Fringe elements	Surfaces only periodically	Mainstream debate
Intent: Explicitly not now but . . .	Implicitly not never	Explicitly if X happens	Explicitly not never

into mainstream political debate. Some states in this position, such as India, ultimately adopt an active proliferation strategy. Others, such as Sweden, conclude at the precipice that nuclear weapons are not in its interest and abandon nuclear pursuit all together.[10]

Table 2.1 lists some key indicators for the varieties of hedging. Not all indicators need to be present in each case, and states may vary in their technical work within each category. Nevertheless, table 2.1 suggests how to distinguish among the varieties of hedging.

Categorizing types of hedgers in real time may be difficult because the activities that distinguish hard hedging from insurance hedging, for example, consist of technical work and deliberation that is likely done in secret. In practice, most external observers may assume that anything resembling soft technical hedging could very well be hard hedging. Even if measurement in real time is difficult, the three types of hedging strategies are analytically distinct and important to disaggregate because, as I argue below, the *reasons* why states select a particular variety of hedging differ and are crucially important. Further, identifying the conditions that ought to generate a particular variety of hedging provides insights into what might trigger a shift to an active weaponization strategy or, alternatively, encourage abandonment

10. See Thomas Jonter, *The Key to Nuclear Restraint: The Swedish Plans to Acquire Nuclear Weapons during the Cold War* (London: Palgrave Macmillan, 2016).

of a nuclear weapons program. For example, knowing that a state relying on extended deterrence via an ally is likely an insurance hedger and not a hard hedger implies that changes in the alliance commitment or a heightened severity of threat might trigger nuclear weapons breakout. To take another example, I argue that hard hedgers often stall due to domestic political fissures. This provides a different mechanism to trigger nuclear weaponization or induce nuclear abandonment.

In terms of nuclear weapons proliferation, hedging is a transitory strategy, albeit one that some states can adopt indefinitely. Hedging over the long term may allow a state to reap some deterrent benefits without paying the costs of overt proliferation, such as sanctions, reactive proliferation by adversaries, and the financial costs of maintaining an overt deterrent. For example, when India was a hard hedger it may have reaped some deterrent benefits against Pakistan by virtue of how close it was to being a nuclear state.[11] Other hedging strategies, particularly insurance hedging, may be both a latent deterrent to an underlying threat and a coercive tool toward a superpower ally. A state that goes from "maybe" wanting nuclear weapons to "definitively not" wanting nuclear weapons exits the universe of cases, that is, its intent to pursue nuclear weapons evaporates.[12] A state that ultimately wants to weaponize a nuclear capability, however, must switch to one of three active development strategies: sprinting, sheltered pursuit, or hiding.

SPRINTING

The first active strategy of proliferation is sprinting. Sprinting is an open and determined march to develop a nuclear weapons capability as quickly as possible. It is the stereotypical strategy of proliferation that much of the literature assumes all states follow. Sprinters almost always attempt tactical obfuscation to protect the integrity of research and production facilities and activity but seldom attempt to mask either their intent or capability to develop nuclear weapons. The state is free to openly develop uranium enrichment or plutonium reprocessing work for expressly military purposes, as well as delivery vehicles and organizational routines to manage nuclear weapons. Sprinting is a strategy which, if available to a state, almost certainly leads to a nuclear weapons capability. It may take some states longer than

11. See Vipin Narang, *Nuclear Strategy in the Modern Era: Regional Powers and International Conflict* (Princeton: Princeton University Press, 2014), chap. 10.

12. On this point, see Levite, "Never Say Never Again."

others for technical or organizational reasons, but if a state directs the necessary resources to a nuclear weapons effort and is immune from economic or military preventive action, its prospects for achieving its goals are very high.[13] To date, scholars have largely assumed or implied that sprinting is the proliferation default. Sprinting is, in fact, a rare strategy of proliferation. In reality, few nuclear pursuers have had the favorable geopolitical position that allowed the United States, Soviet Union, or China to sprint for nuclear weapons, immune from counterproliferation efforts. Some nuclear aspirants sprint at the end of their quest for nuclear weapons, but few after the first-generation proliferators (i.e., the major powers constituting the Permanent Five states) have started and finished with a sprinting strategy.

SHELTERED PURSUIT

Sheltered pursuit enables a state to build nuclear weapons shielded by the tolerance and protection of a major power—often a superpower, but possibly other major powers such as China—which both forgoes its own efforts to stop the nuclear aspirant and deters, dissuades, or undermines the efforts of others to do so. A state that adopts a sheltered pursuit strategy either cultivates or exploits shelter from a major power to attempt to develop nuclear weapons before the shelter evaporates. The major power is not usually a formal ally of the state, since major powers often prefer their formal allies not to possess nuclear weapons so that they can alone control nuclear use and escalation within their alliance blocs. Instead, the state may find itself in an opportunistic client-patron relationship with the major power. Sheltered pursuit requires the proliferator to have a major power that is complicit in, or at least tolerant of, its nuclear weapons pursuit. Not only does the great power exercise forbearance toward the proliferator, but it also shields the state from preventive military, diplomatic, or economic action by other actors. For example, the shelterer can refrain from imposing sanctions or attacking the state itself, or it can undermine sanctions if others attempt to coerce the proliferator or help deter attack on the proliferator by increasing the risk that the shelterer might intervene militarily.

The proliferator may strategically cultivate shelter, or shelter may materialize for exogeneous reasons. Either way, the state must seize the potentially temporary opportunity to pursue the bomb before the patron abandons it. Shelter often arises for reasons that have nothing to do with the nuclear

13. See Hymans, *Achieving Nuclear Ambitions*, for states like China, which was able to develop nuclear weapons rather efficiently, immune from serious preventive threats.

program—the United States, for example, never truly wanted states like Israel or Pakistan to possess nuclear weapons[14]—but because the proliferator has found itself useful to a major power for other domestic or geopolitical reasons that override nonproliferation concerns.[15] The major power patron extends the state forbearance for some window during which it can attempt to develop nuclear weapons. In addition, the major power patron provides the proliferator with protection and diplomatic cover to lend the proliferator plausible deniability to others. Proliferators use a sheltered pursuit strategy to attain a nuclear weapons capability before the major power patron potentially abandons or turns on the state.

Sheltered pursuit is attractive for states that can find suitable shelter, since it allows a state to proliferate without fear of reprisal. Israel and Pakistan are the quintessential sheltered pursuers, both using American shelter to develop nuclear weapons. North Korea's pursuit and successful attainment of a nuclear weapons capability would likely have been impossible absent Chinese shelter, which preferred a nuclear North Korea over a collapsed North Korea. Sheltered pursuers have a high chance of successfully achieving a nuclear weapons capability, certainly higher than hiders, who risk a violent fate if discovered by a major power. However, if the major power patron abandons the sheltered pursuer, then the program could stall or be terminated by external powers, including by the former protector itself (as the United States tried to goad the Soviet Union into doing in the early 1960s to China).[16] A hider whose nuclear weapons program is discovered may also search for protection and attempt a sheltered pursuit strategy to avoid punishment, but this requires the state to swiftly "turn" a previously unwilling power capable of protecting it to suddenly extend shelter.

HIDING

A hider seeks to build nuclear weapons in a fashion that privileges secrecy over speed. Hiders fear prevention or coercion if their activities and capabilities are discovered by other states, particularly by the major powers but especially by active counterproliferators such as the United States or, if in

14. See Gavin, "Strategies of Inhibition."

15. See Or Rabinowitz and Nicholas L. Miller, "Keeping the Bombs in the Basement: U.S. Nonproliferation Policy toward Israel, South Africa, and Pakistan," *International Security* 40, no. 1 (Summer 2015): 47–86.

16. See William Burr and Jeffrey T. Richelson, "Whether to 'Strangle' the Baby in the Cradle: The United States and the Chinese Nuclear Program, 1960–64," *International Security* 25, no. 3 (Winter 2000–2001): 67–72.

the Middle East, Israel. Often, the very same menacing threats that motivate the pursuit of nuclear weapons force the program underground. Hiders may also fear reactive proliferation by their rivals if their efforts are known and seek to preserve as much of a head start as possible. The ideal outcome for a hider is to present the fait accompli of a nuclear weapons capability to its adversaries and the world before it is discovered, or at least achieve sufficient progress to deter prevention. Hiders tend to prefer pathways to nuclear weapons that are easier to conceal, often sacrificing speed and efficiency to maximize secrecy. Uranium enrichment technologies are often presumed to be easier to disperse and conceal, but some hiders such as Taiwan and Syria have attempted to conceal plutonium reactors or reprocessing capabilities.[17] Syria's bold attempt, nearly successful, to conceal the al Kibar nuclear reactor within the view of Israeli and American satellites is the most striking example of a hider attempting to conceal a plutonium pathway. Few plutonium hiders, however, would presumably be as daring as Bashar al-Assad and attempt to hide an aboveground reactor. They may instead try to hide a secret reprocessing facility—the capability to covertly separate plutonium from the spent fuel of a civilian reactor—which is likely easier than hiding a dedicated military reactor. Nevertheless, although clandestine uranium enrichment like Iran's centrifuge program is still perhaps the preferred pathway of hiders, plutonium pathways plausibly exist as well.

Hiding is a high-risk, high-reward strategy. If a state succeeds in hiding and presents its nuclear weapons as a fait accompli, nuclear weapons offer the ultimate security benefit to a state without facing the external duress of the proliferation process. Once presented with a fait accompli, the international community may have little choice but to accept the state's nuclear weapons capability, since nuclear weapons at the very least provide protection against existential threats[18] (though states may contemplate trying to destroy small nuclear arsenals after they are developed, this has never occurred due to the uncertainty about how many weapons the state may have and whether a strike will succeed in eliminating them all). If a hider is caught, however, diplomatic or military mobilization against the proliferator may be more likely because of the perceived illegitimacy of hiding a nuclear capability. Hiding has rarely been successful because the requirement to maximize secrecy can

17. See David Albright and Corey Gay, "Taiwan: Nuclear Nightmare Averted," *Bulletin of the Atomic Scientists* 54, no. 1 (February 1998): 54–60.

18. Vipin Narang, "What Does It Take to Deter?: Regional Power Nuclear Postures and International Conflict," *Journal of Conflict Resolution* 57, no. 3 (June 2013): 478–508.

TABLE 2.2. Typology of the Strategies of Nuclear Proliferation

Strategy	Intended Outcome
Varieties of Hedging	Develop the option for a weapon
Sprinting	Weaponize as quickly as possible
Sheltered Pursuit	Weaponize before abandonment by patron
Hiding	Weaponize without being discovered

induce inefficiencies, and maintaining complete secrecy for many years in the face of counterproliferators' sophisticated intelligence and military tools has proven to be difficult.[19] Only South Africa has ever successfully built nuclear weapons while using a hiding strategy,[20] but even a small prospect of success may continue to tempt states to attempt hiding because the payout upon success is extremely high.

Table 2.2 indicates the varied goals of these strategies. Speed is the paramount priority in only one of the four strategies: sprinting. For example, hedgers intentionally slow down or even pause the weaponization process, while hiders choose to sacrifice speed to maintain secrecy. Sheltered pursuers are in a middle category that balances the desire for speed and secrecy, while their patron state protects them from nonproliferation efforts.

This typology is mutually exclusive—nuclear pursuers fall into one category or another at a given time. While, for example, a hedger can have hidden features of the program, the state is coded as hedging and not as a hider until the decision to culminate nuclear development is taken. Furthermore, hiders are, by definition, not sprinting. And only sheltered pursuers are developing nuclear weapons under protective cover. The typology is also empirically exhaustive. Each nuclear pursuer in the historical record has chosen a strategy in table 2.2, and it is difficult to imagine a future proliferator choosing anything else. The only theoretically plausible omission is *direct foreign acquisition* of an already functional nuclear arsenal—as opposed to a deluxe do-it-yourself kit—which theoretically offers a quick and cheap route to nuclear weapons, while placing the recipient's security at the mercy of the provider. The problem, of course, is finding a nuclear weapons state that is willing to place part of its own arsenal under the sovereign control

19. See Jeffrey T. Richelson, *Spying on the Bomb: American Nuclear Intelligence from Nazi Germany to North Korea* (New York: W. W. Norton, 2007).

20. See, for example, Peter Liberman, "The Rise and Fall of the South African Bomb," *International Security* 26, no. 2 (Fall 2001): 45–86.

of another state. Libya's Gaddafi is rumored to have sent an aide to ask China on March 24, 1970, to sell him nuclear weapons.[21] Zhou Enlai flatly refused. Leaving aside NATO nuclear-sharing arrangements that envisioned wartime transfer, all of the nuclear weapons states have similarly balked at outright transfer—no state wants to make itself a target for potential nuclear retaliation due to the decisions of another state—and there is little reason to think that this is likely to change, despite persistent rumors of, for example, a Saudi arrangement with Pakistan.[22] Other possibilities, such as "bluffing"—pretending to have greater capability than one actually has—are not strategies of proliferation but rather strategies of deterrence, and therefore distinct. Furthermore, *tactics* such as foreign assistance or joint development can be part of a strategy, but they are means to an end and do not define a strategy itself.

One important implication of this typology is that various strategies of proliferation are distinguishable by their unique political and strategic considerations: the choice of technology flows from the strategy of proliferation. That is, my approach is a challenge to the technological determinist perspective, which argues that states try to proliferate using whichever technology they can acquire or develop and that that drives the process of proliferation—and variations in success and failure are a function of available technology and a state's technical competence. My argument is exactly the reverse: states select their preferred strategy of proliferation and, based on that strategy, search for the appropriate technical pathway and generate the requisite competence. There is certainly variation in the technical ability of states to *implement* these strategies, and some do so more efficiently than others, but case evidence shows that the choice of technical pathway flows from the strategy of proliferation rather than the reverse. In the case of sprinting, for example, states choose the pathway that is most expedient, whether plutonium or uranium or both. Hedgers and sheltered pursuers have the latitude to choose different routes as well. Today, hiders find the uranium pathway attractive because they can more easily conceal and disperse uranium enrichment facilities. However, they learned this tactic through experience, either directly or indirectly. Some hiders such as Syria

21. See Richelson, *Spying on the Bomb*, 325.

22. Transferring nuclear weapons to the sovereign control of another state is risky for the supplier state because it could be held responsible for the actions of the recipient. Direct transfer of nuclear weapons to the sovereign control of another state is distinct from *stationing* nuclear weapons on foreign soil, or from inheriting foreign weapons without control of them, as Belarus, Kazakhstan, and Ukraine did. It is also distinct from nuclear assistance, such as China's assistance to Pakistan, which may accelerate the nuclearization of a state but does not involve transfer of weapons.

and Taiwan attempted hidden plutonium pathways and they were perhaps more easily discovered as a result.[23] The conventional wisdom is that hiders often fail because they are technically incompetent.[24] My framework suggests that the strategic choice to maintain a small signature in a nuclear weapons program to avoid external coercion *forces* a state into technically inefficient pathways, which prolongs the proliferation process and increases the likelihood of detection. The choice of technical pathway follows from the choice of proliferation strategy, rather than the reverse. That hiding is a strategic response to external coercion is a sign that global counterproliferation efforts have been successful. The billions of dollars that states expend to track others' nuclear activities pushes proliferators to the least promising pathways.

Proliferation Strategy Theory

Once states decide to pursue nuclear weapons, why do they select a particular strategy of proliferation over the others? This section presents a theory for the strategies of proliferation, hereafter simply Proliferation Strategy Theory (PST). It is structured as a decision tree that, from the view of the state's political leaders, asks: Given the external and domestic political environment, which is the optimal strategy of proliferation for the state? The decision tree makes a prediction for the strategy chosen by a given state at a given point in time, based on the values taken by a sequence of variables at that time. Because the value of each variable can change (e.g., a state's threat environment may change), these predictions are not static. Indeed, if a change in a variable occurs while a state is pursuing nuclear weapons, the theory would predict a corresponding shift in the state's proliferation strategy.

In the tradition inspired by neoclassical realism, the theory privileges systemic variables but recognizes that unit-level variables are necessary to capture the rich variation in state decisions.[25] I take care, however, not to introduce unit-level variables in an ad hoc fashion. I also avoid perceptual

23. See, for example, David Makovsky, "The Silent Strike: How Israel Bombed a Syrian Nuclear Installation and Kept It Secret," *New Yorker*, September 17, 2012; on Taiwan, see Albright and Gay, "Taiwan: Nuclear Nightmare Averted."

24. Målfrid Braut-Hegghammer, *Unclear Physics: Why Iraq and Libya Failed to Build Nuclear Weapons* (Ithaca: Cornell University Press, 2015).

25. See Gideon Rose, "Neoclassical Realism and Theories of Foreign Policy," *World Politics* 51, no. 1 (October 1998): 144–72; Randall L. Schweller, *Deadly Imbalances: Tripolarity and Hitler's Strategy of World Conquest* (New York: Columbia University Press, 1998); William C. Wohlforth,

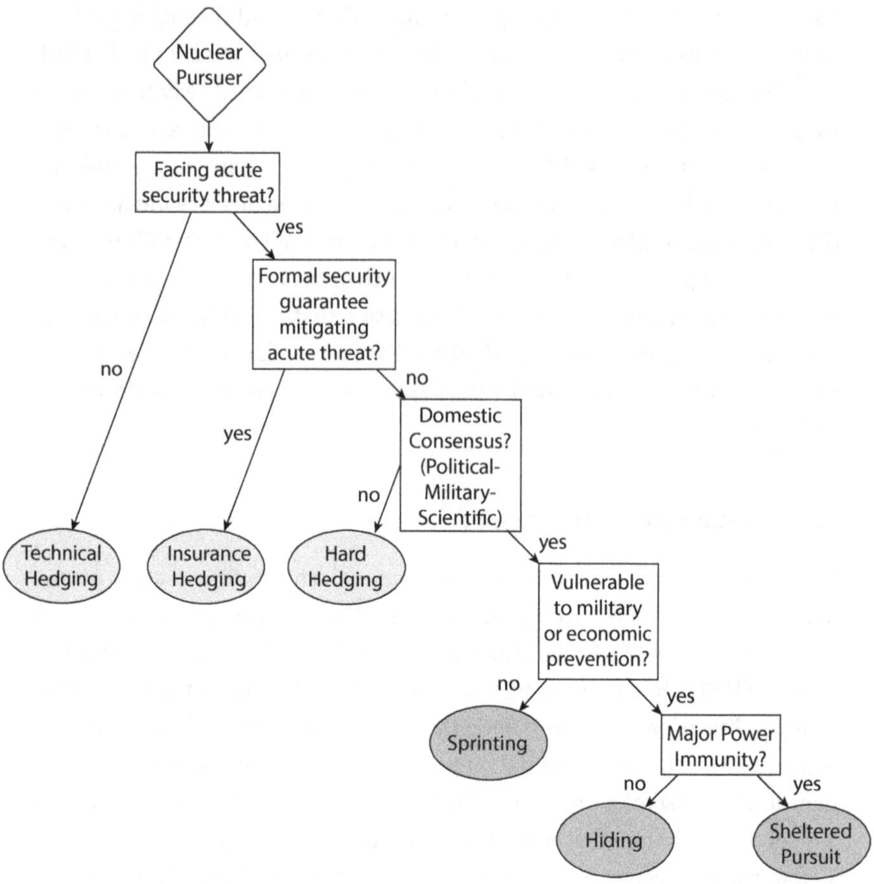

FIGURE 2.1. Proliferation Strategy Theory.

variables, which are often the source of theoretical indeterminacy and degeneration. Instead, I specify when and where unit-level variables might intervene and develop ex ante indictors for those variables so the theory remains both testable and falsifiable. Elsewhere, I employed this broader theoretical approach to predict which strategies of *deterrence* states might select.[26] Figure 2.1 outlines my theory, Proliferation Strategy Theory, for which strategies of *proliferation* states ought to select to develop nuclear weapons in the first place.

The Elusive Balance: Power and Perceptions during the Cold War (Ithaca: Cornell University Press, 1993); and Narang, *Nuclear Strategy in the Modern Era*.

26. See Narang, *Nuclear Strategy in the Modern Era*, chap. 2.

In deciding how to pursue nuclear weapons, states must consider: (1) their external security constraints and opportunities, (2) internal domestic context, and (3) international nonproliferation constraints and opportunities. The first two variables in figure 2.1 capture the intensity of demand generated by a state's immediate security environment, and the third variable measures whether the state's key and relevant political-scientific-military elites agree that nuclear weapons are necessary for the state to achieve its security needs.[27] These variables determine whether a state is a type of hedger, or whether it is on the active weapons development part of the chain, selecting between sprinting, hiding, or sheltered pursuit.

This theory prioritizes a state's security environment, the first necessary condition for active nuclear pursuit, but explicitly argues that domestic political consensus is also necessary: the decision to actively pursue nuclear *weapons* must be filtered through, and subject to, a domestic political process in which a consensus for weaponization congeals. This may not be an easy or expedient process, as cases such as India and Sweden will later show. Security environment and domestic politics determine, in combination, whether a state will seek to weaponize its nuclear capabilities. If a state is ambivalent about its desire for nuclear weapons, due to either a permissive external security environment or lack of domestic consensus, then the state should pursue a variety of hedging. For states that face an acute security threat alone and have the domestic consensus for a nuclear weapons capability, the nature of the nonproliferation or counterproliferation environment the state encounters will determine how the nuclear aspirant goes about active nuclear weaponization. Risk of military prevention or other coercive measures and the possibility that a state has immunity from a major power patron dictate the optimal active proliferation strategy. I now explore each of the variables, explaining how, when, and why each should influence the choice of proliferation strategy.

Facing Acute Security Threat Alone? The first two variables determining a state's strategy are the totality of its security environment. There are two considerations, in sequence. First, does the state confront an acute security environment? That is, does it face a conventionally superior proximate offensive threat that can pose an existential threat to the state or a primary adversary that itself possesses nuclear weapons? Second, if so, does

27. For an active strategy of proliferation to be sustainable, the theory thus posits that an acute security threat and domestic political consensus are necessary. The other hypothesized source of demand, prestige, should not generate an active pursuit of nuclear weapons if the other two variables are not present.

it confront that security threat alone or does it have a formal alliance with a superpower that mitigates the severity of the underlying threat? According to the theory, a high-threat security environment is a necessary condition for an active nuclear weapons strategy. If a state is not facing an acute security threat alone—either because there is no such threat or because the state has a formal superpower guarantee mitigating a threat—then there ought to be little consideration of an active nuclear proliferation strategy. In such circumstances, a state should choose either technical or insurance hedging.

Hedging should appear ideal to states that are not facing an acute security environment alone because it leaves future options open without running the risks—the window of vulnerability—of an active proliferation strategy. States that do not face an acute security threat at all should be technical hedgers that demonstrate at most fringe interest in nuclear weapons and no significant domestic push for weaponization. These are the states that should be most likely to abandon pursuit on their own, without outside influence. States with no acute security threat have weak demand for nuclear weapons but, for idiosyncratic domestic reasons or because they are tempted by the potential of their civilian energy program, flirt with the idea of a nuclear weapons capability.[28]

If a state faces an acute security environment but enjoys the formal protection of a superpower, then it should pursue insurance hedging, which offers both a source of leverage to compel the ally's continued protection and an insurance policy in the event that the state is ever abandoned. The quintessential example of nuclear hedging where a pursuer faces an acute security threat but benefits from a formal alliance is Japan, which faces underlying security threats from nuclear-armed China and North Korea but enjoys a formal alliance and nuclear umbrella from the United States. Japan thus uses the implicit threat of nuclear breakout with its insurance hedge to elicit stronger commitments from the United States, but also to put pieces in place for an independent nuclear deterrent should it ever face abandonment.[29]

How do I measure these security variables? Two considerations in sequence define the intensity of a state's security environment. The first subcomponent of a state's security environment is whether it faces an *acute security threat*. This variable takes a positive value, "yes," if a state faces a primary adversary that itself is believed to have, or be close to having, nuclear

28. See Fuhrmann, *Atomic Assistance*.

29. See Richard J. Samuels and James L. Schoff, "Japan's Nuclear Hedge: Beyond 'Allergy' and Breakout," in *Strategic Asia, 2013–2014: Asia in the Second Nuclear Age*, ed. Ashley J. Tellis, Abraham M. Denmark, and Travis Tanner (Seattle: National Bureau of Asian Research, 2013), 233–66.

weapons *or* an adversary that poses a proximate conventional offensive threat to the state. An adversary's nuclear status is relatively straightforward to measure. I further specify conventional offensive threat as an existential ground threat from a proximate or bordering state, against which nuclear weapons may be a valuable deterrent. Geographic buffers such as the Himalayan Mountains or large bodies of water can attenuate the severity of the conventional threat.[30] For example, China is not coded as an existential ground threat to India, but India is coded as posing one to Pakistan. India's security environment is still "acute" because one of its principal adversaries, China, attained nuclear weapons in 1964. India is coded as having an acute security threat since then. Either of these conditions—a primary adversary with nuclear weapons or a proximate conventional threat—should cause a state to consider initiating a nuclear weapons program. While the variable is coded as binary, there can be perturbations that increase the severity of one's threat—if, for example, another adversary develops nuclear weapons, or if a nuclear adversary also emerges as a proximate offensive conventional threat. The hypothesized relationship between severity of threat and the urgency with which a state tries to develop nuclear weapons is monotonically increasing.

The second component of a state's security environment is the presence or absence of a *formal security guarantee* from a superpower. Is the state (e.g., Japan, Germany) protected against an acute security threat by a *formal* security guarantee and nuclear umbrella? This condition is readily observable, since formal security guarantees are public by necessity as a signal to adversaries. States with underlying acute security threats but with a formal security guarantee should pursue insurance hedging.

For a state facing an acute security threat alone, however, additional variables determine its choice of nuclear proliferation strategy. One option for a state in this position is to seek a formal superpower protector or a nuclear umbrella—India attempted this in the 1960s and 1970s and ultimately failed. If no protector can be found, the state will likely consider an active pursuit strategy.

Domestic Consensus? If a state faces an acute security threat alone, the next crucial variable is whether there is domestic consensus for nuclear weaponization. That is, do relevant political elites, the military, and scientific organizations agree that nuclear weapons are a solution to the state's

30. See, for example, John J. Mearsheimer, *The Tragedy of Great Power Politics* (New York: W. W. Norton, 2001), chap. 4.

security problems?[31] Nuclear weapons are difficult, expensive, and time-consuming to develop; they can also alter a military's missions and arsenal or threaten the budgets of state bureaucracies. Active pursuit of nuclear weapons requires consensus among the political leaders—the head of state and his/her party, as well as potential veto players, such as coalition parties or the legislature in democracies or any veto players in autocracies—as well as among the military leadership, and key scientific bureaucracies. These constituencies must agree that nuclear weapons at least partially solve a state's security concerns.

An extremely acute security environment may catalyze domestic consensus,[32] but the external security environment is not always reflected without distortion in a state's internal politics. In other words, whether or not a state can achieve domestic political consensus to actively pursue nuclear weapons is surely influenced by the external security environment, but other internal factors—regime type and politics, the fundamental battle over resources and power—play a role as well. Even in the face of an acute security threat, domestic consensus can be difficult to obtain or lag behind the emergence of the threat. For one, as Saunders argues, threat uncertainty can retard the formation of domestic consensus.[33] Additionally, political leaders or the general public in democracies may have ideological or economic preferences against weaponization, as in Sweden and Switzerland in the 1960s.[34] At the elite level, several cases, including the Indian case in the next chapter, show that individual leaders can stall or veto weaponization for personal or idiosyncratic reasons. Scientists may not believe they can deliver on the promise of nuclear pursuit in a reasonable time frame, or worry that it might divert resources from other pursuits or threaten civilian energy programs. Militaries may worry that nuclear weapons may cannibalize their conventional missions and budgets. And often, getting these

31. For demand-side work on domestic consensus and nuclear weapons, see Solingen, *Nuclear Logics*; and Hymans, *Psychology of Nuclear Proliferation*.

32. Peter A. Gourevitch, "The Second-Image Reversed: The International Sources of Domestic Politics," *International Organization* 32, no. 4 (Autumn 1978): 881–912.

33. Elizabeth N. Saunders, "The Domestic Politics of Nuclear Choices—A Review Essay," *International Security* 44, no. 2 (Fall 2019): 146–84.

34. The role of mass public opinion with regard to weaponization is beyond the scope of my theory. It could be the case that the general public takes their cues from elites when it comes to favoring or opposing the pursuit of nuclear weapons. Some scholars posit such a process regarding public opinion toward armed intervention. See Adam J. Berinsky, "Assuming the Costs of War: Events, Elites, and American Public Support for Military Conflict," *Journal of Politics* 69, no. 4 (November 2007): 975–97.

various constituencies to agree on pursuing nuclear weapons is not a trivial exercise. Whatever the reason, if a consensus never emerges, state leaders will be unable to order the pursuit of nuclear weapons, as domestic opponents could always threaten to publicize the program or simply stall, thereby effectively killing it from within.

Even in the absence of domestic consensus on nuclear weaponization, a state facing an acute security threat alone should at least pursue a hard hedging strategy. Domestic political "fracture" inhibits active pursuit strategies, but domestic constituencies that prefer nuclear weapons as a solution to the state's security problems should be able to act independently to put some pieces in place for a hard hedging strategy even without total consensus. Sweden essentially followed this path in the late 1950s.[35] Where Sweden's hard hedging strategy arose as a result of pro-weapon constituencies pushing the program as far as possible within their exclusive purview, hard hedging may also emerge as a compromise between opposing constituencies, as in India after 1964.

It is difficult to identify a generalizable causal explanation for the formation or fracture of domestic consensus over nuclear weapons, especially across various regime types and constellations of veto players found in states that have pursued nuclear weapons. Consensus for nuclear weapons will look different within and across presidential and parliamentary democracies, party authoritarian, and personalist dictatorships. Nevertheless, even if there is no underlying theory for what causes domestic consensus to form, the basic structure of a regime may at least provide some indication about which constituencies must support active nuclear pursuit for a functional consensus to exist. Table 2.3 lists the key constituencies across various regime types required for "domestic political consensus" in favor of nuclear weapons.

In my theory, all that matters is whether domestic political consensus or fracture exists in a particular regime. "Fracture" means that at least one of the key constituencies at the domestic level disagrees that nuclear weapons are at least a partial solution to the state's security problems, inhibiting the constituencies that favor nuclear weapons from selecting an active pursuit strategy. The ease with which domestic consensus may be achieved varies across regime types. For example, parliamentary democracies with messy coalition politics may find it difficult to achieve consensus for a project as significant, controversial, and demanding as a nuclear

35. See Jonter, *The Key to Nuclear Restraint*, chap. 3.

TABLE 2.3. Measuring Domestic Political Consensus for Nuclear Weapons across Regime Types

Regime Type	Constituencies Required for Domestic Political Consensus for Nuclear Weapons
Presidential Democracy	Executive, Legislature, Military, Scientists
Parliamentary Democracy (Coalition)	Prime Minister, Coalition Parties, Military, Scientists
Parliamentary Democracy (Single Party)	Prime Minister, Military, Scientists
Military Dictatorship	Head of State, Military Selectorate
Party Authoritarian	Head of State, Party Selectorate
Personalist Dictatorship	Head of State

weapons program.[36] A single-party parliamentary democracy with a powerful prime minister, however, may find the decision nearly as centralized as it would be under a personalist or military dictatorship. The other regimes lie somewhere along a spectrum in the middle in terms of the ease with which domestic consensus for a nuclear weapons program can be achieved by a head of state. Domestic political consensus for nuclear weapons—however operationalized in a particular regime type or state—is, however, required for a state to actively pursue nuclear weapons.

How do I measure domestic consensus? In practice, it is easier to observe fracture than consensus. Significant opposition or even coalition party obstruction to pursuing nuclear weapons, military or scientific opposition due to budgetary concerns, or strong disapproval from the public against nuclear weapons all suggest fracture. Examining parliamentary debates, public opinion polls, and speech evidence from political and military leaders may shed light on this. In some cases, the head of government may evince ambivalence about developing nuclear weapons. Public speech evidence from leaders helps reveal their thinking. In autocracies, measuring the presence or absence of opposition from key veto players is one of the only ways to determine the extent of domestic political fracturing. This can admittedly be difficult. Still, leaders' statements—whether autocrats or democrats—help reflect whether consensus has emerged, including whether the leader himself or herself has overcome their doubts. Because the sources of consensus and fracture are likely to vary across regime types and myriad domestic

36. See Vipin Narang and Paul Staniland, "Democratic Accountability and Foreign Security Policy: Theory and Evidence from India," *Security Studies* 27, no. 3 (2018): 410–47; and Barbara Geddes, Joseph Wright, and Erica Frantz, "Autocratic Breakdown and Regime Transition: A New Data Set," *Perspectives on Politics* 12, no. 2 (June 2014): 313–31.

political configurations, I operationalize and measure this variable on a case-by-case basis.

Domestic consensus is a powerful master variable in the proliferation process and suggests that powerful security pressures must pass through a strong filter at home *before* a state decides to shift from hedging to an active nuclear weapons strategy. If and only if a state facing an acute security threat alone has, or can manufacture, domestic consensus for weaponization can the state pursue an active proliferation strategy. The question, then, is which one. The answer depends on the counterproliferation environment the state faces.

Concerns about external prevention feature prominently in the last two steps of the theory, which predicts *how* active pursuers will pursue the bomb.[37] I assume that states intuitively understand the "window of volatility" around nuclear proliferation that I empirically demonstrated in chapter 1 and therefore take measures to preempt, evade, or hoodwink adversaries and counterproliferators in order to survive that window and emerge with a nuclear weapons capability.

Vulnerable to Economic or Military Prevention? If a proliferator's pursuit of nuclear weapons were discovered by another state or coalition of states, could those external actors make nuclear proliferation economically cost-prohibitive or, more dramatically, end the program by force? The relationship between economic vulnerability and nuclear proliferation has been explored elsewhere.[38] Some states' economies—outwardly looking states in particular—are sufficiently vulnerable to international economic sanctions that achieving a nuclear weapons capability could be incredibly costly, perhaps even crippling. Economic vulnerability may not deter a determined nuclear aspirant, but it should change the *strategy*.

States pursuing nuclear weapons may also be vulnerable to military prevention, if an adversary or major power can attack critical facilities and cripple the program. Vulnerability to military or kinetic prevention is a dynamic variable that depends on the capabilities of both the preventer and the pursuer.[39] First, a potential preventer must have sufficient confidence that they can identify and characterize the full scope of the proliferator's

37. See Debs and Monteiro, *Nuclear Politics*. They argue that prevention determines who succeeds and fails in developing nuclear weapons. Here, I show that it determines *how* they attempt to develop nuclear weapons as well.

38. Solingen, *Nuclear Logics*; Nicholas L. Miller, "The Secret Success of Nonproliferation Sanctions," *International Organization* 68, no. 4 (Fall 2014): 913–44.

39. See Fuhrmann and Kreps, "Targeting Nuclear Programs in War and Peace."

nuclear program. This was especially difficult early in the nuclear era when intelligence capabilities were poor,[40] but it remains challenging as nuclear aspirants have learned how to conceal critical facilities. Second, the structure of nuclear weapons programs varies across states, and different structures are innately more or less vulnerable to military prevention. Some programs could be vulnerable to covert action or sabotage; others require a single or sustained air strikes to destroy. Other nuclear programs are dispersed and expansive enough to require a full-scale ground invasion, or regime change, to terminate. The more difficult the military mission, the less vulnerable a pursuer. Nuclear pursuers with few proximate adversaries, expansive territory, and strong defenses are in a better position to avoid military prevention than those with smaller territories, limited nuclear infrastructure that is easy to locate and destroy, and weak air defense capabilities.

When a state calculates that it is not vulnerable to economic or military prevention, it should pursue nuclear weapons openly and prioritize speed of development, because it is immaterial if other states are aware of its intentions and capability. Few states have this luxury. In fact, it may be that all the states in the system that meet these criteria already possess nuclear weapons: the United States, Britain, France, Soviet Union, China, and, at the end of its pursuit, India. Perhaps Australia, with vast territory, a remote location, and defensible sea borders, meets the conditions to be a start-to-finish sprinter if it were ever to actively pursue nuclear weapons. Japan and Germany may meet the conditions as well, if they ever choose to shift from insurance hedging to active weaponization.

To measure economic vulnerability, I estimate the costs of potential sanctions should a state's nuclear weapons program be discovered. If sanctions can substantially hurt the state, especially its elites—that is, if it is an export-dependent economy, or a weak economy dependent on critical inputs that can be sanctioned—then I code it as vulnerable to economic coercion.[41] External sanctions regimes have also become stronger over time, most notably in U.S. legislation in 1976 and 1977 (the Symington and Glenn Amendments to the Foreign Assistance Act). Nicholas Miller shows that

40. See Richelson, *Spying on the Bomb*.

41. See Solingen, *Nuclear Logics*. This variable is measured similarly to Solingen's economic vulnerability, or global economic orientation variable. The difference between my theory and Solingen's is that, because I am interested in the strategies of proliferation, and not the motivations, her theory elides the fact that the Middle East countries that pursued nuclear weapons may not have been economically vulnerable to coercion, but they were militarily vulnerable, which pushed them into hiding strategies.

more states are vulnerable to economic coercion post-1977 than before due to these changes.[42]

I code a state as vulnerable to military coercion if the state is militarily too weak to defend its nuclear program or the infrastructure is so concentrated that it is easy to destroy. This indicator varies from case to case. It requires an assessment of the nature of a state's potential nuclear weapons infrastructure, its vulnerability to an external power's capacity to launch long-range attacks (usually in the air), and the cost ratio of offense to defense. Major powers are often less vulnerable to economic and military coercion and thus often have the luxury to sprint relatively openly for nuclear weapons. Weak powers tend to be vulnerable on at least one, if not both, of these dimensions and therefore cannot openly sprint for nuclear weapons. This vulnerability forces many weak powers into inefficient and risky strategies such as sheltered pursuit or hiding. Medium powers tend to vary much more on these indicators, and this is where the vulnerability variable has its greatest leverage on a case-by-case basis.

Most contemporary states that might contemplate active pursuit, for example, states in East Asia or the Middle East, are vulnerable to prevention for two interrelated reasons. First, the efficacy of the nonproliferation and sanctions regime has improved over time, so this variable is more powerful today than it was in, for example, the 1960s.[43] Second, today's potential proliferators are often relatively weak compared to the major powers and thus more susceptible to these more powerful military and economic nonproliferation tools. How do these vulnerable states pursue nuclear proliferation?

Major Power Immunity? The strategy chosen by states that are actively pursuing nuclear weapons but are vulnerable to prevention depends on a final variable: whether the state has a major power patron—usually a superpower, but possibly another major power such as China or contemporary Russia—that is willing to tolerate its nuclear pursuit, deterring potential counterproliferators and shielding the pursuer from efforts at prevention.[44] A major power patron may choose to tolerate or be complicit in a state's proliferation for a variety of domestic political or geopolitical reasons that

42. Miller, "The Secret Success of Nonproliferation Sanctions."

43. Ibid.

44. In the United States, there may be variation in levels of this immunity based on, for example, partisan affiliation of the executive; i.e., Republicans during the Cold War may have been more tolerant of proliferation than their Democratic counterparts were. I thank Robert Jervis for this point.

outweigh the major power's nonproliferation objectives. A proliferator can actively attempt to cultivate major power patronage, or it may find itself an important client state for entirely incidental reasons. For example, after the Soviet Union invaded Afghanistan in 1979, Pakistan suddenly found itself on the front line of the Cold War and took advantage of U.S. shelter to redouble its efforts to build nuclear weapons.[45] Importantly, the proliferator should not be in a position where its nuclear weapons threaten, or threaten the freedom of action of, its patron.[46] As a result, states within formal alliances such as NATO, where the senior partner may worry about nuclearization leading to independence of action or recklessness by the junior partner, should not generally expect to receive shelter if they pursue nuclear weapons—in fact, quite the opposite. Major power shelter is therefore distinct from the formal alliance variable mentioned above. Certain client states may enjoy patronage sufficient to facilitate nuclear weapons development under major power shelter.[47] It is also distinct from nuclear *assistance*. The provision of nuclear technology or nuclear weapons assistance is neither necessary nor sufficient to qualify as extending shelter. For example, China assisted Pakistan's nuclear program but it was the Reagan administration that shielded it, both from external powers and from the U.S. Congress.

If a proliferator enjoys major power shelter, it should select sheltered pursuit, which allows a relatively open pursuit of nuclear weapons under major power protection, increasing its likelihood of attaining nuclear weapons. The proliferator may construct facilities and engage in activities that are consistent only with weaponization while claiming (incredibly) to other states that its facilities are energy infrastructure for nonmilitary purposes—or more brazenly, that its centrifuges are textile factories or goat sheds, as in the Israeli and Pakistani cases, respectively.[48] The major power protector

45. See Secretary of State George Schultz to President Reagan, "How Do We Make Use of the Zia Visit to Protect Our Strategic Interests in the Face of Pakistan's Nuclear Weapons Activities," November 26, 1982, in William Burr, ed., *New Documents Spotlight Reagan-Era Tensions over Pakistani Nuclear Program*, NSA EBB 377, doc. 16, https://www.documentcloud.org/documents/347090-doc-16-11-26-82.html; also Feroz Hassan Khan, *Eating Grass: The Making of the Pakistani Bomb* (Stanford: Stanford University Press, 2012), 124–25.

46. Kroenig, *Exporting the Bomb*, chap. 1.

47. Often, this has empirically been development but just short of a full-blown test. See Rabinowitz and Miller, "Keeping the Bombs in the Basement"; also see Gavin, "Strategies of Inhibition."

48. See "We have been misbehaving a little," U.S. Embassy Tel Aviv telegram 574 to State Department, December 23, 1960, Secret, National Archives, Record Group 469, U.S. Operations Mission to Israel, Executive Office Classified Central Files 1952–1961, box 10, Atomic Matters 1960,

becomes complicit in this often implausible deniability and chooses to remain silent or engage in willful denial.[49]

Sheltered pursuit allows states to avoid the typical dangers associated with proliferation in two ways. First, the major power's shelter and complicity allow the nuclear pursuer to consistently deny intent and capability regarding weaponization, sowing doubt among other states regarding its intentions and thereby giving it a wider berth to proliferate. Second, and more importantly, the pursuer's alignment with a major power protector shields it from both the shelterer, who refrains from economic or military coercion, and external powers. A major power shelterer can dilute third-party efforts at economic coercion and deter efforts at military prevention by raising the risk of drawing a major power into military confrontation over some other state's nuclear program. Simply put: states that might otherwise have moved to destroy a nuclear aspirant's atomic dreams decide against attempting to do so.

A sheltered pursuer's statements about its peaceful nuclear intentions are usually at least minimally plausible, given what other states know at the time. Eventually, however, sheltered pursuers lose the ability to convincingly deny the reality of their nuclear weapons programs and depend on the shelterer to shield it from external coercion. Likewise, when the existence of a sheltered nuclear program becomes widely known, the shelterer cannot continue in willful denial indefinitely, often engaging in convenient fictions surrounding the nuclear status of the sheltered pursuer. The crux of a successful sheltered pursuit strategy, therefore, is for the proliferator to attain a nuclear weapons capability, or reach a point sufficiently close to it such that external powers are deterred from preventive attempts by the mere possibility that it has crossed the nuclear threshold, before the shelter evaporates.

For states vulnerable to prevention but lacking major power immunity, the only available remaining strategy is hiding. Proliferators in this position

---

http://nsarchive.gwu.edu/nukevault/ebb510/docs/doc%2015.pdf; and President Zia quoted in Narang, *Nuclear Strategy in the Modern Era*, 59.

49. Under these circumstances, the major power declines to publicize its knowledge of the pursuer's activities. Allison Carnegie and Austin Carson term this "obfuscation." They argue that states deliberately overlook proliferation activities when one of two conditions arises. First, states "obfuscate" when they fear that publicizing violations will threaten other states' beliefs in nonproliferation norms. Second, states look the other way when they worry that publicity will cause a cascade of proliferation among states nearby. My theory does not address this question. The circumstances under which major power patrons might "obfuscate" and therefore permit sheltered pursuit are beyond the scope of my inquiry. On "obfuscation," see Allison Carnegie and Austin Carson, "The Spotlight's Harsh Glare: Rethinking Publicity and International Order," *International Organization* 72, no. 3 (Summer 2018): 627–57.

have to ensure that their weapons programs remain hidden to avoid preventive attempts against them. Hiders must hope their programs remain hidden until they are sufficiently advanced to present a fait accompli to potential counterproliferators. Should their facilities or intent be discovered, they run the risk of crippling preventive action. A hider may attempt to explain away their program after it is discovered, but the fact of discovery of previously clandestine capabilities undermines the plausibility of such denials. A failed hider may then search for major power immunity, but this might prove difficult if it could not find one prior to pursuit. For recent nuclear proliferators, such as Iran and Syria, hiding is the most common strategy given the potency of the nonproliferation and counterproliferation regimes against the states that the major powers least want to possess nuclear weapons—those often finding themselves in the crosshairs of the major powers.

How do I measure major power shelter? This condition takes a positive value of "yes" if the state is not a formal ally of a superpower but is otherwise of critical geopolitical value to either a superpower or a major power—which it can cultivate through its own efforts or find itself suddenly enjoying if fortune smiles upon them. Israel and Pakistan fulfilled this condition for the United States in the past, and Saudi Arabia does today. Active nuclear pursuers may enjoy major power immunity for a variety of idiosyncratic reasons. They may reside in a region of critical importance. Or they may find themselves involved in a dispute with global ramifications. Sometimes superpowers provide immunity for domestic political reasons unrelated to international concerns. In other cases, superpowers grant shelter to pursuers in the aftermath of a sudden development that makes the client state discontinuously valuable to a major power patron. Whatever the underlying reason, major power shelter materializes when the nuclear aspirant offers such value to the major power that it outweighs typical concerns about nonproliferation. This creates conditions that enable the proliferator to more openly and efficiently pursue nuclear weapons under the shelter of superpower protection. If major power shelter evaporates before a state successfully attains nuclear weapons, the previously sheltered pursuer may end up facing the same consequences as a caught hider. But so long as that immunity exists, the state can select a sheltered pursuit nuclear proliferation strategy. If no such immunity is forthcoming, the state has no option but to select a hiding strategy and hope that it attains nuclear weapons before it is discovered by foreign powers.

Proliferation Strategy Theory provides a framework for thinking about how states pursue nuclear weapons. It necessarily sacrifices some parsimony in order to capture the complexity of the proliferation process, distilling the key variables that in sequence should inform a strategy of proliferation.

Based on the values of these variables, it generates a determinate prediction for which proliferation strategy a state might pursue, from a particular variety of hedging to a specific active strategy of pursuit. It also identifies which variables could change to cause a state to shift its strategy. I now turn to the empirical record, showing that the theory explains the nuclear proliferation strategy chosen in the vast majority of cases.

Observed Strategies of Nuclear Proliferation: The Empirical Record

Which proliferation strategies have states selected and when? To establish the universe of cases, I include states that credibly explored or pursued nuclear weapons. Based on data sets by Christopher Way as well as Philipp Bleek, I ultimately identify a total of twenty-nine states as nuclear aspirants.[50] Entry into this universe is obviously not random. These states were all exploring or pursuing nuclear weapons for a reason. This selection effect would be problematic if the reasons for nuclear pursuit correlated with the ultimate choice of strategy (e.g., if all states that pursued nuclear weapons for security motivations chose a sprinting strategy, or if the advent of a stronger nonproliferation regime forced all states into hiding). As noted earlier, however, this is not the case, and the correlation between why states pursue nuclear weapons and how they go about doing so is weak. Therefore, it is reasonable to treat the selection of a strategy of proliferation as a de novo decision once states decide to embark on it. Furthermore, though the number of active nuclear pursuers has decreased over time—some states have already succeeded and the increasingly robust U.S.-led nonproliferation regime has deterred others from even exploring nuclear weapons options[51]—a significant number of states have continued to seek nuclear weapons.

50. Christopher Way, "Nuclear Proliferation Dates," working paper, June 12, 2012, http://falcon.arts.cornell.edu/crw12/documents/Nuclear%20Proliferation%20Dates.pdf; Sonali Singh and Christopher R. Way, "The Correlates of Nuclear Proliferation: A Quantitative Test," *Journal of Conflict Resolution* 47, no. 6 (2004): 859–85; Bleek, "Does Proliferation Beget Proliferation?" Although Way, Singh and Way, and Bleek make a distinction between explorers and pursuers, for my purposes, I include both categories so long as the explorer expresses a basic level of intent such that it "seriously considered building nuclear weapons." Cases of pure technical latency with no serious intent to develop nuclear weapons are excluded. One requires at least a minimal level of intent in order to devise a strategy of nuclear proliferation. The Way and Bleek data sets include Indonesia, which I do not, because it lacked the capability to seriously consider building nuclear weapons. Bleek also includes Nazi Germany, which I exclude for reasons I discuss in chapter 4. Way further excludes four crucial cases that I include: Norway, Japan, West Germany, and Italy.

51. Miller, "The Secret Success of Nonproliferation Sanctions."

TABLE 2.4. Empirical Codings of Strategies of Nuclear Proliferation

	Proliferation Strategy	Country (Approximate Years)
Hedging Strategies	*Technical Hedging*	Argentina (1968–1976)
		Brazil (1953–1976)
		Iran (1974–1978)*
		India (1948–1964)
		Libya (1970–1981)
		Norway (1946–1962)*
		South Africa (1969–1974)
	Insurance Hedging	Australia (1956–1973)
		France (1945–1954)
		Italy (1955–1959)
		Japan (1954–present)
		Romania (late 1960s–1989)
		South Korea (1975–present)
		Taiwan (1967–1974)
		West Germany/Germany (1956–present)
		Yugoslavia (1948–1960)*
	Hard Hedging	Argentina (1977–1990)
		Brazil (1977–1990)
		Egypt (1955–1980)
		India (1964–1989)
		Iran (2003–present)
		Iraq (1973–1981)
		Israel (1949–1955)
		Pakistan (1954–1971)
		Sweden (1945–1966)
		Switzerland (1945–1969)
Weaponization Strategies	*Sprinting*	**China** (1958–1964)
		France (1954–1960)*
		India (1989–1998)
		USSR (1945–1949)
		United Kingdom (1945–1952)
		United States (1940–1945)

TABLE 2.4. (*continued*)

	Proliferation Strategy	Country (Approximate Years)
	Sheltered Pursuit	China (1955–1958)
		Israel (1956–1967)
		North Korea (1979–2006)
		Pakistan (1980–1990)
	Hiding	Algeria (1986–1992)*
		Iran (1987–2003)
		Iraq (1981–1991)
		Libya (1981–2003)*
		Pakistan (1972–1979)
		South Africa (1974–1979)
		South Korea (1970–1974)
		Syria (2000–2007)
		Taiwan (1974–1988)
		Yugoslavia (1974–1987)

Note: Cases with an * denote cases Proliferation Strategy Theory mispredicts relative to alternative explanations (6 of 46 strategies, or a success rate of over 85 percent). Cases in bold successfully attained nuclear weapons.

Twenty-nine nuclear aspirants have explored or pursued nuclear weapons. Some states have shifted strategies over time, providing additional observations (forty-six in total) and allowing me to isolate the causes of shifts in strategies of proliferation. Table 2.4 shows the empirical distribution of proliferation strategies, while figure 2.2 depicts these strategies over time. Some types of aspirants, such as insurance hedgers, can persist indefinitely with a proliferation strategy to guard against a change in their extended deterrence arrangements. Others, such as Saudi Arabia and Turkey, are on the cusp of entering the data set but do not qualify at the time of writing. A state "exits" the data set when it either abandons its pursuit of nuclear weapons or "becomes" a nuclear weapons state.

There can be considerable disagreement about when a particular state "becomes" a nuclear weapons power—the point of attainment or possession.[52] For clear and consistent cross-national comparison, I define the finish

52. Jacques E. C. Hymans, "When Does a State Become a 'Nuclear Weapon State,' *Nonproliferation Review* 17, no. 1 (2010): 161–80; also see Abraham, "The Ambivalence of Nuclear Histories." As an aside, the literature frequently uses the term "nuclear acquisition" to refer to a state's attainment of a nuclear weapons capability. I eschew the word "acquire" or "acquisition"

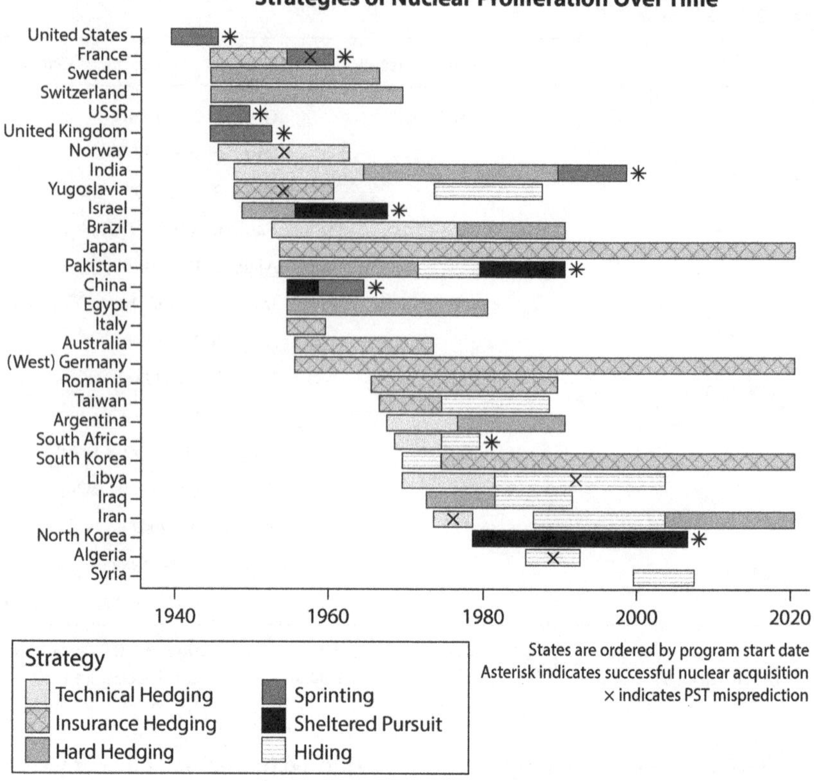

FIGURE 2.2. Strategies of Nuclear Proliferation over time.

line as the year in which a state either (a) tests a nuclear weapon, or (b) is credibly believed to be able to test its first fission nuclear weapon.[53] Some nuclear powers—such as the United States, the Soviet Union, Britain, China, France, North Korea—tested as soon as they were able to do so. In these

---

where possible, since it connotes that a state buys or acquires from a private entity or from abroad a nuclear weapons capability like it does with, for example, fighter aircraft. While components and material may be "acquired," nuclear weapons have thus far been "built," "developed," or "attained" through indigenous national efforts, or nuclear weapons capability "achieved" or "weaponized." The term "acquire" or "acquisition" understates the challenge and effort required to achieve a nuclear weapons capability. This terminology is a departure from Vipin Narang, "Strategies of Nuclear Proliferation: How States Pursue the Bomb," *International Security* 41, no. 3 (Winter 2016–17): 110–50.

53. I define a nuclear weapon as a nuclear capability intended for military purposes. This excludes nuclear "devices" such as India's 1974 peaceful nuclear explosion, which was not a militarily useful capability given its size and instability.

cases, I use the actual test date as the point of nuclearization. Others, India and Pakistan, were capable of testing nuclear weapons before they finally did so in 1998, while some, Israel and South Africa, never openly tested (the unconfirmed 1979 Vela incident notwithstanding). In these cases, I use the date when it is widely believed they were capable of testing a nuclear weapon to code them as nuclear weapons powers. I use the development of the first nuclear weapon as the finish line, rather than construction of a second-strike arsenal or a fully reliable aircraft or missile delivery capability. For one, states can no longer be practically "prevented" after building their first fission nuclear weapons. Second, a state's choices about how to develop its full nuclear force posture and strategy after it possesses the capability to produce nuclear weapons are not necessarily correlated with the strategy of proliferation they chose.[54] Thus, for the sake of theoretical coherence and uniform cross-national comparison, I use the development of a state's first nuclear weapon as the standardized finish line for when it "becomes" a nuclear weapons state in this book, though it is an admittedly imperfect criterion.

There are several important observations about the distribution of strategies. First, sprinting from start to finish is a strategy chosen by—and perhaps only available to—the early proliferators. Only three states—the United States, the Soviet Union, and Britain after it was exiled from the Manhattan Project—sprinted from start to finish, an exceptionally low frequency given that it is presumed to be the default strategy by the bulk of the proliferation literature. These early sprinters were the system's major powers and did not face the serious threat of preventive military strikes when they were developing nuclear weapons or the teeth of a coordinated nonproliferation regime. The states that could choose sprinting had to be relatively powerful and geographically expansive, with the sanctuary to openly pursue nuclear weapons. Since most states that meet these conditions already possess nuclear weapons, there are few, though not zero, possible start-to-finish sprinters left in the system. There are, however, states such as China and India that pursued other strategies before shifting to a sprint at the end.

Second, after the Nuclear Nonproliferation Treaty (NPT) came into force in 1968, the distribution of non-sprinting strategies has not been highly skewed toward any particular one. The frequency of hiding strategies has unsurprisingly risen in the so-called third generation of pursuers that have emerged since the end of the Cold War, but hedging and sheltered pursuit strategies are still selected in the contemporary proliferation landscape.

54. For sources of nuclear strategy, see Narang, *Nuclear Strategy in the Modern Era.*

Third, although my core dependent variable is the proliferation *strategy*, and not whether a state successfully develops nuclear weapons, the differential success rates of these strategies is striking. Hedgers are not failed proliferators, they are simply warming up and deciding whether they will even run the race. But, contrary to the conventional wisdom that successful nuclear proliferation is rare, over *half*—ten of nineteen—of the active proliferators succeeded in developing nuclear weapons. Within active proliferators, sprinters and sheltered pursuers have never failed to get the bomb, illustrating that states that can select these strategies are optimizing their chances of success. Hiding, however, is the refuge of states for whom the very threats that motivate them to seek the bomb drive them to do so clandestinely, for fear of murder. And although many hidden programs have been killed along the way, as I discuss in detail in subsequent chapters, even a small chance of success—South Africa is the only successful hider thus far, though some have come tantalizingly close—tempts hiders to keep trying. This variation alone suggests why classifying and determining the sources of proliferation strategies is so important to understanding the future nuclear landscape.

No theory can explain all forty-six strategies coded in table 2.4. The process of proliferation is too complex. My Proliferation Strategy Theory, though, explains the vast majority—more than 85 percent—of the empirical strategies, and for the correct hypothesized reasons.[55] Of course, there are exceptions. For example, it is not clear that the theory explains the case of Algeria, whose alleged pursuit of nuclear weapons with the construction of the secret Es-Salam reactor in the late 1980s is highly murky.[56] If Algeria was pursuing a hiding strategy, it is unclear which state posed an acute security threat to it. Mapping Algeria's threats in this period to the objective indicators set forth earlier—a conventionally superior proximate offensive threat or a primary adversary with nuclear weapons—is difficult.

Another exception is France, which, according to my theory, should have maintained an insurance hedging strategy. In the early 1950s, France was a formal U.S. ally, protected under NATO's nuclear umbrella.[57] The theory

55. A full coding appendix is available from the author upon request. The cases the theory mispredicts are denoted with an asterisk in table 2.4. This suggests the theory correctly predicts 40 of 46 strategies, or a success rate of over 85 percent.

56. See William Burr, ed., "The Algerian Nuclear Problem, 1991: Controversy over the Es Salam Nuclear Reactor," National Security Archive, Electronic Briefing Book, no. 228, September 10, 2007, http://nsarchive.gwu.edu/nukevault/ebb228/.

57. By comparison, because the United Kingdom's nuclear program begins simultaneously with that of the United States, before the post–World War II architecture emerges, the UK is correctly coded as a sprinter and explained by the theory; Sweden and Switzerland stood outside

predicts that France would use the threat of breakout to compel greater nuclear sharing or receive security assurances from the United States as, for example, West Germany did.[58] Instead, France decided to abandon insurance hedging and sprint to develop an independent nuclear arsenal. Given its experience under German occupation during World War II and subsequent French experiences at Dien Bien Phu and the 1956 Suez Crisis, France's fear of U.S. abandonment overrode the reassurances provided by NATO's nuclear umbrella. My theory would correctly predict France's strategy if it accounted for French leaders', especially de Gaulle's, *perception* that the United States was an unreliable alliance partner. But, without adding a perceptual variable, the theory has a difficult time accounting for France.[59] I explore where the theory went wrong in the French case in chapter 4. Outliers aside, Proliferation Strategy Theory explains the overwhelming majority of the proliferation strategies selected by states. The subsequent chapters show that Proliferation Strategy Theory powerfully explains the proliferation strategies of many important states, highlighting cases within each strategy to test the theory's predictions and hypothesized mechanisms.

Alternative Explanations

Proliferation Strategy Theory relies on five core variables at specific nodes. It sacrifices some degree of parsimony to capture the complexity of the empirical record. It is a broadly neoclassical realist-inspired theory in that it prioritizes and emphasizes a state's threat environment and the threat of preventive action against it. It highlights, however, the crucial role that state-level domestic political consensus and demand play in mediating the effect of the international environment to determine how and when a state decides to actively proliferate. Considering these variables in sequence distinguishes my theory from strictly top-down realist and strictly bottom-up domestic political, or regime type, explanations for nuclear proliferation. My theory draws from both, admittedly introducing more complexity but offering far greater and richer explanatory power.

---

of NATO as neutral states and thus potentially faced the Soviet Union alone but stalled at hard hedging due ultimately to the lack of domestic consensus on nuclear weaponization.

58. See Gerzhoy, "Alliance Coercion and Nuclear Restraint."

59. On French threat perception and fears of abandonment from the United States, see Narang, *Nuclear Strategy in the Modern Era*, chap. 6; and Hymans, *Psychology of Nuclear Proliferation*, chap. 4.

I lay out several alternatives from the broader international relations literature against which I test my theory. Since the strategies of proliferation typology is also a novel contribution of this book, no alternative explanations for precisely the same field of variation exist in the literature. I derive alternative explanations following from the larger available family of theories: a strictly realist theory where proliferation strategy is entirely determined by the international structure, technological determinism where strategy and pace of proliferation are determined by available technology, and the evolution of the international nonproliferation regime where proliferation strategies might shift uniformly over time due to the changing nature of the regime. In some important cases, there may be a country-specific alternative explanation for its proliferation strategy, and I take care to test my theory against those as well.

It is important to note that, except for technological determinism, my theory is not inconsistent with these alternative explanations. Indeed, security variables and nonproliferation regime variables are a key part of my theory, channeling in at various points—security at the apex, and potential coercive efforts at a lower node. Where my theory departs from these alternatives is that I specify when and where these variables should intervene and argue that, by themselves, these alternatives only paint an incomplete portrait of the varied and rich proliferation strategies in the empirical record. But throughout the book, I test to see if my more complex theory is necessary to capture the observed strategies of proliferation or whether these more parsimonious explanations are sufficient.

Structural Realism. Structural realism as a general theory of international relations holds that state behavior is driven by the structure of its security environment and that, under a condition of anarchy, states must engage in self-help behavior to ensure their survival. Nuclear weapons hold a privileged place in structural realist theories. For structure realism, attaining a nuclear weapons capability is the most important self-help measure an insecure state can take to ensure its survival given the destructive and deterrent power nuclear weapons can generate. For structural realists of most stripes, this insurance against extinction is the ultimate goal for states. However, structural realist theories usually have more to say about the *fact* of proliferation than the *method* of proliferation. Structural realists argue that conventionally inferior states or those facing a primary nuclear adversary should pursue nuclear weapons in order to deter conventional invasion and nuclear use, respectively.

But *how* do states pursue nuclear weapons according to structural realism? If security pressures are strong enough to require nuclear weapons, a structural realist theory should predict that all proliferators attempt to build nuclear weapons as quickly as possible—everyone sprints. Structural realism should be allergic to the notion of hedging for any state facing an acute security threat. Likewise, the possibility that domestic politics might systematically result in hedging is anathema to realism because it prevents an insecure state from actively pursuing nuclear weapons. Even subsetting to only active pursuers, a realist theory would suggest that states should optimize for speed if they are pursuing nuclear capabilities, so as to quickly attain the most powerful deterrent available. Debs and Monteiro highlight the importance of the threat of prevention but do not interrogate how the threat of prevention slows states down and pushes them into *hiding* which, although rarely successful, compels many aspirants to gamble on their ability to obfuscate a program just long enough to present the world with a plausible nuclear fait accompli.[60] For Debs and Monteiro, states facing significant potential coercion—the threat of murder—should be deterred from even trying to pursue nuclear weapons in the first place. A strictly realist theory of proliferation expects few if any hiders. Yet there are many. In general, structural realism is agnostic, and almost always indeterminate, about the method of pursuit. If it makes any prediction, it often overpredicts sprinting.

Technological Determinism. Whereas structural realism argues that the broad material contours of the international system should drive state behavior and nuclear proliferation, technological determinism argues that micro-material considerations drive state development of nuclear weapons. Technological determinist theories make more nuanced predictions about *how* states might proliferate and, indeed, is the strongest challenge to my theory. Technological determinism, most generally, would contend that the method of proliferation is determined by the available technologies and competence of a state's scientists and technical communities.[61] If uranium enrichment is the only pathway available due to supply constraints, then states will employ that method of proliferation and look like hiders. If a state can master the fuel cycle and a civilian nuclear energy program, then sprinting or sheltered pursuit is the pathway that states will take. A technological determinist theory would predict that states hedge only when scientists are unable to develop a weapons program due to incompetence or technological constraints. It would have difficulty explaining why a state with the technical capacity to develop nuclear weapons chooses to hedge rather than reach

60. See Debs and Monteiro, *Nuclear Politics*.

61. See treatment of this in Meyer, *The Dynamics of Nuclear Proliferation*.

the finish line, because technological determinism subordinates political strategy and prioritizes technical capability to explain behavior. To test my theory against technological determinism, I look for evidence that a state's proliferation strategy is dictated strictly by the technology available to it and the competence of its technical community.

My theory departs from technological determinism by arguing that a state chooses a political strategy of proliferation first and then *seeks* or *develops* the technologies necessary to carry out that strategy. In a hiding strategy, for example, I argue that a state's leaders first decide on the strategy and then seek to develop the light-footprint technical pathways which support that particular strategy, rather than vice versa. Of course, as the international supply of nuclear technology has changed over time, some technical pathways are easier to acquire or develop than others. However, I argue and show that international supply or scientific competence has rarely been a meaningful constraint, let alone the driver of strategic choice. The critical disagreement between my theory and technological determinism is about whether technical considerations shape strategy or are shaped by it.

Nonproliferation Regime. Changes to the international nonproliferation regime over time do affect how states pursue nuclear weapons. My theory explicitly accounts for the international nonproliferation regime, in the vulnerability to prevention variable. The international community's ability to impede proliferators has improved over time. Signatories to the Nuclear Nonproliferation Treaty (NPT) coordinate economic sanctions against suspected pursuers. Due to domestic laws passed in the 1970s after the emergence of the NPT, U.S. leaders have little choice but to clamp down on any remaining states—inside or outside the NPT—that might be pursuing nuclear weapons.[62] Though the nonproliferation regime is important in shaping strategic choices of nuclear proliferators, I contend that it is an incomplete explanation.

If the evolution of the nonproliferation regime is individually sufficient to determine strategies of proliferation, we should see secular changes in the popularity of certain strategies. When the nonproliferation regime is weakest, prior to the NPT, all pursuers should be sprinters; after the NPT legally proscribes all subsequent proliferation, all pursuers should be either technical hedgers with civilian infrastructure under IAEA safeguards or hiders attempting to evade the monitoring and enforcement mechanisms ushered in by the broader nonproliferation regime. In the years before the NPT comes into force, we might also expect to see some long-term insurance

62. Miller, "The Secret Success of Nonproliferation Sanctions."

hedgers attempt to develop nuclear weapons capabilities, in anticipation of more robust nonproliferation measures that would neuter their threat of nuclear breakout if abandoned by allies.

The empirical record shows some clear secular trends that could be attributed to the nonproliferation regime: start-to-finish sprinting almost entirely predates the NPT, and hiding is certainly a strategy that dominates later generations of proliferators. The decline of the sprinters, however, is also a consequence of structural and sequencing effects that do not have to do with the NPT: the group of states with sufficient relative power to sprint in a post-NPT world almost all had nuclear weapons before 1974 (and, indeed, they erected the inequitable regime to try to lock in their oligopoly). The strongest effects of the nonproliferation regime may be in determining whether a state enters the world of nuclear pursuit to begin with. Miller shows that the evolution of a more robust U.S.-led nonproliferation regime *deterred* many states from becoming nuclear aspirants.[63] For those that chose to pursue nuclear weapons despite the international nonproliferation regime—many beyond the reach of U.S. leverage—their choice of strategy depends on more than the NPT, since the regime is already priced in. Strategies such as hard hedging and sheltered pursuit occur commonly in later generation proliferators but are difficult to fit into a pure nonproliferation regime theory. Indeed, the possibility of sheltered pursuit suggests that major powers are differentially tolerant of proliferation even after the nonproliferation regime grows stronger. My theory also outperforms a strictly nonproliferation regime alternative because it can explain variation in active pursuit strategies (i.e., non-sprinting) prior to the NPT, as well as instances of sprinting or sheltered pursuit after the NPT and the congressional Glenn and Symington amendments. The nonproliferation regime no doubt constrains states in some ways, but I show that it alone is an unsatisfactory explanation for strategies of proliferation.

Conclusion

How states pursue nuclear weapons is as important as *why* they do so, because different strategies of proliferation create different challenges for proliferators, allies, and adversaries alike. This chapter offers a novel typology and theory for how states pursue nuclear weapons. The theory notes that many states initially develop nuclear capabilities to explore their options rather than to immediately pursue a weapon, emphasizing that varieties of

63. Ibid.

hedging are crucial, purposeful waypoints on the path to attaining a nuclear weapons capability for many states—but also one at which states can pause indefinitely, or even make a U-turn.

Each proliferation strategy has different points of vulnerability that can be exploited by nonproliferation efforts. For example, as I show in the case study of India, keeping domestic consensus fractured by making even nominal progress on universal disarmament or keeping key adversaries non-nuclear may forestall a hedger's decision to weaponize. It follows that if, in the future, Japan believes it is facing abandonment from the United States, keeping its domestic consensus fractured would be critical to preventing an active weaponization strategy. Predicting strategies of proliferation based on easily observable variables also provides a boon to counterproliferation efforts. Knowing, for example, that a given state is likely to be a hider if it pursues nuclear weapons primes the intelligence community to look for signatures that indicate a hidden nuclear program. Scholars and policymakers miss this insight when they assume that all nuclear proliferators follow the same path to the bomb. My typology of different strategies of proliferation suggests that how states pursue nuclear weapons matters to international security and is a rich and important area for research on nuclear proliferation and nonproliferation.

The following chapters test my theory, Proliferation Strategy Theory, against the above alternatives by systematically digesting the empirical record in nearly twenty in-depth cases. These chapters establish the validity of the theory and answer this question: Why do states select the proliferation strategy they do? The final chapters of the book explore the consequences of choosing each strategy—hedging, sprinting, sheltered pursuit, and hiding—for the proliferator and for external actors, including allies, adversaries, and international nonproliferation proponents. They show why strategies of proliferation are crucial to understanding the nuclear landscape and international politics. In combination, these chapters explore the causes and consequences of proliferation strategies, adding texture to an issue of tremendous global importance that has thus far been overlooked in favor of a research program focused almost entirely on why states want the bomb. My theory shows that substantial variation in the *intensity* and *nature* of demand, not just the fact of demand, influences how a state pursues nuclear weapons. Strategies of nuclear proliferation themselves are, however, largely independent of a state's initial motivations to initiate pursuit of nuclear weapons. I show that how states pursue the bomb is frankly more important than the often-studied *why*, both for scholars seeking to understand the nuclear landscape of the future and for practitioners seeking to shape it.

3

The Varieties of Hedgers

INDIA, JAPAN, WEST GERMANY, BRAZIL AND ARGENTINA, SWEDEN AND SWITZERLAND

This chapter explores the varieties of hedging and the pathways that lead states to particular hedging strategies. Hedging is a rich and important strategy of proliferation—one that seeks to purposefully keep a bomb option open without fully exercising it—and is a crucial waypoint on the path to nuclear weapons for many states. Hedging is often treated as a distinct phenomenon in the proliferation literature. One of the key aims of this book is to demonstrate that hedging is in fact a point on the proliferation continuum that should be folded into an integrated treatment and theory of proliferation strategies. The previous chapter identified three distinct varieties of hedging—technical, insurance, and hard hedging—unified by a common characteristic: they deliberately shorten a state's future path to nuclear weapons but intentionally stop short of outright weapons development. But some choose to unpause their pursuit and develop nuclear weapons, while others decide to abandon the journey, and still others decide to park the hedge in neutral and remain there indefinitely. This chapter illuminates these different trajectories: why states hedge in a particular way, and what might trigger them to nuclearize or give up.

The varieties of hedging are distinct in several ways. Most importantly, they result from different causes—either from technical temptation, to insure a state against allied abandonment, or because the state itself has not generated internal consensus for a bomb, yet. They also differ in how much technical progress they make toward a working weapon. Technical hedgers usually flirt with the idea of a weapons program since they possess a civilian nuclear program, but they undertake no work on weapons-grade enrichment or reprocessing, nor do they make progress on the organizational or technical architecture required for a nuclear weapons program. Interest in nuclear weapons is limited to the fringes of the domestic political arena. This is closest to the concept of nuclear "latency," a technical condition that implies little thought to the international political purpose of that technology. Insurance hedgers may undertake some enrichment and reprocessing work but explicitly stop short of a dedicated weapons program. They want to be able to quickly close potential windows of vulnerability if their security situation deteriorates either due to the loss of an ally or due to intensification of a preexisting security threat. Hard hedgers are the closest to weaponization. They are essentially "threshold nuclear states" or turnkey nuclear weapons states that stop short because of domestic political reasons rather than external security conditions. These are the states that structural realists assume will develop nuclear weapons. For idiosyncratic domestic political reasons, however, they intentionally stop short of the final stretch while domestic consensus is litigated. The implicit conditions for nuclear breakout vary across hedging types as well. Insurance hedging implies that a state would shift to active pursuit if its external security environment changed, whereas hard hedging implies that active pursuit would likely result from changes in domestic political debate.

Why do states hedge, and why do they adopt one variety of hedging over another? The theory I developed in the previous chapter hypothesizes that hedging strategies are adopted by states whose demand for nuclear weapons is neither nonexistent nor fully congealed, for either external or internal reasons. Perhaps these states do not face an acute security threat. Perhaps they do, but they also enjoy the formal security backing of a superpower, which mitigates the severity of their underlying threat. Under these conditions, they should adopt, respectively, technical and insurance hedging strategies. In cases where a state faces an acute security threat alone but it nevertheless lacks domestic political consensus for nuclear weapons as a solution to that security environment, it should adopt hard hedging. Figure 3.1 depicts the theory's branches for the varieties of hedging.

This chapter tests these mechanisms and hypotheses on seven cases: India, Japan, West Germany, Brazil and Argentina, and Sweden and

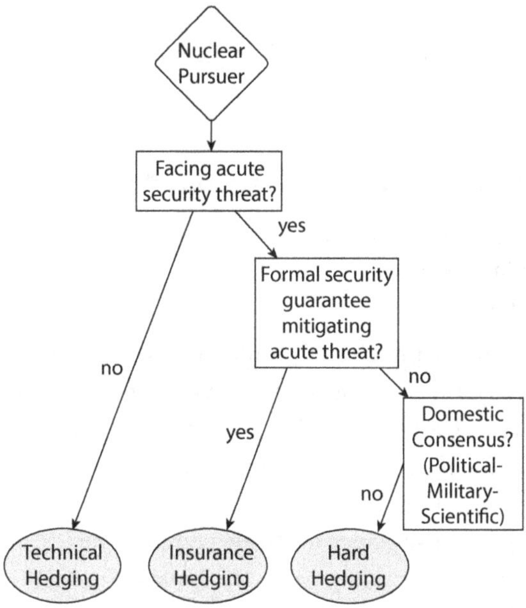

FIGURE 3.1. Proliferation Strategy Theory's pathways to the varieties of hedging.

Switzerland. I chose these cases because they provide a wide distribution of values on the independent variables and represent the different varieties of hedging. There are also new data emerging on these cases, which are interesting in their own right and allow for better testing of the hypothesized mechanisms than previously possible. In each of the seven cases in this chapter, I first describe the dependent variable value—the hedging strategy the state adopts—and then test whether the historical record and justification for adopting that strategy match the hypothesized reasons. I find that my theory does a better job explaining the fact, form, and rationale for each state's hedging strategies than alternative explanations.

Hedging is an important strategy of proliferation. It can either be a transitory strategy as states shift their answer to whether they want nuclear weapons from "maybe" to "no" or "yes" in which case they either exit the proliferation track—as Sweden, Switzerland, Brazil, and Argentina did—or shift to an active strategy of proliferation to weaponize their nuclear capabilities, as India chose to do. It can also persist indefinitely if a state refuses to definitively foreclose the option of nuclear weapons in the future, such as Japan and Germany today. Understanding what type of hedger a state is critically illuminates when and *why* it might shift to an active proliferation strategy—as the rich case of India demonstrates below. Thus, bringing hedging back in as a central, rather than peripheral, proliferation strategy has both theoretical and policy importance.

India: The Reluctant Nuclear Weapons Power

Technical Hedging, 1948–64
Hard Hedging, 1964–89
Sprinting, 1989–98

India adopted three strategies of proliferation over time. I track not only why India selected the strategies of proliferation it did but whether changes in the variables in Proliferation Strategy Theory were responsible for its *shifts*.[1] These shifts in India's strategy over time allow me to explore a variety of mechanisms hypothesized by the theory in a single case, while holding potentially important variables relatively constant, such as India's primary threats and its dominant ruling party, the Indian National Congress. India is a hard case for Proliferation Strategy Theory because the conventional wisdom on India's proliferation trajectory focuses on technological incompetence or organizational dysfunction to explain its half-century journey to attain nuclear weapons. Instead, I show that the delay was an intentional result of strategic calculation, a fact missed by most existing accounts.[2] By focusing on India's strategies of proliferation, I revise our understanding of a major case of nuclear proliferation and present novel data on India's 1989 decision to shift strategies and finally sprint for nuclear weapons.

TECHNICAL HEDGING: 1948–64

India pursued a technical hedging strategy from 1948 to 1964, focusing on civilian nuclear technology—a reactor and reprocessing facility—for economic development. India's scientists and even Prime Minister Jawaharlal

1. On India's nuclear history, see George Perkovich, *India's Nuclear Bomb: The Impact on Global Proliferation* (Berkeley: University of California Press, 1999); Abraham, *The Making of the Indian Atomic Bomb*; Raj Chengappa, *Weapons of Peace: The Secret Story of India's Quest to Be a Nuclear Power* (Delhi: Harper Collins, 2000); Gaurav Kampani, "New Delhi's Long Nuclear Journey: How Secrecy and Institutional Roadblocks Delayed India's Weaponization," *International Security* 38, no. 4 (Spring 2014): 79–114; Bharat Karnad, *Nuclear Weapons and Indian Security: The Realist Foundations of Strategy* (Delhi: Macmillan, 2002); K. Subrahmanyam, "India's Nuclear Policy 1964–98 (A Personal Recollection)," in *Nuclear India*, ed. Jasjit Singh (Delhi: Knowledge World, 1998), 26–53; and Sumit Ganguly, "India's Pathway to Pokhran II: The Prospects and Sources of New Delhi's Nuclear Weapons Program," *International Security* 23, no. 4 (Spring 1999): 148–77.

2. Work representative of this view is Kampani, "New Delhi's Long Nuclear Journey."

Nehru understood that these technologies could have future military applications. Although Nehru is often portrayed as an idealist who abhorred nuclear weapons—which he did—he also understood that, absent universal disarmament, India could ill afford to ignore the possible military applications of inherently dual-use nuclear technology. He stated in legislative debates in 1948, "We must develop [atomic energy] for the purpose of using it for peaceful purposes. . . . Of course, if we are compelled as a nation to use it for other purposes, possibly no pious sentiments of any of us will stop the nation from using it that way."[3] In the mid-1950s, Nehru sanctioned the building of India's plutonium reactor purchased from Canada (no international safeguards existed at the time), as well as a reprocessing facility at Trombay in the early 1960s, which could theoretically produce weapons-grade plutonium. India's chief nuclear scientist, Homi Bhabha, had a keen interest in India being viewed as a modern scientific state and, like many nuclear scientists of that era, saw the ability to develop nuclear weapons as the pinnacle of scientific achievement.[4]

Nehru did not actively discourage Bhabha's interest, and he understood that intrinsically dual-use nuclear technologies left open the option of nuclear weapons in the future. Indian activity during this period, however, never went beyond technical hedging because India's demand for nuclear weapons was weak. Nothing in the immediate security environment pushed Nehru to overcome his abhorrence of nuclear weapons and authorize weapons-related work, limiting any discussion of developing nuclear weapons to the political fringes. India enjoyed conventional superiority over its main adversary, Pakistan, and, in the 1940s and 1950s, did not yet face an acute security threat from China, which was weak and unable to project ground power against India. At the same time, it is clear that Nehru sincerely wanted to explore the peaceful applications of nuclear technology in this period, saying in the lower house of parliament: "We are not interested in making atom bombs, even if we have the capacity to do so, and that in no event will we use atomic energy for destructive purposes."[5]

Nehru was not naïve, however. He understood that he was putting the pieces in place for a military program if it ever became necessary, but in a reversible and manageable way: "The fact remains that if one has these

3. Jawaharlal Nehru, *Constituent Assembly of India (Legislative Debates)*, book 1, vol. 5, April 6, 1948, pp. 3333–34, quoted in Perkovich, *India's Nuclear Bomb*, 20.

4. See Abraham, *The Making of the Indian Atomic Bomb*.

5. Jawaharlal Nehru, *Lok Sabha Debates*, July 24, 1957, quoted in Perkovich, *India's Nuclear Bomb*, 34.

fissionable materials and if one has the resources, then one can make a bomb."[6] However, he stated that while "we will have the competence and equipment to make them . . . we have *deliberately decided* not to do it."[7] Nehru therefore prevented Bhabha from working on anything explicitly related to nuclear weapons. India's strategy in this phase was explicitly not now, but implicitly not never. In other words, a classic technical hedger.

HARD HEDGING: 1964–89

India shifted to a hard hedging strategy in 1964—two years after losing the Sino-Indian War—when China's first nuclear test galvanized mainstream domestic political constituencies to advocate for nuclear weapons against the reservations of Prime Minister Lal Bahadur Shastri. Shastri, who became prime minister following Nehru's death in May 1964, professed an even stronger aversion to nuclear weapons than had Nehru, whose abhorrence of nuclear weapons was counterbalanced by his recognition that India could not be the lone proponent of nuclear abolition in a nuclear-armed world. But with the emergence of the Chinese threat, plus Delhi's unsuccessful attempts to receive a nuclear guarantee from either the United States or the Soviet Union,[8] Bhabha and India's opposition parties pressed Shastri to move at least from technical hedging to hard hedging to counter the threat of a now conventionally superior and nuclear-armed power on India's borders. As predicted by my theory, this shift came in response to a material change in the severity of India's security environment. Once it became apparent that there would be no formal allied protection to enable an insurance hedging strategy, India had to shift at least to a hard hedging strategy, beginning significant theoretical and physical work on a nuclear weapons program. Shastri, however, as the leader of the essentially unchallenged Congress party in parliament, prevented India from achieving a domestic political consensus to weaponize. He, virtually alone, stopped India short of an active strategy to develop nuclear weapons.

Only under significant public pressure, from the popular Bhabha as well as from the opposition party Jan Sangh and even within the Congress Party itself, Shastri was forced to relent on two key points that pushed India into

6. Ibid.

7. Nehru quoted in Karnad, *Nuclear Weapons and Indian Security*, 195, emphasis added.

8. See Andrew B. Kennedy, "India's Nuclear Odyssey: Implicit Umbrellas, Diplomatic Disappointments, and the Bomb," *International Security* 36, no. 2 (Fall 2011): 120–53; also Ganguly, "India's Pathway to Pokhran II," 153–55.

a hard hedging strategy in 1964. First, he publicly announced a policy of nuclear weapons hedging, saying: "I cannot say the present policy is deep rooted. . . . If there is a need to amend what we have said today, then we will say—all right, let us go ahead and do so."[9] Second, he authorized Bhabha and India's scientists to explore the possibility of using peaceful nuclear explosives for development purposes. Shastri's authorization green-lighted theoretical and engineering work to develop weapons-grade fissile material and implosion techniques. In its new strategy, India explicitly generated the option of pursuing nuclear weapons as a domestic political compromise but paused short of pursuing a functional weapon.

Shastri's moral aversion to nuclear weapons, coupled with his firm belief that the financial cost of the program would be unbearable, kept India's nuclear weapons program from moving to active pursuit. His authorization for theoretical work on the Subterranean Nuclear Explosion for Peaceful Purposes (SNEPP) program was a hard hedge, driven by pressure from domestic constituencies to address the newly acute threat from China. India's nuclear scientists understood this for what it was: a license to work on nuclear explosions that were not "weapons" in terms of the engineering they required but still required the same theoretical mastery. As George Perkovich notes, the emergence and crystallization of the Chinese threat in 1962–64 caused India's Congress Party to choose a middle-ground strategy: "[They] wanted neither to undertake nor exclude a bomb program but instead to study the issue seriously and enhance technological preparedness."[10] The only constraint on weaponization was a fractured domestic consensus—particularly at the prime ministerial and cabinet level—on whether India should develop nuclear weapons or seek universal global nuclear disarmament to denuclearize China and prevent Pakistani nuclearization. Indeed, after a subsequent Chinese nuclear test in 1966, Foreign Minister Swaran Singh stated to parliament: "The government still feels that the interests of . . . our own security are better achieved by giving all support to the efforts for world nuclear disarmament than by building our own nuclear weapons."[11] Work on peaceful nuclear explosives continued, however, and debate about whether India should develop nuclear weapons was now both salient and public.

With the theoretical work for the SNEPP proceeding in the late 1960s, and plutonium being reprocessed without any safeguards at Trombay,

9. Shastri quoted in Chengappa, *Weapons of Peace*, 95.

10. Perkovich, *India's Nuclear Bomb*, 81.

11. Singh quoted in Abraham, *The Making of the Indian Atomic Bomb*, 127.

Shastri's successor, Indira Gandhi, authorized a test of a "peaceful nuclear explosion" (PNE) in October 1972. With no real urgency, it took two years to prepare for the May 1974 explosion, partly because of apparent difficulties with the initiator for the device and partly because of the shifting leadership at India's Atomic Energy Commission (AEC).[12] The PNE demonstrated that India was a nuclear capable, but not yet a fully nuclear weapons, state—a distinction with a critical difference. India had demonstrated mastery of a controlled fission detonation. But at roughly four feet in diameter and weighing 1,400 kilograms, the PNE device was unstable and too big to be a reliable deliverable weapon. Pakistan, if erring on the side of caution, might have reasonably assumed that India could deliver a single bomb via a highly delayed, risky one-way mission using a cargo plane.

However, the PNE was not the basis for a reliable nuclear arsenal: it dramatically suggested that India had the fundamental technical capacity to weaponize its nuclear capabilities but that it had not yet chosen to do so. In extensive debate in the upper house of parliament in the months following the PNE, K. C. Pant, the junior minister of energy, stated: "There is no question of our going in for nuclear weapons," and that India's PNE was "exclusively for peaceful purposes." He also stated that India's refusal to sign the NPT was a response to its discriminatory structure—separating nuclear haves from have-nots—not a result of India wanting nuclear weapons, yet.[13] Brajesh Mishra, who would later serve as national security advisor when India tested nuclear weapons in 1998, stated to the Conference on Disarmament in Geneva days after the 1974 PNE that while India, like all states with nuclear energy, may be a "nuclear power . . . India has no intention of becoming a nuclear *weapon* power. At the same time, it retains the right to promote the fullest development of all peaceful uses of nuclear energy."[14] For its part, Pakistan was unpersuaded by these assurances. Prime Minister Zulfiqar Ali Bhutto cut to the heart of the matter, writing Indira in June: "You will, however, appreciate that it is a question not only of intentions but of capabilities. . . . It is well established that the testing

12. Subrahmanyam, "India's Nuclear Policy," 30.

13. K. C. Pant, "Rajya Sabha Extensive Debate on India's Peaceful Nuclear Explosion," August 21, 1974, History and Public Policy Program Digital Archive, Institute for Defence Studies and Analyses (ISDA), Rajya Sabha Q&A Documents, pp. 251–53, http://digitalarchive.wilsoncenter.org/document/119760.

14. "Official Announcement made by Brajesh Chandra Mishra in the Conference on the Committee on Disarmament Regarding the Underground Peaceful Nuclear Explosion Conducted by India," May 21, 1974, Geneva, Document 1826, in *India-Pakistan Relations 1947–2007, A Documentary Study, Vol. I–X, Published in Cooperation with Public Diplomacy Division, Ministry of External Affairs*, ed. Avatar Singh Bhasin (New Delhi: Geetika Publishers, 2012), 4460.

of a nuclear device is no different from the detonation of a nuclear weapon. Given this indisputable fact, how is it possible for our fears to be assuaged by mere assurances, assurances which may in any case be ignored in subsequent years?"[15] Indira stopped short of weaponizing India's nuclear program, but the PNE nevertheless accelerated Pakistan's search for its own bomb; the culmination of Pakistan's efforts would eventually push then-PM Rajiv Gandhi over India's nuclear weapons precipice.

Hard hedging persisted across the tenures of several prime ministers. Indira Gandhi led India after Shastri's death in 1966 until she was assassinated in 1984, except for the period between 1977 and 1979, when India was led by opposition leader Morarji Desai. After her assassination, Indira was succeeded by her son Rajiv Gandhi. Indira and, more so, Rajiv enjoyed large parliamentary majorities and were essentially dictatorial figures in the dominant Congress Party. During their governments, domestic political consensus on how to proceed with developing nuclear weapons depended almost exclusively on their individual preferences. Desai and the two Gandhis persisted with hard hedging as a strategy, stopping short of an explicit weapons program. They continued to authorize theoretical work on nuclear devices, and in 1983, Indira initiated a parallel missile program for possible delivery capabilities. They also continued to publicly hedge by opting out of the NPT—a visible indicator that India refused to legally forswear the nuclear weapons option—despite Indira being one of the original proponents of the regime.

Two features of the Indian nuclear program in this period are emblematic of hard hedging: ambivalence about nuclear weapons at the highest political levels, and centralization of the program to inhibit advances on nuclear weaponization without prime ministerial approval. First, key actors—in this case India's prime ministers—had not yet decided that nuclear weapons were the solution to India's security issues. Like her father and Shastri before her, Indira Gandhi personally abhorred nuclear weapons and felt, in the aftermath of the PNE, that she had been misled by her scientists and advisors about the domestic political benefits.[16] Perkovich reports that a high-ranking official in her government stated: "After 1974, she didn't want to hear anything about nuclear at all. . . . People say her refusal to allow other tests was

15. "Reply Letter from Pakistan Prime Minister Z. A. Bhutto to Prime Minister Mrs. Indira Gandhi," June 6, 1974, Islamabad, Document 1829, in *India-Pakistan Relations 1947–2007, A Documentary Study, Vol. I–X, Published in Cooperation with Public Diplomacy Division, Ministry of External Affairs*, ed. Avatar Singh Bhasin (New Delhi: Geetika Publishers, 2012), 4463.

16. Perkovich, *India's Nuclear Bomb*, 188.

due to U.S. pressure and so on, but it wasn't. She genuinely felt horrified by the bomb."[17] In late 1982 or early 1983, India's scientists approached Indira Gandhi to request approval for a series of nuclear-related experiments—failing to mention that they really wanted to initiate a series of tests for weapons development.[18] After tentatively agreeing, she realized the implications of what she was asked to approve and retracted the authorization within hours according to Defence Research and Development Organisation head V. S. Arunachalam.[19] She was evidently so furious at the incident that she subsequently "refused to entertain meeting with [the scientists] on that subject."[20] She would later tell Arunachalam, "I am basically against weapons of mass destruction."[21] Her view was actually more conflicted. She did not shut down the scientists' theoretical work, for example, and it was Indira who initiated the dual-use missile program that later provided the basis for missile delivery of nuclear weapons. Despite whatever personal misgivings she may have had about nuclear weapons, she ensured India would not close its options given the threats it faced from a more powerful nuclear-capable China and from a Pakistan openly determined to get the bomb.

Scholars agree that when Morarji Desai was prime minister from 1977 to 1979, he "intensified the principled aversion to nuclear weapons . . . [and he] remained effectively unchallenged on nuclear policy."[22] Desai prohibited further peaceful nuclear explosions and slowed work on them because he was aware that "the history of development of nuclear research has shown that the temptation to switch over from peaceful to non-peaceful purposes has proved difficult to resist."[23] He ensured that India would resist that temptation under his brief tenure by refusing to authorize any further advances in the program. Interestingly, though, Desai's foreign minister, Atal Bihari Vajpayee, foreshadowed his own future prime ministerial tenure when he controversially stated to a newsmagazine, *Blitz*, that he was from the party

17. Quoted in ibid.

18. Ibid., 242–43.

19. Ibid., 243; also see Arunachalam to Kampani, cited in Kampani, "New Delhi's Long Nuclear Journey," 91. It should be noted that whether Indira ever actually gave consent to test, or actively considered it, is disputed in Chengappa, *Weapons of Peace*, 257–60.

20. Former high-ranking official quoted in Perkovich, *India's Nuclear Bomb*, 244.

21. Arunachalam quoted in Chengappa, *Weapons of Peace*, 260.

22. Perkovich, *India's Nuclear Bomb*, 224.

23. Morarji Desai, "Rajya Sabha Q&A on the Nuclear Explosion at Pokhran in 1974," December 21, 1978, History and Public Policy Program Digital Archive, Institute for Defence Studies and Analyses (ISDA), Rajya Sabha Q&A Documents, p. 136, http://digitalarchive.wilsoncenter.org/document/119759.

that was "for the bomb" and that India "cannot for all time to come foreclose its nuclear option."[24] Though Desai was personally opposed to the development of nuclear weapons, he too maintained a hard hedging strategy as a domestic political compromise.

Rajiv Gandhi became prime minister after his mother's assassination in 1984. According to Perkovich, he "had no intention of moving toward a nuclear arsenal and requisite operational doctrine. This stemmed from his personal aversion to nuclear weapons, his sense that India had greater priorities, and his determination—like his predecessors—to keep the military from taking a significant role in nuclear policymaking."[25] Cabinet Secretary B. G. Deshmukh says that Rajiv put the brakes on any effort to "exercise [the nuclear] option" but equally "did not want India to give up [the] option for going nuclear" so long as Pakistan was proceeding apace.[26] Although it was derided internationally, Rajiv Gandhi's Action Plan in the late 1980s calling for universal nuclear disarmament stemmed from a genuine belief that global nuclear disarmament served India's national security interests better than developing nuclear weapons; India enjoyed conventional parity in theater against nuclear-China and, more importantly, conventional superiority over Pakistan, which could be neutralized only if Pakistan attained nuclear weapons.[27] Rajiv's primary efforts were therefore directed at trying to eliminate China's nuclear weapons and to prevent Pakistan from developing them under the auspices of universal disarmament, rather than authorizing Indian nuclear weaponization. All the same, Rajiv allowed India's scientists to maintain a very "minimum state of readiness" through the late 1980s,[28] although much of their work focused on protecting India's infrastructure and military installations from a nuclear attack.[29]

The second main indicator of hard hedging in this fifteen-year period was the careful concentration of decision making within the prime minister's office, allowing each of the three prime ministers to control—and

24. Vajpayee quoted in "Letter from General Zia-ul-Haq to Prime Minister Morarji Desai," March 3, 1979, Islamabad, Document 1832, in *India-Pakistan Relations 1947–2007, A Documentary Study, Vol. I–X, Published in Cooperation with Public Diplomacy Division, Ministry of External Affairs*, ed. Avatar Singh Bhasin (New Delhi: Geetika Publishers, 2012), 4474.

25. Perkovich, *India's Nuclear Bomb*, 275.

26. Deshmukh quoted in ibid., 282.

27. Interview with member of Rajiv Gandhi's Prime Minister Office advisory staff, New Delhi, June 2015.

28. See Chengappa, *Weapons of Peace*, 303.

29. Ibid., 304.

restrain—the nature and pace of the program.[30] Gaurav Kampani correctly notes that "the process of weaponization and operational planning within the Indian state in this period was characterized by inefficiency, delay, and dysfunction" as well as tremendous amounts of secrecy.[31] Key members of Rajiv Gandhi's advisory circle say this situation was not accidental. Although concerns about prying U.S. satellites and nonproliferation pressure existed, they were secondary to Rajiv's desire to centrally manage the program in order to prevent India's scientists and military from entrepreneurially progressing beyond the point that India's prime ministers had so carefully calibrated.[32] Centralization was a deliberate tactic designed to regulate the pace of the program and to make it impossible to advance the nuclear program without authorization of the prime minister. Under the threat of being fired, Rajiv told the scientists that at "every step you have to inform [me personally] and seek approval."[33] Rajiv augmented control by preventing coordination at levels below the prime minister's office: the various scientific and military organizations were disconnected, operating in isolation. Rajiv created a system where "the left hand didn't know what the right hand was doing" so that the two could not decide to "clap on their own."[34]

The military expressed frustration at being left out of nuclear decision making, but this too was by design. Civilian control increased even more after the 1986–87 Brasstacks Crisis, during which Rajiv Gandhi believed that the military, led by Gen. Krishnaswamy Sundarji, almost dragged India into a war with Pakistan as a result of unsanctioned freelancing in a series of large conventional military exercises.[35] On nuclear weapons matters, Rajiv wanted to prevent any similar freelancing.[36] As such, the AEC and the Defense Research and Development Organization were not allowed to conduct experiments or develop bomb components—though they surely worked

30. See Bhalchandra Gopal Deshmukh, *A Cabinet Secretary Looks Back* (New York: HarperCollins Publishers India, 2004), 171.

31. Kampani, "New Delhi's Long Nuclear Journey," 88.

32. Naresh Chandra, interview by the author, New Delhi, December 30, 2015. This is a key difference in motivations from the military account deftly illuminated by Kampani. The military may have believed the secrecy was due to potential counterproliferation efforts, but my own interviews suggest that the civilian managers were much more concerned with siloing the program to manage its pace internally.

33. Rajiv Gandhi quoted in Vinay Sitapati, *Half Lion: How P. V. Narasimha Rao Transformed India* (Delhi: Penguin India, 2016), 281.

34. Rajiv Gandhi's Prime Minister Office advisory staff, interview; this point was also reiterated and emphasized in Chandra, interview.

35. Rajiv Gandhi's Prime Minister Office advisory staff, interview.

36. Chandra, interview.

through the theoretical foundations—for weaponization of the nuclear program. Development of delivery systems, to the extent it occurred, was undertaken without input from the military services that would eventually have to field them. For example, the dual-use missile program initiated in 1983 (the Integrated Guided Missile Development Program) worked in parallel, not in conjunction with, the military and the AEC. Whether the early missiles produced through this program were even considered for potential nuclear delivery is unclear. Unlike the dedicated nuclear missiles in the Agni family, the dual-use Prithvi missile has such a short range that it would have to be deployed very near the Pakistan border in areas where its survivability is questionable. Further, the air force was kept isolated from the scientists designing the early generation gravity bombs.[37] These groups would have had to organize a hasty "arranged marriage" between the gravity bombs and their delivery aircraft if the need to weaponize suddenly arose. Kampani colorfully notes one air chief's awareness that there was little he could do about being in the dark: "No air chief wants to approach the prime minister about nuclear issues only to be told to go mind his own business!"[38] Pro-bomb figures such as Sundarji and K. Subrahmanyam were tasked with "endless studies," according to Naresh Chandra, to keep them occupied and away from the Prime Minister's Office.[39]

Thus, even as they authorized significant steps to facilitate a compressed-timeline weapons program at a later date, India's political leaders stopped short of weaponization from 1964 through 1989. So long as India's prime minister was ambivalent about nuclear weapons, there could be no culmination of weaponization. But the pieces were always available to assemble should that decision come—India kept itself at a technological and organizational point where it was several months from a nuclear test, and several years from a reliable deliverable weapons capability. Indeed, in October 1985, on the sidelines of the United Nations General Assembly meeting in New York, Rajiv raised the issue of advancing Pakistani weaponization with President Zia.[40] Zia retorted that it "applies to both countries," to which Rajiv replied: "But we know that we are not doing it. . . . We have absolutely no

37. See Kampani, "New Delhi's Long Nuclear Journey."

38. Ibid., 94–95.

39. Chandra, interview.

40. "Record of the Meeting between Prime Minister Rajiv Gandhi and President Zia-ul-Haq," October 23, 1985, New York, Document 1081, in *India-Pakistan Relations 1947–2007, A Documentary Study, Vol. I–X, Published in Cooperation with Public Diplomacy Division, Ministry of External Affairs*, ed. Avatar Singh Bhasin (New Delhi: Geetika Publishers, 2012), 2860–61.

interest in going in for nuclear weapons. Every argument is against it . . . our whole foreign policy will be affected. We don't want it at all."[41] Rajiv would repeatedly state, when referring to Pakistan's advancing nuclear weapons program: "India has the capability, but we have demonstrated . . . that we are not willing to turn that capability into a weapon system" for the moment.[42] The veiled implication, however, was that if Pakistan were to indisputably weaponize, Rajiv would have no choice but to pull the trigger on Indian weaponization. This was the strategy of hard hedging: explicitly not now, but explicitly not never. And the decision point was fast approaching by the late 1980s.

FINAL SPRINT: 1989–98

In March 1989, India abandoned its hard hedging strategy and shifted to an active pursuit of nuclear weapons with a sprinting strategy. The specter of Pakistan possibly achieving a nuclear weapons capability had loomed throughout the decade. Concern about Pakistan was noted in a secret Ministry of External Affairs report as early as 1979, which said that the U.S. government was "absolutely certain" that Pakistan had an advanced project to develop a nuclear bomb—"there was no doubt about this," the memo categorically stated.[43] Evidence of Pakistan's growing centrifuge and enrichment capabilities, as well as material assistance from China and a blind eye from Washington, accumulated through the mid-1980s. Zia openly declared to *Time* in 1987 that Pakistan "could build a bomb whenever it wishes" but

41. Ibid.

42. "Extract from the Speech of Prime Minister Rajiv Gandhi at the National Defence College on Pakistan's Nuclear Programme," November 17, 1987, New Delhi, Document 1865, in *India-Pakistan Relations 1947–2007, A Documentary Study, Vol. I–X, Published in Cooperation with Public Diplomacy Division, Ministry of External Affairs*, ed. Avatar Singh Bhasin (New Delhi: Geetika Publishers, 2012), 4541.

43. "Briefing by the American Embassy in Islamabad to American Journalists on Pakistan's Nuclear Programme," April 8, 1979, Embassy of India, Islamabad, Document 1836, in *India-Pakistan Relations 1947–2007, A Documentary Study, Vol. I–X, Published in Cooperation with Public Diplomacy Division, Ministry of External Affairs*, ed. Avatar Singh Bhasin (New Delhi: Geetika Publishers, 2012), 4480. Yogesh Joshi cites an August 1981 Ministry of External Affairs report noting its own first internal assessment. See "Pakistan's Nuclear Programme," Ministry of External Affairs, National Archives, New Delhi, August 19, 1981, quoted in Yogesh Joshi, "How Technology Shaped India's Nuclear Submarine Program," working paper, 2016; also see Kargil Review Committee, *From Surprise to Reckoning: The Kargil Review Committee Report* (New Delhi: Sage Publications, 2000), 187–88; and Avatar Singh Bhasin, ed., *India-Pakistan Relations 1947–2007, A Documentary Study, Vol. I–X, Published in Cooperation with Public Diplomacy Division, Ministry of External Affairs* (New Delhi: Geetika Publishers, 2012), vol. VI (Nuclear).

stopped short of stating that it had definitively done so—just enough wiggle room to allow Rajiv to exercise continued forbearance.

The semantic games began to end in March 1988, when Rajiv Gandhi quietly received nearly definitive intelligence of Pakistan's weaponization, which had likely crossed the threshold and assembled nuclear weapons during or shortly after the Brasstacks Crisis the previous year.[44] As Rajiv told a key advisor, "If Pakistan gets the bomb, even I cannot stop India from going nuclear."[45] Yet, even this intelligence on Pakistan did not compel Rajiv to weaponize India's nuclear capabilities immediately. It was only after Rajiv's Action Plan—a final effort to advance global nuclear disarmament that he believed was the last chance to stop Pakistan from definitively nuclearizing—fell on deaf ears at the United Nations in June 1988 that Rajiv began to consider changing India's proliferation strategy.

In March 1989, nine months after his failed UN speech, Rajiv publicly stated for the first time that he was now "one hundred percent convinced that [Pakistan's program] is a nuclear weapons programme" and implied that there was no way to stop it.[46] Rajiv had waited until the last possible moment to make a decision on India's nuclear future, but time was now up. It was thus precisely that same month, perhaps even the same week, that Naresh Chandra, Rajiv's newly appointed defense secretary,[47] states that Rajiv ordered him to take India's nuclear program over the finish line, giving the "green light" that "resulted in a dramatic change of pace in India's nuclear weapons plans."[48] Cabinet Secretary Deshmukh indicated that the

44. Indian intelligence assessed that Pakistan probably possessed "at least three nuclear devices" in March 1988, with varying estimates of the size of the arsenal, but likely all within single digits. See Kargil Review Committee, *From Surprise to Reckoning*, 190. Also see Deshmukh, *A Cabinet Secretary Looks Back*, 170.

45. Rajiv Gandhi's Prime Minister Office advisory staff, interview.

46. "Remarks by Prime Minister Rajiv Gandhi that Pakistan's Nuclear Programme Was a Nuclear Weapons Programme," April 2, 1989 (remarks made on March 18–19, 1989), New Delhi, Document 1872, in *India-Pakistan Relations 1947–2007, A Documentary Study, Vol. I–X, Published in Cooperation with Public Diplomacy Division, Ministry of External Affairs*, ed. Avatar Singh Bhasin (New Delhi: Geetika Publishers, 2012), 4552.

47. Chandra quipped that he had become defense secretary the month before, having just come from the Ministry of Water Resources. That prior experience actually came in handy when he had to creatively describe "cattle herding" projects in the Rajasthani desert to conduct work at the Pokhran test site. Chandra, interview.

48. Chengappa, *Weapons of Peace*, 335; Shekhar Gupta, "How We Built the Bomb," *Indian Express*, August 19, 2006, http://archive.indianexpress.com/news/how-we-built-the-bomb/10875/0. These details were confirmed in the author's interview with Naresh Chandra. Chandra indicated that not even Minister of Defence K. C. Pant was aware of this order at the time,

steps were now clearly laid out: "when the trigger would be ready, what type of platform would carry the bomb, how the bomb was to be mated to a delivery vehicle, the type of electronic checks and the command and control system needed. A carte blanche was given for expenses but every time a milestone was crossed, the prime minister was to clear the next step."[49] Chandra indicates that Rajiv's directive was informal—he never put it in writing—but it was clear: "Get things ready in case we want to test" a nuclear weapon.[50]

The goal of this final sprint was to get India's program in a position to test its first-generation nuclear weapons within seventy-two hours of a decision to do so, down from "more than t-minus 100 days," which is where India's preparations were in 1989.[51] This was a concerted effort fortuitously led by Chandra, a permanent bureaucrat who lasted through the churn of ministers and governments, and who would later become the powerful cabinet secretary—allowing him to direct and control the entire weaponization project personally and centrally after Rajiv lost his parliamentary majority at the end of 1989, giving way to several years of weak, distracted governments. He and Rajiv (and subsequent prime ministers, particularly P. V. Narasimha Rao) were perhaps the only ones with a complete picture of India's weaponization activities.[52] The program remained centralized domestically to control its pace, not to ensure secrecy. The goal of getting India within seventy-two hours of a test required work and coordination—particularly at the test site—that could not be fully hidden, especially from U.S. satellites.[53] Rajiv also approved a slate of highly visible public tests for explicitly nuclear-capable missiles, particularly the longer-range Agni missile, beginning in

---

because Rajiv instead preferred to empower a civil servant such as Chandra who would be able to "marry" the scientific community with the necessary funding bodies, and then ultimately with the military. The military was also "deliberately kept out of the loop because, in any case, they were unnecessary in this phase."

49. Chengappa, *Weapons of Peace*, 335.

50. Chandra, interview.

51. Ibid. Chandra says he initially preferred a goal of t-minus 30 days because anything beyond that risked international detection especially at the test site (cables, digging, instrumentation, etc.). But as further evidence that international detection was only a secondary concern, he adhered to Rajiv's directive to take India to t-minus 3 days from being able to test.

52. Ibid. Indeed, Chandra notes that he explicitly kept the air force out of the loop on delivery because he was afraid they would "blab to the *Express*," leading to parliamentary questions about India's nuclear weapons, which Rajiv did not want to deal with. Other advisors such as Deshmukh, G. Parthasarthy, and Ronen Sen were likely aware of various components of the activity according to Chandra.

53. Ibid.

May 1989.[54] That India was now seriously contemplating open weaponization was obvious to all but the willfully blind. This was not a hiding strategy but a final sprint to swiftly take India from a nuclear hedger to a nuclear weapons state. India's open sprint led it to the brink of nuclear tests in 1995 and 1996, before finally going over the precipice in 1998.

The sprinting strategy involved reprocessing and machining weapons-grade plutonium for weapons cores and doing all the necessary work for the production, management, and delivery of nuclear weapons. Chandra indicates that India's scientists had largely completed the weaponization of its nuclear capabilities sometime in 1993 or 1994, putting India in a position to test its fission weapons; higher-yield boosted fission designs would be completed several years later.[55] Once fission weapons were complete, the air force was given the mission of delivering India's first-generation gravity bombs with Mirage aircraft, while the missile program moved forward, albeit slowly.[56] As Kampani shows, India certainly paid a price for the stovepiping instituted during the hard hedging phase. In one instance, the scientists who designed India's initial gravity bombs had no contact with the air force and were therefore unfamiliar with the rotation problems (such as tailstrikes) their designs might cause during takeoff,[57] which led to some "acceptable delays" in reliable delivery, according to Chandra. Coordination issues aside, by 1994 India had compressed its time to retaliate with nuclear weapons from a baseline of many days in 1989—and even that would have "been a highly improvised affair"—to less than twenty-four hours.[58]

It took India about five years to complete the weaponization process once it began sprinting—not much longer than other nuclear weapons states—even as it clearly faced challenges along the way due to the compartmentalized structure India's nuclear establishment originally built to accommodate a long-standing hedging strategy.[59] Although India did not formally test until May 1998, it was in a position to do so much earlier, at the very latest in 1995, when Prime Minister Narasimha Rao allegedly aborted a nuclear test.[60] India did face pressure from the United States not to test, with Rao worrying

54. See Vipin Narang, "Pride and Prejudice and Prithvis: Strategic Weapons Behavior in South Asia," in *Inside Nuclear South Asia*, ed. Scott D. Sagan (Stanford: Stanford University Press, 2009), chap. 4.

55. Chandra, interview.

56. Kampani, "New Delhi's Long Nuclear Journey," 97.

57. Ibid.

58. Chandra, interview.

59. See Kampani, "New Delhi's Long Nuclear Journey," 93–95.

60. See Sitapati, *Half Lion*, chap. 14.

that sanctions might affect India's nascent economic liberalization effort.[61] Rao's concern was not intense enough for him to consider rolling back its program; it was just a matter of waiting until the economy might be in a better position to withstand the inevitable sanctions after a highly visible test. For all practical purposes, India's nuclear weapons sprint initiated in 1989 was complete by 1994.[62] In May 1998, however, Bharatiya Janata Party (BJP) prime minister A. B. Vajpayee, who twenty years earlier as foreign minister had declared that he was for the bomb and that India could not forever foreclose the nuclear option, would leave no doubt.

TESTING PROLIFERATION STRATEGY THEORY

My theory identifies the reasons for India's different proliferation strategies and why they shifted over time. Although India had faced a conventionally superior, nuclear-armed China for decades, which forced it to select a hard hedging strategy, it was the prospect of Pakistani weaponization coupled with the recognition that universal disarmament was a nonstarter that ultimately killed Rajiv's opposition and generated domestic consensus for weaponizing India's nuclear program.[63] It was only at this point that India undertook a sprinting strategy. The perturbations in India's security environment only prompted a final sprint to nuclear weapons once they were strongly refracted through a domestic political prism. A realist explanation for India's proliferation process purposely excludes domestic political factors and therefore fails to explain India's stuttered march to nuclear weapons. Once Rajiv decided to weaponize, its leaders did not have to fear their country becoming the target of counterproliferation efforts given India's size, power, and geography. The result was a relatively open weaponization of India's nuclear capabilities over the next five to six years, including

61. Ibid. Also see Rabinowitz and Miller, "Keeping the Bombs in the Basement." Chandra further notes in the author interview that "testing when our economy could not withstand potential sanctions was also a problem. Rao said that there is never a good time to test [during the initial liberalization period] . . . but by 1998 the economy was in much better shape."

62. See Narang, *Nuclear Strategy in the Modern Era*, chap. 4.

63. There is certainly evidence of Gourevitch's second image reversed in this case. But domestic consensus for developing nuclear weapons nonetheless took almost a decade to form. As noted previously, the Indian Ministry of External Affairs had, as early as 1981, recognized that Pakistan was in the process of weaponizing its nuclear capability. When Rajiv finally agreed to weaponization in 1989, the proximate cause was his realization that universal disarmament—India's preferred security solution to Chinese and Pakistani nuclear weapons—was a fantasy. Domestic consensus for nuclearization therefore lagged significantly behind India's security pressures.

regular and public tests of explicitly nuclear-capable missiles beginning in May 1989.[64]

Absent an acute threat, India's energy needs caused its scientists to look to nuclear energy as a potential solution to its economic development challenges in the years after independence. The inherently dual-use nature of the pursuit pushed India toward being a technical hedger, with interest in a nuclear weapons program limited only to the political fringes and to scientists like Bhabha. The combination of India's military defeat by China in the 1962 war and China's 1964 nuclear test provided a shock to India's security environment. Lacking any formal allies, India confronted this acute security threat alone. But the severity of the threat was insufficient to overcome domestic political—particularly prime ministerial—opposition to nuclear weapons. Absent domestic consensus among key decision makers, especially a succession of reluctant prime ministers, India shifted only as far as a hard hedging strategy, as my theory predicts, where it remained a prime ministerial decision away from weaponization for almost a quarter century. The hard hedging strategy included the recognition that India needed to be in a position to weaponize if necessary. None of this was hidden. But successive prime ministers ensured that the final steps on warhead development and weaponization were prohibited—until 1989.

In addition to the structural realist story—which fails to adequately explain India's nuclear journey—there are three other alternative explanations for India's nuclear proliferation saga. The first is technological determinism, which argues that India took decades to weaponize because its scientific enclave was slow and incompetent.[65] The evidence, however, suggests otherwise. India's progress toward nuclear weapons was slow because of intentional political decisions to choose different strategies over time, two of which were hedging strategies where the aim was not to develop nuclear weapons but to maintain the option to do so. When Rajiv decided to order the weaponization of India's nuclear capabilities, India had a reliable, deliverable capability within roughly five years. The challenges that India did face during its final sprint were mostly caused by compartmentalization of different elements of the program. The silos that made it hard for the air force to collaborate with the gravity bomb designers, for instance, were

64. On the challenges India faced in operationalizing its nuclear weapons, see Kampani, "New Delhi's Long Nuclear Journey."

65. Kampani's argument focuses on the need for secrecy leading to organizational dysfunction but is consistent with the view that India's delay was largely due to that dysfunction, rather than being strategically motivated. See ibid.

created during the hard hedging phase as a feature, not a bug, to forestall weaponization—when the military was finally tasked with marrying the bombs to the delivery aircraft, India's progress in the sprinting phase was not significantly slower than that of other nuclear weapons states. Indeed, Naresh Chandra (though perhaps self-servingly) disputes the "incompetence" narrative, claiming that once a concerted decision to weaponize was taken, India needed roughly the same amount of time to implement it as did the other nuclear weapons powers.[66] The typology and theory introduced here suggest, and the evidence demonstrates, that India's slow march to nuclear weapons was both strategically and politically motivated.

Another alternative explanation for India's slow attainment of nuclear weapons is that India was inhibited by international nonproliferation norms. There is no doubt that the perceived discriminatory nature of the NPT influenced India's nuclear weapons approach. But India's strategy shifted in response to external security and domestic political variables and remained stable through critical junctures in the international nonproliferation regime. India first shifted from technical hedging to hard hedging because of major changes in its immediate security environment, fully a decade before the NPT. The second shift from hard hedging to sprinting was caused by Rajiv Gandhi's change of heart after seeing evidence of Pakistani weaponization coupled with his failed effort to make progress on global nuclear disarmament. Once this combination changed his mind, a domestic consensus for weaponization solidified. Hedging until 1989, and sprinting thereafter, was not a product of global nonproliferation norms or efforts—in fact, it was the opposite. International and U.S. pressure, as well as debates surrounding the Comprehensive Test Ban Treaty and the indefinite extension of the NPT, affected the timing of India's nuclear tests, but not its progress toward weapons development. It did not change India's proliferation strategies or force India to hide or roll back its program.[67] Instead, the perceived discriminatory nature of these treaties empowered those in India who wanted to accelerate testing before they might go into force. To the extent that nonproliferation norms affected India's trajectory, they seem to have been most powerful at the individual level: successive Indian prime ministers seemed to evince discomfort with nuclear weapons, particularly Shastri, Desai, and even Rajiv Gandhi. Rajiv only ordered weaponization

66. Chandra, interview. He also noted that several years were lost during the V. P. Singh and Chandra Shekhar governments because they were short-lived coalition governments where neither prime minister was terribly interested in the details of the advancing weaponization effort.

67. See Hymans, *Psychology of Nuclear Proliferation*, chap. 7.

when the security threat became so undeniable that it swamped his moral aversion to nuclear weapons.

The final alternative explanation, virtually unique to the case of India, is Jacques Hymans's theory of oppositional nationalism, which is a domestic political explanation focusing on differences between the "oppositional" nationalism of the BJP and the "sportsmanlike" nationalism of the Congress Party.[68] Hymans's theory would predict that India, under Congress leadership, would be eternally content with hedging and would seek nuclear weapons only under the oppositional nationalist BJP. This may explain when India tested nuclear weapons, but it cannot explain India's proliferation strategies. Prior to March 1998, the BJP never held power for longer than two weeks. Atal Bihari Vajpayee, who had been prime minister for only two months when India conducted the Pokhran tests in 1998, would not have had anything to test if not for Congress prime ministers' management of India's nuclear program to that point. Rajiv Gandhi ordered nuclearization, and Rao continued to sprint after Rajiv was assassinated in 1991 and almost tested a weapon in 1995. Hymans counters that Rajiv's authorization was more like a "flashing yellow" light, and it was only Vajpayee who took India over the line by testing in May 1998.[69] Chandra, however, indicates that Rajiv gave him a clear and unmistakable mandate to develop an arsenal of nuclear weapons. Certainly, steps and budgets had to be cleared along the way, and several weak coalition governments between 1989 and 1991 paid little attention to the work Chandra was doing, but the end goal of developing nuclear weapons and the reliable means to deliver them were indisputable after March 1989.[70] The BJP was keener than the Congress Party to test nuclear weapons for the reasons Hymans suggests.[71] However, it inherited ready-to-test nuclear weapons from Congress. Prime Minister Vajpayee put it bluntly: "Rao told me the bomb was ready. I only exploded it."[72] Psychological differences between Congress and the BJP leaders do not explain India's proliferation strategies. Although India's tests were a BJP affair, attaining a nuclear weapons capability was a Congress affair. Proliferation Strategy Theory best captures the distinct strategies of India's nuclear proliferation over time and why Indian leaders shifted strategies when they did.

68. Ibid.
69. Ibid., 190.
70. Chandra, interview.
71. See also Narang, "Pride and Prejudice and Prithvis."
72. Vajpayee quoted in Sitapati, *Half Lion*, 279.

Insurance Hedgers: Japan and (West) Germany

I now turn to the cases of two insurance hedgers, Japan and West Germany, formal allies of the United States who maintained—and continue to maintain—nuclear options to hedge against the possibility of American abandonment and used the threat of breakout as a coercive tool to elicit stronger reassurance guarantees from Washington. These cases illuminate and test the mechanisms that lead to insurance hedging and carry implications for theories of alliance management and theories of nuclear proliferation. I also offer insights about key dynamics in East Asian security and regarding the security and behavior of states under formal nuclear umbrellas.

Japan and West Germany both faced long-running, severe security threats: China (as well as more recently nuclear North Korea) in the case of Japan, and the Soviet Union in the case of West Germany. But neither state faced the threat alone: both enjoy a formal military alliance with the United States, which had—and still has—formal instruments committing to the defense of both Japan and (West) Germany, including explicit extended nuclear guarantees (though conditions of nuclear use in their defense are nevertheless ambiguous). Japan has gone beyond simply the development of civilian nuclear energy technology in order to put itself closer to a nuclear weapons option should it ever need it—should it face outright abandonment from the United States or if the severity of its underlying threats increases to the point that the alliance with the United States no longer meets its security needs. In the case of West Germany, it is often forgotten that Bonn's nuclear status was the animating dilemma of the early Cold War. West Germany seriously explored the possibility of nuclear weapons in order to extract historically unique nuclear-sharing procedures from the United States in the late 1950s. Those arrangements largely persist with post–Cold War Germany, which continues to be an insurance hedger in the event it is forced to confront a resurgent Russian threat alone.

Both Japan and West Germany were clearly insurance hedgers. Putting themselves in a position to explicitly exercise a nuclear weapons option under the U.S. nuclear umbrella had—or, in the case of Japan, has—twin benefits. First, as I stated earlier, states that actively pursue nuclear weapons face a period of heightened danger when they undertake this process. Other states are likely to attempt to stop them. Insurance hedging can help mitigate this problem. It inches a state closer to nuclear weapons, compressing the window in which others might be able to act to arrest their progress if they actively pursue weapons in the future. Insurance hedging makes states better equipped to react if they face a grave new threat or sudden abandonment. Second, Japan's and West Germany's implicit—and in some cases explicit—threats to develop (or in Germany's case weaponize through joint development) nuclear weapons helped Tokyo and Bonn secure key concessions from the United States. Washington heightened its commitments to both states to reduce their fears of abandonment. As Japanese and West German leaders well knew, the United States always strongly opposed the development and possession of nuclear weapons by formal U.S. allies. Washington wished to exert sole control over nuclear use and escalation within its alliance system in the event of conflict.[73] This gave its allies leverage when it came to potential nuclear proliferation—and they used, and can continue to use, it.

JAPAN (1954–PRESENT): ALLERGY OR ADDICTION?

Because of its experience as the only state on which nuclear weapons were used in war, Japan is often portrayed as having a nuclear "allergy" and being a staunch proponent of nuclear disarmament and nuclear nonproliferation.[74] However, accumulating historical evidence and new scholarship suggest that Japan has had a much more complicated relationship with the possibility of nuclear weapons development. Despite being diagnosed with an "allergy," Japan has fed on a steady diet of all things nuclear since the 1950s, developing a robust civilian nuclear energy sector, as well as eventually indigenous uranium enrichment and plutonium reprocessing facilities (first at Tokaimura, and subsequently Rokkasho) that impart Japan full indigenous control of the fuel cycle. Today, the nuclear proliferation literature is replete with references to the "Japan Model," which refers not to its erstwhile status as an economic powerhouse but rather to having all the requisite pieces in place to develop nuclear weapons but refraining from doing so—hedging, in other words. In fact, Ariel Levite refers to Japan as "the most salient

73. Gavin, "Strategies of Inhibition"; Miller, *Stopping the Bomb*; Rabinowitz and Miller, "Keeping the Bombs in the Basement"; Gerzhoy, "Alliance Coercion and Nuclear Restraint." These recent works all suggest that the United States was deeply opposed to even British, French, and certainly West German nuclearization. On the unique cases of Pakistan and India, see Thomas P. Cavanna, "Geopolitics over Proliferation: The Origins of US Grand Strategy and Their Implications for the Spread of Nuclear Weapons in South Asia," *Journal of Strategic Studies* 41, no. 4 (June 2018): 576–603.

74. On the use of the "allergy" epithet by proponents of nuclear weapons in Japan, see Glenn D. Hook, "The Nuclearization of Language: Nuclear Allergy as Political Metaphor," *Journal of Peace Research* 21, no. 3 (September 1984): 259–75.

example of nuclear hedging to date." Japan "hardly tried to conceal its hedging strategy."[75]

This section performs three tasks. First, it demonstrates that, as scholars such as Richard Samuels and James Schoff, Takaaki Daitoku, and Mayumi Fukushima have shown through newly available Japanese archival sources, Japan's leaders conceived of intentional nuclear weapons hedging in the late 1950s, much earlier than is generally appreciated.[76] Second, I show that Japan adopted a strategy of insurance hedging, a variety of hedging that served the twin purposes of compelling a stronger alliance commitment from the United States while simultaneously compressing Japan's window of vulnerability—or breakout time to actual weaponization—should the alliance no longer meet Japan's calculated security needs. Third, it demonstrates the power of my theory in explaining why Japan opted for insurance hedging, as opposed to hard hedging or an active proliferation strategy, providing a superior explanation to alternative theories such as technological determinism. It should be noted that scholars such as Jacques Hymans and Llewelyn Hughes who focus on the domestic fissures keeping Japanese nuclearization at bay are not incorrect: my theory suggests that, should Japan shift out of insurance hedging, it would first have to transition through a nontrivial hard hedging phase, during which it would have to undertake the arduous task of assembling domestic consensus for nuclear weapons.[77] My theory offers a more complete explanation for what Japan has done, and the domestic political challenges it would have to surmount in order to pursue nuclear weapons should conditions change.

Contrary to conventional wisdom that points to the bombings of Hiroshima and Nagasaki, and the postwar constitution, notably Article 9, banning offensive military capabilities, to suggest that Japan is allergic to nuclearization, Japan has in fact carefully crafted a nuclear hedging strategy that

75. Levite, "Never Say Never Again," 71. Curiously, however, Levite lists Japan under nuclear reversal, despite the fact that its hedging strategy persists.

76. See Samuels and Schoff, "Japan's Nuclear Hedge," 233–64; Takaaki Daitoku, "Resorting to Latency: Japan's Accommodation with Nuclear Realities," in *Uncovering the Sources of Nuclear Behavior: Historical Dimensions of Nuclear Proliferation*, ed. Andreas Wenger and Roland Popp (Washington, DC: Georgetown University Press, forthcoming); and Mayumi Fukushima, "Japanese Nuclear Ambition: An Important Decision Yet to Be Made?" unpublished manuscript, May 26, 2015.

77. See Jacques E. C. Hymans, "Veto Players, Nuclear Energy, and Nonproliferation: Domestic Institutional Barriers to a Japanese Bomb," *International Security* 36, no. 2 (Fall 2011): 154–89; Llewelyn Hughes, "Why Japan Will Not Go Nuclear (Yet)," *International Security* 31, no. 4 (Spring 2007): 67–96; and Mike M. Mochizuki, "Japan Tests the Nuclear Taboo," *Nonproliferation Review* 14, no. 2 (July 2007): 303–28.

has put all the technological pieces in place to exercise a nuclear weapons option should it ever decide to do so. As early as 1957, Prime Minister Nobusuke Kishi's cabinet not only declared that the possession of nuclear weapons for defensive purposes—specifically tactical nuclear weapons—would be consistent with Article 9 of the Japanese constitution, but the prime minister went so far as to tell U.S. ambassador Douglas MacArthur II that he "believed it was essential that Japan have (a) nuclear" weapons arsenal, even though Japanese leaders were only exploring the idea at the time.[78] His successor, Prime Minister Ikeda, made similar remarks in private.[79] In December 1964, several months after the first Chinese nuclear test, Prime Minister Sato told U.S. ambassador Edwin Reischauer that "if other fellow nations had nuclears [*sic*] [weapons] it was only common sense to have them oneself."[80] He repeated this to President Johnson directly several weeks later in January 1965, stating to him that "if the Chicoms had nuclear weapons, the Japanese should also have them."[81] Even as the NPT was being negotiated between 1968 and 1970, Japan's signature and ratification were not a foregone conclusion, and Vice Foreign Minister Shimoda, according to Daitoku, "insisted that Japan should 'reserve the option' of going nuclear even in case of acceding to the NPT."[82] Publicly, Prime Minister Sato declared the Three Non-nuclear Principles in 1967 while two years later privately referring to them as "nonsense" to U.S. ambassador U. Alexis Johnson.[83] In 1970, a Japanese Defense Agency White Paper, commissioned by its then director and future prime minister Yasuhiro Nakasone, stated: "as for defensive nuclear weapons, it would be possible in a legal sense to possess small-yield, tactical, purely defensive nuclear weapons without violating the Constitution."[84] Over the course of a little over a decade, Japanese leaders had rationalized

78. "Japan Discussed Acquisition of 'Defensive' Nuclear Weapons in 1958," *Japan Times*, March 17, 2013, http://www.japantimes.co.jp/news/2013/03/17/national/history/japan-discussed-acquisition-of-defensive-nuclear-weapons-in-1958/#.VeBpyZd3AlM. For the formal policy guidelines, see Richard J. Samuels, *Securing Japan: Tokyo's Grand Strategy and the Future of East Asia* (Ithaca: Cornell University Press, 2007).

79. See Fukushima, "Japanese Nuclear Ambition," 5.

80. Tokyo 2067, December 29, 1964, *Foreign Relations of the United States* [hereafter *FRUS*], *1964–1968*, vol. XXIX, part 2 (Washington, DC: U.S. GPO, 2006), doc. 37.

81. Sato quoted in Kurt Campbell and Tsuyoshi Sunohara, "Japan: Thinking the Unthinkable," in *The Nuclear Tipping Point: Why States Reconsider Their Nuclear Choices*, ed. Kurt M. Campbell, Robert J. Einhorn, and Mitchell Reiss (Washington, DC: Brookings Institution Press, 2004), 222.

82. Daitoku, "Resorting to Latency."

83. Ibid.

84. Nakasone quoted in Campbell and Sunohara, "Japan: Thinking the Unthinkable," 222.

the potential possession of not only strategic nuclear weapons for defense if necessary but tactical nuclear weapons as well which, if ever developed, could obviously support both defensive and offensive strategies.

Earlier than many realize, Japanese leaders overcame any so-called "allergy" to nuclear weapons and began to evaluate nuclear policy based on their security situation. They considered the possibility of developing nuclear weapons if conditions required, and they lay the technological foundation for nuclear optionality through the development of a robust civilian nuclear energy program and by obtaining control of the full nuclear fuel cycle. A 1968 and 1970 two-volume internal Cabinet Research Staff report titled *The Basic Studies of Japan's Nuclear Policy* was tasked with examining the costs and benefits of a nuclear weapons capability.[85] It concluded that although Japan could attain an indigenous nuclear capability in "five to six years" and that it was "possible and rather easy [to] produce a small number of atomic bombs,"[86] the technological, political, and security costs were too great and that Japan should not develop an independent deterrent. Rather, it should continue to rely on the U.S. extended deterrent and advocate for universal disarmament to best achieve its security. Nevertheless, in 1969, an internal study for the Foreign Ministry titled "An Outline of Japanese Foreign Policy" concluded, according to Mochizuki, that Japan should "maintain always not to restrict the economic and technological potential to produce nuclear weapons."[87] One official inside the ministry's policy planning staff outlined the nascent hedging strategy in this period, which persists today: "We will continue to use nuclear power for peaceful purposes, on the one hand. On the other, we should be in a position where we can continue to develop fast breeder reactors and other relevant installations so as to make nuclear weapons instantly in case of need."[88] So although Japan eventually acceded to the NPT in 1970 and ratified it in 1976, it nevertheless persisted in pursuing and obtaining full control of the fuel cycle, which would be critical for a potential future indigenous nuclear weapons capability. Japan not only rejected the technical constraints of the NPT but also did not believe the regime was politically durable and thus would not constrain its ability to go nuclear if it ever needed to do so.[89]

85. See Yuri Kase, "The Costs and Benefits of Japan's Nuclearization: An Insight into the *1968/70 Internal Report*," *Nonproliferation Review* 8, no. 2 (Summer 2001): 55–68.

86. Daitoku, "Resorting to Latency," 17.

87. Quoted in Mochizuki, "Japan Tests the Nuclear Taboo," 311; also see Daitoku, "Resorting to Latency," 18.

88. Quoted in Daitoku, "Resorting to Latency," 19.

89. See Fukushima, "Japanese Nuclear Ambition," 35–37.

In the post–Cold War era, Japan has faced acute security threats at various moments, including an errant North Korean Taepodong missile test that overflew the Sea of Japan in 1998 and a series of long-range North Korean missile tests as Kim Jong Un expanded and improved the DPRK's missile force in 2017, which renewed at least private discussion about nuclear weapons. In 1994, in the midst of the Agreed Framework and upcoming talks on the indefinite extension of the NPT, one Diet member stated, with the consent of the prime minister: "To tell the truth, of course, Japan has already had the capability for creating nuclear-armed forces. But we have restrained ourselves from doing so."[90] Although internal government reports commissioned in 1995 and 2006 again concluded against nuclear weaponization, Japan's hedging strategy has persisted and deepened, both in latent technical capability and in policy goals. Japan's capabilities to support a potential nuclear weapons force have only improved over time, as it now possesses roughly 48 tons of reprocessed reactor-grade plutonium (which could be further purified for weapons grade)—about 10 tons on Japanese territory alone—capable of generating thousands of nuclear weapons, uranium enrichment facilities, and an array of advanced nuclear-compatible aircraft and long-range missiles derived from its space program.[91] It is unknown how advanced research on pit fabrication and the nonfissile components for warheads has progressed, but given Japan's technical and industrial capabilities, these are not prohibitive or time-consuming hurdles.

Furthermore, Japan's leaders have periodically kept the fact of the nuclear hedge publicly salient. In 2002, then deputy chief cabinet secretary and future prime minister Shinzo Abe said in an interview to *Asahi Shimbun* that "the Japanese government's official position is that the possession of nuclear weapons is not necessarily forbidden by the constitution if they are small, of tactical nature and being kept to a minimum size," though he then reiterated Japan's commitment to not possessing nuclear weapons at the moment, performing the now-perfected hedging pirouette.[92] Even after the horrific events of the Fukushima nuclear crisis, Ishiba Shigeru, a former Japan Defense Agency chief, stated: "I don't think Japan needs to possess nuclear weapons, but it is important to maintain our commercial reactors because it would allow us to produce a nuclear warhead in a short amount of time. It is a tacit nuclear

90. Ooki Hiroshi (LDP), quoted in Daitoku, "Resorting to Latency," 26.

91. See Samuels and Schoff, "Japan's Nuclear Hedge," 240–43; and Campbell and Sunohara, "Japan: Thinking the Unthinkable," 243–45.

92. Shinzo Abe quoted in *Asahi Shimbun*, June 8, 2002, trans. Mayumi Fukushima, August 28, 2015.

deterrent."[93] He later stated in 2012 that "it would be possible to create nuclear weapons in the relatively short time of several months to a year."[94]

Japan, like India before it, has carefully laid the foundation for transitioning from a peaceful nuclear program to the development of nuclear weapons if necessary. In 1968, *Basic Studies* had estimated Japan's "breakout" time to be five to six years. By 2012, those responsible for managing Japan's nuclear hedge, such as Ishiba (after leaving office), had publicly reduced that breakout time to under a year, possibly even several months, though estimating the exact time frame is fraught with uncertainties. A sitting defense minister, Satoshi Morimoto, stated that Japan's nuclear energy program was the foundation for Japan's "latent deterrent" and that it must be maintained.[95] While Japan has publicly continued to forswear nuclear weapons—for now—and consistently highlighted public opposition to nuclear weapons, its leaders have carefully emplaced Japan as a threshold nuclear state as a conscious strategic choice as early as the mid-1950s.

But what variety of hedging has Japan adopted? Here I show that it has explicitly adopted insurance hedging—hedging because another country has offered a nuclear umbrella, not because of domestic fracture—putting all the pieces in place for a nuclear weapons program both to elicit stronger extended deterrence reassurance from a United States that does not generally wish to see its allies develop independent nuclear capability and to compress its window of vulnerability to regional adversaries should American security guarantees disintegrate or no longer meet Japan's security needs. The hedge is an insurance policy against these two specific contingencies. The general strategy and particular type of Japan's nuclear hedge are succinctly illuminated and described by Samuels and Schoff:

> Over the past four decades, Japan has maintained viable—and *unconcealed*—options for the relatively rapid acquisition of nuclear weapons . . . *each time* the regional security environment has shifted—such as after China's first nuclear test in 1964, the end of the Cold War, North Korea's nuclear breakout in the 2000s, or the 2010 U.S.-Russia

93. Ishiba Shigeru quoted in Chester Dawson, "In Japan, Provocative Case for Staying Nuclear," *Wall Street Journal*, October 28, 2011, http://www.wsj.com/articles/SB10001424052970203658804576638392537430156.

94. Ishiba Shigeru quoted in Linda Sieg, "Japan Atomic Power Defenders: Keep Ability to Build Nuclear Weapons," Reuters, February 13, 2012, https://www.reuters.com/article/japan-nuclear-arms/japan-atomic-power-defenders-keep-ability-to-build-nuclear-weapons-idINL4E8DA2ZK20120213.

95. Samuels and Schoff, "Japan's Nuclear Hedge," 241.

> New Strategic Arms Reduction Treaty (START) agreement limiting warheads and launchers—Tokyo has re-examined its policy before *signaling for (and accepting)* U.S. reassurance on extended deterrence.[96]

Japan has not hidden its latent nuclear capabilities. It has developed them openly and clearly with the intention of creating leverage that can be used to ensure that American extended deterrence meets its security needs. Green and Furukawa argue that Japan has consistently used "the 'nuclear card' as a hedge and a signal or warning to the United States to sustain a strong extended deterrence commitment."[97] Because of the difficulty of credibly extending deterrence—and allies' infinite appetite for reassurance—Japanese leaders have almost always questioned the reliability of America's nuclear umbrella.[98] Building an insurance hedge lends credibility to Japan's threat to build nuclear weapons if American extended deterrence is insufficient. This in turn motivates Washington to maximize the credibility of its extended deterrent to Japan. (Separately, Japanese leaders employed the threat of breakout as a means of compelling the United States to concede control over the island of Okinawa.)[99] But the threat of breakout is more than leverage. The same technical work that gives Japan leverage against the United States comprises a very real, and potentially swift, pathway to a nuclear weapons arsenal in the event of a rapid deterioration in Japan's security environment, either because its underlying threats—China and North Korea—become unbearably menacing or because the U.S. alliance is insufficient to meet Japan's security needs (or both).

With respect to insurance against American abandonment, Prime Minister Sato's shocking statements to Ambassador Reischauer and President Johnson about Japanese nuclear weapons may have been a calculated manipulation to elicit an explicit American extended deterrence guarantee. Japanese historian Ayako Kusunoki writes: "It is unlikely, however, that Sato was serious about acquiring nuclear weapons. . . . He hinted at ambitions of nuclearization, but knew beforehand that Washington would react unfavorably to such desires."[100]

96. Ibid., 234–35, emphasis added. Also see Samuels, *Securing Japan*, 176.

97. Michael J. Green and Katsuhisa Furukawa, "Japan: New Nuclear Realism," in *The Long Shadow: Nuclear Weapons and Security in 21st Century Asia*, ed. Muthiah Alagappa (Stanford: Stanford University Press, 2008), 348.

98. See Fukushima, "Japanese Nuclear Ambition," 11; Green and Furukawa, "Japan: New Nuclear Realism," 352.

99. See Tristan A. Volpe, "Atomic Leverage: Compellence with Nuclear Latency," *Security Studies* 26, no. 3 (July 2017): 517–44.

100. Ayako Kusunoki, "The Sato Cabinet and the Making of Japan's Non-nuclear Policy," *Journal of American-East Asian Relations* 15, no. 1 (2008): 31.

When Sato asked Johnson explicitly about a guarantee should Japan suffer any form of attack—including nuclear—he replied "affirmatively" and "understood Japan's position and did not want to increase the number of nuclear powers."[101] Kusunoki further illuminates this episode, writing, "Not until [Sato] had unequivocal confirmation of the credibility of this nuclear deterrent did the prime minister withdraw his previous remarks to Ambassador Reischauer about going nuclear."[102] The conditions for keeping Japan an insurance hedger were established early and explicitly by two heads of government: Japan would go nuclear without an unequivocal American security guarantee.

Japan conceived of this strategy much earlier than is generally appreciated. In 1971, Takuya Kubo, a defense official, wrote a memo explicitly linking Japan's hedge to a U.S. guarantee: "when Japan has acquired enough capabilities for the peaceful use of atomic energy to be able to develop substantial nuclear forces at any time (as Japan already has in fact), the United States, for fear of destabilized international relations provoked by nuclear proliferation, will desire to maintain the U.S.-Japan security treaty with nuclear extended deterrence."[103] Though it is unclear how widespread across the government and political parties this linkage and strategy were at the time, Japan's behavior—trotting out Japan's status as a virtual nuclear state when it required reassurance from the United States—has been consistent.

In the late 1970s, the Carter administration was faced with a dilemma: how should the United States deal with Japan's insistence that it be allowed to reprocess plutonium—nominally for fast breeder reactor technology and independent of uranium supply for its civilian program—which would give Japan a ready capability and potential supply for plutonium nuclear weapons and allow it to occupy a unique status within the NPT that persists today? William Burr narrates the debate within the Carter administration over the government of Japan's reprocessing request—which was an increasing irritant in the bilateral relationship—with the administration ultimately relenting in order to preserve the alliance: "By 1979, Gerard C. Smith, the president's representative on nonproliferation policy, wanted Japan to be given leeway so it could reprocess without getting U.S. consent. Worried that Japan and other close allies perceived the United States as an

101. Johnson quoted in ibid.

102. Ibid.

103. Takuya Kubo, "A Point of View Regarding Japan's Defense Capabilities," World and Japan Database, University of Tokyo Institute of Oriental Culture, February 20, 1971, cited and translated by Fukushima, p. 27, original (Japanese), http://www.ioc.u-tokyo.ac.jp/~worldjpn/documents/texts/JPSC/19710220.O1J.html.

'unreliable' nuclear supplier, Smith hoped to avoid 'major damage' to the relationship with Tokyo."[104] Whatever doubts there may have been in the rest of the Carter administration, the subsequent Reagan administration had no qualms about granting Japan this unique capability, with Ambassador Mike Mansfield writing: "Even though it would represent a *significant shift in our nuclear policy*, I believe there is one *thorn in the Japanese side* which we should completely remove as soon as possible. I refer to the Japanese Government's wish to operate without interference its Tokai Mura pilot plant for the reprocessing of spent nuclear fuel and to construct a still larger plant for this purpose."[105] This is precisely what the Reagan administration would allow. Knowing it had leverage with the United States, Japan was able to convince the Carter administration, which was relatively hawkish on nonproliferation, and then the more amenable Reagan administration to allow it to carve out a unique and unprecedented capability to possess an indigenous nuclear weapons potential should it ever need it, as a concession to maintaining the U.S.-Japan alliance and remaining non-nuclear for the time being.

As Samuels and Schoff noted in the excerpt quoted above, any time there has been a perturbation in the external security environment that causes Japan to question America's extended deterrent, Japanese leaders—across all parties—have not so subtly publicly mentioned the threat to go nuclear if American security guarantees were deemed insufficient to Tokyo. Writing in *Foreign Affairs* just as North Korea was testing long-range missiles, one of which would errantly overfly the Sea of Japan, and several months after the Indian and Pakistani nuclear tests in 1998, former prime minister Morihiro Hosokawa stated: "It is in the interest of the United States, so long as it does not wish to see Japan withdraw from the NPT and develop its own nuclear deterrent, to maintain its alliance with Japan and continue to provide a nuclear umbrella."[106]

Japanese leaders have justified their position in ways that mirror my theoretical predictions. First and foremost, my theory predicts that a state's acute security environment—specifically rivals with nuclear weapons—should be a

104. William Burr, "Japan's Plutonium Overhang," *Wilson Center NPIHP Research Updates*, June 8, 2017, https://www.wilsoncenter.org/publication/japans-plutonium-overhang.

105. U.S. Embassy Japan Telegram 01311 to State Department, "U.S. Policy toward Japan," January 26, 1981, Secret, https://nsarchive.gwu.edu/dc.html?doc=5731918-National-Security-Archive-Doc-04-U-S-Embassy, emphasis added.

106. Morihiro Hosokawa, "Are U.S. Troops in Japan Needed? Reforming the Alliance," *Foreign Affairs*, July/August 1998, p. 5, https://www.foreignaffairs.com/articles/asia/1998-07-01/are-us-troops-japan-needed-reforming-alliance.

key point of discussion when a state considers pursuing nuclear weapons. In 2006 amid renewed concerns about North Korean nuclear weapons, former prime minister Nakasone did just that. "There is a need to also study the issue of nuclear weapons," he said. "There are countries with nuclear weapons in Japan's vicinity. We are currently dependent on U.S. nuclear weapons (as a deterrent), but it is not necessarily known whether the U.S. attitude will continue."[107] Even more directly, Foreign Minister Taro Aso—although he subsequently denied it—was reported to have told Vice President Cheney around the same time: "If North Korea continues its nuclear development, even Japan would need to arm itself with nuclear weapons."[108] The goal was clear: to directly convey to the United States that a deterioration in Japan's security environment or a belief that Washington was not doing enough to protect Japanese security could be met with nuclear weapons development. Under the conditions that I predict, Japan explicitly embraced an insurance hedging strategy. The insurance has served its purpose so far. Each time Japan has questioned U.S. guarantees and raised the prospect of potentially culminating the weaponization process, the United States has obliged in reaffirming Japan's request for an "unshakeable nuclear umbrella."[109]

This consistent pattern over decades makes Japan the quintessential insurance hedger in the international system. Japan is not just a generic nuclear hedger. Rather, it is a nuclear hedger with a very specific aim: to insure against changes in its external security environment, most notably American abandonment. In doing so, Tokyo has reduced the probability of such abandonment occurring. But it has emplaced itself very close to a nuclear weapons capability if it ever deems it necessary.

Japan does not hedge simply because it is tempted by its civilian energy program, like some of its Western European counterparts. Nor does it do so because its elite domestic consensus is fractured despite clear, acute security

107. Yasuhiro Nakasone quoted in "Nakasone Proposes Japan Consider Nuclear Weapons," *Japan Times*, September 6, 2006.

108. See "Japan Denies Official Made Pro-Nuke Comments," *Nuclear Threat Initiative*, March 9, 2006, https://www.nti.org/gsn/article/japan-denies-official-made-pro-nuke-comments/.

109. Abe quoted in Samuels and Schoff, "Japan's Nuclear Hedge," 245. Conditions that affect Japan's belief in the reliability and credibility of the U.S. nuclear umbrella not only include the severity of Japan's proximate threats but also issues such as the state of the U.S. nuclear force posture generally and in Asia, and the China-U.S. nuclear balance. Just as during the Cold War with Britain and France worrying about American extended deterrence once the Soviet Union achieved the ability to hit the U.S. homeland, a more robust Chinese ability to target the U.S. homeland could exacerbate anxieties in Tokyo about the credibility of American extended nuclear guarantees.

threats that it faces alone (though it would undoubtedly have to pass through that phase in the future should it move off of insurance hedging), as in India. Rather, Japan adopts hedging as a strategy to simultaneously manipulate its senior ally, the United States, and to insure its security should unforeseen shocks to its security suddenly emerge. Samuels and Schoff document the regularity with which "Japanese policymakers often remind their U.S. and regional counterparts (both privately and publicly) about the importance of the U.S. nuclear umbrella and Japan's own ability to go nuclear if necessary."[110] Identifying the character of Japanese hedging as insurance hedging is critical: it clarifies that there are two target audiences—Japan's potential adversaries and its superpower ally, the United States—and specifies the conditions under which Japan may move off hedging toward an active weaponization strategy.

TESTING PROLIFERATION STRATEGY THEORY

My theory explains Japan's choice of this specific form of hedging. Japan resides in one of the most hostile security environments in the world—threats to Japan's security have, over time, ranged from the Soviet Union and China, both nuclear and aggregately conventionally superior states over Japan, and now include China and nuclear North Korea. If Japan ever had to face that underlying threat environment by itself—without a superpower ally—there is no question that it would have extremely strong security demand for nuclear weapons. However, that otherwise acute security environment is attenuated by a superpower ally, the United States, which has formally committed to the defense of Japan and goes to great lengths—including forward deployment of forces on permanent bases—to assure Tokyo of that commitment. In its formal alliance arrangements, the United States prefers to be the only state with control of nuclear weapons—to retain sole authority over nuclear use and escalation—and has therefore historically been strongly opposed to allied pursuit of nuclear weapons.[111] This empowers its allies to use the threat of nuclear proliferation to manipulate and extract greater commitments from the United States. Insurance hedging enables the junior ally to prepare for potential abandonment while also taking steps to reduce the chance that such an eventuality comes to pass.

110. Ibid., 244.

111. See Gavin, "Strategies of Inhibition"; Miller, *Stopping the Bomb*.

My theory predicts that Japan's particular security situation is exactly the one required for a state to select insurance hedging, putting all of the pieces of a nuclear weapons program in place and openly laying out the conditions under which nuclear possession will be culminated and the insurance policy exercised. An insurance hedge may serve as a virtual deterrent to adversaries and to the superpower from abandoning the state. A finely tuned realist explanation might capture Japan's current insurance hedging strategy, but a narrow security explanation should reject the notion that a state in an otherwise hostile security environment might outsource its security to a patron. Similarly, technological determinism fails to explain why Japan might develop all of the pieces and technologies to weaponize its nuclear capabilities but then intentionally stop short, which is clearly a political decision made at the highest levels of government. A normative explanation that focuses on Japan's aversion to nuclear weapons after suffering nuclear use against it at Hiroshima and Nagasaki would have the opposite problem: it cannot explain why Japan would go as far as it has with its insurance hedge, emplacing itself—uniquely within the NPT regime—within months of a bomb if it chose to exercise the option. As a state with a self-professed nuclear allergy, Japan has nevertheless fed on a steady diet of nuclear technology, coming right up to the line of a military potential without exercising it.

My theory also uniquely provides a template to consider what might occur if Japan's security environment severely deteriorates—whether because the underlying threat environment becomes so severe that Japan decides it needs to protect itself without the United States or because it believes the United States has abandoned Japan or no longer meets its security needs. Both realism and technological determinism would predict that Japan, in that scenario, would sprint for a bomb as quickly as possible. Given Japan's extensive technological preparation, the sprint would be short: perhaps culminating in attaining nuclear weapons in several months. My theory, however, predicts that Japan might stall due to a lack of domestic consensus. Hymans and Hughes both identify major domestic constraints on Japanese nuclearization from institutional veto players, the military, and public opinion.[112] These constraints are meaningful. Japan would undoubtedly transit a hard hedging phase in which it would have to assemble domestic consensus for an active weaponization strategy, even as it marched steadily toward an overt nuclear weapons program from a technological perspective. Achieving

112. Hymans, "Veto Players, Nuclear Energy, and Nonproliferation"; Hughes, "Why Japan Will Not Go Nuclear (Yet)."

a consensus for weaponization might be an arduous task, even in a severe security environment. As Samuels and Schoff note, "constraints are multiple and significant," though "they are not fixed."[113] Campbell and Sunohara write that "although public sentiment against nuclear weapons remains strong, its ability to fully inhibit the decisions of Japanese leaders should not be exaggerated."[114]

In the event of a significant shift in its security or alliance portfolio, Japan would transition from insurance hedging to hard hedging—working on at least some parts of the weaponization process and putting Japan closer to a nuclear weapons capability, but stopping short of openly nuclearizing while domestic consensus was being built. If and when domestic consensus is assembled, only then would Japan be able to sprint for a nuclear weapon. It is plausible that acute deterioration in Japan's security environment which pushes it to a hard hedging strategy might itself quickly congeal domestic consensus over nuclear weapons. My theory, however, highlights the domestic hurdles to overt weaponization generally faced by political elites and predicts a phased approach should Japan ever have to abandon insurance hedging for a more active nuclear weaponization strategy. Technological determinism and realism, under these conditions, would simply predict a much faster Japanese sprint to the bomb. My theory predicts a more deliberate approach that might increase Japanese strategic vulnerability for a period, because it recognizes that a Japanese prime minister would be risking his or her government if Japan openly nuclearized without overcoming domestic opposition to the bomb.

This insurance hedging story would essentially apply to the other formal ally in America's East Asia security architecture as well. South Korea initially pursued a clandestine nuclear weapons effort in the early 1970s—when it feared American abandonment—involving potential reprocessing capabilities from France as well as uranium enrichment experiments. This discovery triggered substantial pressure from its formal ally—the United States—to terminate its activities "to obtain capability eventually to produce nuclear weapons."[115]

113. Samuels and Schoff, "Japan's Nuclear Hedge," 251.

114. Campbell and Sunohara, "Japan: Thinking the Unthinkable," 242.

115. See William Burr, ed., "Stopping Korea from Going Nuclear, Part I," National Security Archive, Briefing Book, no. 582, March 22, 2017, https://nsarchive.gwu.edu/briefing-book/henry-kissinger-nuclear-vault/2017-03-22/stopping-korea-going-nuclear-part-i; also U.S. Embassy in Republic of Korea telegram 4957 to Department of State, "Korean Accession to NPT," July 30, 1974, Confidential, https://nsarchive.gwu.edu/dc.html?doc=3513489-Document-01-U-S-Embassy-in-Republic-of-Korea.

South Korea is also under the American nuclear umbrella in East Asia and hosted tactical nuclear weapons on its soil through the end of the Cold War. However, South Korea is different from Japan in two ways. First, South Korea does not have the technical ability to reprocess plutonium the way Japan does. In fact, South Korea had been caught attempting laboratory-scale experiments with uranium enrichment during the Cold War, which created tension with the United States and elicited both greater reassurance and significant berating from Washington.[116] So South Korea would have a more difficult time breaking out than would Japan, and may have to do so clandestinely to avoid American pressure. Second, public support for South Korean nuclear weapons is remarkably high due to the North Korean conventional and nuclear threat. Historically, some 60–70 percent of the South Korean public supports possessing independent nuclear weapons, which is remarkably high compared to most states.[117] South Korean fears of abandonment, and questions about the reliability of America's extended nuclear deterrent, were stoked by the United States itself under the Trump administration when the president repeatedly discussed removing American troops from the Korean Peninsula because he believed they were a waste of money, questioning their value and purpose and demanding that South Korea pay $5 billion in cost sharing to support the extended deterrence mission.[118] In many ways, South Korea may be more willing to pursue an active weaponization strategy if it continues to fear abandonment and with such high levels of public support for nuclear weapons. The limitation for South Korea would be developing fissile material, which Japan has in abundance already. While Tokyo may have a short sprint if it ever decided to develop nuclear weapons, Seoul might fear coercive efforts not only from North Korea or China if it attempted to pursue nuclear weapons but also from the United States, which might strongly oppose its ally's possession of nuclear weapons, as it has in the past. This would force South Korea into hiding in all likelihood.

116. See Miller, *Stopping the Bomb*, 110–12.

117. See Byong-Chul Lee, "Don't Be Surprised When South Korea Wants Nuclear Weapons," *Bulletin of the Atomic Scientists*, October 23, 2019, https://thebulletin.org/2019/10/dont-be-surprised-when-south-korea-wants-nuclear-weapons/.

118. Mark Landler, "Trump Orders Pentagon to Consider Reducing U.S. Forces in South Korea," *New York Times*, May 4, 2018, p. A1; Michael R. Gordon and Gordon Lubold, "Trump Administration Weighs Troop Cut in South Korea," *Wall Street Journal*, July 17, 2020, https://www.wsj.com/articles/trump-administration-weighs-troop-cut-in-south-korea-11595005050.

(WEST) GERMANY (1956–PRESENT): NUCLEAR SHARING IS NUCLEAR CARING

Contemporary scholars of proliferation and nonproliferation often forget that the dominant nuclear question in the early Cold War was the nuclear status of West Germany. On the front lines of Cold War Europe, partitioned, with the status of Berlin outstanding and persistently challenged, most models of nuclear proliferation would predict that West Germany ought to seek and develop its own nuclear weapons. West Germany could ill afford to rely on a potentially shaky external security guarantee because, more so than other Western European states, West Germany was directly exposed to and threatened by the massive conventional military might of the Soviet Union and the Warsaw Pact. West German leaders were seized with the fear of American conventional abandonment and nuclear abrogation at the potential moment of truth, particularly as the Soviet Union developed the ability to hold the American homeland at risk—would the United States trade Boston to save Bonn? As Chancellor Adenauer put it in 1956, German troops unequipped with nuclear weapons, unlike their frontline American and British counterparts, would face the brunt of the Soviet conventional attack and be "cattle for the slaughter."[119] Indeed, it is a genuine puzzle for the causes of proliferation literature as to why France and Britain pursued an independent nuclear weapons capability while West Germany stopped short with a hedge. Focusing on West Germany's strategy of proliferation helps resolve this puzzle: insurance hedging between the mid-1950s through late 1960s enabled West Germany to extract virtually unprecedented and unique nuclear devolution and sharing procedures from the United States that mitigated its need to develop an indigenous nuclear arsenal, which surely would have triggered Soviet reprisals.

This section outlines the fine line West German leaders, particularly Chancellor Adenauer, walked between initiating the outright indigenous pursuit of nuclear weapons from 1956 through 1969—a possibility that gave the Soviet Union paroxysms—and using that threat to maximize nuclear protection from the United States, culminating in a unique nuclear arrangement that would essentially transfer American nuclear weapons to German

119. Adenauer quoted in Hans-Peter Schwarz, *Konrad Adenauer: A German Politician and Statesman in a Period of War, Revolution and Reconstruction*, vol. 2, trans. Geoffrey Penny (Providence, RI: Berghahn Books, 1997), 264.

personnel during a crisis or war.[120] West Germany never abandoned the foundation for ultimately developing its own nuclear weapons—control of the fuel cycle and basic understanding of nuclear weapons designs and delivery systems—should it deem it necessary and was therefore the ultimate insurance hedger through 1969 (and after), paying high premiums to guard against existential disaster: being extinguished by the Soviet Union. I first describe West Germany's strategy of insurance hedging over time, as well as the reactions it elicited from the United States. I then show how the variables I identify—Germany's acutely threatening security environment coupled with a security guarantee from the United States—explain Bonn's behavior.

During the Eisenhower administration, both the United States and Britain were focused on trying to reduce their conventional commitments to Continental Europe (read: West Germany). The so-called Radford proposal by the American Chair of the Joint Chiefs formally studied how the United States could reorient its conventional footprint, cutting 800,000 forces from the U.S. military, and instead increasingly rely on tactical nuclear weapons to offset the Soviet Union's conventional power. For West Germany, American conventional deployments were the critical and credible signal—quite literally, America's skin in the game—that it would commit nuclear weapons to the defense of NATO, and particularly West Germany. Adenauer was terrified of a long-term, even if gradual, reduction in American conventional forces that would be increasingly deterred from using U.S. tactical nuclear weapons in Europe as the Soviet Union became capable of holding American homeland targets at risk.[121] Indeed, according to biographer Hans-Peter Schwarz, he was "almost panic stricken by a far reaching reorientation of the United States' policies towards Europe and Germany."[122] A German force unequipped with nuclear weapons and with no inputs into the use of American nuclear forces on West German territory would indeed be simply "cattle for the slaughter." On July 22, 1956, Adenauer dictated a personal letter to John Foster Dulles in which he stated explicitly: "Germany . . . has lost its confidence in the United States' reliability. These plans are regarded as clear evidence that the United States does not feel itself to be strong enough to keep pace with the Soviet Union. *The political consequences will appear very soon*, unless the United States emphatically dissociates itself from these

120. See Gerzhoy, "Alliance Coercion and Nuclear Restraint," 109–10; and Catherine McArdle Kellher, *Germany and the Politics of Nuclear Weapons* (New York: Columbia University Press, 1975), chap. 5.

121. Schwarz, *Konrad Adenauer*, 313.

122. Ibid., 233; also see Adenauer's personal letter to Dulles, reprinted in ibid., 234–35.

plans."[123] The threat to Dulles was clear: we will pursue the indigenous and independent development of nuclear weapons if your commitment to the conventional and nuclear defense of West Germany is not unshakably firm.

The Eisenhower administration attempted to allay Adenauer's fears by committing that the United States would not reduce the level of American forces in Germany so long as they were welcome there. However, Adenauer's doubts about the reliability of American extended nuclear deterrence naturally persisted, given Germany's precarious security situation and the fact that nothing prevented the United States from abrogating its pledge at any time in the future. Indeed, in September 1956, Adenauer stated in a cabinet meeting that "Germany cannot remain a nuclear protectorate."[124] In December 1956, the United States vacillated on a proposal by some of NATO's European members, including West Germany, to devolve nuclear weapons to the "level of the division," which meant, in practice, transfer of American weapons to European forces.[125] After this meeting, a German cabinet meeting convened in which Adenauer stated: "the Bundeswehr must be built up more rapidly . . . and nuclear weapons must be produced in the Federal Republic of Germany."[126] On April 5, 1957, Adenauer drew a distinction between tactical nuclear weapons and strategic nuclear weapons, which is what he claims to have forsworn in the 1954 Adenauer Declaration (which formally renounced production of atomic weapons *within German borders*, a key caveat). He stated in 1957: "Tactical weapons are nothing more than a further development of the artillery. Naturally, we cannot commit ourselves to saying that our troops will do without the latest developments of normal armaments. We do not have the large weapons, however."[127] Schwarz recounts that "during these months, Adenauer, beset by doubts about the reliability of the U.S. nuclear shield, was ready to listen to anything."[128]

One of the wilder, though short-lived, proposals was the so-called France-Italy-Germany (FIG) nuclear consortium around November 1957. Germany's foreign minister stated that European states should have nuclear weapons available to them such that "in the event of war armed forces would be appropriately equipped." Adenauer expressed stronger interest: "We

123. Adenauer to John Foster Dulles, in ibid., 234–35, emphasis added.

124. Adenauer quoted in ibid., 239.

125. Ibid., 265.

126. Adenauer quoted in Matthias Küntzel, *Bonn & the Bomb: German Politics and the Nuclear Option* (Boulder, CO: Pluto Press, 1995), 5.

127. Adenauer quoted in Schwarz, *Konrad Adenauer*, 266.

128. Ibid., 319.

must produce them."[129] But given his 1954 renunciation, Germany could not produce nuclear weapons on its soil. Enter France. After the 1956 Suez Crisis, France accelerated its pursuit of nuclear weapons to carve out an independent position from the United States. At the time, needing German financial support and perhaps technical knowledge (it is unclear what Italy brought to the table other than softening the image of a Franco-German axis), French prime minister Gaillard proposed a nuclear-sharing stockpile that would be hosted on French soil.[130] On April 7, 1958, in Rome, the FIG treaty was signed to assist in the financing of a future shared stockpile. It disintegrated quickly, however, since as soon as de Gaulle came to power in November of that year, he canceled the agreement, opting instead for a completely indigenous French nuclear weapons program.

One consequence of the not-so-secret French-German (and Italian) negotiations was that the Eisenhower administration was motivated to further devise and evolve nuclear-sharing agreements within NATO to give Germany greater input—and ability—into the use of nuclear weapons in a conflict. This was one of Adenauer's key objectives. In December 1957, after learning of initial Franco-German negotiations, the Eisenhower administration proposed a NATO stockpile sharing plan. The briefing for the NATO meeting stated that the "best assurance . . . lies in our allies actually having a share in this power close at hand and *a capability to employ it effectively*."[131] This single shift reoriented NATO's stewardship and potential nuclear release procedures, particularly in Germany. As Trachtenberg elaborates, this agreement meant that "over the next few years NATO allies were given effective control over American nuclear weapons," and since the lion's share of tactical nuclear weapons were deployed on West German soil, this essentially bequeathed Bonn a significant nuclear weapons arsenal in wartime.[132] Indeed, German pilots on quick reaction alert (QRA) "were sitting on runways, armed with American nuclear weapons . . . [with] a lone American sentry standing on the tarmac, armed only with a rifle, not even knowing what to aim at if the pilot tried to take off without authorization . . . this is what American custody of those weapons had come to

129. Adenauer quoted in ibid.

130. Ibid., 320.

131. "Nuclear Policy" background paper for NATO meeting prepared by Department of State, Policy Planning, December 4, 1957 quoted in Marc Trachtenberg, *A Constructed Peace: The Making of the European Settlement 1945–1963* (Princeton: Princeton University Press, 1999), 194, emphasis added.

132. Ibid.

mean."[133] Furthermore, Trachtenberg questions whether the "dual-key" system for medium-range strategic systems was actually "dual" by this point and whether, in reality, the "American government had the physical ability to prevent the use of [these] weapons."[134] In essence, the United States was ceding nuclear use to the Germans, in Germany, in the event of a conflict, at the request of the Germans. This was not an accident. It was Eisenhower's solution to keeping Germany nominally non-nuclear and avoiding triggering a Soviet aneurysm.[135] It was a remarkable and unprecedented evolution of nuclear control procedures and nuclear sharing to allay German fears of abandonment and to forestall an independent German nuclear arsenal.

Did Adenauer's statements merely amount to a bargaining tactic with the Americans? Or did he genuinely hope to obtain an independent deterrent? These motives are not mutually exclusive—a credible drive for an independent deterrent gave Adenauer more leverage to bargain with the United States. Matthias Küntzel reports that German politicians in this period understood the value of their threats in extracting greater commitments from the United States: "We undoubtedly have much more to gain from being 'persuaded' not to build the bomb than we would have once we actually started . . . the threat that 'we just might do it yet' has proved quite a bargaining card."[136] To be sure, there was strong domestic political and scientific opposition to Adenauer's hints that Germany should pursue an independent nuclear arsenal.[137] This limited Adenauer's ability to truly embark on an indigenous nuclear weapons program. But it did not stop him from using the threat of initiating such a program, which Germany had the industrial and scientific base to do, in order to improve its nuclear-sharing position within NATO and vis-à-vis the United States.

The Kennedy administration had a fundamentally different view of control of nuclear weapons in Europe. Kennedy and McNamara preferred centralized American control of nuclear weapons and took steps to limit Germany's ability to use the weapons by installing Permissive Action Links (PALs).[138] In some cases, the arming plugs for the QRA weapons

133. Ibid.

134. Ibid., 195.

135. Ibid., 196–97.

136. Küntzel, *Bonn & the Bomb*, 7.

137. See Schwarz, *Konrad Adenauer*, 267–69. Not only did the SPD oppose Adenauer's proclamations, but there was strong scientific opposition due to Nazi origins of German nuclear research.

138. See Trachtenberg, *A Constructed Peace*; also Jenifer Mackby and Walter B. Slocombe, "Germany: The Model Case, a Historical Imperative," in *The Nuclear Tipping Point: Why States*

were removed and kept under American custody so they could not be used without presidential authority.[139] How effective were these efforts? It is unclear. This generation of PALs were essentially combination locks and any components that were removed from the weapon (such as arming plugs) were stored on the same bases.[140]

As another possible way to satisfy the Germans, the Kennedy and Johnson administrations continued to dangle the idea of a so-called Multilateral Force (MLF), which originated under Eisenhower. The Americans eventually settled on the vision of a "sea-based NATO MRBM force under truly multilateral ownership and control."[141] Given the complicated arrangements and release procedures, the MLF would require full and equal German participation in NATO's Nuclear Planning Group, which was a welcome possibility in Bonn as a reassurance mechanism. But the complexity of the MLF, particularly at sea, would become its undoing over time. Ultimately, the United States preferred keeping release authority and use under an American officer, the Supreme Allied Commander, Europe. They agreed to include West Germany in NATO's Nuclear Committee and eventually Nuclear Planning Group on the theory that "greater access to information about U.S. nuclear capabilities and plans in the NATO context would make the Germans more confident in the credibility of the U.S. deterrent."[142] All of this is to suggest that German threats to develop an independent deterrent were credible enough to successive U.S. administrations that they went to great lengths to keep Germany at bay as an insurance hedger.

According to my theory, insurance hedging should not hinge on changes in individual leadership. Chancellor Adenauer's passing from the German political scene in 1965 offers an opportunity to observe whether this is the case. The new West German chancellor, Ludwig Erhard, is portrayed as having been more amenable to American arrangements for the sake of

---

Reconsider Their Nuclear Choices, ed. Kurt M. Campbell, Robert J. Einhorn, and Mitchell B. Reiss (Washington, DC: Brookings Institution Press, 2004), 190.

139. See "History of the Custody and Deployment of Nuclear Weapons July 1945–September 1977," Office of the Assistant to the Secretary of Defense (Atomic Energy), February 1978, chap. 9, https://nsarchive2.gwu.edu/nukevault/ebb442/docs/doc%201A%20custody%20and%20deployment%20history%2078.pdf.

140. See Mark E. Bleck and Paul R. Souder, "PAL Control of Theater Nuclear Weapons," Sandia National Laboratory, March 1984, https://www.cs.columbia.edu/~smb/nsam-160/Theater_Control/Theater_Control.pdf.

141. "The Developing Atlantic Partnership," *Department of State Bulletin*, April 23, 1962, p. 668, cited in Mackby and Slocombe, "Germany," 191.

142. Mackby and Slocombe, "Germany," 195.

maintaining good relations with the United States. But even Erhard was unhappy with the Johnson administration's decision to let the MLF die and its increasingly heavy pressure on Bonn to join the NPT. It was "impossible to assume that Germany will go forever without a nuclear deterrent," Erhard complained to Lyndon Johnson.[143] Erhard, like Adenauer before him, initially insisted on a "hardware solution" to the nuclear-sharing agreement but would ultimately have to acquiesce to essentially a "software solution."[144] Gene Gerzhoy suggests that there was a great deal of coercion by the United States in getting West Germany to come around to this softer position, using the threat of abandonment to moderate Bonn's insistence on nuclear sharing and to sign and eventually ratify the NPT.[145]

Through these debates of the mid-1960s, Adenauer and his successors did not deviate into a more aggressive nuclear proliferation strategy. Although Adenauer seems to have seriously sought independent control of nuclear weapons—either American or otherwise—Bonn took few concrete steps to expand its efforts. It did not move to acquire or develop the capability to separate weapons-grade plutonium, for example.

Only in 1967, once U.S.-German negotiations over the NPT were in full swing, did Erhard and then Chancellor Kiesinger lay the foundation for a program in which Germany could, if it chose, produce weapons-grade plutonium on short notice.[146] Again, the personality or party of the German leader in power mattered little. Chancellor Willy Brandt of the historically anti-nuclear SPD "linked [Bonn's] 1969 signature [to the NPT] to some nineteen restrictive interpretations, including reservations intended to preserve West Germany's civilian nuclear industry and hence its technological basis for a military nuclear program."[147] The Americans and the Germans worked together to carve out exceptions in the NPT itself so that Germany could persist with a unique nuclear-sharing agreement. Non-nuclear states, such as West Germany, were allowed to host American nuclear weapons and to participate in dual-key control procedures

143. Chancellor Erhard in Johnson-Erhard Meeting, "Memorandum of Conversation," December 20, 1965, *FRUS, 1964–1968*, vol. XIII, doc. 119, https://history.state.gov/historicaldocuments/frus1964-68v13/d119.

144. "Letter from President Johnson to Prime Minister Wilson," December 23, 1965, *FRUS, 1964–1968*, vol. XIII, doc. 121, https://history.state.gov/historicaldocuments/frus1964-68v13/d121.

145. See Gerzhoy, "Alliance Coercion and Nuclear Restraint."

146. Mackby and Slocombe, "Germany," 197. The time frame of a month or even a week seems exaggerated, but the point remains.

147. Ibid., 199.

under grandfather clauses. During a war, this would essentially birth West Germany as a nuclear weapons state overnight, while still being consistent with the letter of the NPT.

At the same time, the Americans secured their top priority: keeping Germany non-nuclear, at least for the moment. As National Security Advisor Walt Rostow informed CDU parliamentarian Rainer Barzel in the latter's visit to the White House: "The simple fact is that Germany depends, and must depend, on collective nuclear defense. If you would not sign [the NPT], and decided to defend yourself with your own nuclear weapons, you would (a) tear apart the Alliance and (b) face a very difficult period during which you might well be destroyed [by the USSR]."[148] In short, West Germany, faced with veiled abandonment threats—and the window of vulnerability that that would rip wide open—ultimately acceded to signing the NPT. It did, however, insist upon dual-key control, and indigenous civilian hedging—including control of the full fuel cycle and tons of plutonium on German soil—should the alliance and American nuclear guarantees dissipate.

West Germany's signature and ultimate ratification of the NPT in 1975 essentially terminated the active portion of its insurance hedging strategy. Nevertheless, as Mackby and Slocombe rightly point out, "there is no question that Germany today has the technical capacity to develop nuclear weapons quickly, if it chose to do so."[149] West Germany persisted with a passive insurance hedge after it ratified the NPT: there was no will to militarize the program, some fringe voices notwithstanding, but the underlying technical capacity certainly existed to ensure that the United States abided by its extended nuclear deterrence commitments. Although, as Mackby and Slocombe continue, "with German accession to the NPT, the question of a distinctly national nuclear capability was laid to rest . . . Bonn continued to be deeply concerned about maintaining the effectiveness of NATO's nuclear guarantee."[150] Although West Germany drops out of most "proliferation" data sets at this point, unified Germany today still possesses the basis for an independent nuclear weapons capability should it ever perceive abandonment from the United States and a threat from, for example, a resurgent or revisionist Russia. Save some vocal fringe politicians, there is presently very little domestic political resonance for a German nuclear capability,

148. Walt Rostow and Rainer Barzel, "Memorandum of Conversation," February 23, 1968, *FRUS, 1964–1968*, vol. XV, doc. 248, https://history.state.gov/historicaldocuments/frus1964-68v15/d248.

149. Mackby and Slocombe, "Germany," 201.

150. Ibid., 202–3.

but the foundational technical capabilities persist and Mackby and Slocombe write that "some observers have speculated that Germany would reconsider its nuclear renunciation if the U.S. nuclear umbrella were to be withdrawn . . . particularly if Russia were somehow to reemerge as a threat in such a context."[151] The bullying behavior of the Trump administration toward its allies, and especially toward Germany on burden sharing, certainly resurrected questions about Germany's indefinite reliance on American extended deterrence.[152] If American extended deterrence evaporated, Germany would, like Japan, have to pass through a difficult and tumultuous hard hedging phase before it could adopt an active proliferation strategy. But, although Germany is typically coded as terminating weapons pursuit in 1969, it maintains an insurance hedging capability that serves to ensure the United States' formal nuclear commitment to Germany.

TESTING PROLIFERATION STRATEGY THEORY

What explains West German nuclear insurance hedging? My typology and theory explain German behavior in ways previously underappreciated. Given the severity of Germany's proximate threat—West Germany would have been the battleground in any NATO–Warsaw Pact conflict—Adenauer had one objective: West Germany must control nuclear weapons use in a conflict, because millions of German lives would be at stake if the United States failed to fulfill its security commitment when the time came. Adenauer sought German inputs into the use of nuclear weapons, either American bombs or, failing that, other European forces (e.g., French), or in the ultimate case, Germany itself. Independent pursuit of nuclear weapons, as Rostow so bluntly said, exposed West Germany to reactive proliferation by Eastern Bloc countries at best or to complete destruction by the Soviets in a preventive war at worst. The United States was seized by the fear of an independently nuclear Germany that would induce Soviet paroxysms and paranoia and could pull NATO into nuclear war. Therefore, Germany's optimal strategy was indeed ensuring that the United States abided by its nuclear commitments to Germany and that Germany could have some voice in that arrangement. Leveraging the threats of joint pursuit with the French and independent pursuit compelled the United States to erect unique

151. Ibid., 207.

152. See Ulrich Kuhn, "The Sudden German Nuke Flirtation," Carnegie Endowment for International Peace, December 6, 2016, https://carnegieendowment.org/2016/12/06/sudden-german-nuke-flirtation-pub-66366.

devolution and dual-key arrangements that provided credible assurance to the Germans that NATO would not abdicate on the use of nuclear weapons should a conventional war break out. France did not face potential preventive destruction from the Soviet Union—and therefore had the option to sprint for an independent nuclear weapons capability rather than accept even extensive American nuclear-sharing arrangements, as I show in the next chapter. Germany was much more highly constrained by its hostile geography and neighbors, and its best option was to leverage an insurance hedge to elicit unprecedented U.S. nuclear-sharing procedures.

Alternative explanations fail to account for Germany's insurance hedging strategy. Realists of all stripes long predicted—and even advocated—an independent nuclear Germany, even after the end of the Cold War.[153] Realism assumes alliances are fundamentally unreliable compared to self-help or an independent nuclear force. Indeed, faced with the weight of the Warsaw Pact right on its borders, no state had more to lose than West Germany in a European war. But contrary to clear and forceful predictions from both offensive and defensive realists, Germany never pursued an independent nuclear arsenal, choosing instead to use the threat of proliferation to optimize and maximize the assurance of allied nuclear commitments.

Technological determinism would, like in the case of Japan, predict that West Germany would have broken out in the 1950s and 1960s when it controlled the fuel cycle. German scientists were not lacking in expertise on nuclear weapons design or manufacturing. Instead, Germany stopped short, developing the basis for a military program—a basis that persists today—but consciously and credibly signaled that it would not develop nuclear weapons so long as the United States fulfilled its security commitments.

Finally, did anti-nuclear norms in German domestic politics shape West Germany's nuclear proliferation strategy? There is no denying that the anti-nuclear parties such as the SPD would have presented substantial opposition to an independent nuclear arsenal if the domestic debate reached that point during the Cold War. However, even Willy Brandt, when he became chancellor, was very clear about maintaining German inputs into American nuclear weapons on German soil. Brandt had no hesitation in either laying the foundation for an independent nuclear capability in the late 1960s or threatening the United States with nuclearization if German security requirements necessitated it. And, although there was no nonproliferation

153. See John J. Mearsheimer, "Back to the Future: Instability in Europe after the Cold War," *International Security* 15, no. 1 (Summer 1990): 5–56.

regime when West Germany sought its insurance hedge from the United States in the 1950s and 1960s, when the NPT was negotiated in the late 1960s, exceptions were carved out specifically with West Germany in mind to grandfather in any existing nuclear-sharing arrangements—including transfer of nuclear weapons from a recognized nuclear weapons state, the United States, to a non-nuclear weapons state within war.[154] Not only did nonproliferation norms fail to constrain or shape German leaders in their pursuit of insurance hedging, they were ignored within the NPT itself to allow Germany to effectively "become" a nuclear state in war through the preexisting nuclear-sharing arrangements.

For West Germany, a looming security threat—perhaps one of the most severe any state in the system has experienced to date—coupled with a formal American nuclear guarantee pushed Germany into an insurance hedging strategy until it was sufficiently reassured by America's forward deployment and nuclear stewardship arrangements that it did not acutely fear abdication. The hedge persisted until Bonn had access to American nuclear weapons on its soil, even if nominally under American control during peacetime. The threat to openly pursue indigenous capability forced Washington to accede to remarkable and unprecedented nuclear-sharing procedures with the Germans that temporarily included a virtual German nuclear weapons capability with the QRA during the Eisenhower years. The Germans themselves must have been surprised at how loose centralized control had become by 1960. These procedures were so remarkable and terrifying to the Kennedy administration that they were reined in through the 1960s. But the concept of dual-key control and at least enough of an illusion of German inputs into planning and release persisted to sufficiently assure Bonn of American nuclear guarantees, thereby forestalling an independent German nuclear force. Had West Germany not pursued joint development with the French or implicitly (sometimes explicitly) threatened to develop a national force, it is unlikely that the United States would have ever acceded to such arrangements. In this case, the insurance hedge worked to optimize Germany's deterrent posture: it bought it inputs into NATO nuclear planning and release without exposing it to Soviet preventive efforts. Indeed, this suggests a template for Japan's contemporary experience. Should Tokyo perceive an

154. See "NATO and the Nonproliferation Treaty," NATO Fact Sheet, March 2017, p. 2, https://www.nato.int/nato_static_fl2014/assets/pdf/pdf_2017_03/20170323_170323-npt-factsheet.pdf.

existential threat from China, it may force the United States to develop "novel" sharing procedures with the Japanese to forestall them breaking out of their modern-day insurance hedge.

Pieces of Germany's insurance hedging capability indeed persist today, though there is little will and appetite for an independent capability except perhaps at the fringes of German domestic politics, particularly during the Trump administration which called for greater cost sharing and actually did reduce the American footprint in Germany. Should that continue and Germany perceive a resurgent Russia as a threat, it may not indefinitely remain an insurance hedger.

Brazil and Argentina: Temptations of Technical Hedging and the Treaty of Tlatelolco

Brazil	**Technical Hedging, 1953–76**
	Hard Hedging, 1977–90
Argentina	**Technical Hedging, 1968–76**
	Hard Hedging, 1977–90

I now turn to two cases, Brazil and Argentina, in which states did not objectively face acute security threats but nevertheless flirted briefly with the possibility of nuclear weapons programs when fringe military interest in nuclear weapons became more central following military coups in both countries. They faced a rival—each other—but not an enemy, and each had civilian nuclear programs. Under these circumstances, we should observe a strategy of technical hedging. As in the section on West Germany, I first describe Argentine and Brazilian behavior, with occasional reference to the factors driving it. Then I discuss the causal logic behind their actions in greater depth. I treat these cases together because their causal chains are intimately intertwined.

Brazil and Argentina both developed civilian nuclear energy sectors with foreign assistance, and some constituencies in both states briefly toyed with the idea of military applications of those technologies in the early 1980s, largely as a hedge against each other. For most of their existence as nuclear programs, I code these as technical hedges against each other. The programs never went far, even under the military juntas in each country during the early 1980s. Once both were able to commit to only peaceful use of nuclear energy in 1990, Argentina followed Brazil and pledged to ratify a formal agreement, the Treaty of Tlatelolco, that made Latin America a nuclear weapons–free zone. Brazil and Argentina were, as Mitchell Reiss puts it, "rivals, not enemies."[155] They contemplated the idea of nuclear weapons programs only when each worried that the other might be developing nuclear weapons. These cases show that technical hedgers, under the right domestic political configurations, can veer toward hard hedging as the temptation of some leaders to flirt with the notion of nuclear weapons based on an underlying technical capacity proves seductive.

For a brief period in the early 1980s, as the rivalry intensified and both anticipated potential future security threats from each other, the two countries briefly shifted to hard hedging where work on technology relevant to nuclear weapons was initiated by the military juntas—though this also never went terribly far because there was no military or domestic consensus for nuclear weapons and neither country would seriously contemplate nuclear weapons development unless the other went first. During this brief hard hedging phase, the goal was to establish the military basis of the program under the guise of uranium enrichment for submarine nuclear reactors and as an indigenous supply for power reactors in the event they faced an international cutoff, which was a serious possibility. This hard hedging had the virtue of compressing both states' time to weapons-grade fissile material if they ever had to go nuclear. With Argentina as the weaker power, and having lost the 1982 Falklands War to the United Kingdom, Reiss argues that its hedge was probably "harder" in this phase with a primary aim "to hedge against the possibility of a Brazilian nuclear bomb."[156]

However, in response, the Brazilian military seems to have also loosely had a military (primarily navy) uranium enrichment "parallel program" to its IAEA-safeguarded West German nuclear reactors. There were suspicions of a test shaft dug at the remote Amazonian Cachimbo Air Force Base, but uranium enrichment never went past the laboratory-scale, and Reiss writes that Brazil "did not even have the nonnuclear components for a 'cold' test."[157] But the logic in Brazil was that "it had to have the capacity to build the bomb, in case Argentina were to do so."[158] Because Argentina was not perceived as a serious threat and, according to Michael Barletta, "only extreme and uninfluential nationalist sectors in Argentina favored construction of atomic weapons . . . Brazil reportedly never engaged in research necessary

155. Mitchell Reiss, *Bridled Ambition: Why Countries Constrain Their Nuclear Capabilities* (Washington, DC: Woodrow Wilson Press, 1995), chap. 3.

156. Ibid., 45.

157. Ibid., 51.

158. Michael Barletta, "The Military Nuclear Program in Brazil," Stanford CISAC Working Paper, August 1997, https://fsi-live.s3.us-west-1.amazonaws.com/s3fs-public/barletta.pdf, p. 15.

to develop employable weapons."[159] Navy Minister Fonseca stated bluntly: "We don't need the bomb now, since there is no foreign enemy in sight. What we need is to retain the technology to have the capability to fabricate it should circumstances require."[160] The general message Brazil wanted to signal to Argentina was simply: "Watch your step; I can do it too, and I'm bigger than you are."[161] Barletta concludes that the "preponderance of evidence . . . leads to the conclusion that what the Brazilian government and military services sought was the nuclear option . . . Brazilian efforts sought only the technical capacity to permit a subsequent government decision to go for the bomb."[162] Argentina was therefore hedging against a Brazil that was hedging against Argentina.

But for both countries, there was never any real consideration of an active strategy of nuclear weaponization except during brief junta periods and, even then, from a minority of leaders. Roberto Ornstein, head of international affairs at Argentina's National Atomic Energy Commission (CNEA) in this period, noted that "in Argentina, some crazy elements [in the army] even thought that the only defense against Brazil was precisely to develop nuclear armament, since it was the only possible equalizer, but it did not go beyond that."[163] This is a case where technical hedging took on a momentum toward hard hedging until both countries realized that if they mutually verified a nuclear weapons–free zone, they would be better-off.

Reiss describes this dynamic: "There was no real conflict between the two countries. Their last war had ended in 1828; Brazil and Argentina had never seen each other as enemies and certainly never envisioned a nuclear war with each other."[164] Argentina was at a disadvantage in any potential arms race anyway, as "provoking an unwinnable arms race with a much larger and wealthier Brazil made little sense."[165] As for Brazil, it made little sense to nuclearize once it knew that doing so would trigger Argentinian nuclearization and neutralize Brazil's conventional superiority. Thus, these cases represent an interesting proliferation dynamic. Legitimate civilian

159. Ibid.

160. Quoted in ibid., 16.

161. Quoted in ibid., 15.

162. Ibid., 29.

163. Ornstein in Rodrigo Mallea, Matias Spektor, and Nicholas J. Wheeler, eds., *The Origins of Nuclear Cooperation: A Critical Oral History between Brazil and Argentina* (Washington, DC: Wilson Center, 2015), 124–25.

164. Reiss, *Bridled Ambition*, 52.

165. Ibid.

nuclear technologies in both countries generated technical hedging. This, in turn, gave rise to the fear—especially under military governments—that the other might in the future develop nuclear weapons. In response, the security situation deteriorated in a self-fulfilling prophecy and both countries pursued hard hedging. Eventually, both countries recognized that mutual nuclearization would be strategically senseless for both.

What explains this sequence? Supply-side explanations, in which the availability of nuclear technology tempts states into pursuing programs, as Fuhrmann posits, do not fully account for these events. Rather, the emergence of military regimes in both countries pushed events in a specific direction. Each regime reinforced the other's sense of threat. In response, hard hedging with nuclear weapons appealed to both countries as a means to address the threat.

What was the character of the initial technical hedging? Both Argentina and Brazil, through the Atoms for Peace program, initiated civilian nuclear power programs in the 1950s. Argentina had built several research reactors with international assistance from West Germany and Canada, one of which, Atucha I, built in 1968 under the first round of military governments, was a natural uranium-fueled heavy water reactor that could potentially generate plutonium for nuclear weapons. But in the 1960s and 1970s, Brazil and Argentina actually enjoyed a high degree of nuclear cooperation and coordination. Their mutual concern was not each other but what they perceived to be an "unjust nuclear order imposed by the nuclear weapons states" that constrained their ability to develop nuclear technology.[166] Argentina even supported Brazil's landmark nuclear agreement with West Germany for up to eight power reactors and technology to control almost the entire fuel cycle, at least at the pilot scale. However, with the advent of Argentina's military junta a year later, Argentina subsequently secretly built a uranium enrichment facility employing gaseous diffusion at Pilcaniyeu, as well as a pilot plutonium reprocessing facility at Ezeiza.[167] The motivation for both of these facilities, according to Ornstein, was to ensure an indigenous fuel supply for Argentina's reactors should it face an international cutoff.[168] The secrecy surrounding both of these installations was claimed to be due to the

166. James E. Doyle, "Argentina and Brazil," in *Nuclear Safeguards, Security, and Nonproliferation: Achieving Security with Technology and Policy*, ed. James E. Doyle (Oxford: Elsevier, 2008), 315.

167. See ibid., 311–12.

168. Ornstein in Mallea, Spektor, and Wheeler, *The Origins of Nuclear Cooperation*, 87–89.

fear that American pressure "would be so strong as to make the project fail even before it could bear fruit."[169]

However, the military junta in Argentina was certainly concerned that the West German deal would lay the groundwork for a Brazilian nuclear weapons program, and the deal, according to James Doyle, "raised suspicions concerning Brazil's nuclear intentions."[170] This agreement began Argentina's shift to hard hedging and Brazil's corresponding shift to the same as it erected a parallel enrichment program under full military control and not under safeguards. In particular, the enrichment facility at Pilcaniyeu did not amount to nothing. Jacques Hymans's claim that Argentina was never pursuing nuclear weapons turns on his interpretation that Pilcaniyeu was only configured to enrich uranium to 20 percent, not 90 percent for weapons.[171] But uranium enrichment is nonlinear, and being capable of enriching to 20 percent is only a hop, skip, and a jump from 90 percent; though it may require some reconfiguration and greater time, it is not a technical hurdle by any means and, in fact, enriching uranium to 20 percent is actually 90 percent of the separative work to weapons-grade uranium, as figure 3.2 depicts. Pilcaniyeu was a harder hedge than Hymans admits. Although it was never configured to produce weapons-grade uranium, it laid the foundation to easily do so. Clarifying this is important because it highlights how threat perception informed Buenos Aires's activities.

For its part, Brazil's representative to the IAEA at this time, Luiz Augusto de Castro Neves, says that Argentina's Ezeiza reprocessing facility posed no proliferation concern to Brazil at the time because "through visits to Ezeiza, including due to the very dimensions of the plant, it became clear that nothing that could be harmful to the Brazil-Argentina relationship could come from there."[172] On Pilcaniyeu, which had the theoretical capability to enrich weapons-grade uranium, Castro Neves says "there was [initial] surprise . . . however, afterwards it was understood that it was an attempt at ensuring supply for the research reactors . . . it was concluded that there were no conditions to enrich in a significant scale because there was not enough energy to power the compressors."[173] Castro Neves goes on to say about the Argentinian enrichment and reprocessing activities: "although some in the

169. Ibid., 87.

170. Doyle, "Argentina and Brazil," 313.

171. See Jacques E. C. Hymans, "Of Gauchos and Gringos: Why Argentina Never Wanted the Bomb, and Why the United States Thought It Did," *Security Studies* 10, no. 3 (Spring 2001): 153–85.

172. Castro Neves in Mallea, Spector, and Wheeler, *The Origins of Nuclear Cooperation*, 74.

173. Ibid., 90.

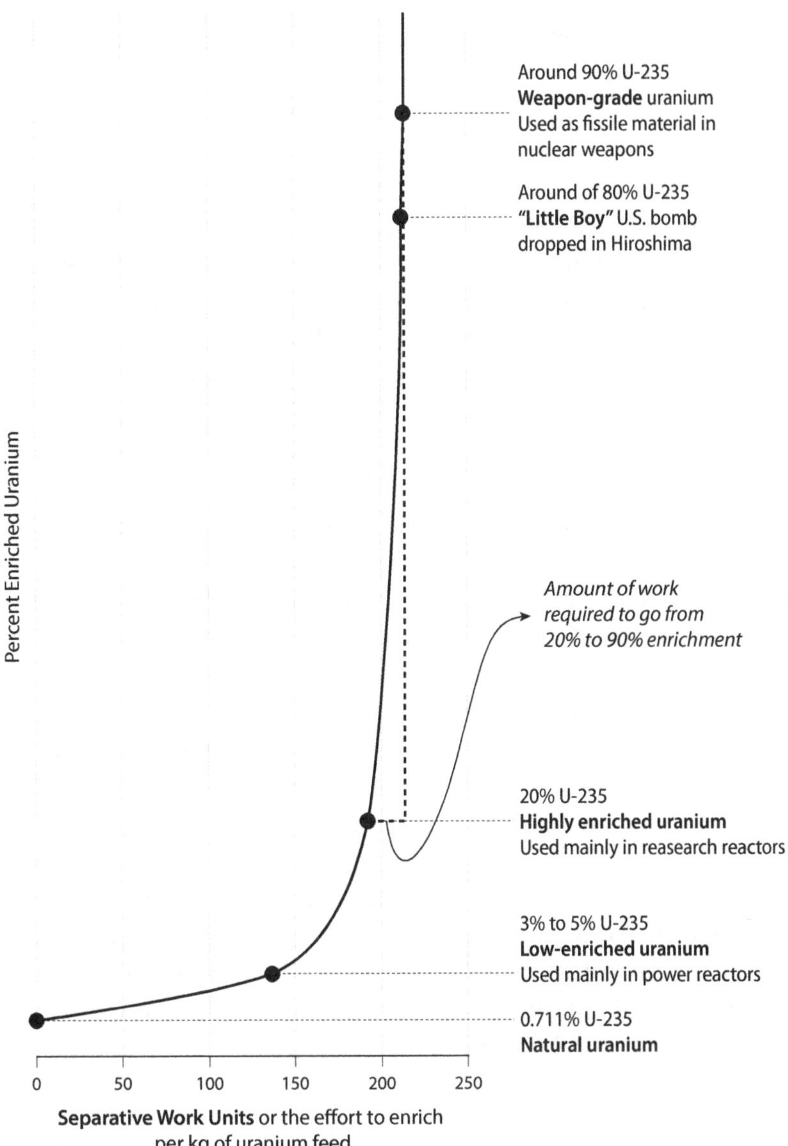

FIGURE 3.2. The nonlinearity of uranium enrichment, illustrating that, for example, 20 percent enriched U-235 is roughly 90 percent of the separative work to weapons-grade uranium.

military sectors from one or the other side always lived a little fiction that the space of rivalry still permitted it to be said that both countries would have to develop a nuclear device as a counterpoint for the eventual threat posed by the other . . . this never went beyond bravado on both sides."[174]

But even if the Brazilians perceived it as just bravado, the Brazilian military government nevertheless erected a limited parallel uranium enrichment program outside of international safeguards through each of its services, with the navy being the most advanced with lab-scale gas centrifuges. Details of the navy's enrichment program are the only service efforts still redacted in a U.S. Special National Intelligence Estimate.[175] Castro Neves notes that when the Pilcaniyeu facility was disclosed, Brazil had exactly eight centrifuges in operation, each one apparently named after a Brazilian actress.[176] The military's parallel program in each of the services seems to have been a hard hedge to put Brazil in a position to enrich weapons-grade uranium if the Argentinians did. But just as Brazil's civilians were seemingly unfazed by Argentina's enrichment and reprocessing activities, the knowledge of the parallel program caused little concern. Ornstein says the parallel program in fact "seemed absolutely logical to us" because the West German deal did not include indigenous "national development" and he believed the Brazilians would always seek indigenous supply for its power and submarine reactors.[177] For him, "the idea that Brazil wanted to develop an autonomous technology was not only something accepted but also considered inevitable."[178] A 1985 American Special National Intelligence Estimate on the Brazilian program noted, "On balance, we do not believe that the Brazilian Government has decided to produce nuclear weapons. A segment of recent reports, however, taken together do suggest that segments of Brazil's nuclear establishment, particularly the military, are now intent on acquiring facilities and expertise that would give them the capability to produce nuclear weapons. . . . The indigenous national nuclear program could, as structure, provide the technical base for a nuclear weapons program."[179] The program

174. Ibid., 74.

175. "Special National Intelligence Estimate SNIE 93–83, 'Brazil's Changing Nuclear Goals: Motives and Constraints,'" December 1985, History and Public Policy Program Digital Archive, National Security Archives, pp. 4–5, http://digitalarchive.wilsoncenter.org/document/121397.

176. Castro Neves in Mallea, Spector, and Wheeler, *The Origins of Nuclear Cooperation*, 91.

177. Ornstein in ibid., 92–93.

178. Ornstein in ibid., 93.

179. "Special National Intelligence Estimate SNIE 93–83," 6.

was judged to have accelerated in the early 1980s under junta rule but, as of 1985, was still active despite the transition to a civilian government.

In Brazil and Argentina, the military junta periods took both states from technical hedging—when the "crazy elements" were outside the government—to hard hedging, where at least some of those elements were guiding national policy. The junta pathology of fearing the worst from other states and militaries resulted in a higher threat perception between the joint juntas. This led to the pursuit of parallel programs outside of international safeguards that had both legitimate grounds—indigenous fuel supply—but also a stronger hedge for nuclear weapons by compressing the time to break out if necessary. It was only when Brazil's military government yielded to Jose Sarney in 1985 that the pre-1977 spirit of mutual nuclear cooperation reemerged. The regime changes in Brazil and Argentina put both states back on the path toward nuclear cooperation and formally forswearing nuclear weapons, culminating in the 1990 Argentinian pledge to follow Brazil and ratify the Treaty of Tlatelolco, which maintained Latin America as a nuclear weapons-free zone.

TESTING PROLIFERATION STRATEGY THEORY

My theory explains the initial proliferation strategies of both Brazil and Argentina. There was no real security threat perceived between the two states, certainly not one that—except for fringe elements in the Argentinian military—would generate any pressures for nuclear weapons. Both states, however, sought to build robust nuclear energy sectors as part of their development strategies. As the international nuclear supply controls tightened in the 1970s, both states sought the means to control the fuel cycle so that they could indigenously produce uranium fuel for their power and research reactors, and potentially reprocess their own plutonium. These efforts, though advanced on paper, amounted to nothing more than technical hedging. There was very little will in either country to explore the development of nuclear weapons. However, shortly after the Brazilian military junta signed the nuclear deal with West Germany—which was initially supported by Argentina because it would set a precedent to allow Argentina access to the same technologies—Argentina also experienced a military coup. Some elements within the Argentinian military, perhaps fearing the proliferation implications of the unprecedented West German deal, shifted to a harder hedging strategy. It developed pilot reprocessing capabilities and an enrichment facility at Pilcaniyeu, neither of which was ipso facto a nuclear weapons facility but lay the foundation for them should a future Argentinian government decide to go forward. Even within the Argentinian government, however, there was no domestic consensus for nuclear weapons development. Thus, Argentina stopped short of an active proliferation strategy and, in this period, settled on hard hedging. It is certainly the case that the exogenous shift in Argentina to a military junta, coupled with Brazil's existing military government, heightened threat perceptions and pushed Argentina to hedge harder against the uncertainty of Brazil's program.

In turn, Brazil's military government, once it discovered the reprocessing facility at Ezeiza and the enrichment program at Pilcaniyeu, correspondingly shifted to a hard hedge. This is consistent with my theory, as there was a shift in the severity of the potential threat with the emergence of an Argentinian military junta, but domestic consensus was still lacking for an active weaponization strategy. In response to these discoveries, the Brazilian military government initiated a parallel program under each military service for uranium enrichment, the most promising of which resided with the navy and its gas centrifuge program. These programs had a legitimate ground to possibly fuel submarine reactors, but they also compressed the time to an active nuclear weapons program should it become apparent that Argentina was pursuing nuclear weapons as well. Some of the activities maintained tactical secrecy, but there was broad awareness in both countries of the hard hedge that the other side maintained in this phase. My theory would predict that this hard hedging phase would shift back to technical hedging once the severity of the security threat posed by each party dissipated. This is what we observe. The shift back to democracy in both Argentina in December 1983 and then Brazil in 1985 dampened each country's sense of threat. The mutual democratization of Brazil and Argentina enabled both governments to engage in a substantial degree of nuclear cooperation—and blame the juntas for whatever suspicious work had been done to move to hard hedging—until they built enough mutual confidence to both agree to implement the Treaty of Tlatelolco in the 1990s.

Neither a strict realist explanation nor technological determinism fully accounts for Brazilian and Argentinian behavior. A strictly security explanation would either underpredict pursuit, since Brazil and Argentina did not pose acute security threats to each other when the energy programs were initiated, or overpredict outright weaponization during the overlapping military junta period because of the heightened security competition. Either way, it is incapable of explaining the historical record and a shift from nothing more than technical hedging to a brief period of hard hedging that gave way to mutual renunciation after both democratized. Technological determinism also does not capture the shift from technical to hard hedging because it was a political decision in both countries to develop uranium enrichment technologies under the juntas—nominally to provide for indigenous fuel supply but with the ancillary effect of exploring technologies that could one day be useful to enrich weapons-grade uranium. Neither does the nonproliferation regime explain the shift in strategies—particularly its timing—since there was no limitation on pursuing these sensitive technologies either earlier or later. The timing was entirely dictated by domestic political shifts, particularly the emergence of military regimes, which heightened the security competition to a degree that triggered this "harder" hedge but not so much that there was domestic political consensus for the outright pursuit of nuclear weapons. Only my theory captures this distinction and the fascinating cases of Brazil and Argentina: the reluctant enrichers.

Sweden and Switzerland: Domestic Politics and the Bomb

Sweden and Switzerland were both neutral states outside of NATO's Cold War security architecture. Both potentially faced the threat of Soviet ground forces in the event of a general European war, Sweden through the Northern Flank, and Switzerland through the Central Front. Without the extended nuclear guarantees of NATO that countries such as Germany and Norway enjoyed, these states faced a potentially existential threat from the Soviet Union, and faced it alone. Any security model of nuclear weapons would predict that both states should seriously consider pursuing nuclear weapons. Though it is often forgotten, both in fact did. I choose these cases because they are both surprisingly understudied in the proliferation literature, and they also powerfully demonstrate the crucial role domestic political consensus plays as a necessary bridge between hard hedging and an active weaponization strategy—even in avowedly neutral states facing an acute security threat alone. Neither Sweden nor Switzerland ever built nuclear weapons, but they refrained because of domestic politics, not because their original security motivations had dissipated.

In the 1950s and 1960s, both Sweden and Switzerland leveraged substantial civilian nuclear technology to lay the foundation for the potential production of nuclear weapons—especially compact advanced tactical nuclear weapons—as a deterrent to a Soviet ground invasion. While the Swedish and Swiss militaries were keen on developing tactical nuclear weapons, and already envisioned an asymmetric escalation nuclear strategy (backed in some ways by the general strategic nuclear power of the United States), there was deep domestic division in both states about nuclear weapons development. This explains why both states adopted hard hedging but proceeded no further. Both ultimately lacked the domestic political consensus for the development of nuclear weapons despite the potential existential Soviet threat. Both persisted with hard hedging during fractured domestic political conditions in the 1950s and early 1960s. Eventually, opponents of nuclear weapons were victorious, ending their weapons hedges. These two cases illustrate the power of domestic politics in halting states from an outright active proliferation strategy even when the security environment—quite severe for both states in the 1950s when a Soviet threat to Western Europe was an especially real possibility—suggests that they should develop nuclear weapons. They show how domestic politics can condition the *strategy* of proliferation: both states allowed theoretical research on nuclear weapons to continue and intentionally delayed decisions on explicit weaponization simply to "keep the option open" until it no longer became domestically politically tenable.

SWEDEN (1945–66): STOCKHOLM'S STOCKPILE

Sweden pursued a strategy of hard hedging for two decades. In this section, as in the previous ones, I describe Swedish behavior and then discuss how Proliferation Strategy Theory successfully accounts for it. In 1945, Sweden began research on nuclear power and broadly on the issue of nuclear weapons—focusing primarily on how Sweden could protect itself in the atomic age but also on the issue of developing its own nuclear weapons.[180] Swedish scientists pursued these efforts as two separate research tracks—officially designated the protection and development tracks, respectively—within the newly created Swedish National Defense Research Establishment (FOA). This enabled Sweden to conduct research that might hedge against the development of nuclear weapons under the guise of pursuing "protection." An official history of this program was conducted by Thomas Jonter, who provides the most credible and detailed data on what precisely the Swedes did and when. Given the expectation that nuclear weapons would

180. Thomas Jonter, "Sweden and the Bomb: The Swedish Plans to Acquire Nuclear Weapons, 1945–1972," Swedish Nuclear Power Inspectorate (SKI) Report, 01:33, September 2001, p. 21, https://www.stralsakerhetsmyndigheten.se/contentassets/bda8f1ac1d914cd9a27c846c8b524fb1/200133-sweden-and-the-bomb.-the-swedish-plans-to-acquire-nuclear-weapons-19451972.

quickly proliferate, and cursed by geography on the potential front lines of the Cold War, Swedish prime minister Tage Erlander, writes Jonter, "for several years in the late 1940s and early 1950s . . . supported a nuclear weapons program for Sweden."[181] Sweden's approach to its nuclear program is described by Jonter:

> In December 1945, the head of Department 1 at FOA, Gustaf Ljunggren, presented a proposal that led the way for the entire Swedish nuclear weapons program. . . . Sweden should do the same as the United States—but the other way around. In the United States, civilian exploitation of nuclear energy was a "spin off" of the nuclear weapons program, in which plutonium production held a central position. Ljunggren's view took the *opposite approach* and argued that the *main aim* should be the generation of nuclear energy, with plutonium production, which would make possible the manufacture of nuclear weapons as a side effect.[182]

Over the course of the next several years, research groups were formed to explore the various energy- and weapons-related activities that would be required should the political leadership decide to authorize a nuclear weapons program. The Chief of Defense Staff ordered FOA in February 1948 to estimate the time and cost of a nuclear weapons program; given Sweden's large natural uranium deposits, a graphite moderated (later, heavy water) reactor fueled by natural uranium was estimated to be the most efficient power-producing and plutonium-producing option.[183] The estimated timeline for the reactor was three to four years, and if a weapons option were ever authorized, eight years after that to produce nuclear weapons.[184] Furthermore, regardless of whether there was ever a dedicated weapons program, the energy program under the public-private consortium AB Atomenergi (AE) would employ plutonium reprocessing to be fed back into the reactors to "enable a more efficient use of the natural uranium."[185] That is, civilian energy equipment was deliberately chosen to complement and support a hedging strategy.

Sweden's progress was retarded in the next several years as Swedish scientists and industry were thwarted in their efforts to seek American

181. Thomas Jonter, "The Swedish Plans to Acquire Nuclear Weapons, 1945–1968: An Analysis of the Technical Preparations," *Science & Global Security* 18 (2010): 62.

182. Ibid., 63, emphasis added.

183. Ibid., 64.

184. Ibid.

185. Ibid., 65.

and British assistance in the development of their civilian program. It was not until 1953 that a subsequent study was commissioned by FOA on the potential for nuclear weapons development. This report triggered Sweden's first open debate about whether to pursue nuclear weapons. The military's supreme commander argued in a 1954 report that "Sweden [should] obtain nuclear weapons in order to uphold its non-aligned policy."[186] The logic was that if Sweden truly valued its neutrality it had to be able to provide for its own defense in the event of a Soviet invasion through the Northern Flank, and the only option to avoid being overrun was essentially the development of tactical nuclear weapons to defeat oncoming Soviet forces. In the 1954 parliamentary debate, Prime Minister Erlander "acknowledged that Sweden was conducting research on how to protect itself from nuclear weapons. However, he did not openly admit that FOA was also conducting research on possible Swedish nuclear weapons production."[187] The research on development continued, with a major study in 1955 by FOA investigating the timeline (eight to ten years) and requirements for the development of one hundred nuclear weapons, "tactical nuclear weapons . . . regarded as transportable and could be used in both missiles and torpedoes" or delivered by aircraft.[188] This study, according to Jonter, "established that it was technically possible from then on to produce a Swedish nuclear weapon, given access to plutonium."[189]

In 1955, three out of the four main political parties in Sweden supported funding nuclear weapons research; by 1957 most of the fourth party (Social Democrats) also supported nuclear weapons research.[190] Jan Prawitz notes, "In the early days, the issue was when rather than if Sweden should acquire its own atomic bombs."[191] This period was the closest Sweden came to achieving domestic consensus for an active nuclear weapons proliferation strategy. Indeed, the CIA recognized the domestic political impediments to weaponization but concluded that it was still likely that Sweden would make a decision to pursue a dedicated nuclear weapons program down the road: "There is also strong opposition, and the government has not reached a decision. We believe that discussion and agitation will probably continue for

186. Cited in ibid., 68.

187. Ibid.

188. Ibid., 69.

189. Ibid., 70.

190. Maria Rost Rublee, *Nonproliferation Norms: Why States Choose Nuclear Restraint* (Athens: University of Georgia Press, 2009), 170.

191. Jan Prawitz, *From Nuclear Option to Non-Nuclear Promotion: The Sweden Case* (Stockholm: Swedish Institute for International Affairs, 1995), emphasis added.

some time, and there is a good chance that at some point in the next decade Sweden will initiate a limited [nuclear weapons] program."[192]

There was still, however, no political sanction to actively pursue this development, since "the Swedish parliament had not yet decided to launch the nuclear program" and Erlander did not enjoy the latitude and dominance that, for example, India's prime ministers did to simply dictate nuclear weapons policy.[193] Research was permitted on the justification that any nuclear weapons would be defensive and "non-offensive."[194] But the decision point was fast approaching by 1958 because FOA would need political clearance to continue some of the design-level work and experimentation required for the nuclear weapons (the "device program"), as opposed to just the protection, track. If authorized, the targeted completion date for Sweden's first nuclear weapon was estimated to be 1966 (delays would push this estimate even further back to 1972).[195] But Jonter writes that Prime Minister Erlander "began to have doubts about equipping the Swedish military with nuclear weapons as early as 1957."[196] His foreign minister, Osten Unden, was a staunch proponent of universal disarmament, and the partner Social Democratic Party also opposed the development of nuclear weapons. Jonter notes that "Erlander prioritized the achievement of broad political consensus on the nuclear weapons issue, which meant that the social democratic party would decide the matter together with the centrist and right-wing parties."[197] While the protection program was allowed to continue, the device program was strictly limited in what it could do—just as in the Indian case—though, later, Prime Minister Olaf Palme suggested that it was difficult to define the precise line where "research aimed at protecting the Swedish population against nuclear arms" blurred into developing its own deterrent.[198]

By 1959, Jonter reports that public opinion was mobilizing toward a "'no' to Swedish nuclear weapons" while a parliamentary committee that represented both proponents and opponents of Swedish nuclear weapons

192. "Memorandum for the Disarmament Staff," Central Intelligence Agency, April 3, 1957, p. 7, http://nsarchive.gwu.edu/nukevault/ebb433/docs/1.pdf.

193. Jonter, "The Swedish Plans to Acquire Nuclear Weapons," 71.

194. Prime Minister Tage Erlander, quoted in Gary Lee, "Sweden Admits Nuclear Tests, Says It Will Not Build Bomb," *Washington Post*, April 27, 1985, https://www.washingtonpost.com/archive/politics/1985/04/27/sweden-admits-nuclear-test-says-it-will-not-build-bomb/29ecd3bc-80fe-4786-848c-c995ad6192c5/.

195. Jonter, "The Swedish Plans to Acquire Nuclear Weapons," 72, 76.

196. Ibid., 73.

197. Ibid.

198. Prime Minister Olaf Palme, quoted in Lee, "Sweden Admits Nuclear Test."

essentially decided not to decide one way or the other, concluding that "Sweden had breathing room until at least the mid-1960s [to decide], when international developments would guide decision making."[199] (By international developments, the committee meant Sweden's security situation. Opponents and proponents identified that as a major factor in their decision making.)[200] Furthermore, and critically, while parliament indicated that "defense research should continue," it also "specified that no *design research* aimed directly at the manufacture of nuclear weapons should be carried out."[201] As Maria Rublee argues, "Rather than commit to immediate nuclear weapons procurement (which would have been practically difficult anyway) or funding for nuclear weapons research, the Swedish government decided on a course of keeping the nuclear option open without making any clear commitment to a weapons program."[202] Similar to India's hard hedging phase, there were clear restrictions on what Sweden's scientists were allowed to do, though in both cases they would push the envelope on the theoretical work that they could do. Nevertheless, Paul Cole's important work on the program concludes that "available evidence . . . points to a large, expensive, and comprehensive [nuclear] weapon research program."[203] Cole concludes that Sweden had assembled all the pieces in place for a nuclear weapons program at this point, except one critical ingredient: domestic political consensus and sanction to actually produce them:

> By the late 1950s, Sweden's nuclear program had achieved significant advances. Reactors, intended to provide an indigenous source of plutonium, had been constructed, and detailed cost projections for plutonium and weapon production calculated. Swedish weapons designers had perfected implosion technology, while military strategists devised plans to prepare for the deployment and use of nuclear weapons. *The only component lacking was a clear-cut political commitment to a full-scale production program.*[204]

199. Jonter, "The Swedish Plans to Acquire Nuclear Weapons," 74.

200. See ibid., 72–73.

201. Ibid., 74.

202. Rublee, *Nonproliferation Norms*, 171.

203. Paul Cole, "Atomic Bombast: Nuclear Weapon Decisionmaking in Sweden 1945–1972," Henry L. Stimson Center Occasional Paper, no. 26, April 1996, p. 10, https://www.stimson.org/wp-content/files/file-attachments/Occasional%20Paper%20No.%2026%20April%201996.pdf.

204. Ibid., emphasis added.

But, with broader political consensus fracturing, even the military consensus for nuclear weapons began to fray by 1961. Jonter's evidence suggests that "the formerly strong consensus, within the military, in favor of equipping the Swedish defense forces with nuclear weapons was now beginning to disintegrate . . . [for] several reasons," mostly having to do with interservice rivalries where the army and navy feared budgetary cuts since the air force "was expected to be awarded the bulk of additional nuclear related budgetary resources since the nuclear weapons were primarily to be mounted on aircraft."[205] However, even the air force feared cannibalization of its conventional assets and platforms should nuclear weapons be developed. The military consensus was further fractured by perceived shifts in American strategy away from massive retaliation, with aggressive nuclear first use, to the Kennedy administration's flexible response that called for stronger conventional defense—a strategy seized upon by the Swedish services to justify expansion and larger budgets (little did they know that in reality, American nuclear strategy shifted very little). A 1961 U.S. National Intelligence Estimate (NIE) picked up on the increasingly fractured domestic debate: "Sweden has so far avoided making any clear-cut decision in regard to a nuclear weapons program . . . the economic and financial costs, the strong opposition within the bulk of the SDP, and the fact that it will probably be at least several years before enough domestically produced plutonium becomes available even to conduct a test, have all combined to keep a clear-cut decision in abeyance."[206]

This momentum toward a decision not to pursue weapons would accelerate. It ultimately led to the political termination of FOA's "freedom of action" on the device program. By 1964, the United States NIE noted this growing domestic hesitation from the outside, judging: "Sweden will continue its peaceful nuclear program, but we believe the chances of its developing nuclear weapons during the next decade are less than even."[207] It continued: "The Social Democratic Party, which was returned to power in a recent parliamentary election, is on record as wishing to postpone a decision on nuclear weapons as long as possible."[208] By 1966, the United States NIE was

205. Jonter, "The Swedish Plans to Acquire Nuclear Weapons," 75.

206. "Nuclear Weapons and Delivery Capabilities of Free World Countries Other than the US and UK," National Intelligence Estimate, NIE 4-3-61, September 21, 1961, http://nsarchive.gwu.edu/NSAEBB/NSAEBB155/prolif-6b.pdf.

207. "Prospects for a Proliferation of Nuclear Weapons over the Next Decade," National Intelligence Estimate, October 21, 1964, NIE 4-2-64, *FRUS, 1964–1968*, vol. X, doc. 57, https://history.state.gov/historicaldocuments/frus1964-68v10/d57.

208. Ibid.

further predicting against Swedish proliferation due to growing domestic opposition: "The Swedish Government has repeatedly deferred a decision to develop nuclear weapons. . . . The government follows a policy of keeping its hands free to take action should Sweden's security position deteriorate, while working actively for effective international disarmament."[209] At this point, the NIE estimated that Sweden could produce a nuclear weapon "two years after a decision to undertake a program,"[210] though estimates varied from two to seven years.[211] Later that year in 1966, in fact, the Swedish government rejected FOA's proposal for "phased procurement" (the most cost-effective plan they had studied), and in doing so, "the Swedish nuclear weapons planning was, in practice, terminated."[212] By 1968, the government's defense plan explicitly noted that "acquiring nuclear weapons was not in line with Sweden's interests" and, when parliament concurred, "the policy of freedom of action was removed from the field of security activities."[213] The proponents of international disarmament, including Prime Minister Erlander, who had by now changed his mind on Swedish nuclear weapons—shifting to a mobilization strategy against nuclear weapons, as Saunders terms it—not only terminated Sweden's hard hedging activity but also generated momentum for signing the NPT in August 1968.[214] The domestic consensus for nuclear weapons in Sweden never congealed because Erlander fractured it and mobilized the necessary allies, once he decided Sweden should forswear the option.

Curiously though, even as Sweden was ratifying the NPT in 1972, which Cole writes marked a "moratorium,"[215] not an end, to the Swedish nuclear program, reports later emerged that Swedish scientists allegedly conducted ten gram-scale underground plutonium implosion tests as part of its "research" on defending the Swedish population from nuclear arms.[216] There is substan-

209. "The Likelihood of Further Nuclear Proliferation," National Intelligence Estimate, NIE 4-66, January 20, 1966, p. 9, http://nsarchive.gwu.edu/nukevault/ebb401/docs/doc%203.pdf.

210. "The Proliferation of Missile Delivery Systems for Nuclear Weapons," National Intelligence Estimate, NIE 4-67, January 26, 1967, p. 12, http://nsarchive.gwu.edu/NSAEBB/NSAEBB155/prolif-14b.pdf.

211. George C. Denney Jr. to the Secretary, "Swedish Decision to Cut Military Spending Causes Defense Review, Reduces Likelihood of Nuclear Weapons Acquisition," REU-16, March 20, 1967, Confidential, http://nsarchive.gwu.edu/dc.html?doc=2830717-Document-15C-George-C-Denney-Jr-to-the-Secretary.

212. Jonter, "The Swedish Plans to Acquire Nuclear Weapons," 80.

213. Ibid.

214. See Saunders, "The Domestic Politics of Nuclear Choices—A Review Essay."

215. Cole, "Atomic Bombast," 30.

216. Lee, "Sweden Admits Nuclear Tests."

tial evidence, according to Cole, that even after "the program was abandoned officially . . . additional research continued in secret."[217] Specifically, believing they had broad authority to continue to conduct research until Sweden officially ratified the NPT in 1972, Cole finds that, even early on, "Swedish designers perfected and tested both the implosion technology and the high-speed camera techniques required to monitor tests of the conventional explosives." That is, Sweden was essentially conducting cold tests by the late 1950s and then, piecing together the evidence of underground small-scale plutonium implosion tests in 1972, even possibly miniscule yield-producing nuclear tests.[218] Sweden's nuclear weapons program, in retrospect, appears to have been an incredibly hard hedge and much closer to a nuclear weapons capability than is generally appreciated or publicly known. It is unclear if Swedish leaders were even aware of the research and activity that continued after they believed they had halted Sweden's nuclear weapons program.

There is no question that Sweden developed a program to seriously consider—and lay the foundation for—Swedish nuclear weapons between 1945 and 1972.[219] The civilian energy equipment, particularly the nuclear reactors, was chosen with a keen eye toward potential weapons-grade plutonium production. But the political will for nuclear weapons never congealed and the option was ultimately not only never exercised but de facto foreclosed in 1968, and then formally in 1972, when Sweden decided that its security was better met through the NPT than through neutrality plus nuclear weapons. Jonter concludes: "From a strict, formal point of view, they were only plans, because no decision to start a serial production of nuclear weapons was taken . . . the Swedish case only covered research, planning and experimental evaluations. But if we take into account the whole concept to place the military manufacture within the framework of civilian development of nuclear energy, it could be argued that it was indeed a program."[220] It was a program: a hard hedging program, one that seems to have made substantial progress, such that Sweden could have exercised a nuclear option relatively quickly if the government decided to do so. When the political—and military—consensus for nuclear weapons not only failed to congeal but in fact frayed further in the course of public debate, the program, and Sweden's hard hedging strategy, was terminated, or perhaps more accurately placed on Scandinavian ice.

217. Cole, "Atomic Bombast," 10.

218. Ibid., 12.

219. Ibid.

220. Jonter, "The Swedish Plans to Acquire Nuclear Weapons," 81.

TESTING PROLIFERATION STRATEGY THEORY

My theory accounts for the Swedish case reasonably well. Outside of the NATO architecture but buffered only by a vulnerable Finland against the weight of a Soviet Union that had explicit invasion plans through the Northern Flank, Sweden faced an acute security threat alone after World War II. The potential development of tactical nuclear weapons—backstopped by America's strategic nuclear arsenal if the balloon ever went up—made eminent strategic sense. Sweden, however, wrestled with domestic consensus for nuclear weapons. The initial prime ministerial decision to authorize research activity and studies for both nuclear protection and nuclear devices occurred at a level that did not require broader parliamentary or public consensus. It was therefore able to proceed for several years without a political decision point.

When a decision point came as to whether to fund the program in the 1960s, FOA and Prime Minister Erlander required parliamentary approval. There were parties, such as the Social Democrats, which opposed nuclear weapons on normative, or what the U.S. government termed "emotional," grounds,[221] as well as economic grounds since a nuclear weapons program might threaten social welfare programs. There were bureaucratic reasons why military consensus for nuclear weapons fractured as well, with the navy and army worrying that a nuclear-equipped air force would attract the lion's share of the defense budget. There were growing security reasons as well that helped coalesce domestic political opposition to nuclear weapons, including the fact that a tactical nuclear-armed Sweden could become an early preemptive target for the Soviet Union. The Kennedy administration's perceived shift away from tactical nuclear weapons and toward stronger conventional forces as the first line of defense fueled Swedish military opposition to nuclear weapons. The Swedish military wished to grow their conventional footprint and believed a nuclear program would cannibalize their budgets and forces. There were variegated and multidirectional pressures that frayed domestic political consensus for Swedish nuclear weapons in the mid-1960s. Indeed, the consensus shifted to supporting the NPT and arms control rather than Swedish armament. Once that occurred and Swedish domestic politics settled against nuclear weapons, the hard hedging strategy initiated in 1945 ended. The Swedish case indeed illustrates the power of domestic forces in conditioning how states pursue nuclear weapons.

221. "Prospects for Further Proliferation of Nuclear Weapons," Atomic Energy Commission, October 2, 1974, http://nsarchive.gwu.edu/NSAEBB/NSAEBB181/sa08.pdf.

A security model would predict that Sweden should have pursued and developed nuclear weapons—realism does not countenance abandoning the ultimate deterrent for domestic political reasons. Sweden would have certainly had to fear Soviet prevention against a nuclear weapons program, but it had an overwhelming security rationale to develop nuclear weapons. And a hiding strategy would have made some sense if a security-only model were accurate. However, Sweden openly hedged on whether to actually pull the trigger on a nuclear weapons program and did so for domestic political reasons, which put the brakes on a dedicated weapons program with increasing force through the 1960s until it came to a halt by 1968. Strict security models that take no account of domestic politics would have a hard time accounting for the Swedish case of hedging rather than active pursuit.

Similarly, technological determinism does not adequately explain the Swedish decision, which was intensely political. The parliament decided to put the brakes on further weapons research and even terminated the hard hedge before Sweden had enough plutonium for a nuclear weapon. Indeed, weapons research seems to have been largely productive before the program was terminated—it was not halted due to incompetence or technological hurdles. Only my theory which predicts hard hedging behavior offers a satisfactory account of the fascinating Swedish nuclear weapons program after World War II until the signing of the NPT.

The emerging NPT provided the opportunity for Sweden to bring its domestic political debate to a climax, but there is little evidence that it abandoned the military aspects of its nuclear program *because* of the NPT, although the international debate over the looming treaty may have empowered the domestic political opponents to the bomb in Sweden. Indeed, the domestic political decision to suspend the military aspects of the bomb in 1966 predated and likely enabled Sweden's accession to the NPT two years later when the treaty was established, rather than vice versa. Nevertheless, Sweden is a fascinating case of a highly threatened state outside of a formal alliance structure that should have actively pursued—and in retrospect actually came quite close to—nuclear weapons but hedged and ultimately refrained for domestic political reasons.

SWITZERLAND (1945–69): SWISS SCANDALS AND THE BOMB

Switzerland's experience with nuclear weapons proliferation again underscores the power of domestic politics. Like Sweden, Switzerland valued its international neutrality. Having eschewed NATO membership, Bern could turn to no one for a guarantee of its security. If a domestic political consensus formed for nuclear weapons, Switzerland ought to have pursued nuclear weapons, according to my theory. It almost did. Indeed, for a time, it appeared that this would come to pass. Switzerland adopted a strategy of hard hedging and—like Sweden—stood on the precipice of developing nuclear weapons. And then a domestic scandal brought all that to a halt. The so-called Mirage Affair in 1964 shook parliament's faith in the military and the Swiss Federal Council. Until the scandal, Swiss leaders expressed serious interest in going nuclear, particularly inside the military. They hoped to develop tactical nuclear weapons to thwart a Soviet invasion. The Mirage Affair, however, shone a light on the advancing nuclear weapons program and mobilized domestic opposition, ultimately resulting in its termination.

I present the Swiss nuclear odyssey in abbreviated form to demonstrate the importance of domestic political consensus in moving a hedger to an active weapons strategy—and how a fractured consensus led Switzerland to abandon the military aspects of its nuclear program. Through the late 1950s and early 1960s, research on nuclear weapons was allowed to proceed with approval from the Federal Council, the Swiss executive branch of government. Parliament exercised little oversight. When the Mirage Affair occurred, which was essentially a financial scandal that cost several high-level officers and Federal Council members, particularly Paul Chaudet, their jobs, it tightened financial oversight over military programs. As a result, parliament choked funding for nuclear weapons research and the oversight resulted in a termination of the hard hedge when Switzerland signed the NPT in 1969, ultimately ratifying it in 1977.

Switzerland's security situation was perhaps even more precarious than Sweden's. According to Jürg Stüssi-Lauterberg, who authored the official history of the Swiss nuclear weapons program, Switzerland faced the threat of a "Soviet invasion from the Danube, through Switzerland to the Rhone—and thus the avoidance of the use of French nuclear weapons which could with certainty be expected against the Soviet troops in Switzerland."[222] Swiss physicists were involved in the fundamental research that underlay the development of nuclear weapons in the 1940s and, as early as 1945, Switzerland began thinking about developing nuclear weapons as well—also under the assumption that all states would eventually field them. The initial forays

222. Jürg Stüssi-Lauterberg, "Historical Outline on the Question of Swiss Nuclear Armament" (report prepared for the Swiss Federal Council [Federal Administration: Bern], translated by the United States Department of State, December 31, 1995), 48, http://www.alexandria.admin.ch/bv001147186.pdf.

into nuclear weapons research were largely theoretical, though the military always had a keen interest in tactical nuclear weapons, going so far as to even think about aircraft types for delivery.[223] As Stüssi-Lauterberg writes, "It is certain the *Atomic Energy Study Commission* was working on basic principles as early as 1945. The Federal Council . . . emphasized the military aspects of the question clearly enough, but [Federal Councilor Karl Kobelt] also stated that Switzerland had no plans to develop its own nuclear weapons, which practically went without saying under the conditions of 1946 and the objective resources required."[224] Given the structure of Swiss democracy, the executive Federal Council could allow this research to continue among the military and atomic energy actors without parliamentary approval so long as significant budget outlays were not required.

By 1955, however, there was growing public opposition to nuclear weapons, particularly in the French-speaking cantons, and Stüssi-Lauterberg notes that around this time, "there must have been a certain slowdown in efforts to develop a Swiss atom bomb."[225] After the Soviet Union crushed the Hungarian Revolution, on March 29, 1957, the Federal Council tasked the Swiss military, led by Chief of the General Staff Louis de Montmollin, to investigate "the possibility of acquiring nuclear weapons in Switzerland."[226] At the same time, multiple public petitions were gathering substantial popular support against the possibility of Swiss nuclear weapons. In response, the Federal Council incredibly stated in a 1958 Basic Declaration that, "in accordance with our centuries-old tradition of defensive capability, the Federal Council is therefore of the opinion that, to defend our independence and to protect our neutrality, the Army must be equipped with the most effective weapons. These include nuclear weapons. Consequently, the Federal Council has ordered the Federal Military Department to *continue its investigation* of the introduction of nuclear weapons in our army, and at the appropriate time to submit a report and motion to the houses of Parliament."[227] This included the search for uranium deposits, and sizing the potential nuclear force, but no authorization for actual development. At this point, this was a largely unfunded mandate since it had not received any budgetary appropriation from parliament.

223. Ibid., 3–4.
224. Ibid.
225. Ibid., 4.
226. Ibid., 5.
227. Quoted in ibid.

For the next several years, the military investigated a variety of options, including the fantastical notion to "request proposals from the USA, Great Britain, and the Soviet Union [the envisioned adversary!] for the sale of nuclear weapons to Switzerland on a commercial basis, and to offer France and Sweden, on the other hand, cooperation in the area of 'tests.'"[228] Unsurprisingly, the Federal Council "rejected such ideas out of hand."[229] On July 7, 1961, the Federal Council clarified: "This question will remain open until the opportunity arises. . . . That is currently not the case. Decisions with regard to acquisition . . . have therefore not been made, nor will they be considered in the near future."[230] The Federal Council and military were frustrated by public opposition to nuclear weapons, rejecting the notion that the issue of nuclear weapons, a military matter, should be subject to the "passionate atmosphere of a referendum [which] is irresponsible," thereby spitting at the essence of Swiss democracy. But they could not avoid or ignore parliamentary opposition.[231] The Federal Council and the parliament declined to decide whether or not to proceed with an indigenous Swiss nuclear weapons capability. Meanwhile, the military continued to do what militaries do and planned for potential weaponization, submitting a report in 1964 that recommended developing "50 50–100kT aerial bombs (Mirage)." From a strictly nuclear strategy perspective, this made little sense. The Swiss military sought not just a tactical nuclear force but a strategic one. But given Soviet retaliatory potential, this would amount to strategic suicide—though the strategy could have been derived from the French concept of "proportional deterrence" to hold at risk as much of the Soviet Union as Switzerland was worth.[232]

However, whatever consideration may have been given to a potential nuclear weapons program by the military and the Federal Council came to a relatively abrupt halt in April 1964 with the so-called Mirage Affair. The military and Federal Council were playing fast and loose with the defense budget in their request for Mirage aircraft, asking for an additional—and unaccounted—outlay of 576 million Swiss francs (roughly $1.5 billion in 2020 dollars). The nuclear program would become a casualty of and collateral damage from the Mirage Affair. On the same day that he requested new French fighter planes, the Chief of the General Staff requested a 20 million Swiss franc appropriation for uranium deposit exploration and research on

228. Ibid., 7.
229. Ibid.
230. Ibid., 7–8.
231. Ibid., 8.
232. Ibid., 10.

centrifuges and "nuclear weapons technology as well as the possibility of conducting nuclear tests."[233] The outlay request for Mirages triggered Switzerland's first parliamentary investigation of the Federal Council and the military, resulting in the resignations of the Chief of the General Staff and the Commander of the Air Force.[234] Parliament strictly curbed the freedom of the Federal Council on military matters thereafter. Stüssi-Lauterberg writes that by late 1965, the Federal Council had "clearly abandoned the 1958 doctrine. On November 1, 1965, [Federal Councilor] Chaudet reported to his colleagues as follows: The emphasis must be placed on the civilian aspect (energy production). Solution C ['a certain "potential" would be created for the manufacture of nuclear weapons, without having to make a decision about their actual production'] is considered by the Military Committee to be the correct basis on which to continue research."[235] Like in India and Sweden, parliament severely restricted the Federal Council's, but especially the military's, ability to do research on nuclear weapons qua nuclear weapons and its tasks would thereafter be "narrowly drawn."[236] At this point, Stüssi-Lauterberg reports that the lack of personnel, training, and equipment along with financial choking "resulted in a reduction of the pace to a typically slow and deliberate 'Swiss' speed."[237]

Paul Chaudet, who was under attack for the Mirage Affair among other things, was replaced as head of the Military Department in 1967 by Nello Celio. Celio was much more "skeptical about the acquisition of nuclear weapons."[238] This reflected the shifting opinion of the Federal Council, which was becoming more opposed to the idea of Swiss nuclear weapons. Federal Councilor Julius Binder explicitly noted in a December 1967 speech: "Is an effective national defense possible without nuclear weapons? The answer to this question is yes. No one thinks that our Army has to be equipped with nuclear weapons."[239] Certainly, the situation could change, so laying the technical foundation for future development might be prudent, but the Federal Council was shifting closer to public opinion and parliament on settling the nuclear weapons question in the negative. Indeed, even in response to Binder's proposal to hedge, Federal Councilor Willy Spühler argued that

233. Ibid., 10–11.
234. Ibid., 11–13.
235. Ibid., 15, 22–23.
236. Ibid., 23.
237. Ibid., 26.
238. Ibid., 90.
239. Binder quoted in ibid., 40–41.

such a "small country [cannot] support such a load without adverse effects on its economic growth."[240] Indeed, when Celio shifted to becoming head of the Finance Department, he terminated research on the military dimensions of nuclear energy completely. There were definitely perturbations in the Cold War security situation that pointed in the same direction as Swiss domestic politics. But the shock of the Mirage Affair coupled with growing public opposition to nuclear weapons played the most powerful roles in fracturing domestic consensus for authorizing a Swiss nuclear weapons program. Stüssi-Lauterberg concludes the official history of the Swiss program with: "On a political level, the Federal Council of Ministers closed the gap in policy that had already narrowed substantially since the Mirage-affair, by its decision to sign the treaty on nonproliferation of nuclear arms on 27 November 1969."[241] For all practical purposes, the Swiss nuclear weapons program terminated with this signature and was formally foreclosed when Switzerland ratified the NPT in 1977.

TESTING PROLIFERATION STRATEGY THEORY

Like Sweden, Switzerland was a neutral country without the formal protection of NATO and a serious existential assault by the Soviet Union during the Cold War was eminently plausible. It therefore had a strong security incentive—perhaps one of the strongest in Cold War Europe along with Finland, West Germany, and Sweden—to explore the possibility of developing nuclear weapons. There was very serious consideration of the possibility by the Swiss military and early incarnations of the seven-member Federal Council, which sanctioned research into how Switzerland might produce nuclear weapons and what the force size and mission might look like. But despite a massive security threat, the domestic politics in Switzerland never aligned to green-light Swiss nuclear weapons.

Granted, there were strictly security arguments against nuclearization. Seeking the bomb might make Switzerland a target of prevention prior to, or early in, a war. If this factor were decisive in dissuading the Swiss from going nuclear, we would expect to observe senior Swiss leaders saying as much. Despite its parochial concerns, the military ought to have taken this into account as well. In reality, I find neither kind of evidence.

240. Spühler quoted in ibid., 41.

241. See Stüssi-Lauterberg, "Historical Outline on the Question of Swiss Nuclear Armament: Extract," April 1996.

But the overwhelming reason for the abandonment of what was, at least within the military, serious interest in developing a nuclear weapons program—moving from its hard hedge, which included open interest in nuclear weapons in 1958, to what ended up being effectively abandonment—was a fractured domestic consensus, which actually ended up solidifying against nuclear weapons development by 1969. As with Sweden, security and technical explanations cannot capture the texture of the Swiss nuclear weapons program. Only my theory which highlights the security motive but then requires strong domestic consensus for nuclear weapons captures the story of the Swiss nuclear weapons program.

Conclusion

This chapter shows that hedging is an important waypoint in the proliferation process, and any analysis of nuclear proliferation must account for states that seek not a bomb but a bomb option. Explaining why some choose to exercise that option while others refrain from doing so paints a much more complete portrait of the nuclear landscape than focusing on strictly the aspirants who are seeking weapons outright. Understanding what drives hedgers to weaponize, forswear nuclear weapons, or continue to hedge indefinitely is central to nuclear proliferation. The chapter laid out the three distinct varieties of nuclear hedging and showed that they are characteristically different—the varieties of hedging are diverse and emerge from *different* strategic logics. Some hedgers such as Brazil and Argentina were just flirtatious technical hedgers that were briefly tempted by the idea of nuclear weapons—illustrating the risk that technical hedgers subjected to the right domestic and regional political conditions can be seduced by the weaponization potential of their preexisting technical capacity. Others, like Japan and West Germany, were forced to develop insurance hedges in the face of an underlying acute security threat to ensure that they would have a compressed window of vulnerability should they face abandonment from a superpower ally. The insurance hedge has the significant benefit of having a coercive effect on the superpower, reducing the probability of the very event it is hedging against: abandonment. Still others, like India, Sweden, and Switzerland, stall at the threshold of nuclear weapons development as their domestic politics serve as a speed bump or roadblock to final weaponization.

The different mechanisms illustrated here show two things. First, hedging is an important part of the nuclear proliferation process that manifests as three different hedging strategies. Second, these varieties of hedging imply *different reasons* why states might be hedging—not all hedgers hedge for the same reason or against the same thing. The implication of this is that the trigger for what might push a particular type of hedger to exercise its bomb option systematically differs as well. Locating hedging on the proliferation spectrum and disaggregating the various types of hedging is a crucial goal of this book.

The differences are important because the variables that lead a state to adopt a particular form of hedging are distinct. In turn, the variables that might push Japan, an insurance hedger, over the precipice into active pursuit of nuclear weapons are different from those that pushed India, or might have pushed Switzerland, both hard hedgers. Understanding the differences in hedging allows one to craft policies that can keep hedgers hedging. Hedging is an important waypoint on many states' paths to nuclear weapons, and the different forms it takes are of practical, not just intellectual, importance: the hedging phase offers the greatest opportunity to forestall or dissuade states from pursuing active weaponization, but because states adopt different hedging varieties for distinct reasons, a one-size-fits-all counterproliferation approach to hedgers would certainly fail.

The chapter also importantly illuminates the power of a fractured domestic consensus in causing states to stall on their path to nuclear weapons. For outsiders, this suggests a point of leverage: keeping domestic consensus fractured. Indeed, I will show that this is precisely what the world has attempted to do with Iran once it was caught with a clandestine nuclear program. Even hard hedgers—those that believe they have compelling reasons to obtain nuclear weapons—can be moderated by a fractured domestic consensus. For instance, India faced a conventionally superior nuclear adversary—China—and had fought three wars with a nuclearizing Pakistan. And yet, for fifteen years, India lacked the internal will to move forward with nuclear weapons, despite having gone as far as exploding a peaceful nuclear device. The case of India also hints that domestic consensus matters—in some form—across political systems: India's heads of government, not democratic opposition, the voting public, or the military-scientific enterprise, were the last obstacles to a nuclear consensus. Domestic variables crucially affect the trajectory of a state's nuclear proliferation strategies. Above all, this chapter demonstrates that nuclear proliferation is a spectrum and the varieties of hedging are critical waystations within it. The next chapters explore the active weaponizers, starting with the quintessential proliferators depicted in the literature: the sprinters.

4

The Sprinters

SOVIET UNION, FRANCE, AND CHINA

This chapter explores sprinting, the stylized strategy that the bulk of the proliferation literature assumes is universal. Sprinters are the states that pursue nuclear weapons openly and seek their development as quickly as possible. I focus in detail on the Soviet Union, France, and China, the second, fourth, and fifth nuclear weapons powers, respectively. All three countries openly pursued nuclear weapons for security reasons (although France had strong status motivations as well) and sought a bomb as quickly as possible; in some cases they mortgaged their economies and other projects to do so. Although each of these cases ultimately fit the stylized versions of nuclear pursuit that realist theories in particular assume characterize proliferation, domestic political consensus was a critical regulator in the timing of each nation's sprint to the bomb. Domestic politics matters even in the most determined and structurally unconstrained proliferators. The choice of sprinting over other active weaponization strategies was driven by the relative invulnerability to prevention. Most sprinters were the major powers who possessed vast territories on which to build nuclear weapons and that sought nuclear weapons when nonproliferation considerations were not particularly salient, when counterproliferation intelligence was low quality, and when preventive capabilities were limited. Many, though not all, of the nuclear aspirants in the system with the motive and opportunity to sprint have already done so. Proliferation Strategy Theory's pathway to sprinting is depicted in figure 4.1.

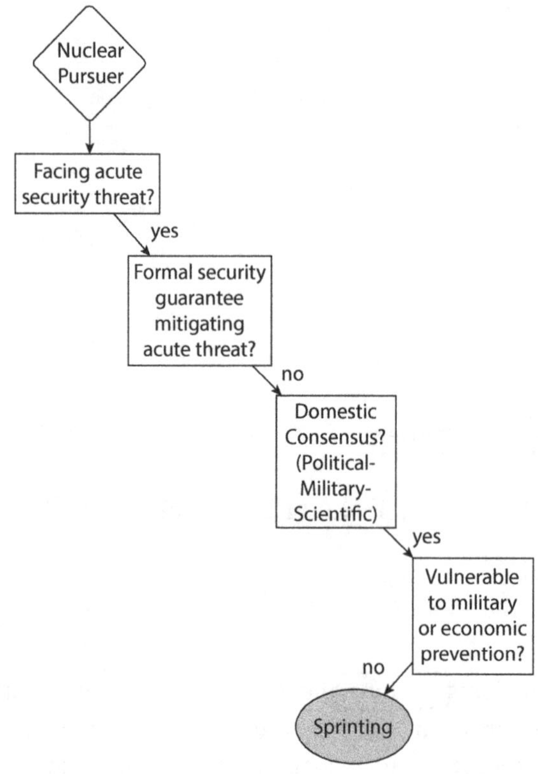

FIGURE 4.1. Proliferation Strategy Theory's pathway to the sprinting strategy.

In the Soviet Union, domestic politics delayed the start of a sprint. Key senior scientists were begging Stalin to sprint for a bomb in 1943 once they understood how far along the Americans were, and once the tide had turned in the war against Nazi Germany. But Stalin was unimpressed and did not fully grasp the impact of nuclear weapons on Soviet security or international politics until Hiroshima—an event that in itself had no direct impact on the balance of power for the USSR but dramatically convinced Stalin that the Soviet Union could not allow an American nuclear monopoly for long. France is an interesting case because my theory actually predicts that it should have remained an insurance hedger, leveraging its threat to break out to compel greater reassurance from its nuclear patron, the United States. But France defies my theory and elected to sprint, unsatisfied with even the most extensive nuclear-sharing arrangements Washington would offer—the very same arrangements that managed to keep West Germany an insurance hedger. France was in a "goldilocks" position to sprint: facing an objectively acute threat from the Soviet Union that motivated the sprint but with a buffer—West Germany itself—that enabled it to do so without fear of prevention. However, even the French sprint was paced by domestic political considerations. The revolving door of leadership in the Fourth Republic between 1954 and 1958 made even the simple things difficult: France embarked on something more akin to the 110-meter hurdles, slowing down every time there was a new government. Only when de Gaulle returned to power in 1958 did France begin a more straightforward final sprint. De Gaulle shifted France's political system from a parliamentary democracy to a more centralized and powerful quasi-presidential system, making domestic consensus for nuclear weapons easier for de Gaulle to assemble and direct. China may be the sprinter that most resembles the stereotypical proliferation case: Mao decided China would have its own bomb after perceived American nuclear coercion and did everything possible to attain it in only five years, despite the internal turmoil of the Great Leap Forward.

I chose these cases because they are the first cases of non-wartime nuclear pursuit. There were three cases of nuclear pursuit during World War II: Nazi Germany, and the combined United States and British effort in the Manhattan Project. I leave them aside here, because I assume that the considerations driving proliferation strategies during a world war are different from the peacetime considerations I describe in my theory. The case of Nazi Germany nuclear pursuit is fascinating but complicated by its circumstances: in the midst of a two-front war, Hitler's Germany could not, thankfully, get very far in a nuclear project—Hitler did not believe he could achieve a bomb in time for it to make a difference in the war and focused on conventional rockets instead. The Nazi nuclear bomb project remained largely theoretical and experimental by the time the Red Army and allied forces crashed down on it.[1] The Manhattan Project was initially a combined American and British effort to race against the fear of a Nazi bomb, conducted in the sanctuary of the New Mexican desert.[2] It was undoubtedly a sprint, led by the United States and aided by the British. The British were eventually frozen out—but only after they had seen what doors to push on

1. See Richelson, *Spying on the Bomb*, chap. 1; Vince Houghton, *The Nuclear Spies: America's Intelligence Operation against Hitler and Stalin* (Ithaca: Cornell University Press, 2019), chaps. 1–3; and Mark Walker, *Nazi Science: Myth, Truth, and the German Atomic Bomb* (New York: Springer Books, 1995).

2. See Richard Rhodes, *The Making of the Atomic Bomb* (New York: Simon and Schuster, 1986).

and how to develop the bomb. There is little new ground one can tread on the Manhattan Project, and it is a complicated case for theories of proliferation in general. Not only was it a wartime effort designed to win World War II, it was undertaken without a full appreciation for the power of nuclear weapons. In this way, the Soviet Union was actually the first "proliferator," the first nation to attempt to build the bomb after the United States showed that it could be done and demonstrated the immense power it held at Hiroshima and Nagasaki.

The United Kingdom would be the second proliferator, but it is not a clean case for any theory of proliferation due its incredibly close cooperation with the United States during the Manhattan Project, codified by the 1943 Quebec Agreement for joint production. London quite literally rode the momentum of the project to develop its own bomb—partly to show that it could do so independently after being frozen out by the United States, which benefited from extensive British assistance during the war and then excluded London from the final product.[3] Being shut out of the final stages of the Manhattan Project certainly triggered British anxiety about the reliability of the American commitment to it, but Britain also enjoyed the security buffer of the English Channel no matter what the postwar order might look like. The British coupling to the Manhattan Project and its decision to simply build the bomb right where it left off after 1945 makes it fall outside the scope conditions for a generalizable theory of proliferation, though my theory does happen to predict its sprinting strategy correctly. As Scheinman puts it, "The British program was for all intents and purposes absorbed into the American program after 1943, [and] the decision to continue to pursue an atomic development program with a specific military content was reaffirmed as a matter of course in late 1945."[4] The United Kingdom became the world's third nuclear power in 1952, but only six years later, in 1958, it essentially made itself an adjunct force of the United States by subjugating production and coordination to Washington—a condition that largely persists until today. The only things British about present-day British nuclear weapons are the fissile material and perhaps some warhead components: the submarines are American Trident designs, and the United States and Britain share a common missile pool that is loaded onto British ballistic missile submarines in Kings Bay, Georgia.

3. Matthew Jones, *The Official History of the UK Strategic Nuclear Deterrent, Volume 1: From the V-Bomber Era to the Arrival of Polaris, 1945–1964* (London: Routledge, 2017), chap. 1.

4. Lawrence Scheinman, *Atomic Energy Policy in France under the Fourth Republic* (Princeton: Princeton University Press, 1965).

This chapter is therefore a study of the three most significant independent sprinters after World War II—the major powers who could build nuclear weapons openly and without fear of prevention. All built nuclear weapons within roughly five years of a leadership decision to so, approximately matching the pace of the Manhattan Project. These are the states that had the incentive and luxury to sprint from start to finish—though it took France some searing experiences of perceived abandonment from its superpower ally, the United States, to shift gears. Many of the states that can sprint from start to finish have already done so, save perhaps Australia. But as the previous chapter showed, states such as India sprinted in their final years of attaining nuclear weapons, and existing hedgers such as Japan and Germany may still opt for a sprinting strategy should they ever decide to weaponize their nuclear capabilities. It is therefore still an important and relevant strategy of proliferation. The chapter proceeds in chronological order beginning with the first proliferator: Stalin's Soviet Union.

Soviet Union (1945–49): Stalin's Sprint

The Soviet Union was the first successful "proliferator" after the United States showed the world that it was indeed possible to develop nuclear weapons. On August 29, 1949, slightly four years after the United States developed a nuclear weapons capability and employed it in wartime against Japan, the Soviet Union broke America's nuclear monopoly. Although the Soviet Union had conducted early research into nuclear fission and the possibility of atomic weapons, the Nazi invasion of the Soviet Union in June 1941 redirected all of Stalin's, and the Soviet Union's, energies to first surviving the Nazi assault, and then crashing down on Germany's eastern front like a tsunami by 1945. Due to incredibly successful espionage, the Soviet Union was well aware of the Manhattan Project but did not focus on nuclear weapons until after Hiroshima, when Stalin finally understood the full implications of nuclear weapons on international politics—believing that the United States employed nuclear weapons to at least partially induce Japanese surrender before the Soviet Union could invade and capture its spoils in the Far East.[5] Stalin immediately recognized that American nuclear monopoly could be exceptionally dangerous to Soviet interests in the already emerging Cold War and decided that the Soviet Union must develop the bomb as quickly as possible.

5. David Holloway, *Stalin and the Bomb: The Soviet Union and Atomic Energy, 1939–1956* (New Haven: Yale University Press, 1994), 132.

Stalin ordered the atomic program to be accorded highest priority and initiated the world's first non-wartime sprint to nuclear weapons. The United States consistently misjudged how long it would take the Soviet Union to attain nuclear weapons, partly because it was unaware of the degree to which the Manhattan Project had been penetrated by Soviet intelligence assets, who even handed Moscow the plutonium bomb design that the Soviet Union would essentially copy for its first nuclear test. Even months before the Soviet Union would test its first nuclear weapon, the United States believed the Soviet Union was years away from being able to do so.[6] Stalin and the Soviet Union made no secret of its general pursuit of the bomb but operated with significant tactical secrecy and dispersion across the interior of the Soviet Union, making it difficult for the United States to penetrate the program or obtain quality assessments of how far along the program was, let alone contemplate preventing it from attaining nuclear weapons. It was largely a foregone conclusion in the United States that the Soviet Union would break its monopoly at some point, it was just a matter of when, not if.

This case explores the Soviet sprint to the bomb, relying largely on the best historical treatment of the program, David Holloway's masterful *Stalin and the Bomb*, which leverages a significant number of Soviet sources. It describes a successful effort to attain a nuclear weapons capability as quickly as possible—at great cost to the Soviet Union, which was still rebuilding after the war—because the Soviet Union could not allow the United States to maintain a monopoly on nuclear weapons as its sole peer competitor, nor allow it to gain such an advantage in nuclear weapons as to make the risk of prevention greater.

Soviet scientists were aware of the research being done across primarily Europe on nuclear fission by the late 1930s. But whatever wartime effort the Soviet Union may have wished to mount to develop an equivalent to the Manhattan Project was shelved with Hitler's betrayal of Stalin when he invaded the USSR with Operation Barbarossa in June 1941. Stalin was not surprised at Hitler's duplicity, but he was certainly shocked at the timing, believing that the Molotov-Ribbentrop Pact would buy him more time after the military purges to rebuild the Red Army—and he never believed Hitler would invade the Soviet Union until Britain was first defeated.[7] Once the initial shock wore off, Stalin was confronted with stunning early losses

6. See Richelson, *Spying on the Bomb*, chap. 3; and Houghton, *The Nuclear Spies*, chap. 4.

7. See David Stahel, *Operation Barbarossa and Germany's Defeat in the East* (Cambridge: Cambridge University Press, 2009).

despite ordering a full mobilization of the Red Army. Before the end of the year, Holloway notes that Germany "had gained control of the territory on which 45 percent of the Soviet population lived and 60 percent of Soviet coal, iron, steel, and aluminum were produced."[8] The Soviet Union's leading scientists, including Igor Kurchatov, who would ultimately be critical to the Soviet bomb effort, "decided to drop his research on fission, and his laboratory was disbanded. . . . Most nuclear scientists abandoned their research to work for the war effort."[9] In December 1941, there was a real possibility that many of these laboratories and scientists outside Moscow would fall under Hitler's control; they were saved only by the winter, which froze Germany's advances. The initial fundamental research on fission and the Uranium Commission to discover and mine uranium in the Soviet hinterland were suspended to focus on the primary goal of simply surviving Hitler's onslaught.

While the British and American efforts raced ahead in the sanctuary of New Mexico, attempting to beat a (disjointed) German effort to the bomb, the Soviet Union was simply trying to survive. The next two years, writes Holloway, were "a very difficult time for the Soviet Union. Although the German advance had been stopped on the outskirts of Moscow in December 1941, the country was still in mortal danger" as Stalin's counteroffensives stalled.[10] The Soviet Union was similarly concerned about the Nazi atomic bomb effort but was in little position to do anything materially to match it because there was simply no ability to find and mine uranium as the country was fighting for its life.[11]

It would not be until January 1943, in the middle of the Battle of Stalingrad, that the Soviet Union would nominally make the decision to start a nuclear weapons program.[12] But the effort was minimal, as Holloway notes that "the small project Stalin initiated in 1943 could not lead quickly to a Soviet bomb. . . . when the fortunes of the war had turned [at Stalingrad], it is extremely unlikely that Stalin thought a Soviet bomb could affect the outcome of the war with Germany."[13] Without uranium, or a nuclear pile to produce plutonium, this program was still theoretical and there is little

8. Holloway, *Stalin and the Bomb*, 74.

9. Ibid., 75.

10. Ibid., 85.

11. Ibid., 85–86.

12. Ibid., 89. Also see "Decree No. 2352CC of Ukrainian State Committee of Defence," September 28, 1942, Atomic Project of USSR: Documents and Materials, vol. 1, part 1, document no. 128, p. 269, obtained and translated for NPIHP by Oleksandr Cheban, https://digitalarchive.wilsoncenter.org/document/121637.

13. Holloway, *Stalin and the Bomb*, 90.

evidence that Stalin prioritized it in any way, believing it did not fundamentally alter the correlation of forces or the balance of power. Stalin believed in the power of Soviet conventional might and quantitative superiority and may not have believed that a "bigger" bomb would or could change much. Soviet scientists, led by especially Kurchatov, began studying the intelligence the USSR had obtained on British scientific advances by 1943, which showed that fissile isotope separation and a sustained exothermic reaction (the boom part) were possible. But this was all theoretical for Kurchatov and Soviet scientists, since there was no national effort to produce a bomb or, more importantly perhaps at this time, to obtain uranium[14] or enough pure graphite for the experimental nuclear pile to produce plutonium.[15] Holloway writes that "the Soviet leadership was not treating the uranium problem as a matter of high priority. Kurchatov was especially distressed by the gap between the Soviet project and the Manhattan Project. He was in a better position than anyone else to understand how wide this gap really was."[16]

What was proceeding apace, however, was Soviet penetration of, and espionage on, the Manhattan Project. Spies such as Klaus Fuchs were keeping their Soviet handlers apprised of the advances and challenges in the American program—particularly the gun-type uranium design and the need to focus on implosion for the plutonium pathway due to the risk of spontaneous fizzles.[17] Worried at the pace of the American effort in May 1945, months before Hiroshima and Nagasaki, Holloway reports that Soviet scientists "proposed that extraordinary measures be taken and that the nuclear project be given 'the most favorable and advantageous conditions' in order to speed up the research and development work."[18] Even at this point, however, Stalin and members of his inner circle such as Beria and Molotov "showed no urgency about expanding the Soviet effort" because Stalin viewed Germany as the primary threat. He did not believe the atom bomb would materially affect international politics and viewed the intelligence that the Soviet Union was

14. "Letter, Igor V. Kurchatov, Director of the Soviet Nuclear Program, to Lavrenti Beria," September 29, 1944, History and Public Policy Program Digital Archive, I. N. Golovin, "Kurchatov—uchenyi, gosudarstvennyi deiatel', chelovek" ["Kurchatov—Scholar, Government official, Man"], in Materialy iubeleinoi sessii uchenogo soveta tsentra 12 ianvaria 1993 g. [Materials of the Jubilee Session of the Academic Council of the Center, 12 January 1993] (Moscow: Russian Scientific Center "Kurchatov Institute," 1993), 24–25, http://digitalarchive.wilsoncenter.org/document/115921.

15. Holloway, *Stalin and the Bomb*, 100.

16. Ibid., 103.

17. Ibid., 107–8.

18. Ibid., 115.

collecting on the Manhattan Project with suspicion, paranoid that it could be a disinformation campaign to distract and divert the Soviet Union down a cul-de-sac.[19] Holloway writes that "neither Stalin, Beria, nor Molotov understood the role that the atomic bomb would soon play in international relations" and thus had not—even if they perceived an emerging acute threat from the United States—formed the necessary domestic consensus to sprint for a bomb.[20]

This would all change in July and August 1945. On July 24, roughly a week after the Trinity test in the New Mexico desert, President Truman and his advisors decided to tell their wartime ally, Stalin, that it had the bomb but wanted to "give as little as possible away,"[21] with Secretary of State Byrnes writing that Truman believed "it would be regrettable if the Soviet Union entered the [Pacific] War, and. . . . he was afraid that if Stalin were made fully aware of the power of the new weapon, he might order the Soviet Army to plunge forward [into the Far East] at once."[22] Truman therefore nonchalantly informed Stalin that the United States "had a new weapon of unusual destructive force."[23] What Stalin said in reply is a matter of dispute, with Truman reporting that he said "he was glad to hear it and hoped we would make 'good use of it against the Japanese,'"[24] while British foreign secretary Anthony Eden reports that Stalin just nodded his head and said "thank you."[25] Stalin did not act surprised because he was not—the Soviets had known about Trinity and the fact that the Manhattan Project had reached the finish line. But it is unclear that the full import of the atomic bomb had been impressed upon Stalin at Potsdam. Holloway concludes that "the impact of the American bomb on Soviet policy did not become apparent until after Hiroshima."[26]

On August 6, 1945, the United States used the uranium bomb, Little Boy, on Hiroshima. A day later, Stalin expedited Soviet entry into the Far East and ordered the Red Army to attack the Japanese in Manchuria.[27] In an August 8 meeting with U.S. ambassador Averell Harriman and George Kennan in

19. Ibid.

20. Ibid.

21. See Rhodes, *The Making of the Atomic Bomb*, 690.

22. Byrnes quoted in ibid.

23. Truman quoted in Holloway, *Stalin and the Bomb*, 116–17.

24. Harry S. Truman, *Memoirs by Harry Truman, Volume 1: Year of Decisions* (New York: Doubleday, 1955), 416.

25. Eden quoted in Holloway, *Stalin and the Bomb*, 117.

26. Ibid., 118.

27. Ibid., 127–28.

Moscow, Holloway writes that Stalin implied "we have entered the war, in spite of your attempt to end it before we did so," to which Harriman implied "the atomic bomb will end the war; we have it, and it was very expensive to build; it will have a great impact on postwar international relations," and Stalin essentially retorted that "Japan was about to surrender anyway, and the secret of the atomic bomb might be hard to keep."[28] The next day, the United States dropped Fat Man, the plutonium bomb, on Nagasaki.

Stalin now fully understood the importance of the bomb and that an American monopoly on nuclear weapons would upset the balance of power against the Soviet Union for two reasons. First, he finally realized its military value, with the British ambassador to the USSR colorfully saying "the three hundred [Soviet] divisions were shorn of much of their value."[29] Second, the longer an American nuclear monopoly persisted, the greater the risk to the Soviet Union and that, according to Campbell Craig and Sergey Radchenko, "in a few years, the United States would have more—and more powerful—bombs, and would be more willing to go to war and use them against the USSR."[30] Once Stalin understood the security threat of conceding a nuclear monopoly to the United States, the domestic consensus—essentially Stalin's sole privilege—congealed quickly, as he unilaterally ordered the Soviet Union to sprint for nuclear weapons with all key constituencies agreeing without hesitation, especially the scientists and Beria, the reviled spymaster who would manage the program. Holloway writes that "there is no evidence of any discussion in the political leadership—at this time or later—about the wisdom of this decision. It was assumed that if the United States had the atomic bomb, the Soviet Union needed to have it too."[31] Once Stalin internalized the acute security threat of American nuclear weapons, he could and did unilaterally birth the Soviet effort to develop nuclear weapons as quickly as possible. Holloway concludes that "Stalin had not taken the atomic bomb seriously until Hiroshima had shown in the most dramatic way that it could be built. The Soviet Union now mobilized its resources to catch up" and had a system—a planned, state-mobilized industrial economy with considerable scientific and technical capability—that was optimized precisely for scientific-industrial projects such as a nuclear weapons effort.[32]

28. Ibid., 128–29.

29. Quoted in Debs and Monteiro, *Nuclear Politics*, 117.

30. Campbell Craig and Sergey Radchenko, *The Atomic Bomb and the Origins of the Cold War* (New Haven: Yale University Press, 2008), 110.

31. Holloway, *Stalin and the Bomb*, 131.

32. Ibid., 132.

The Soviet sprint began immediately. After Hiroshima, Stalin told Kurchatov and others: "Comrades—a single demand of you. Get us atomic weapons in the shortest possible time. As you know, Hiroshima has shaken the whole world. The balance has been broken. Build the bomb—it will remove the great danger from us!"[33] On August 20, the State Defense Committee ordered "all work on the utilization of the intra-atomic energy of uranium" and stood up the First Chief Directorate to coordinate all the state's efforts to develop nuclear weapons as quickly as possible.[34] Despite the enormous expense of the project amid the Soviet rebuilding effort—much of the nation lay in ruins after the war—Stalin "did not stint the project," imploring Kurchatov to come to him for any requirement: "If a child doesn't cry, the mother doesn't know what he needs. Ask for whatever you like. You won't be refused."[35] Kurchatov and his scientists told Stalin that it would likely take five years to develop a Soviet atomic capability.[36] It took them four.

The first order of business was to find and mine uranium in Soviet territory while efforts to build isotope separation facilities and nuclear reactors progressed simultaneously. Valuable time was likely shaved off thanks to data gathered from espionage on the Manhattan Project that detailed the most efficient pathways to enrich uranium, reprocess plutonium, and design the bomb. This information may have cut one or two years off a de novo effort. Holloway notes that the "Manhattan Project had proved successful, and the Soviet Union possessed a great deal of information about it. Soviet technical choices were strongly influenced by what the Americans had done" notably on uranium enrichment but especially the plutonium bomb design, a blueprint of which had essentially been passed on directly by Klaus Fuchs.[37] There were debates about the wisdom of copying the American approach, or the Soviet understanding thereof, but as Holloway describes, "the Soviet Union wanted the bomb as soon as possible, and was prepared to pay virtually any price to obtain it. It made sense to exploit the intelligence information about the Manhattan Project rather than search for a new Soviet way to build the bomb. In the interest of speed, it also made sense to pursue redundant paths to the bomb, rather than adopt a single plan of attack."[38] The effort was slightly hampered by the Soviet domestic surveillance apparatus,

33. Stalin quoted in Richelson, *Spying on the Bomb*, 64.
34. Holloway, *Stalin and the Bomb*, 129.
35. Stalin quoted in ibid., 131–32.
36. Ibid., 132.
37. Ibid., 137–38.
38. Ibid., 140.

which was suspicious about scientists, but this was a double-edged sword: in addition to enforcing basic patriotism, the surveillance programs motivated scientists to sprint as fast as they could—failing risked the gulags or death—but surveillance certainly did impose immense psychological stress on the scientists. In January 1946, Stalin told Kurchatov "to build the bomb quickly, and not to count the cost,"[39] and the implication was clear: Stalin expected "results from this investment and political loyalty from scientists."[40] This was a determined sprint to the bomb, with Soviet characteristics and a tailwind from intelligence pilfered from the United States.

The program continued at impressive speed, especially given the state of the Soviet nation and American efforts such as trying to corner the global market on uranium to deny the USSR the material basis for the bomb.[41] But General Leslie Groves, leading that U.S. effort, underestimated the Soviet Union's own natural uranium deposits. By 1946, the Soviet Union had begun mining natural uranium across its vast territory, from Ukraine to the Caucasus to the Urals, but also in Eastern Europe, which the Soviet Union now effectively owned. East Germany alone accounted for 45 percent of Soviet-accessible uranium, raising a terrifying counterfactual about the Nazi bomb.[42] Only once the uranium ore was mined, enriched, and fabricated into uranium metal could the reactor project get underway. This was a massive organizational endeavor.[43] The Soviet Union pushed three enrichment methods in a high-cost effort to maximize its prospects for sustainable success: electromagnetic separation, thermal diffusion, and gaseous diffusion. Construction on the nuclear reactor began in parallel, and an experimental reactor went critical in December 1946, laying the groundwork for an actual production reactor to supply plutonium for the Soviet nuclear arsenal. This would only be built and go critical in the summer of 1948. The reprocessing plant to extract plutonium from the reactor's spent fuel was

39. "Notes on the discussion between I. V. Kurchatov, lead scientist for the Soviet nuclear effort, and Stalin," January 25, 1946, History and Public Policy Program Digital Archive, from personal notes of I. V. Kurchatov, Archive of the Russian Scientific Center "Kurchatov Institute," Fond 2, Opis 1/c, Document 16/4, printed in Yuri Smirnov, "Stalin and the Atomic Bomb," *Voprosy istorii estestvoznaniiai tekniki* [Questions on the History of Science and Technology] 2 (1994): 125–30, http://digitalarchive.wilsoncenter.org/document/111533.

40. Holloway, *Stalin and the Bomb*, 148.

41. Houghton, *The Nuclear Spies*, 167–68.

42. Holloway, *Stalin and the Bomb*, 176–77.

43. "Decree of the USSR Council of Ministers, 'Questions of Reactive Weaponry,'" May 13, 1946, History and Public Policy Program Digital Archive, published in Sergeev (1994), 227–33, selected, edited, and annotated by Asif Siddiqi, and translated by Gary Goldberg, http://digitalarchive.wilsoncenter.org/document/121064.

ready by December of that year, putting the Soviet Union months from the bomb—unbeknownst to the United States, whose intelligence on Soviet progress was of very poor quality.[44] The plutonium became available before weapons-grade uranium, setting the stage for the First Lightning test in 1949.

In terms of bomb design, the Soviets shortcut the process by essentially copying the Trinity test design Klaus Fuchs handed over. While plutonium was first being separated in the winter of 1948–49, the bomb design team conducted a series of cold tests to ensure that the design they were copying would work, particularly the geometry and positioning of the explosive lenses.[45] Within months, in June 1949, enough plutonium had been reprocessed and fabricated into two subcritical hemispheres for a full-blown test. The final bomb assembly took place at the test site in Kazakhstan itself, with the plutonium hemispheres, initiator, and lenses being emplaced in position at the site before being raised on the shot tower. On August 29, 1949 only four years after a decision to sprint for the bomb—and while simultaneously working on missiles and aircraft delivery capabilities—the Soviet Union broke the American nuclear monopoly with the First Lightning test. It was an impressive sprint, all the more so given the Soviet Union's postwar economic and human devastation. As Beria, the terrifying spymaster who managed the program, quipped after rewarding the scientists who achieved the success, "those who were to be shot in case of failure were now to become Heroes of Socialist Labor," the highest order of the state.[46] Failure was not an option, and speed was of the utmost urgency.

The Soviet Union did not hide its intention or determination to break the American nuclear monopoly. The United States consistently lacked intelligence on the effort and underestimated how quickly the Soviet Union was moving—partly because it had no idea how much information had been stolen from the Manhattan Project.[47] In July 1948, the director of the CIA, Admiral Roscoe Hillenkoetter, wrote to Truman estimating: "the earliest date by which it is remotely possible that the USSR may have completed its first atomic bomb is mid-1950, but the most probable date is believed to be mid-1953."[48] The CIA stuck with this estimate the following year, on July 1, 1949, erroneously predicting two months before the first Soviet test that such an event was one to four years away. The United States was aware that

44. Holloway, *Stalin and the Bomb*, 186–88; also Houghton, *The Nuclear Spies*, 124–25.

45. Holloway, *Stalin and the Bomb*, 199.

46. Beria paraphrased in ibid., 218.

47. See Richelson, *Spying on the Bomb*, 76–77; also Houghton, *The Nuclear Spies*, 145–48.

48. Quoted in Holloway, *Stalin and the Bomb*, 220.

the Soviet Union was working on the bomb—it is hard to hide, as Holloway puts it, an "all-out project" that was the product of "an enormous undertaking in an economy that had been devastated by the war," and one that Stalin gave the "highest priority" and ordered to be organized on "Russian scope" to not only develop a bomb but to do so "as quickly as possible."[49] Soviet penetration of the Manhattan Project certainly helped, offering guidance on promising directions for enrichment and bomb design, but such information shaved off a year or two at most.[50] It is hard to envision how the Soviet Union would have failed even absent that espionage.

The United States consistently underestimated Soviet progress toward the bomb but, more importantly, there was simply little that could be done to stop it. Although General Groves tried to slow down the Soviet Union by trying to starve it of global uranium supplies, the Soviet Union was able to discover and mine it on its own territory and those of its client or occupied states in Eastern Europe. The vastness of Soviet territory and geographic dispersion of the program further meant the effort was impregnable to American military prevention. As Debs and Monteiro write: "Stalin's openness about the existence of the Soviet nuclear program was possible because a preventive U.S. strike against the Soviet Union [especially in a climate of post–World War II war weariness] entailed tremendous costs, and was therefore highly unlikely."[51] I would upgrade their assessment to: it was virtually impossible. The United States lacked the conventional capability to invade the Soviet Union, had very few nuclear weapons, and lacked the delivery capability to reach the Soviet interior. The Soviet Union could also hold much of Continental Europe at risk conventionally if the United States had attempted any preventive strike. Prevention was a nonstarter. This enabled the Soviet Union to sprint in the open and become the second state—the first "proliferator" following the lead of the United States—to develop nuclear weapons.

TESTING PROLIFERATION STRATEGY THEORY

Proliferation Strategy Theory essentially collapses to the narrow structural realist prediction in the case of sprinters like the Soviet Union. The acuteness of the security threat should generate domestic consensus for weaponization

49. Ibid., 220–21.
50. Ibid., 222.
51. Debs and Monteiro, *Nuclear Politics*, 119.

quickly, and if a state is not vulnerable to economic and military prevention, it should sprint for a bomb. But even in the Soviet case, the nuance provided by Proliferation Strategy Theory proves valuable. Why did Stalin not initiate the sprint for a bomb in 1943 once he had clear intelligence that the Manhattan Project was moving at a rapid pace, and once the Soviet Union had turned the tide on the Nazis? Debs and Monteiro's realist theory has no clear explanation, for example. But Proliferation Strategy Theory highlights the importance of domestic consensus for weaponization. In the 1940s Soviet system, domestic consensus was coterminous with Stalin's own opinion. Before Hiroshima, Stalin simply did not believe that nuclear weapons would fundamentally alter international politics, so domestic consensus did not exist. In terms of the balance of power, Hiroshima—the precipitating event for the USSR's sprint—changed little directly for the Soviet Union. Stalin had intelligence on the Trinity test weeks before but was unmoved by it. However, it was a dramatic use in war, against third-party Japan, that crystallized Stalin's focus on the need to build a nuclear weapons capability as quickly as possible. Only once that "domestic consensus" was achieved did the Soviet Union sprint. Even a sophisticated realist account has a difficult time accounting for why the *Soviet Union*, a superpower led by a hyperrational, if paranoid, realist, delayed pursuit of nuclear weapons for two years. Proliferation Strategy Theory at least identifies the variable responsible for that delay, even if it is for idiosyncratic Stalinesque reasons.

Technological determinism actually fares pretty well in these early sprinters. The Soviet Union managed to develop nuclear weapons about as fast as it technically could, and even received a tailwind from its espionage efforts to shortcut some of the trial-and-error process. And Holloway writes that "the length of time the Soviet Union needed to develop the atomic bomb was determined more by the availability of uranium than by any other factor. As soon as uranium became available in sufficient quantity, Kurchatov was able to build and start up the experimental reactor."[52] There is no doubt that the Soviet Union essentially maxed out efficiency to the bomb, given the state of the nation after World War II. One value of Proliferation Strategy Theory versus technological determinism here is explaining why Stalin did not order a concerted effort to discover and mine uranium prior to 1945. His scientists implored him in 1943 to do so, knowing it would be the rate-limiting step, but it was just not accorded high priority given the state of the war. That is obviously reasonable, but it is possible that if Stalin had understood the

52. Holloway, *Stalin and the Bomb*, 223.

impact of nuclear weapons on international politics that, after Stalingrad when the Soviet Union had some breathing room, it could have found uranium earlier. Nevertheless, after 1945, the Soviet nuclear program was well organized and efficient, as Hymans's theory would predict, and was only limited by uranium availability and then plutonium production.

At this time, there was little international concern about the spread of the atomic bomb, and very little effort was made to stop the Soviet Union diplomatically or normatively, as efforts such as the Baruch Plan were stillborn. Stalin would not have been stopped in any case. There was some American arrogance about how long it might take the Soviets to build the bomb, with estimates reaching into the mid-1950s, out of what Truman believed was backwardness. Vince Houghton writes that Truman was incredibly orientalist about the Soviet Union: "He was convinced that the Soviets, or 'those Asiatics,' as he called them, would never match the scientific accomplishments of the United States and build their own atomic bomb."[53] But he did little to try to stop them militarily, diplomatically, or normatively.

In sum, even the most quintessential sprinter—Stalin's Soviet Union—has a nuclear proliferation process that is better captured by Proliferation Strategy Theory than by even sophisticated realist or technological determinist accounts of the program. The key advantage of Proliferation Strategy Theory is a theory-native explanation for why Stalin waited until 1945 to initiate the sprint, even though his scientists implored him in 1943 to do so when the Soviet Union had the ability and breathing room from Hitler to do so. It took Hiroshima—an event that did little to change the threat to the Soviet Union or the overall balance of power given common knowledge of the existence of the bomb—for Stalin to grasp the impact of nuclear weapons. It was only then that he decided that he must have it, and as quickly as possible. It was only once he made that decision that the Soviet Union sprinted to the bomb.

France: The "Abandoned" Ally

Insurance Hedging: 1945–54
Sprinting: 1954–60

France, the fourth state to possess nuclear weapons, is a fascinating case of proliferation strategies. French scientists had been involved with the early research on nuclear fission, but the German occupation suspended France's exploration of nuclear technology during World War II while the United

53. Houghton, *Nuclear Spies*, 162.

States, the Soviet Union, and Britain continued largely apace during and especially after the war. France was protected by the emergence of the European security architecture in the early Cold War that extended American nuclear deterrence to Western Europe. This protection should have—according to Proliferation Strategy Theory—kept France firmly as an insurance hedger like West Germany, not an active nuclear weapons proliferator. While Britain's development of nuclear weapons largely rode the momentum of participating in the Manhattan Project, France was much further from the bomb when the contours of NATO and a formal extended deterrence guarantee from Washington emerged. As Scheinman writes, "France, then appears to be in a special category as a [World War II] military nuclear power, for despite an incipient prewar atomic program and the creation of an atomic energy agency in early 1945, the question of nuclear weapons was not given serious consideration for nearly a decade to come," and by then France had the option to remain under America's extended nuclear deterrence umbrella.[54] According to Proliferation Strategy Theory, France should have remained an insurance hedger—using the threat of breakout to elicit greater reassurances and guarantees from the United States. Yet France, as France usually does, defies international relations theorizing. It elected to sprint to a nuclear weapons capability beginning in 1954, culminating in a nuclear test in the Algerian desert on February 13, 1960.

Why does Proliferation Strategy Theory mispredict France's nuclear proliferation trajectory? Why was Paris not content with indefinite insurance hedging, or simply developing a capacity for a nuclear weapons program but refraining from active weaponization in favor of reliance on America's forward-deployed and strategic nuclear weapons? A series of foreign policy crises through the 1950s—perceived American abandonment of France at Dien Bien Phu in 1954 and the Suez Crisis in 1956—convinced Paris that the United States would never wage a war, let alone a nuclear war, on France's behalf. Especially once the Soviet Union developed the ability to hold the United States homeland at risk with intercontinental ballistic missiles, de Gaulle would "himself [ask] whether we would be ready to trade New York for Paris."[55] Foreseeing this problem, France concluded that relying on American security guarantees risked French security and that, in light of the failure of its treaty partner to come to its aid in Indochina and the Suez,

54. Scheinman, *Atomic Energy Policy in France under the Fourth Republic*, xi–xii.

55. Memorandum of Conversation, President John F. Kennedy and General Charles de Gaulle, *FRUS*, Paris, May 31, 1961, https://history.state.gov/historicaldocuments/frus1961-63v14/d30.

its best option was to develop an independent nuclear deterrent. This is in contrast to West Germany, which concluded—albeit with extensive nuclear-sharing procedures similar to those that Eisenhower was in fact willing to offer France—that insurance hedging could meet its even more acute security needs, partly because West German nuclearization might spark a Soviet attack in ways that French nuclearization did not.[56]

Once Paris made the decision to develop an independent nuclear weapons capability in 1954, a decision then reinforced after Suez, France openly sprinted for nuclear weapons. In 1958, de Gaulle penned a memo to President Eisenhower essentially declaring his intent to fully develop a nuclear deterrent independent of the U.S. arsenal because France no longer considered "that NATO in its present form meets the conditions of security of the free world and notably its own."[57] It made little attempt to hide it from either the United States or the Soviet Union, even though neither superpower was thrilled about the prospect. Washington wanted to retain the sole capability among its allies to initiate and escalate a nuclear war in Europe, worried that a nuclear France might start a war that chain-ganged the United States into a nuclear exchange with the USSR. Moscow worried that French nuclearization complicated the European nuclear landscape and its nuclear planning but ultimately believed that it did not fundamentally alter the balance of power. The United States was not happy about one of its allies getting out of the nuclear barn, but Richelson notes that its reaction "was one of resignation and regret,"[58] which seems to have largely mirrored Moscow's reaction as well with the added bonus that Khrushchev "guessed rightly when he told the French '[y]our atomic force . . . is meant to annoy the Americans'" by complicating NATO's nuclear management.[59]

Proliferation Strategy Theory correctly predicts French insurance hedging until 1954 but has a more difficult time accounting for France's decision to sprint after perceived American abandonment at Dien Bien Phu triggered domestic consensus for weaponization to congeal. The consensus was formed on the belief that a formal extended nuclear guarantee—and even nuclear forces stationed on French territory—was fundamentally insufficient to meet French security needs.

56. See Trachtenberg, *A Constructed Peace*, 111.

57. President de Gaulle to President Eisenhower, *FRUS*, 1958–1960, Western Europe, vol. VII, part 2, September 17, 1958, https://history.state.gov/historicaldocuments/frus1958-60v07p2/d45.

58. Richelson, *Spying on the Bomb*, 201.

59. Beatrice Heuser, *Nuclear Mentalities? Strategies and Beliefs in Britain, France, and the FRG* (London: Palgrave Macmillan, 1998), 119–20.

FRENCH INSURANCE HEDGING

Frédéric Joliot-Curie was one of the scientists involved in discovering atomic fission and the basics of sustained nuclear chain reactions that were fundamental to the development of nuclear weapons in the mid- and late 1930s. In 1939 and 1940, Joliot-Curie had secured natural uranium and heavy water to undertake research on atomic fission. However, the German invasion and occupation of France in May 1940 suspended French exploration of the atomic bomb. Joliot-Curie fled to Britain along with much of France's heavy water, while the uranium oxide made its way to a Moroccan mine.[60] Until the end of the war, France had little involvement with nuclear weapons or the Manhattan Project. As the French provisional government began to rebuild after the war, Charles de Gaulle established the Commissariat à l'Énergie Atomique (CEA) in October 1945 to explore atomic energy with a nuclear reactor. Its initial aim was to develop a 100,000-kilowatt reactor that, according to Richelson, "could produce 5 percent of the electricity France had consumed in 1938."[61] Much of the uranium exploration took place in France's African colonies. The basis for France's atomic energy program—and for nuclear weapons—was laid.

Although the effort was entirely civilian in this period, the type and extent of nuclear research nonetheless had obvious military potential. There was, however, no decision to pursue nuclear weapons. At this point, de Gaulle "neither ruled in nor ruled out a French bomb drive during his first stint in power," according to Hymans.[62] Instead, he simply stated that "we have time" to decide this question.[63] When de Gaulle resigned in 1946 and Joliot-Curie managed the CEA, it had "purely peaceful" intentions.[64] Joliot-Curie, the CEA's first commissioner, had "become increasingly hostile to the notion of France developing atomic weapons" itself, notes Richelson, largely because he was an actual communist who feared that France might use them against the Soviet Union.[65] The French military similarly had little interest in nuclear weapons at this point, believing that they would cannibalize its conventional missions and that nuclear weapons were a political instrument solely for the superpower competition.[66]

60. Richelson, *Spying on the Bomb*, 196.
61. Ibid., 197.
62. Hymans, *Psychology of Nuclear Proliferation*, 87.
63. De Gaulle quoted in ibid.
64. Alexandre Parodi, French ambassador to the United Nations in 1946, quoted in ibid., 88.
65. Richelson, *Spying on the Bomb*, 198.
66. Hymans, *Psychology of Nuclear Proliferation*, 89.

At the dawn of NATO in 1949, France had still refrained from making a decision to develop its own nuclear weapons, relying instead on American atomic power. But the German question, specifically the issue of German rearmament, made the weapons debate salient. It is easy to forget that in this period, although France viewed the Soviet Union as a potential security threat, its more acute threat was still perceived to be a rearmed Germany—after all, it was not the Red Army that twice invaded France and made the Champs-Élysées its marching ground.[67] French acquiescence to NATO and American forward presence in 1949 was, to paraphrase Lord Ismay's famous quip, as much about "keeping Germany down" as it was about "keeping Russia out," even if that meant allowing the Americans in and placing France under a broader European security architecture and American extended nuclear deterrence.

Trachtenberg argues that France went along with the American-led security architecture and discussions of a broader European Defense Community (EDC) (later rejected by France) in the early 1950s after receiving "assurances about maintaining an American military presence in Europe. But the other side of this coin was a blunt warning to France that a collapse of the EDC could lead to an American withdrawal from the continent. The French were also told that if the EDC failed, the United States, together with Britain, would simply rearm Germany by themselves."[68] This left France with little choice but to accept American-led NATO arrangements, eventual West German accession into NATO, and American extended deterrence. The price of America's commitment to France—to keep Germany weak and non-nuclear with a forward American presence there—was that France had to nominally commit to Article 107 of the EDC treaty, which limited the use of nuclear technology to peaceful purposes.[69] Although it maintained the basis of a nuclear weapons program via its civilian energy capability—one that could be broken out if Paris required greater reassurance from the United States—Hymans writes that "the French had signed away the right to sovereign nuclear weapons in exchange for the certainty that Germany could never have them either."[70]

This was a variant of insurance hedging, to be sure. France agreed to keep its nuclear weapons program in an icebox for American-led European protection and extended deterrence. Most important to France was having American forces physically in Germany to limit German rearmament

67. Trachtenberg, *A Constructed Peace*, chaps. 3 and 4.

68. Ibid., 122.

69. Scheinman, *Atomic Energy Policy in France under the Fourth Republic*, 103.

70. Hymans, *Psychology of Nuclear Proliferation*, 91.

and American-controlled nuclear weapons stationed there to prevent West German nuclear weapons pursuit. In order to extract greater reassurance, France could threaten to nuclearize and "annoy" Washington. Paris did not relinquish the technological basis for a nuclear weapons program by any means—France approved a five-year civilian nuclear energy plan in 1952 that retained military potential, should France ever require it, at the same time that it signed the EDC treaty[71]—but it tied its own hands militarily in order to tie Germany's hands as well. This is what Proliferation Strategy Theory would predict for France. So far so good.

FRENCH FEARS AND A SPRINT TO NUCLEAR WEAPONS

By 1954, France became uneasy with the European security architecture and outsourcing its security, particularly its nuclear security, to the United States. Three things came to a head around 1954, leading France to question whether *any* American reassurance including stationing nuclear weapons on French territory could meet French security needs: perceived abandonment at Dien Bien Phu, concerns about the credibility of Eisenhower's massive retaliation nuclear strategy, and growing fears of German rearmament. Insurance hedging is predicated on the assumption that a formal alliance provides a level of reassurance that will meet a client state's security needs. If a client state decides that depending on its patron for extended nuclear deterrence can never meet its security needs, then it is, for all intents and purposes, making strategic decisions as if it faces a security threat alone. This is precisely what France did—the only insurance hedger thus far to make this calculation.

What were the series of events that led France to reconsider its insurance hedging strategy and opt to sprint for nuclear weapons? The first event was the perception that, as France's position in its colonial periphery collapsed, the United States abandoned France at Dien Bien Phu. In the spring of 1954, a desperate France sent a delegation to Washington led by Foreign Minister Georges Bidault and General Paul Ély to request American military assistance and even the use of nuclear weapons if required.[72] President Eisenhower had supported the French war, even materially, on the belief that western forces could not afford further losses to communism in Asia.

71. Scheinman, *Atomic Energy Policy in France under the Fourth Republic*, 86.

72. George C. Herring and Richard H. Immerman, "Eisenhower, Dulles, and Dienbienphu: 'The Day We Didn't Go to War' Revisited," *Journal of American History* 71, no. 2 (September 1984): 346–47.

The French complained that American assistance was simply Washington's way to "control" the French strategy.[73] But when faced with this final siege at Dien Bien Phu, Eisenhower essentially cut American losses and demurred from assisting the French, deciding against using nuclear weapons in French defense of Indochina. The British supported Eisenhower's decision, raising concerns that American nuclear use might expose Britain to Soviet nuclear retaliation against U.S. forces stationed in the United Kingdom.[74] Shortly thereafter, Dien Bien Phu fell.

In a case where the French perceived a vital national security interest, it found itself at the mercy of Washington, begging it to come to its aid and provide nuclear assistance. Without its own nuclear forces, Paris could not entirely decide for itself what constituted a circumstance when nuclear weapons might be employed to protect French security interests. Avery Goldstein writes that this experience taught France that its "two most important allies had demonstrated that there were limits to the circumstances in which they would provide support."[75] And it raised the specter of a danger to which France had succumbed twice earlier in the century: divergence in allied perceptions of vital national interests can leave France abandoned and vulnerable. This time it was Dien Bien Phu, but next time it could be Paris.

This concern was amplified by growing doubts about the credibility of Eisenhower's massive retaliation nuclear strategy, which nominally threatened massive American nuclear retaliation for any attempted conventional salami slice or nuclear use against its European allies.[76] For Eisenhower, the idea to "blow the hell out of them in a hurry" was a mechanism to reduce the American conventional footprint in Europe and Asia and offset it with nuclear weapons. The problem, of course, lay in making such a threat credible in defense of allies when the stakes—or salami slices—did not justify such a massive nuclear use, and when the U.S. homeland was held at risk by Soviet nuclear forces, as it soon would be. On the heels of Dien Bien Phu, it was reasonable for France to wonder whether the United States would decide that fighting a nuclear war to defend Bonn or Paris was unappealing, especially if it risked losing Boston or Pittsburgh in the process. Outsourcing

73. Ibid., 347.

74. Avery Goldstein, *Deterrence and Security in the 21st Century: China, Britain, France, and the Enduring Legacy of the Nuclear Revolution* (Stanford: Stanford University Press, 2000), 189.

75. Ibid.

76. See Scott D. Sagan, *Moving Targets: Nuclear Strategy and National Security* (Princeton: Princeton University Press, 1989), 23. Also see Francis J. Gavin, *Nuclear Weapons and American Grand Strategy* (Washington, DC: Brookings Institution Press, 2020), chap. 5.

nuclear deterrence to a superpower patron means that that patron decides when to use nuclear weapons, and the client sacrifices the ability to independently decide what is in their national security interest. Put bluntly, France was concerned that the United States would sooner sacrifice Continental Europe to the Soviet Union than risk destruction of its homeland—a concern that little gray island Britain did not face as acutely due to the "stopping power of water."[77]

The third triggering event for an independent French nuclear weapons program was the rehabilitation of West Germany. A combination of potential German rearmament, which was resurrected after the EDC collapsed in France's parliament—which led to West German accession to NATO—and the prospect of France being subordinate to Britain and the United States in the NATO military, and nuclear, architecture and "reduced to the rank of Germany" led French leaders to question the value of U.S. extended deterrence.[78] Already, France had accepted second-tier status within the western nuclear hierarchy, and American refusal to assist France in nuclear technology, according to Goldstein, "could not but help contribute to French doubts about the dependability of security based on a deterrent to be provided by this same ally."[79] This "freezing out of France" was amplified when French prime minister Mendès France was pressured by the Western allies at an October 1954 London Conference to forswear the right to build nuclear weapons, as Chancellor Adenauer had done.[80] This was something that France could not continue to do.

After French experiences at Dien Bien Phu (to which Mendès France actually owed his elevation to prime minister), Mendès France had had enough. Doubts about America's willingness to use nuclear weapons when France deemed it necessary were growing, and France was increasingly wary of the codified inequity of the NATO nuclear structure—which Mendès France was being pressured to formalize—while the prospect of German rearmament continued to loom. He would note that although the scientists might have opposed nuclear weapons, the military increasingly supported it, and he was, according to Hymans, "warming up to the idea."[81] Only three days after the London Conference, on October 26, 1954, Mendès France officially put France off to the races for an independent nuclear weapons

77. Mearsheimer, *The Tragedy of Great Power Politics*, 114.

78. Pierre Mendès France quoted in Hymans, *Psychology of Nuclear Proliferation*, 102.

79. Goldstein, *Deterrence and Security in the 21st Century*, 192–93.

80. See Hymans, *Psychology of Nuclear Proliferation*, 98–102.

81. Ibid., 102.

capability. There is no monocausal explanation for this decision, but it seems like a confluence of security and status events led France to abandon insurance hedging and openly sprint for nuclear weapons. On that date, Mendès France created the Commission Supérieure des Applications Militaires de l'Énergie Atomique, which, writes Hymans, "formally requested a precise budget projection for a French bomb without delay. This represented a crucial *green light* for formal contacts between the military and the CEA."[82] A month later, after a trip to the United States, Mendès France reportedly remarked to CEA head Francis Perrin that he felt he was "in a meeting of gangsters. Everyone is putting his gun on the table, if you have no gun you are nobody."[83] The "gun" in question was nuclear weapons, and this experience crystallized Mendès France's decision to initiate a quiet "program to build the bomb."[84]

It would not remain quiet for long. The day after Christmas, 1954, forty top officials were presented with a classified document by Mendès France with the opening statement: "The making of atomic bombs is decided."[85] Incidentally, though it did not seem to matter, the projected cost was 80 billion francs for the first nuclear weapon, a price all were willing to bear (the second five-year plan in 1957 would allocate 200 billion francs to CEA alone).[86] After hearing opposing arguments at this meeting, Mendès France essentially announced his order to his government to pursue an independent French nuclear weapons capability. The meeting led to the creation of a division with the vague name of the "Office of General Studies" (*bureau d'études générales*) within the CEA, funded through the defense budget and with a mandate to develop a nuclear weapon. Although the French government would make no public announcement of this decision to its citizens,[87] Mendès France himself remarked that he made arrangements to "make the Russians and Americans aware" of the decision.[88] There was little effort to hide the program from external actors. Hymans concludes that this meeting,

82. Ibid., emphasis added.

83. André Finkelstein, interview by Avner Cohen, June 17, 1993, *History and Public Policy Program Digital Archive*, Wilson Center, https://digitalarchive.wilsoncenter.org/document/113997.

84. Hymans, *Psychology of Nuclear Proliferation*, 104.

85. Ibid., 105.

86. Ibid.

87. Bruno Tertrais, "'Destruction Assurée': The Origins and Development of French Nuclear Strategy, 1945–1981," in *Getting MAD: Nuclear Mutual Assured Destruction, Its Origins and Practice*, ed. Henry Sokolski (Carlisle, PA: U.S. Army War College, 2004), 54.

88. Pierre Péan, *Les Deux Bombes, ou, Comment la guerre du Golfe a commencé le 18 novembre 1975* (Paris: Fayard, 1982), chap. 4.

and Mendès France's decision, "served as the crucial catalyst for the march to the French bomb."[89] France was off to the nuclear races.

There was initial concern about socialist opposition to the bomb, so domestic consensus was not fully built yet, but there would be little domestic resistance and the key decision makers like Mendès France and his successors had formed an internal consensus for the bomb that would only be reinforced in the coming years. Hymans argues that Mendès France's decision created "substantial, and as it turned out, unstoppable momentum toward a French nuclear arsenal on at least three levels: intra-bureaucratic (within the CEA), inter-bureaucratic (notably between the CEA and the military), and political."[90] Because Mendès France's position on the bomb itself evolved, he had credibility with left-leaning scientists such as Perrin, who initially opposed the bomb but eventually came around. Mendès France ensured that his decision would persist among the revolving door of French prime ministers, with each being "informed of the verbal accord given by his predecessor, for him to confirm verbally."[91] Regional and global security events led Mendès France to overcome whatever hesitations he had, and domestic consensus began to coalesce once he came around and ordered the nuclear program militarized. Nevertheless, the revolving door of coalition parliamentary governments and prime ministers in this phase retarded the development of a stable domestic consensus and leadership for an unimpeded sprint for the bomb—it was more of a 110-meter hurdle, with a new election placed every 10 meters.

The French decision to sprint for the bomb was reinforced by the watershed Suez Crisis in 1956. Only earlier that year, in January, did the Marcoule plutonium production reactor reach full power. Then, on July 26, Egyptian president Gamal Abdel Nasser nationalized the Suez Canal, and the British and French, along with Israel, developed plans to physically recapture the strategically vital artery, unbeknownst to their American superpower ally. When the operation was executed on October 29, the United States went ballistic, orchestrating an attack on the British pound and berating its two NATO allies for behaving like colonial powers.[92] Goldstein writes that "the Suez Crisis was a shocking experience for Britain and France that stirred doubts about the wisdom of overdependence on their alliance with

89. Hymans, *Psychology of Nuclear Proliferation*, 107.

90. Ibid., 109.

91. Albert Buchalet, "Les Premieres Etapes (1955–60)," quoted in ibid., 110.

92. Goldstein, *Deterrence and Security in the 21st Century*, 163.

the United States."[93] The fundamental problem was that what Britain and France deemed to be their vital security interests diverged from what the United States determined to be in its vital national security interest. Yet the former were at the mercy of the latter with respect to their security, particularly France, which did not yet have an independent nuclear capability.

Interestingly, the Suez Crisis generated different conclusions on nuclear weapons for Britain and France. For Britain, Suez reinforced the notion that the junior ally should never diverge from the senior partner again, and Britain chose to essentially subjugate its nuclear force and strategy to the United States only two years later. But for France, Suez once again underlined the lesson that America would only back France if *American* interests were at stake, not French interests alone. The humiliation and abandonment over Suez led Prime Minister Guy Mollet to double down on French nuclear weapons, with Raymond Aron noting that the Suez Crisis did "a great deal to convince our leaders that nuclear armament was indispensable to France."[94] De Gaulle would later tell his American counterparts that Suez showed him that "American nuclear power does not necessarily and immediately meet all the eventualities concerning France and Europe" and that thus France must "equip herself with an atomic force of her own."[95] Whatever lingering doubts anyone in the French political system may have had about an independent nuclear deterrent were laid to rest by American treatment of France during the Suez Crisis.[96] The French government "established a definite military [nuclear] program for the period 1957–1961" after the crisis.[97] The nuclear program was thereafter open, fully funded, virtually unquestioned, and preparing to be weaponized—with Mollet ordering studies and preparations for a test at the earliest possible date.[98] Once the initial studies were complete, on April 11, 1958, Prime Minister Félix Gaillard, who held the post for less than half a year, ordered a nuclear test for the first quarter of 1960, a decision de Gaulle "confirmed" when he took power in July 1958 according to Richelson.[99]

93. Ibid., 164–65.

94. Quoted in Debs and Monteiro, *Nuclear Politics*, 425.

95. Quoted in Wilfred L. Kohl, *French Nuclear Diplomacy* (Princeton: Princeton University Press, 1971), 234.

96. See Hymans, *Psychology of Nuclear Proliferation*, 112–13.

97. Kohl, *French Nuclear Diplomacy*, 26.

98. Debs and Monteiro, *Nuclear Politics*, 427. Also see Richelson, *Spying on the Bomb*, 199. It was only a month later, on November 30, that Mollet ordered the CEA to conduct studies for a test.

99. Richelson, *Spying on the Bomb*, 200.

It is important to note the domestic political challenges of a concerted sprint under the Fourth Republic, which occurred across a series of unstable coalition governments. Kohl writes: "Constantly changing cabinet coalitions rendered ministers impotent and ineffective and the bureaucracy became the principal source of policymaking. However, by the time of the Gaillard decision in 1958 a general parliamentary consensus had developed in support of [developing nuclear weapons] by the government."[100] The sprint "was the result of a series of incremental decisions . . . beginning in 1954 within the French bureaucracy during a period of frequently changing governments and cabinet ministers . . . [the 1958 official order] only ratified what was already *de facto* policy."[101] In addition to challenges associated with coalition governments, the military professed consistent opposition to an independent nuclear capability due to budgetary concerns under the Fourth Republic. Albert Buchalet, the colonel tasked with leading the Office of General Studies, remarked that "most of the military authorities were against the bomb . . . [because] the budget of the army was limited, and everyone saw the bomb as a competitor to their tanks, their boats, and their planes."[102] Indeed, due to his involvement with the nuclear program, when Buchalet rejoined the army after leaving the CEA in 1960, he was so unpopular that he resigned and joined the private sector.[103] Similarly, Bruno Tertrais observes that "for most of the French high command, an independent nuclear program meant diverting resources [and] reducing conventional budgets and forces."[104] Domestic consensus—which is required for the decision tree to predict a sprinting rather than hard hedging strategy—existed insofar as there was a sufficient core of pro-bomb individuals to sustain the program until 1958. Domestic consensus was clearly achieved by the dawn of the Fifth Republic in 1958, however, when General de Gaulle returned to power, erecting a centralized quasi-presidential system initially under his powerful stewardship, and directed a sprint that "accelerated from the autumn of 1958 to the end of 1960" through sheer force of personality and the stability of the government.[105]

When de Gaulle took the helm of the Fifth Republic, he was crystal clear to the United States that French pursuit of an independent nuclear arsenal

100. Kohl, *French Nuclear Diplomacy*, 29.

101. Ibid., 19.

102. Quoted in Péan, *Les Deux Bombes*, chap. 4.

103. Cohen interview, June 17, 1993.

104. Tertrais, "'Destruction Assurée,'" 62–63.

105. Kohl, *French Nuclear Diplomacy*, 82.

was a foregone conclusion, not a ruse to elicit nuclear-sharing agreements or greater reassurance. A memorandum from Assistant Secretary of State for European Affairs Charles Elbrick to Secretary of State John Foster Dulles in June 1958 explicitly noted: "The primary difficulty you should expect to encounter in your talks centers on de Gaulle's determination to have France become the fourth nuclear power. . . . What will be particularly difficult to explain is why we will not provide France with the same nuclear information we intend to supply the British once the French explode a bomb, which may not be far off."[106] This memo was revealing on several levels. It accepted that a French nuclear bomb was essentially inevitable by this point but also inadvertently pointed to the reason that de Gaulle was determined to sprint for one: the United States treated France as a second-tier ally, and this was unacceptable to Paris.

The Eisenhower administration would continue to attempt to offer a prized incentive to stave off a French bomb: nuclear sharing with American nuclear forces physically stationed on French soil under the NATO stockpile plan. Secretary of State Dulles would tell de Gaulle personally that "he was absolutely confident that we would be willing to use our strategic power rather than to see the world conquered bit by bit" and then proposed that the United States "would be prepared to see French forces fully trained in the use of such weapons and French equipment adapted to deliver them."[107] The "purpose was to ensure that a NATO government, such as the French Government, would never have any doubts as to the use of such weapons should French forces be subject to a major attack in Europe."[108] De Gaulle was decidedly doubtful and unmoved, and replied that "the delicate question . . . was that of the disposition of these weapons. If the United States were to make weapons available to be used by the United States and French forces on the condition that the order for their use had to be given by the United States

106. Memorandum from Assistant Secretary of State Charles Elbrick to Secretary of State John Foster Dulles, *FRUS*, 1958–1960, Western Europe, vol. VII, part 2, June 26, 1958, https://history.state.gov/historicaldocuments/frus1958-60v07p2/d27.

107. Memorandum of Conversation, "The Secretary's Talks with General De Gaulle in Paris, July 5, 1958," *FRUS*, 1958–1960, Western Europe, vol. VII, part 2, July 5, 1958, https://history.state.gov/historicaldocuments/frus1958-60v07p2/d34. Also see "Telegram from Secretary of State Dulles to the Department of State," *FRUS*, 1958–1960, Western Europe, vol. VII, part 2, July 5, 1958, https://history.state.gov/historicaldocuments/frus1958-60v07p2/d37.

108. Memorandum of Conversation, "The Secretary's Talks with General De Gaulle," *FRUS*, 1958–1960, Western Europe, vol. VII, part 2, July 9, 1958, https://history.state.gov/historicaldocuments/frus1958-60v07p2/d39.

or by SACEUR, this proposition had little interest."[109] He told Eisenhower explicitly, "[France] obviously cannot entirely trust her life or death to any other state whatsoever, even the most friendly . . . she cannot consent to such [nuclear] projectiles being stored on her territory and used from there unless she herself has complete and permanent control over them."[110] He would later declare that "he would regard even the most flexible and tenuous conditions [on French use] as unacceptable if they operated to limit in any way France's right to command, use and dispose of its nuclear forces, at will and purely for national reasons."[111] Simply put, de Gaulle would state: "The defense of France must be in French hands . . . it is indispensable that it be a French defense and that France defends herself by herself, for herself and in her own manner."[112]

Short of outright sovereign nuclear weapons transfer to France, nuclear sharing was the most extensive form of reassurance a nuclear patron can offer an ally—an offer other insurance hedgers such as West Germany, and to a lesser extent South Korea, seized upon. However, France insisted that this would be insufficient to meet its security needs and national interest because even if American nuclear weapons could be transferred onto French platforms, it was unacceptable if the decision about whether and when to use them rested not exclusively with Paris but with Washington. De Gaulle demanded an independent ability to use nuclear weapons and was "insistent on the necessity for France to have its own atomic weapons" because he felt that, "with the development of intercontinental missiles," the United States would increasingly "be reluctant to use its nuclear weapons against the Soviet Union to defend European countries."[113] The Eisenhower administration concluded that "[de Gaulle] wants, however, more than cooperation from us; his aim is tripartite control of the nuclear deterrent and a veto power on its use. The US

109. Memorandum of Conversation, "The Secretary's Talks with General De Gaulle in Paris, July 5, 1958."

110. President De Gaulle to President Eisenhower, *FRUS*, 1958–1960, Western Europe, vol. VII, part 2, May 25, 1959, https://history.state.gov/historicaldocuments/frus1958-60v07p2/d117.

111. President De Gaulle to President Johnson, August 5, 1963, quoted in "Memorandum from Under Secretary of State George W. Ball to President Kennedy, 'A Further Nuclear Offer to General De Gaulle,'" National Archives, Record Group 49, Records of Undersecretary of State George Ball, box 21, France, August 8, 1963, pp. 3–4.

112. De Gaulle quoted in Wolf Mendl, *Deterrence and Persuasion: French Nuclear Armament in the Context of National Policy, 1945–1969* (London: Faber and Faber, 1970), 61.

113. Memorandum of Conversation, "United States Delegation to the Meeting of Foreign Ministers, Palais des Nations, Geneva 1959," *FRUS*, 1958–1960, Western Europe, vol. VII, part 2, July 31, 1959, https://history.state.gov/historicaldocuments/frus1958-60v07p2/d124.

is not ready to compromise its national security to this extent."[114] Eisenhower would assure de Gaulle personally that the United States would never use any nuclear weapons stored on French territory without the "consent of the French Government," but the fear was precisely the opposite: that the United States would *fail* to use them when France decided doing so was in *its* supreme national interest—both within Europe and outside it where French interests may demand it—a guarantee Eisenhower could never, and would never, ultimately give de Gaulle.[115] What France ultimately demanded was full and sovereign control of either American nuclear weapons—a nonstarter in Washington—or an independent nuclear capability.

As such, de Gaulle stated unequivocally to Secretary Dulles in 1958 that "France would have an atomic explosion within some months; he could not say for certain when this would occur, but in any case he could be certain that France would have [its own] atomic bombs." An independent nuclear deterrent—one wielded solely and entirely by and for France—was "the only effective way of ensuring her territorial integrity and political independence."[116] De Gaulle made no secret of French pursuit of nuclear weapons in this phase, and French parliamentary debates and budgets were largely public.[117] By now, it was now just a matter of technicalities: France began reprocessing plutonium in 1958 and preparing the Algerian test site for the inevitable. On September 4, 1959, de Gaulle told Eisenhower directly: "for the personal and private information of the President, the French would explode their nuclear weapon in March 1960. They have already made all preliminary tests including the detonator and these had been successful. They were as sure as one can be that the test would be successful."[118] Some in the United States were under the misapprehension that France was testing a weapon simply so that it would become eligible for American nuclear

114. Memorandum from Assistant Secretary of State for European Affairs (Merchant) to Secretary of State Herter, "U.S.-French Relations," *FRUS*, 1958–1960, Western Europe, vol. VII, part 2, May 5, 1959, https://history.state.gov/historicaldocuments/frus1958-60v07p2/d111.

115. President Eisenhower to President De Gaulle, *FRUS*, 1958–1960, Western Europe, vol. VII, part 2, September 21, 1959, https://history.state.gov/historicaldocuments/frus1958-60v07p2/d139. See de Gaulle's reply as well: President De Gaulle to President Eisenhower, *FRUS*, 1958–1960, Western Europe, vol. VII, part 2, October 6, 1959, https://history.state.gov/historicaldocuments/frus1958-60v07p2/d141.

116. De Gaulle quoted in Goldstein, *Deterrence and Security in the 21st Century*, 182.

117. President de Gaulle to President Eisenhower, *FRUS*, 1958–1960, Western Europe, vol. VII, part 2, September 17, 1958, https://history.state.gov/historicaldocuments/frus1958-60v07p2/d45.

118. Memorandum of Conversation, "Rambouillet, September 4, 1959," *FRUS*, 1958–1960, Western Europe, vol. VII, part 2, September 4, 1959, https://history.state.gov/historicaldocuments/frus1958-60v07p2/d134.

assistance. De Gaulle would repeatedly insist that he "was not asking for anything."[119] He might have preferred Washington to be more forthcoming on assistance, but France was neither slowed down without it nor seeking an independent nuclear capability as a bargaining chip against its ally. Finally, on February 13, 1960 (not March), roughly five years after a decision to weaponize the program, France conducted its first nuclear test off of a 344-foot tower, a 60–70kT test shot. As de Gaulle was famously quoted as saying, "Hurrah for France!"

TESTING PROLIFERATION STRATEGY THEORY

Why did France sprint while West Germany—facing similar if not more acute security concerns—elected insurance hedging and accepted the nuclear-sharing agreements that France rejected? The most straightforward explanation is that West Germany was susceptible to prevention—especially from the Soviet Union, which would have had an aneurysm if West Germany attempted to develop an independent nuclear capability—while France largely was not. This left West Germany no choice but to accept Washington's sharing arrangements, while France had the space and berth to seek the independent deterrent it thought necessary. And although the United States was not happy about another NATO ally possessing nuclear weapons—recall that Washington and Washington alone wants to make decisions about nuclear use and escalation, especially since it would be the likely target of Soviet retaliation regardless—it ended up being resigned to the fact, unable to stop Paris. The United States, and the entire world, was well aware of French intentions after 1954.[120] The Americans certainly froze France out of technical assistance through the 1950s and "there was not much sympathy for France becoming a nuclear power."[121] Dulles called de Gaulle "increasingly troublesome" and

119. Memorandum of Conversation, "Paris, September 2, 1959," *FRUS*, 1958–1960, Western Europe, vol. VII, part 2, September 2, 1959, https://history.state.gov/historicaldocuments/frus1958-60v07p2/d130.

120. Richelson, *Spying on the Bomb*, 201–6. Also see Goldstein, *Deterrence and Security in the 21st Century*, 194.

121. Memorandum of Conversation, "The Secretary's Forthcoming Meeting with General de Gaulle," *FRUS*, vol. VII, part 2, June 27, 1958, https://history.state.gov/historicaldocuments/frus1958-60v07p2/d28. Interestingly the memorandum lists the cascade concern as one of the reasons the Eisenhower administration was not wild about a French nuclear weapons capability: "The basic issue was not merely opposition to a fourth country producing nuclear weapons, but the fact that this might lead to fifth, sixth and seventh countries entering the field."

Eisenhower "added to watch out for him" being a nuisance to NATO.[122] But it could do little to stop a determined France from nuclearizing. For the United States, an ally out of the barn was a nuisance but not an existential threat to its interests. And there is no doubt the United States was annoyed, as a rather lengthy letter from Eisenhower to de Gaulle on a range of issues including nuclear arrangements and France's withdrawal from certain NATO mechanisms noted: "I frankly must confess that I cannot understand completely your reasoning."[123] But Miller's study on U.S. nonproliferation policy concludes that the Eisenhower administration decided "as a matter of policy" to place "no coercive pressure on France in an effort to halt their nuclear weapons program."[124]

What about the Soviet Union? Similar to the American calculation, an independently nuclear France did not shift the correlation of forces in Europe—whether France was defended by American plutonium or French plutonium made little difference to Moscow. France was not on the frontier, and the Soviet Union could treat the Western alliance, from a nuclear strategy perspective, the same way whether France had independent nuclear weapons or not: hold the United States responsible for any allied nuclear use, which had the added effect of creating trouble for Washington's nuclear management of NATO nuclear forces once France possessed nuclear weapons. This was distinct from Soviet views of the West German nuclear question over which it was ready to start a war. But, in many ways, Khrushchev realized the French nuclear capability was a bigger nuisance for Washington than it was for Moscow, an "instrument of blackmail" over the United States and NATO.[125] There is no evidence the Soviet Union contemplated preventing French nuclearization—a military strike risked American nuclear use and was likely viewed as not worth the cost to prevent something that was more nettlesome to the United States than it was to the Soviet Union.[126]

Faced with a perceived security threat from the Soviet Union (and with residual fears of German rearmament), fearing American abandonment or unwillingness to wage war in defense of French interests, and having no

122. Memorandum of Conference with President Eisenhower, *FRUS*, 1958–1960, Western Europe, vol. VII, part 2, December 12, 1958, https://history.state.gov/historicaldocuments/frus1958-60v07p2/d79.

123. President Eisenhower to President de Gaulle, *FRUS*, 1958–1960, Western Europe, vol. VII, part 2, August 30, 1960, https://history.state.gov/historicaldocuments/frus1958-60v07p2/d197.

124. Miller, *Stopping the Bomb*, 148.

125. Philip Gordon, *A Certain Idea of France: French Security Policy and the Gaullist Legacy* (Princeton: Princeton University Press, 1993), 41.

126. Debs and Monteiro, *Nuclear Politics*, 430–31.

arrangement capable of substituting for an independent nuclear arsenal, France sprinted for nuclear weapons after 1954. The security imperatives and domestic consensus for nuclear weapons had emerged, and France could sprint without significant fear of prevention. Proliferation Strategy Theory fails to explain this choice, given that France enjoyed not just formal extended deterrence via the United States and NATO but also the offer of nuclear-sharing agreements like those erected for West Germany. France declined an offer to station nuclear weapons on French soil under the NATO stockpile plan and potentially make them transferable to French delivery platforms—a back door to French nuclearization, though not entirely under sovereign French control. My theory predicts that France should have accepted this offer and persisted with insurance hedging, since the hedge would have bought *almost* all the nuclear security it sought, sacrificing only the sole ability to determine when American nuclear forces could be employed. Proliferation Strategy Theory does a much better job predicting the insurance hedging phase than the shift to sprinting, though once France concluded (contrary to my predictions) that it was essentially facing an acute security threat alone, Proliferation Strategy Theory is again useful for understanding the path it takes. France was able to sprint for the reasons that the theory predicts: slowly congealing domestic consensus, triggered by a confluence of security and equity concerns, enabled the shift from insurance hedging to sprinting; France determined that it was largely unpreventable and openly pursued a nuclear weapons capability as quickly as possible. It is important to note, however, that the pace of the sprint was retarded by domestic political churn: Mendès France and Mollet led weak coalition governments that attempted to begin a sprint—and sprinting was de facto policy—but domestic political uncertainty tied France's shoelaces together. Only when de Gaulle put on proper track spikes did the program accelerate. It took centralized power, and full domestic consensus led at the top by de Gaulle, to fully power the French run to the bomb.

Structural realist theories, particularly the one advanced by Debs and Monteiro, do a better job predicting France's decision to pursue an independent deterrent. On average, structural theories overpredict both nuclear pursuit in general and sprinting in particular. But in this case, France's leaders were thinking the way realists expect all statesmen to think: allergic to the notion of outsourcing even a small percent of France's security to an ally—no matter how friendly, de Gaulle would say—when the alternative of an independent nuclear weapons capability was readily available. Once the decision to develop an independent deterrent was reached, France was able to sprint thanks to the inability or unwillingness of the United States and Soviet Union to stop France's program. Debs and Monteiro's theory says little about French urgency to develop nuclear weapons but would likely predict sprinting as well after the experiences of Dien Bien Phu and Suez. France, as usual, is a difficult state for general theories of international politics. In this case, a structural realist theory for proliferation strategies does a better job than Proliferation Strategy Theory, even though it tends in general to overpredict pursuit and has difficulty with unfalsifiable predictions on weaponization—states that get the bomb in their theory are, largely by definition, unpreventable. Because my theory focuses on *strategies of proliferation* and not *success* of proliferation, however, the French calculation that it did not face a serious preventive threat and could openly sprint for nuclear weapons is less tautological. Nevertheless, there is no doubt that my theory has difficulty accounting for the French decision to depart from insurance hedging—one that elicited extensive nuclear-sharing offers—to sprint for an independent capability. But France is going to be France, and often defies generalizable theories on nuclear weapons.

Technological determinism explains pieces of France's nuclear weapons trajectory—and often does a good job in general of explaining the permissive conditions for sprinters: building a bomb as quickly as one can is often dictated by the availability of fissile material and bomb design. From 1954 to 1960, France's sprint was limited only by the availability of fissile material; once plutonium at the Marcoule reactor was produced and reprocessed, and bomb designs cold tested, France successfully detonated a plutonium implosion device only five years after a decision to weaponize. But France's technological capability to sprint for the bomb existed prior to 1954, and it was Mendès France's political decision on the heels of Dien Bien Phu that accelerated France's militarization of its civilian nuclear program. The insurance hedging strategy prior to 1954 is not well explained by technological determinism. But it does fare well after that. Once France put its foot on the gas pedal, the only rate-limiting steps were technical and no longer political.

France sought nuclear weapons at a time not only when nonproliferation norms were weak but when the possession of nuclear weapons was believed to enhance a state's status. French pursuit of nuclear weapons was in fact part of its effort to recapture its lost grandeur. Theories of French demand for nuclear weapons include both security and these status—grandeur[127]—

127. See, for example, Gabrielle Hecht, *The Radiance of France: Nuclear Power and National Identity after World War II* (Cambridge, MA: MIT Press, 2009).

motivations, but they are not mutually exclusive of each other and, in fact, can reinforce the demand for nuclear weapons. But, in terms of strategies of proliferation, pursuit of grandeur does not provide a determinate strategy of proliferation—there has always been a desire for grandeur in postwar France, but a constant variable cannot explain sudden shifts in urgency. In contrast, Proliferation Strategy Theory highlights the French experiences at Dien Bien Phu and Suez, resulting in French leaders concluding that only France could provide for its own security. This led to an urgent need to develop nuclear weapons so that France would no longer have to outsource defense of its national interests to Washington. Domestic consensus formed quickly as this security imperative congealed between 1954 and 1956: a revolving door of prime ministers were all committed to an independent French nuclear deterrent. Without any major preventive threats, from either the United States or the Soviet Union, France had the luxury to sprint openly for the bomb, and very quickly broke into the nuclear club once it decided to do so. France certainly achieved grandeur when it tested in 1960, but the urgency was dictated by the belief that no amount of reassurance from Washington—even stationing nuclear forces on French soil under American control—could fully satisfy France's security needs.

Although the nonproliferation regime had not yet taken form, the United States did withhold atomic assistance to France due to the 1954 Atomic Energy Act, which prohibited the United States from assisting non-nuclear states with atomic knowledge or technology. But France's program was entirely indigenous, and technology and knowledge denial did little to slow down its sprint. French scientists were at the cutting edge of nuclear research and were capable of backing out techniques that the British and Americans had used using good old detective work and induction (such as using tributyl phosphate for plutonium separation).[128] The Marcoule reactor design was indigenous and fed by uranium reserves from French colonies. There was little the United States could do to stop France, even if it withheld knowledge and technology. De Gaulle would tell Eisenhower directly that he did not require any atomic assistance, at this point. It is possible that this slowed French bomb design, but only marginally. In terms of "efficiency," France tested a plutonium implosion device as quickly as the United States, Britain, the Soviet Union, and China. If the baseline for a sprinter is achieving a nuclear weapons capability in about five years, France hit the mark even without American atomic assistance.

128. See Richelson, *Spying on the Bomb*, 198.

France is an important test for my theory because it fails to predict that the security events of 1954 would be acute enough to push France from insurance hedging to sprinting. According to my theory, France is a case of a sprinter that should have never gotten off the blocks, one that should have been content to stay warmed up but enjoy American extended deterrence and use its hedge and vast technical expertise to elicit the very nuclear-sharing arrangements that the Eisenhower administration ultimately offered. The implication for the theory is that insurance hedgers may be nudged to active weaponization by a series of cumulative events that may appear independent and idiosyncratic to the patron state—usually the United States—but in the aggregate call into question its willingness to defend the insurance hedger. Few theories can neatly capture France, and a combination of insisting on complete independence on its nuclear force reinforced by a desire to determine its own fate in Europe and around the world led France to run the nuclear race and become the world's fourth nuclear weapons power. But the lesson for the theory and for proliferation is that other insurance hedgers can also do the same if they question America's willingness to come to their defense.

China: Mao's Nuclear March

Sheltered Pursuit: 1955–58
Sprinting: 1958–64

China was the last nuclear weapons power—and the first non-Western state—to succeed in what was essentially a sprint from start to finish. Although it briefly sought shelter and assistance from the Soviet Union in the mid-1950s, the brewing Sino-Soviet split left Mao's China for all intents and purposes on its own to develop nuclear weapons. Nie Rongzhen managed the program effectively, developing both uranium and eventually plutonium pathways to the bomb and locating the infrastructure in China's interior to make it less vulnerable to external threats. China did not try to hide its interest in or pursuit of nuclear weapons—it was well aware that American satellites were scoping the country for its infrastructure. There was, in fact, very serious evaluation in the United States, during the Kennedy and then early Johnson administrations, about whether the United States could prevent China from attaining nuclear weapons through a military—either conventional or nuclear—strike. Given that the Soviets believed that a Chinese nuclear capability was inevitable, with Ambassador Dobrynin saying Moscow took it for "granted," the United States analyzed whether it could prevent China alone.[129] The conclusion was grim but realistic: China's sprint toward nuclear weapons was likely unpreventable, and even the most serious strike would only delay it, at most "perhaps four to five" years.[130] On October 16, 1964, the question essentially became moot when China tested its first nuclear device—a uranium bomb—and became the fifth member of the nuclear club. China was an unlikely sprinter given the deep economic crisis it faced during the Great Leap Forward. However, the case shows that a determined state that does not fear prevention—China had the luxury of extensive interior territory immune from America's growing but still limited intelligence and counterproliferation capabilities—is difficult to stop if it chooses to sprint for the bomb.

The landmark work on China's nuclear weapons program, John Lewis and Xue Litai's *China Builds the Bomb*, dates China's initiation of its pursuit to 1955,[131] several years after the Korean War and on the heels of the first Jinmen and Mazu crisis where Mao perceived American nuclear coercion. M. Taylor Fravel, however, finds that "a consensus among China's top leaders to acquire nuclear weapons formed earlier, by the spring of 1952, directly in response to US nuclear threats during the Korean War."[132] The Korean War impressed upon Mao and the Chinese leadership the utility of nuclear weapons, when they faced a nuclear-armed United States and perceived nuclear blackmail. Although Mao famously derided nuclear weapons as "paper tigers" that did not change the overall correlation of forces or replace the value of "man over weapons," privately he believed that "whatever they have, we must have."[133] Nie Rongzhen stated that "when the Chinese people have this weapon, [the United States'] nuclear blackmail toward the people of the world will be completely destroyed."[134] Mao would repeatedly stress the need to possess nuclear weapons to avoid being "bullied" and having

129. Richelson, *Spying on the Bomb*, 164.

130. Walt Rostow, Policy Planning Staff, U.S. Department of State, to McGeorge Bundy, "The Bases for Direct Action against Chinese Communist Nuclear Facilities," April 22, 1964, enclosing report with same title, April 14, 1964, Top Secret, LBJ Library, National Security File, Countries, box 237, China Memos Vol. I, 12/63–9/64, p. 1, https://nsarchive2.gwu.edu/nukevault/ebb488/docs/Doc%2016%204-22-64%20R%20Johnson%20bases%20for%20direct%20action.pdf.

131. John W. Lewis and Xue Litai, *China Builds the Bomb* (Stanford: Stanford University Press, 1988).

132. M. Taylor Fravel, *Active Defense: China's Military Strategy since 1949* (Princeton: Princeton University Press, 2019), 237.

133. John W. Lewis and Xue Litai, *China's Strategic Seapower: The Politics of Force Modernization in the Nuclear Age* (Stanford: Stanford University Press, 1994), 209.

134. Marshal Nie Rongzhen quoted in Fravel, *Active Defense*, 245.

"others . . . say that you don't count. Fine, we should build a few."[135] Zhou Enlai would later quote a 1951 message from Frederic Joliot-Curie to Mao: "if you want to oppose the atomic bomb, you must possess the atomic bomb."[136] According to Fravel, consensus for active weaponization came early, in 1952, at the height of the Korean War where Chinese and American forces clashed and Mao perceived nuclear coercion from the United States. Once Mao and the top Chinese leadership decided China must possess nuclear weapons and that it was a top priority for the country, China was off to the races.

In March 1952, in the middle of Korean War, Zhou Enlai began initial exploration of "the technological prerequisites for the trial production of the atomic bomb and other sophisticated weapons."[137] Several months later, Zhou Enlai began thinking about where China could acquire or find uranium, the material basis for any domestic nuclear weapons program—to either enrich or fuel reactors for the plutonium route.[138] Without a uranium supply, an indigenous and self-sufficient Chinese bomb program was only an academic aspiration. Over the next two years, Chinese delegations and scientists would request Soviet assistance on a cyclotron to enrich uranium and on an experimental reactor for the plutonium route while searching for domestic uranium deposits.[139] Finally, in the fall of 1954, China hit the proverbial jackpot and discovered natural uranium reserves sufficient for a nuclear program in Guangxi. Fravel writes that "by late August or early September 1954, the decision to pursue the bomb was made informally."[140] The January 1955 official decision was thus enabled by China's discovery of vast natural uranium reserves several months prior. But that search for uranium began earlier—a determined search for the basis of a nuclear weapons program, which Fravel dates to 1952—leading then to the official launching of the nuclear weapons program.

Following the discovery of natural uranium in 1954, the Chinese leadership decided on January 15, 1955, to formally launch its nuclear weapons program, culminating in a "strategic decision" to develop atomic weapons.[141] The organizational heft and acumen that Nie Rongzhen brought to the program resulted in a systematic, bureaucratically efficient, and organizationally

135. Mao quoted in ibid., 246.
136. Quoted in ibid., 250.
137. Quoted in ibid., 248.
138. Ibid.
139. Ibid., 248–49.
140. Ibid., 249.
141. Ibid., 250.

robust approach to the nuclear weapons project. With Mao's political directive and support, this program could not and would not fail.[142] It focused initially on uranium enrichment domestically and anticipated that Soviet assistance on the plutonium route would enable China to develop both pathways to nuclear weapons. Although Khrushchev nominally pledged to assist China with reactor and bomb designs, the Soviet Union pulled back almost immediately and never delivered on his promise, particularly on direct weapons assistance, as the Sino-Soviet relationship frayed from the mid-1950s until the final break in June 1959.

Mao may have hoped for some Soviet shelter to enable the pursuit of nuclear weapons under Moscow's protection, but the competition between the two for leadership of the communist bloc made their imminent split unsurprising.[143] In 1958, after the shelling of Jinmen, Zhou Enlai did not believe that the Soviet Union would come to China's assistance: "The Chinese Prime Minister Zhou Enlai told [Soviet Foreign Minister] Gromyko on 7 September that China was not counting on the Soviet nuclear umbrella. If the United States bombed China, the Chinese leaders did not expect their Soviet allies to get involved."[144] The Soviet Union did provide training and assistance in the mid-1950s, and this did generally lay the foundation for China's scientific and industrial base for a nuclear weapons program, but it was short on specific aid, though the assistance on reactor design and material for the Lanzhou gaseous diffusion plant was likely helpful.[145] Liu Yanqiong and Liu Jifeng, in a detailed analysis of the technical assistance, conclude that "the Soviet Union guided China's efforts during the early stages, though Chinese scientists and technicians solved key problems independently. China could have built its own initial atomic bomb in 1964 or 1965 without this Soviet

142. See Lewis and Xue, *China Builds the Bomb*, 54–59. The sheer organizational breadth of the program is discussed, involving fifteen bureaus and a clear organizational chart. This was a massive industrial effort established and operating during some of the leanest years of the Great Leap Forward to succeed, and do so efficiently.

143. See Zhihua Shen and Yafeng Xia, "Between Aid and Restriction: The Soviet Union's Changing Policies on China's Nuclear Weapons Program, 1954–1960," *Asian Perspective* 36, no. 1 (2012): 95–122.

144. Campbell Craig and Sergey Radchenko, "MAD, Not Marx: Khrushchev and the Nuclear Revolution," *Journal of Strategic Studies* 41, no. 1–2 (February 23, 2018): 217.

145. See Liu Yanqiong and Liu Jifeng, "Analysis of Soviet Technology Transfer in the Development of China's Nuclear Weapons," *Comparative Technology Transfer and Society* 7, no. 1 (April 2009): 66–110. This is an incredibly detailed and helpful piece on what technology and assistance the Soviets did and did not transfer to China. The authors conclude that the assistance was broad, not specific, and therefore helped but was not dispositive as it forced Chinese scientists to solve many technical issues on their own.

technology transfer" if it had embarked on a sustained program in 1956.[146] Even if the timeline is disputable, the general point remains that the Soviet Union very early on limited its assistance on nuclear weapons technology.[147] Lewis and Xue write that "the initial (and secret) Soviet decision to renege came in early 1958" just as China's nuclear program was in its infancy.[148] For a full year, Soviet advisors promised data and a prototype weapon, with no intention of delivering it. Finally, on June 20, 1959, the Soviet Union formally notified the Chinese leadership that it would "not supply the prototype bomb or blueprints and technical data on the bomb."[149] This just formalized what the Chinese scientists and leaders had been sensing for several years, and left China alone to pursue the bomb. Lewis and Xue write that the Chinese Politburo met within two days and "vowed that China would produce its first atomic bomb within eight years."[150] The nuclear program was codenamed 596, in honor of this perceived betrayal, to commemorate June 1959, the month when the Soviet Union left China to pursue the bomb on its own. And China would succeed not in eight years but in five, in an impressive sprint to the bomb that dared both the Americans and the Soviets to stop it.

The nuclear program ballooned to fifty organizations and over three thousand people, and its success, according to Zhang Aiping, demanded national determination and the "vigorous support" of all departments and bureaucracies.[151] The heart of the program was the Lanzhou gaseous diffusion plant, in the middle of China's vast territory, rendering it essentially immune to attack and surveillance; Richelson notes that the spot was deliberately chosen in part because "its interior location made it difficult for U.S. spyplanes to overfly."[152] Lanzhou would enrich uranium that would be supplied from uranium conversion facilities in Inner Mongolia. China's plutonium pathway would follow but would center on the Jiuquan Atomic Energy Complex, located in the remote Gobi Desert. It was initially assumed that the Soviet Union would assist with reactor and reprocessing design for the plutonium pathway, but Richelson notes that "by the time Soviet assistance ceased, in 1960, the Soviets had not delivered a single key component for the plutonium production reactor to be built at Jiuquan,

146. Ibid., 104.
147. Shen and Xia, "Between Aid and Restriction," 117.
148. Lewis and Xue, *China Builds the Bomb*, 61.
149. Ibid., 64.
150. Ibid., 65.
151. Quoted in Fravel, *Active Defense*, 252.
152. Richelson, *Spying on the Bomb*, 139.

much less the 'sample' bomb."[153] China would have to develop and design its own reactor and reprocessing facilities at Jiuquan. Lanzhou would begin enriching weapons-grade uranium in 1964, which led China to test a uranium device first—surprising the world that the uranium path paid off before the plutonium route—while Jiuquan began producing plutonium in 1966, providing the fuel for China's first thermonuclear test a year later.[154] The program simultaneously worked on bomb design—plutonium and uranium implosion designs (which was more difficult and more sophisticated than a uranium gun-type)—so that once fissile material became available in 1964, China could immediately insert it into a November 1963 cold-tested design and conduct a nuclear test.[155]

Despite the pain of the Great Leap Forward and an unfinished battle with Chinese Nationalists, Mao reaffirmed in 1962 that "the research and development of sophisticated weapons should continue, we cannot relax or stop."[156] And it had to be China's bomb. Jacques Hymans writes that "although Mao dearly wanted a Chinese *bomb*, what he really wanted was a *Chinese* bomb. To that end he was willing to mortgage the entire Chinese economy, but not to bow his head to the leadership of the Soviet Union."[157] Indeed, Richelson writes that Mao had decided after the Soviets terminated assistance to "divert the resources necessary, and by 1960 China was actively engaged . . . in constructing its first generation of atomic facilities."[158] The total cost of the nuclear program, according to Lewis and Xue, was equivalent to 37 percent of China's entire 1957 budget, and the equivalent of two years of total defense spending.[159] It was a massive expenditure, and China was relatively open about it. This was not a hiding strategy, nor was it simply technological determinism, as Mao intentionally put his foot on the gas pedal despite the economic impact of the Great Leap Forward, accelerating the program to attain a Chinese nuclear weapons capability as quickly as possible.

Hymans assesses that the priority placed on the nuclear weapons program is why "of all the various large-scale civilian and military scientific-industrial projects that Maoist China undertook, the nuclear weapons project was an

153. Ibid., 141.

154. Hui Zhang, "The History of Fissile-Material Production in China," *Nonproliferation Review* 25, nos. 5–6 (2018): 477–99.

155. See Lewis and Xue, *China Builds the Bomb*, 139, 159–60.

156. Quoted in Fravel, *Active Defense*, 252.

157. Hymans, *Achieving Nuclear Ambitions*, 136.

158. Richelson, *Spying on the Bomb*, 143.

159. Lewis and Xue, *China Builds the Bomb*, 108.

almost uniquely happy experience."[160] The most important factor—the one that set up Nie Rongzhen's "organizational genius" for success—is that, as Hymans summarizes, "Mao gave the nuclear weapons project the highest political priority, assuring it a stable provision of resources and political support even at the expense of the conventional military, not to mention the famine stricken populace."[161] After a yearlong debate during which the nuclear program continued despite growing concerns that the pace and program were mortgaging the entire economy solely for the sake of nuclear weapons amid the turmoil of the Great Leap Forward, Mao doubled down in the summer of 1962 and directed Nie Rongzhen to continue to race for the bomb.[162] Indeed, at this meeting, China's foreign minister, Chen Yi, purportedly and famously said that China will develop nuclear weapons "even if the Chinese had to pawn their trousers for this purpose."[163] Doing so would allow him, in his international negotiations, to "straighten my back," partially giving China the equalizer it needed to confront both the Soviet Union and the United States.[164] The priority placed on developing nuclear weapons, and Mao's ability to resist interfering with the program, instead delegating to Zhou Enlai and Nie Rongzhen, even amid social and economic chaos, meant that, as Hymans concludes, "the nuclear program ran supremely efficiently" and China was well on pace to sprint for the bomb by the turn of the decade.[165] Once Mao reaffirmed his unwavering support for China's sprint to the bomb in 1962, China would test its first device only two years later, a remarkable feat given the effects of the Great Leap Forward.

By now the United States had strategically assessed that China was "energetically developing her native capabilities in the field of atomic energy."[166] The evidence was fragmentary, largely because American intelligence assets did not know what to look for nor where to look precisely, and the U.S. intelligence community had not yet realized that the Soviet Union had terminated assistance. Nevertheless, a December 1960 National Intelligence Estimate judged that China had made substantial progress in developing both

160. Hymans, *Achieving Nuclear Ambitions*, 129.

161. Ibid., 133.

162. Lewis and Xue, *China Builds the Bomb*, 129.

163. Ibid., 130.

164. Ibid.

165. Hymans, *Achieving Nuclear Ambitions*, 137.

166. Director of Central Intelligence, NIE 13-2-60, *The Chinese Communist Atomic Energy Program*, December 13, 1960, p. 1, http://www.foia.cia.gov/sites/default/files/document_conversions/89801/DOC_0001095912.pdf.

the uranium and the plutonium pathways.[167] It assessed that China could generate enough plutonium for a bomb by 1962, but more likely around 1963 or 1964 (which would end up being correct), though it mistakenly assumed that the plutonium pathway would be the likely source for China's first weapons when, in fact, it would be uranium.[168] Although every other nuclear weapons power after the United States would start with plutonium because it was believed to be easier to produce—which is why American intelligence assumed the same with China—Mao's China was pushing on both pathways and would ultimately test whichever delivered fissile material first.

Concern began growing in Washington over what seemed like eventual Chinese nuclear weapons development and the resulting consequences on the Asian balance of power. There were some stillborn proposals for ways to potentially stop China, such as the September 1961 idea floated by George McGhee, director of policy planning at the State Department, that the United States preempt Chinese attainment by assisting India in getting the bomb first: "While we would like to limit the number of nuclear powers, so long as we lack the capability to do so, we ought to prefer that the first Asian one be India and not China."[169] The assumption was that India preempting China would mitigate the impact that Chinese nuclear weapons would have on the Asian balance of power and in energizing communism. Secretary of State Dean Rusk rejected the idea on the basis that the United States could not be seen as assisting in proliferation because it "would start us down a jungle path from which I see no exit."[170]

China's determined march toward nuclear weapons continued briskly, with the United States unclear as to which facilities were involved and with a murky picture of the plutonium and uranium pathways Beijing was pursuing.[171] By January 1963, President Kennedy became more alarmed at what seemed like the inevitability of China possessing nuclear weapons, with National Security Advisor McGeorge Bundy claiming the president believed such an outcome "would so upset the world political scene [that] it would be intolerable."[172] Mao was painted as a "madman" who could not be allowed to

167. Ibid., 1–2.

168. Ibid., 3.

169. George McGhee to Dean Rusk, "Anticipatory Action Pending Chinese Demonstration of a Nuclear Capability," National Security Archive, September 13, 1961, p. 2, https://nsarchive2.gwu.edu//nsa/DOCUMENT/950428.htm.

170. Rusk quoted in Burr and Richelson, "Whether to 'Strangle the Baby in the Cradle,'" 62.

171. Ibid., 64–66.

172. Bundy quoted in ibid., 67.

possess nuclear weapons—a characterization that would foreshadow future pursuers such as North Korea. The Kennedy administration approached the Soviets about applying joint pressure on Mao, with no option left off the table—with proposals ranging from the Partial Test Ban Treaty to imposing costs on a Chinese test, to joint military action. But the Soviets were uninterested at this point, with Dobrynin ultimately saying that Moscow took a Chinese nuclear capability as a given with little interest in stopping it, though it would not assist it.[173]

Could the United States unilaterally prevent China from achieving the bomb? The key to a sprinter's ability to sprint is to avoid prevention from—or being tripped up by—an external actor. It was precisely this question—the possibility of "direct action" by the United States—that the Johnson administration explored in April 1964 as it became apprehensive of China approaching the nuclear finish line. In a Policy Planning study titled "The Bases for Direct Action against Chinese Communist Nuclear Facilities," a variety of scenarios were worked up to examine the prospects of the United States eliminating China's nuclear weapons program. The conclusion was straightforward and simple: "Direct action against the Chinese Communist nuclear facilities would, at best, put them out of operation for a few years (perhaps four to five)."[174] Whether a bolt from the blue strike, an opportunistic strike in the midst of a general conflict, or through covert means (e.g., staged out of Taiwan), the prospects were equally low of dealing a crippling blow to China's nuclear ambitions.[175]

Why were the prospects so low? Even by April 1964, six months before China would test its first uranium nuclear device from weapons-grade uranium that Lanzhou was now enriching, the report stated:

> It is doubtful whether, even with completion of initial photographic coverage of the mainland, we will have anything like complete assurance that we will have identified all significant nuclear installations. Thus, even "successful" action may not necessarily prevent the ChiComs from detonating a nuclear device in the next few years. . . . It seems to be the case that a relatively heavy non-nuclear air attack would be required to put installations "permanently" out of business (i.e., destroy them so completely that any rebuilding effort would have to start virtually from scratch). . . . Could the U.S. mount an

173. Richelson, *Spying on the Bomb*, 164.

174. Rostow to Bundy, p. 1.

175. Ibid., 2–3.

> effective counterforce operation, should that prove necessary, without employing nuclear weapons?[176]

There was the further problem that "there may, moreover, be other facilities which we have so far not identified. It is therefore impossible to assume at present that the U.S. could knock out all nuclear material production."[177] China might already have a "stockpile" of fissile material or even weapons and "it would be impossible to assume that all of these would be destroyed."[178] Essentially, the United States did not know what to hit or where a stockpile might be, and even if it did, it might not be able to completely destroy all the necessary facilities to do anything more than set back China a couple of years without resorting to a massive nuclear strike on the country. China was, by the United States' own assessment, immune to prevention.

Faced with no realistic prospects for unilateral action, Secretary Rusk made a last-ditch effort to try to re-recruit the Soviet Union into joint pressure or action, especially as the rift between China and the Soviet Union had spilled out into the open. Dobrynin was still uninterested, claiming in September 1964, weeks before China would test its first device, that a Chinese nuclear test was "of no importance for his government."[179] As Burr and Richelson conclude, Dobrynin's "negative response effectively settled the argument over direct action."[180] President Johnson and the U.S. government had no choice but to be resigned to a Chinese nuclear capability. They would not have to wait long. Signatures at the Lop Nur test site were blinking red. And on October 16, only weeks later, China would detonate an implosion uranium device and declare itself the world's fifth nuclear power. A sprint that began less than a decade earlier, powered by facilities that broke ground only five years earlier, culminated in an impressively efficient and quick run to the bomb. Three years later, China would join the thermonuclear club.

TESTING PROLIFERATION STRATEGY THEORY

Proliferation Strategy Theory makes an unambiguous prediction that China would adopt a sprinting strategy to the bomb. China believed it faced an acute security threat from the United States during the Korean War. Tens

176. Ibid., 3–4.
177. Ibid., 6.
178. Ibid., 7.
179. Dobrynin quoted in Burr and Richelson, "Whether to 'Strangle the Baby in the Cradle,'" 88.
180. Ibid.

of thousands of American forces were parked on the Korean Peninsula and in Japan and were backing the Nationalist forces threatening to overthrow Mao's communist China. For Mao, the United States was not just an acute security threat, it was an existential threat—both to him and to his country. During the Korean War, as Fravel notes, Mao had already decided that China would require atomic weapons—the only way to combat atomic weapons was to possess atomic weapons, as Joliot-Curie had noted. China's strategy of proliferation is more complicated in the period between 1955 and 1959, when promises of Soviet nuclear assistance raised the possibility of some sort of sheltered pursuit. But China never enjoyed a formal guarantee from Moscow, and not only did any promises of loose shelter evaporate but so did assistance in the nuclear domain. Nuclear weapons also offered China independence from a Soviet Union that had essentially abandoned it within the Communist Bloc. The Chinese leadership congealed quickly around Mao's active pursuit of the bomb, making domestic consensus a foregone conclusion once Mao gave the green light, unofficially in 1952 and officially in 1955. The early signs of Sino-Soviet fissures over the next several years eliminated the possibility of a sustained sheltered pursuit—the shelter was crumbling even before it was fully extended. Mao not only decided that China must possess the bomb, he decided it must have it as quickly as possible and that the program would be accorded highest priority. Determined to build the bomb—even amid political and economic pain during the Great Leap Forward—China showed that even a relatively poor non-Western state could develop the scientific-industrial capacity to quickly and efficiently produce nuclear weapons, even in the 1960s.

The relevant variable for China was whether it was immune from prevention to allow it to sprint in the open or whether it would be forced into hiding. Because China was blessed with vast remote interior territories that enabled it to locate critical infrastructure out of the prying eyes of American spy planes and intelligence assets, as Richelson put it, and with the ability to develop redundant facilities, American intelligence and officials themselves concluded that China was essentially immune from prevention. This enabled China to sprint for nuclear weapons. It made little effort to hide its intent to pursue nuclear weapons, though Nie Rongzhen was smart enough to disperse the facilities in places that obfuscated how far along China was in its sprint and which, and how many, facilities were involved. China was the last country to essentially have the ability to sprint from start to finish in its nuclear program. To be fair, this dovetails with a narrow realist explanation for China's nuclear proliferation strategy. Most realist accounts of China's nuclear pursuit would also predict that it would attempt—and largely be able to succeed because it had little choice—to develop nuclear weapons as quickly as possible.

Do alternative explanations account for China's decision to sprint? Technological determinism again accounts for some features of China's nuclear pursuit—it needed certain technological bases for the program, such as the discovery of natural uranium, and the knowledge and industrial base to construct enrichment facilities and a plutonium reactor as well as a reprocessing facility. But technological determinism does not account again for the *strategic* decision to prioritize the nuclear program and build nuclear weapons as quickly as possible, especially amid the Great Leap Forward, that accelerated the pace of China's nuclear development. It was Mao and Zhou Enlai's insistence to put the foot on the gas pedal, targeting five years from 1959 and instituting a "two year plan" to testing in 1963, that drove the breakneck pace of the program.[181] Contrast the speed with which China built the bomb with the delays and sluggishness of the sea-based SSBN and ballistic missile program, as Lewis and Xue document. Chinese scientists and technicians were equally capable in both programs, but the priority the nuclear weapons program was accorded drove such impressive results. Technological determinism fails to capture the difference in strategic urgency between the two programs. Ultimately, technology was an enabler, but not a determinant, of the strategy.

Hymans's organizational theory in *Achieving Nuclear Ambitions* also identifies critical enablers for China's success: the ability to stand up such a massive scientific-industrial program amid the Great Leap Forward coupled with Mao's ability to simultaneously grant the nuclear program unfettered support but also incredible autonomy no doubt led to success. Hymans points to the uniqueness of the nuclear program in this regard, as no other Chinese scientific-industrial program in this period succeeded. That begs the question, why? Security. A perceived threat from the United States during the Korean War drove Mao to insist that China develop its own nuclear weapons as quickly as possible despite dire economic conditions. Credit is also due to China's relative immunity from external prevention—a variable Hymans fails to consider—that allowed it to sprint out in the open and not be forced into hiding, which would have slowed down its progress considerably. There is no question that Hymans is correct that China's organizational strength, Nie Rongzhen's "organizational genius," and Mao's ability to grant the nuclear

181. Fravel, *Active Defense*, 252.

program autonomy is the intervening variable that led to China's success. But those felicitous conditions were the consequence of strategic decisions, not accident or luck. They reflected China's determination to develop the bomb as quickly as possible; they were not independent forces that caused it.

Finally, nonproliferation-focused theories have little to say about China's pursuit of the bomb, since the nonproliferation regime was in its infancy during China's sprint. The Soviet Union thought nothing of assisting China in developing the bomb and only terminated assistance because Khrushchev believed Mao was a "megalomaniac." The United States' assessments about how to shape China's nuclear strategy focused on prevention, not on any international regimes or norms. Certainly, Mao had no qualms about weaponization or, scarily, even considering nuclear war: "it would hardly mean anything to the universe as a whole, though it might be a major event for the solar system."[182] China's attainment of nuclear weapons *caused* the establishment of the NPT, as the United States and the Soviet Union essentially said enough is enough and began to consider how to slow the growth in the number of nuclear weapons states. But it had little impact on Mao's thinking or strategy.

China's path to the bomb is impressive, given the state of its society and economy during the Great Leap Forward, and it illustrates that a state with the ability and strategy to sprint can quickly build nuclear weapons if it is determined to do so. Luckily, from a proliferation standpoint, there are very few large industrial states with the territorial advantages China had in the 1950s and 1960s that enabled it to sprint to nuclear weapons. But within a decade of a decision to seek the bomb, and within five years of breaking ground on the facilities that would produce the fuel for the bomb, China broke into the nuclear club.

Conclusion

This chapter has shown that sprinting is an exceptionally attractive and potent strategy of proliferation—for those that can choose it. It is the stereotypical version of nuclear proliferation: a determined and open march for a nuclear weapons capability, intended to achieve that capability as quickly as possible. For a nuclear aspirant that can select this strategy, there is often little that the international community can do to stop it. Those that could sprint from

182. Quoted in Michael Krepon, "Mao on the Bomb," *ArmsControlWonk*, February 9, 2014, https://www.armscontrolwonk.com/archive/404038/mao-on-the-bomb/.

start to finish—major powers with substantial industrial-scientific capability and large territories invulnerable from prevention—mostly did so early in the nuclear era, though there are some remaining potential sprinters such as Australia—advanced, isolated—that might be immune to any economic or military prevention. But sprinting as a strategy of proliferation is no longer available to many states. Few can adopt the stylized proliferation strategy that the literature has assumed characterized the proliferation landscape. This is fortunate from a nonproliferation perspective, because sprinters are exceptionally difficult to stop from the outside. There are states, such as India, that were able to sprint after a period of hedging—it jogged, stopped for a water break, and then sprinted the last 50 meters—and it is possible that existing hedgers such as Japan or Germany could have quick sprints to the bomb if they chose to do so. As such, it is not an irrelevant strategy, but it is increasingly rare. The more relevant active weaponization strategies for contemporary nuclear proliferation are sheltered pursuit, in which states take advantage of temporary or permanent great power shielding to develop nuclear weapons, and hiding, where states that fear prevention attempt to present a nuclear fait accompli to the world. These strategies are discussed in the next chapters.

5

The Sheltered Pursuers

ISRAEL, PAKISTAN, AND NORTH KOREA

Active pursuers who cannot sprint for the bomb are forced to carefully and creatively craft their proliferation strategies based on the threats they confront and the opportunities available to them. This chapter explores the proliferation strategy of sheltered pursuit, in which a state attempts to cultivate or take advantage of a great power's protection to develop nuclear weapons with its tolerance or even complicity. The shelter of a great power or superpower patron allows the client state to pursue nuclear weapons more freely, with a lower chance of a successful coercive attempt to stop or destroy its program. The great power not only commits to tolerating the client's possession of nuclear weapons but deters or dissuades other major powers from trying to prevent it, providing military, economic, and diplomatic shelter. Critically, the relationship between the great power and potential proliferator is one of a patron and a client, rather than a formal alliance (or formal nuclear umbrella). As the insurance hedging strategy in chapter 3 suggests, superpowers tend to strongly oppose independent nuclearization within their formal alliance structures, preferring to maintain a single decision center for nuclear use and escalation. For NATO states like Germany, or other formal U.S. allies like Japan and South Korea, sheltered pursuit is not an option. For states that have a superpower patron, but not a preexisting extended deterrence guarantee, sheltered pursuit is a creative strategy of proliferation for nuclear aspirants provided that the proliferator and the major power can walk a fine line. It is a strategy that the existing literature

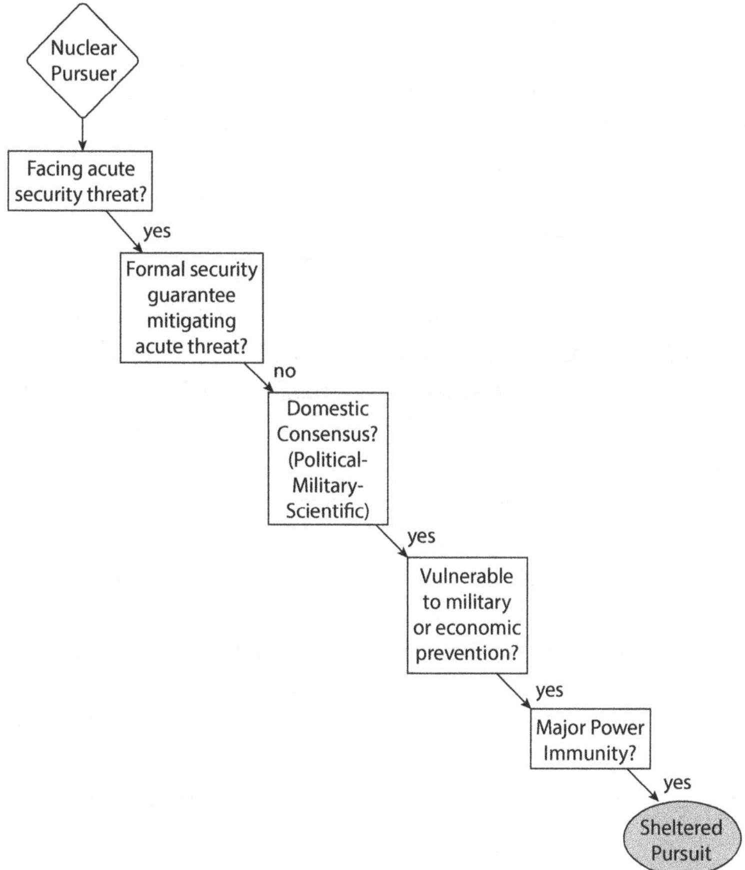

FIGURE 5.1. Proliferation Strategy Theory's pathway to the sheltered pursuit strategy.

has largely overlooked. Figure 5.1 illustrates Proliferation Strategy Theory's hypothesized pathway to the sheltered pursuit strategy.

A sheltered pursuit strategy is available to states outside a formal alliance structure or extended deterrence guarantee but that still enjoy temporary—or sometimes indefinite—protection from a major power, such as Israel and Pakistan from the United States, and North Korea at various times from the Soviet Union and China. These states can select sheltered pursuit strategies after cultivating a patronage relationship or if patronage fortuitously emerges for other reasons. The reasons why a greater power would offer such immunity and protection vary. In cases like Israel, Tel Aviv actively sought and cultivated shelter—especially by nurturing domestic political support for Israel through the U.S. Congress—in order to maximize protection for the Israeli nuclear weapons program against the Soviet Union and its Arab client states, as well as from the United States itself. In other cases like Pakistan, the emergence of shelter was triggered by an exogenous event that suddenly made Pakistan critical to the American Cold War fight against the Soviets, giving Pakistan carte blanche to redouble its efforts to build a weapons capability before the American shield evaporated. Although China and North Korea have a Mutual Aid and Cooperation Friendship Treaty, Beijing has historically viewed its treaty commitments very narrowly and does not offer Pyongyang extended nuclear deterrence.[1] Furthermore, in the years in which North Korea sought the bomb, while China shielded Pyongyang, it did so reluctantly. The crucial point is that, although Pakistan suddenly found itself surprisingly protected for exogenous reasons, the sheltered pursuit strategy can be, and has been, actively crafted—even if painstakingly and rarely—by the nuclear aspirants themselves.

In all three cases, the potential proliferator made, or found, itself useful to the major power for larger geopolitical reasons, forcing the patron to look the other way and tolerate the client state's pursuit of nuclear weapons, even though it may have otherwise opposed or stopped it. This chapter walks through several cases of quintessential sheltered pursuers who were able to develop nuclear weapons under the immunity of greater powers. In each case, they likely would not have succeeded if not for the protection afforded them: Israel during the 1960s, Pakistan in the 1980s, and North Korea in the 1990s and 2000s.

Sheltered pursuit is a strategy that depends on cultivating, or opportunistically taking advantage of, a great power patron that is willing to shield a state's nuclear program from preventive efforts, from both domestic actors in the patron state and other powers. It is a strategy made possible when a specific set of stars align for a state that is contemplating actively pursuing nuclear weapons—when it succeeds in making, or suddenly finds, itself useful to a major power patron for anticipated or unanticipated reasons that override nonproliferation goals. The nuclear aspirant can exploit that window of opportunity to pursue nuclear weapons under the shelter of the greater power. It has been wildly successful for the states that have been able to select it.

1. See Anny Boc, "Does China's 'Alliance Treaty' with North Korea Still Matter?" *The Diplomat*, July 26, 2019, https://thediplomat.com/2019/07/does-chinas-alliance-treaty-with-north-korea-still-matter/; and Ankit Panda, "China and North Korea Have a Mutual Defense Treaty, But When Would It Apply?" *The Diplomat*, August 14, 2017, https://thediplomat.com/2017/08/china-and-north-korea-have-a-mutual-defense-treaty-but-when-would-it-apply/.

Israel (1956–67): The Textile Plant at Dimona

As with the previous cases, I first describe Israel's multidecade interest in—and ultimate attainment of—nuclear weapons. I then explain how Proliferation Strategy Theory accounts for Tel Aviv's actions. Although counterfactual exercises are notoriously difficult, it is plausible that Israel would not possess nuclear weapons today without the active assistance and protection it received first from France after the Suez Crisis but then critically from the United States over the course of a decade, from the waning days of the Eisenhower administration through the Nixon administration. The Kennedy administration made serious efforts to discern the scope of Israel's nuclear activities, but neither the Kennedy nor Johnson administration was willing to threaten the American-Israeli relationship over its pursuit of nuclear weapons, despite clear evidence that Israel was omitting key details about its activities and probably outright lying to American officials about their true purpose. Israel engaged in significant levels of tactical deception on the advancement of its nuclear weapons program—obfuscating the true purpose of key facilities in an effort that eventually became implausibly deniable. As early as 1958 or 1959, the U.S. government knew Israel was undoubtedly pursuing nuclear weapons. Except for Kennedy, American presidents were reluctant to employ considerable U.S. leverage—such as threatening termination of arms sales or outright abandonment—to slow the Israeli nuclear program, before a nuclear-armed Israel became essentially a foregone conclusion by the late 1960s. Even Kennedy exerted limited coercive leverage and deliberately declined to offer Israel a formal security guarantee, knowing full well that such a guarantee was probably the only chance to keep Israel non-nuclear. Successive U.S. administrations willfully turned a blind eye to Israel's nuclear weapons activities—they knew enough to know Israel had both intent and capability to develop nuclear weapons, and what they did not know, they deliberately did not seek to find out.

By the time President Nixon took office, the United States relied even more heavily on Israel as a bulwark in the Middle East against Soviet-backed Arab socialism. Presidents Johnson and Nixon were both unwilling to condition the American relationship—or arms sales, such as F-4 Phantoms—on Israel remaining non-nuclear. While no American administration necessarily wanted Israel to become a nuclear weapons power, they were increasingly willing to tolerate it in the service of broader geopolitical goals, namely having a friend and foothold in the Middle East. This culminated in a secret personal agreement between Nixon and Israeli prime minister Golda Meir in 1969—which reportedly persists until today—that effectively codified American acceptance of Israel's possession of nuclear weapons, provided Israel did not openly declare them, test them, or otherwise incorporate them into its arsenal in ways that might trigger reactive proliferation in the region. In any case, Israel had already crossed the finish line several years prior: Israel reportedly assembled two nuclear weapons during the Six Day War in 1967.[2] Both states have thus far honored the Nixon-Meir agreement, allowing Israel to be the only undeclared nuclear weapons power in the world.

Israel's nuclear weapons pursuit began in earnest with the return of Prime Minister Ben Gurion in 1954.[3] The minutes of a cabinet meeting on December 16, 1954, report that Ben Gurion, who had always had an interest nuclear energy and its potential application to military uses, said: "And another issue that must be given more resources by the state is the development of science. It might be that our ultimate security would rest on that. But I will not talk about it any further. This could be the last thing that may save us."[4] Given its history, small size, and precarious geographic situation, surrounded by Arab states openly committed to its elimination, Israel resides in one of the most hostile security environments in the world. In 1948, five Arab states invaded Israel after Zionist activists declared an independent state. Given the threats it faced since its birth, Israeli motivations for pursuing nuclear weapons to ensure its survival are relatively clear. There was strong domestic consensus for nuclear weapons across parties and across time in the Israeli political leadership once Ben Gurion decided to develop them. Strong prime ministers could centralize, compartmentalize, and direct the highly sensitive and secret development of nuclear weapons. Once Ben Gurion embarked on the program, it was virtually unquestioned.[5] In 1955, Nasser's Egypt, the most powerful Arab state, cemented a massive arms deal with the Czech Republic, as a front for Soviet arms. This further catalyzed Israel's quest to establish a nuclear weapons program. Israel therefore faced an acute security threat. It could rely on no formal ally at this time. Key domestic constituencies were in agreement as to the necessity of nuclearization. All the ingredients to

2. See Avner Cohen and William Burr, "How Israel Built a Nuclear Program Right under the Americans' Noses," *Haaretz.com*, January 17, 2021, https://www.haaretz.com/israel-news/.premium.MAGAZINE-how-israel-built-a-nuclear-program-right-under-the-americans-noses-1.9445510.

3. See Avner Cohen, *Israel and the Bomb* (New York: Columbia University Press, 1998), 42.

4. Ben Gurion quoted in ibid.

5. See Avner Cohen, *The Worst-Kept Secret: Israel's Bargain with the Bomb* (New York: Columbia University Press, 2010).

actively pursue nuclear weapons were present. The question: How could it do so without being stopped?

Through 1955, Ben Gurion endorsed the idea that Israel should think about how to best ensure its survival, noting that "our security problem could have two answers: if possible, political guarantees, but this is not up to us. But on what depends on us, we must invest all our power, because we must have superiority in weapons, because we will never achieve superiority in manpower. All those things that have to do with science, we must do them."[6] No formal alliance or nuclear umbrella was forthcoming to Israel in the 1950s. If it were, perhaps Israel would have gone down the path of Japan and West Germany and stopped at insurance hedging. With the Eisenhower administration's Atoms for Peace program, Israeli leaders saw an opportunity to lay the technical foundation for its nuclear weapons program. At the first Geneva conference related to Atoms for Peace in August 1955, the Israeli team, led by Ernst Bergmann, openly discussed a novel reactor design with the American delegation that would have produced gram-quantities of plutonium (~8 grams per month). The chairman of the AEC, Admiral Lewis Strauss, rebuked the Israelis. He understood what plutonium production might be used for: "You could not do anything that would provide you even the slightest quantities of plutonium."[7] Within the Israeli scientific establishment, Amos de Shalit then argued that "the issue cannot be snuck in through talk about fissile products, power plants, etc. . . . if we're to be allowed to proceed in the direction of plutonium separation it would be better to ask directly for plutonium rather than try to outsmart everyone and build a complicated reactor for that purpose."[8] This was the first hint at the notion of pursuing a sheltered pursuit strategy if Israel could find a willing supplier who would know the purpose of its plutonium reactor and provide separation assistance but was also willing to turn a blind eye to its ultimate purpose.

Enter France. Shimon Peres was the initial architect of the pivot to France for arms in 1953. The arms relationship steadily improved and was formalized between Peres and the new French prime minister, Guy Mollet, in 1956. With France's position in its North African colonies steadily declining and agitation further stoked by Egyptian president Nasser, France and Israel had a common enemy. Nasser's seizure of the Suez Canal in July 1956 gave

6. Ben Gurion quoted in Cohen, *Israel and the Bomb*, 43.
7. Strauss quoted in ibid., 45.
8. De Shalit quoted in ibid., 47.

Israel the opening it needed to try to upgrade the relationship with France to the nuclear field. Though it was not an explicit quid pro quo, Israeli participation in the British-French operation to recapture the Sinai Peninsula ultimately had a nuclear goal. Peres, according to Avner Cohen, chose to "reply in the affirmative [about Israel's participation] because he calculated that this could be the opportunity that would give Israel the reactor."[9] Less than two months later, in September 1956, the French atomic energy commission (CEA) and its Israeli counterpart reached an agreement for a small research reactor. According to Cohen, "there is little doubt that the French understood what the deal was about."[10] They were initially, as Israel had hoped, however, willing to turn a blind eye.

Peres wanted to ensure that Israel got more than simply a small research reactor. At the Sèvres Conference in October 1956, in which the parties finalized plans for the Sinai operation, Peres writes that he met secretly with Mollet and the French defense minister on the sidelines and also "finalized with these two leaders an agreement for the building of a nuclear reactor at Dimona, in southern Israel, and the supply of natural uranium to fuel it."[11] Granted, Israel joined action against Nasser in Suez for reasons beyond the issue of nuclear assistance. But French acquiescence on that front was a welcome bonus, according to Cohen.[12] The details of the reactor and the precise nature of French assistance were vague at this point. However, as the Suez Crisis intensified and the Soviet Union issued direct threats to Israel, Peres leaned on the French to provide, according to Cohen, "nuclear assistance . . . as a security guarantee if Israel withdrew from the Sinai" and diffused the crisis.[13] Over the course of the next year, the contours of the Israeli requests became clearer: a Marcoule-style reactor (40 MWth) and an underground plutonium reprocessing facility below the reactor.[14] Or Rabinowitz writes that the deal consisted of three agreements: the first on December 12, 1956, for the reactor and uranium supply for it for "peaceful purposes"; the second on August 23, 1957, in which "France agreed explicitly to cooperate with Israel in research and production of nuclear *weapons*," of which the French cabinet was not informed; and a third on October 3, 1957, for

9. Ibid., 53.

10. Ibid., 54.

11. Shimon Peres, *Battling for Peace: A Memoir*, ed. David Landau (New York: Random House, 1995), 130.

12. Cohen, *Israel and the Bomb*, 54.

13. Ibid., 55.

14. Ibid., 58.

the reprocessing facility to be built by Saint Gobain.[15] As Cohen concludes, "French officials who were involved in making the Dimona deal understood it for what it was."[16] Though the French foreign ministry forced Israel to sign an instrument declaring that the cooperation was strictly for peaceful purposes, it was a convenient fictional cover: the secret agreement to cooperate on weapons and for a reprocessing facility, which had but a single purpose, allowed Israel to pursue nuclear weapons under French shelter, and with French assistance, at this point. To many, this was not plausible deniability but implausible deniability.

French shelter was not extended for long. Upon assuming office in 1958, French prime minister Charles de Gaulle grasped the unprecedented nature of the cooperation and wanted to terminate "the improper military collaboration established between Tel Aviv and Paris after the Suez Expedition, which permanently placed Israelis at all levels of the French services."[17] Luckily for Israel, the French minister for atomic energy, Jacques Soustelle, was a strong supporter of Israel and slow-rolled de Gaulle on terminating CEA and Saint Gobain's construction of Dimona and the secret reprocessing facility.[18] After a series of meetings between de Gaulle and Ben Gurion directly, followed by Israeli stalling, a compromise was struck whereby CEA would terminate its involvement, but private French companies such as Saint Gobain could continue to fulfill the originally contracted work. This allowed Israel to essentially complete the project, despite de Gaulle's reservations.

Just as the French shelter was decaying, the Eisenhower administration was getting wind of the scale, scope, and purpose of Israel's nuclear activities. A December 8, 1960, National Intelligence Estimate (NIE) noted: "Recent information confirms that Israel is engaged in construction of a nuclear reactor complex in the Negev, near Beersheba. . . . On the basis of all available evidence, including configuration of the complex, we believe that plutonium production for weapons is at least one major purpose of this effort . . . it is intended for the production of weapons grade plutonium, whether or not generation of electric power is involved."[19] The NIE noted the

15. Or Rabinowitz, *Bargaining on Nuclear Tests: Washington and Its Cold War Deals* (Oxford: Oxford University Press, 2014), 74.

16. Cohen, *Israel and the Bomb*, 60.

17. De Gaulle quoted in ibid., 73.

18. Ibid.

19. Special National Intelligence Estimate, "Implications of the Acquisition by Israel of a Nuclear Weapons Capability," No. 100-8-60, December 8, 1960, p. 1, http://www.foia.cia.gov/sites/default/files/document_conversions/89801/DOC_0005796843.pdf.

role of French assistance and ascribed Paris's motives to "bolstering Israel as the only reliable long-term French ally in an area swept by influence hostile to France."[20] By late 1960, just as President Eisenhower was leaving office during the transition to the Kennedy administration, the U.S. intelligence community concluded its assessment of Dimona and understood its key objective: nuclear weapons.

Given how long the French had been involved in the construction of the Dimona complex, the CIA's delayed assessment of the activity there represented an intelligence failure. In 1958, American intelligence began detecting suspicious nuclear activity at the Dimona site. Avner Cohen speculates: "Important information was available but was not disseminated through the system. Israel may also have had friends in high places in the intelligence and nuclear establishments who might have helped to suppress the early information. . . . The Eisenhower Administration had knowledge of the Dimona project as early as 1958–59 but did not act on it, setting the precedent that Israel's nuclear weapons program was *treated as a special case*."[21] Rather than active suppression of information, Austin Long and Joshua Shifrinson blame a set of mutually reinforcing dynamics. The absence of high-quality intelligence failed to win policymaker attention or spur action, which in turn left intelligence agencies with insufficient guidance from policymakers. At the same time, policymakers' ambivalence regarding the spread of nuclear weapons and how Washington ought to treat Israel "left intelligence analysts and diplomats with little incentive to probe other evidence of Israeli nuclear activities and prioritize collection on the program."[22] Whatever the causes of the lapse, it seems clear that, although the CIA had inklings about the potential weapons application of Dimona, other U.S. government agencies, such as the State Department, were largely unaware of this until mid-1960.[23]

There is no doubt that Israeli leaders were not exactly forthcoming about the true purpose of Dimona, with officials and business contacts referring to it alternately as a "textile plant" or a "metallurgical research installation."[24] Through the last months of the Eisenhower administration, a vigorous debate ensued across U.S. agencies about how to gain access to Dimona

20. Ibid.

21. Cohen, *Israel and the Bomb*, 84, emphasis added.

22. Austin G. Long and Joshua R. Shifrinson, "How Long until Midnight? Intelligence-Policy Relations and the United States Response to the Israeli Nuclear Program, 1959–1985," *Journal of Strategic Studies* 42, no. 1 (January 2019): 55–90.

23. Cohen, *Israel and the Bomb*, 101.

24. Ibid., 85.

and inspect the facility. However, given that the realization of Israel's activities came in the twilight of Eisenhower's presidency, Cohen writes that "in [Secretary of State Herter's] first meeting on the subject, it was already possible to discern the president's desire to look the other way with regard to the Israeli case."[25] In the meantime, Israeli officials categorically denied that it was building nuclear weapons, with Ben Gurion stating in the Knesset on December 21, 1960, that "this reactor, like the American reactor [at Soreq], is designed exclusively for peaceful purposes."[26] On the one hand, this statement was largely disingenuous. On the other hand, it provided the Eisenhower administration the public cover to look the other way while privately pressing for inspections of Dimona. Behind closed doors, Ben Gurion played semantic gymnastics with American ambassador Ogden Reid. "Israel has no plans for developing nuclear weapons," Ben Gurion stated, which may have been technically true at the time but was clearly not entirely truthful.[27] But, for the most part, Eisenhower was content to pass the buck to Kennedy because he had neither the interest to deal with the issue nor the desire to arouse the ire of a Congress that was increasingly supportive of the relationship with Israel.[28] Avner Cohen and William Burr conclude in their analysis of the diplomatic record:

> It is apparent that the Eisenhower administration had no appetite to call Ben-Gurion's bluff (either in private or in public). Nor was the departing president interested in escalating the Dimona problem into a diplomatic confrontation, which would not have even been possible with all that was already on his agenda (the Laos and Berlin crises, for example). Because relations with Israel had been relatively good, Israel had significant domestic support within the United States, and, perhaps most significantly, the Eisenhower administration was in its last few days in office, the White House let the State Department deal with the issue, keeping it under diplomatic control until the new Kennedy administration took office.

A determination to avoid a crisis encouraged senior officials such as Assistant Secretary of State G. Lewis Jones to try to "calm down" the

25. Ibid., 89.

26. Ben Gurion quoted in ibid., 91.

27. Ben Gurion quoted in ibid., 95.

28. See Dennis Ross, *Doomed to Succeed: The U.S.-Israel Relationship from Truman to Obama* (New York: Farrar, Straus and Giroux, 2015); also Warren Bass, *Support Any Friend: Kennedy's Middle East and the Making of the U.S.-Israel Alliance* (New York: Oxford University Press, 2003).

> agencies, including CIA, which he believed had been reacting intemperately, and to ensure that no one tried to cut off aid to Israel. At the same time, "calm", secrecy, and the avoidance of publicity might make it possible for Washington to get answers from the Israeli[s] and put quiet pressure on them to open up Dimona to visits by U.S. scientists and to accept safeguards by the IAEA (in fact, the last thing Ben-Gurion and his associates were likely to accept).[29]

The waning days of the Eisenhower administration illuminated the dilemma that would seize the next three American presidents. On the one hand, the United States opposed horizontal proliferation, due to fears of a cascade of proliferation and resulting complications to American policy and freedom of action in the Middle East.[30] On the other hand, the Israeli case was special and sui generis for a variety of reasons. It is certainly not the case that any administration wanted Israel to possess nuclear weapons, but none—save perhaps Kennedy—were willing to trigger a public crisis with this friend in a geopolitically vital region that enjoyed growing domestic and congressional support in order to stop it. Israeli leaders exploited this position. Ben Gurion simply needed to, writes Cohen, "lessen American pressures in order to allow for the completion of the physical infrastructure for a nuclear weapons option. He was willing to say almost anything the United States wanted to hear," and there were many prominent officials across various administrations—despite nonproliferation hawks at State, Defense, and the CIA who vehemently argued for a tougher line—who accepted these fictions as a tactic to delay American pressure and coercion on Israel to roll up Dimona.[31] The contours of American sheltering of Israeli pursuit of nuclear weapons thus began in the Eisenhower administration, were challenged hardest during the Kennedy administration, picked up steam again during the Johnson years, and were finally formalized by President Nixon in an extraordinary personal agreement struck with Israeli prime minister Golda Meir.

When Kennedy took office, his first priority on this issue was establishing secret American inspections of Dimona. The Israelis initially tried to stall the new administration, but two American reactor experts visited Dimona in

29. Avner Cohen and William Burr, "The Eisenhower Administration and the Discovery of Dimona: March 1958–January 1961," National Security Archive Electronic Briefing Book, no. 510, April 15, 2015, http://nsarchive.gwu.edu/nukevault/ebb510/.

30. See Nicholas L. Miller, "Nuclear Dominoes: A Self-Defeating Prophecy?" *Security Studies* 23, no. 1 (2014): 33–73.

31. Cohen, *Israel and the Bomb*, 96–97.

May 1961. In a highly scripted affair, the scientists accepted Israeli assurances that the reactor was strictly for peaceful purposes. The pilot reprocessing facility was necessary to avoid long shipping distances for spent reactor fuel in the future, the Israelis said. The scientists were not shown any sign of the larger underground reprocessing plant, nor did they seek to inquire about it. Cohen writes, "It is striking how uncritically the American technical experts accepted what the Israelis had told them about the project . . . [however], their mission was not to challenge what they were told, but to verify it."[32]

This set the stage for Kennedy's meeting with Ben Gurion in New York. Having seen the scientists' report, Kennedy decided not to push Ben Gurion too hard on Dimona and its purpose. When he asked Ben Gurion about Dimona, the American memorandum of conversation states that Ben Gurion replied: "Our main—for the time being—only purpose is this [desalination] . . . there is no intention to develop weapons capacity now (The Prime Minister spoke rapidly and in a low voice at this point and some of his words were missed by the rapporteur)."[33] The Israeli version of this conversation is a bit clearer, with Ben Gurion choosing his words quite carefully: "We are asked whether it is for peace. For the time being the only purposes are for peace. . . . But we will see what happens in the Middle East. It does not depend on us. Maybe Russia won't give bombs to China or Egypt, but maybe Egypt will develop them herself."[34] Kennedy colorfully prefaced this exchange with the remark "a woman should not only be virtuous but have the appearance of virtue," and reiterated the need to assure the rest of the world that Israel did not intend to use Dimona to develop nuclear weapons.[35] Kennedy was well aware of his intelligence community's conclusion that Dimona was primarily for nuclear weapons, albeit perhaps in the future as Ben Gurion had himself conceded. However, as Cohen writes, "Kennedy did not ask his guest difficult questions on this issue. . . . Both leaders wanted to avoid confrontation, and each had a sense of his own political limits. Based

32. Ibid., 107.

33. "Memorandum of Conversation, 'President Kennedy, Prime Minister Ben-Gurion, Ambassador Avraham Harman of Israel, Myer Feldman of the White House Staff, and Philips Talbot, Assistant Secretary, Near East and South Asian Affairs,'" May 30, 1961, History and Public Policy Program Digital Archive, RG 59, Bureau of Near Eastern and South Asian Affairs, Office of Near Eastern Affairs, Records of the Director, 1960–1963, box 5, Tel Aviv, 1961, obtained by William Burr, http://digitalarchive.wilsoncenter.org/document/123839, emphasis added.

34. Israeli memorandum of conversation quoted in Cohen, *Israel and the Bomb*, 108–9.

35. "Memorandum of Conversation, 'President Kennedy, Prime Minister Ben-Gurion, Ambassador Avraham Harman of Israel, Myer Feldman of the White House Staff, and Philips Talbot, Assistant Secretary, Near East and South Asian Affairs,'" May 30, 1961.

on these understandings, the two leaders created the rules of the game as they were muddling through . . . Kennedy exerted no new pressure."[36]

The key to this exchange was not what Kennedy asked Ben Gurion but what he did *not* ask or pursue. Ben Gurion's biographer notes that, after the meeting, "Ben Gurion felt relieved. The reactor was saved, at least for the time being."[37] Kennedy was unwilling to pressure Israel too hard on this issue because, although offering a formal security guarantee risked significant geopolitical blowback and consequences, he believed the United States shared "a special relationship with Israel in the Middle East really comparable only to that which it has with Britain over a wide range of world affairs . . . [a] close and intimate all[y]."[38] Galen Jackson refers to "the absence of any real effort on the part of the White House to put pressure on Jerusalem to drop its nuclear program prior to mid-1963."[39] The United States and Israel were perfecting the "don't ask, don't tell" pirouette.

American assessment of Dimona's true purpose remained unchanged, however. An NIE issued on October 5, 1961, concluded explicitly: "Israel may have decided to undertake a nuclear weapons program. At a minimum, we believe it has decided to develop its nuclear facilities in such a way as to put it in a position to develop nuclear weapons promptly should it decide to do so. With an increase in the present small plutonium separation facilities and with a continuation of the estimated present level of French technical aid, we believe Israel could have a very few crude weapons deliverable by aircraft in about five years."[40]

How do I code Israeli nuclear weapons activity? By now, Israel had made a decision to continue with the foundation for an active nuclear weapons program, the key indicator being the construction of a major underground reprocessing facility at Dimona. However, this was not insurance hedging. Israel was not threatening breakout to extract greater concessions from the United States but was instead doing the opposite: hiding capabilities from American visiting scientists hoping they would not ask questions, in order to develop nuclear weapons. There is no evidence of any hesitation

36. Cohen, *Israel and the Bomb*, 110.

37. Quoted in ibid., 111.

38. President Kennedy, Memorandum of Conversation, *FRUS, 1961–1963*, vol. XVIII, Near East, 1962–1963, doc. 121, December 27, 1962, https://history.state.gov/historicaldocuments/frus1961-63v18/d121.

39. Galen Jackson, "The United States, the Israeli Nuclear Program, and Nonproliferation, 1961–69," *Security Studies* 28, no. 2 (March 2019): 360–93.

40. "The Outlook for Israel," National Intelligence Estimate, No. 35-61, October 5, 1961, p. 2.

or reluctance by the Israeli leadership to suggest this was a form of hedging. Rather, Israel was determined to develop nuclear weapons and was banking on the United States to at least turn a blind eye to their development. For Kennedy, the Israeli nuclear program was part of a broader global nonproliferation agenda—if Israel were to attain nuclear weapons, it would be assumed that the United States allowed it, and then how could Washington stop Bonn, Delhi, and others that were similarly considering nuclear weapons? But for the next several years, both the United States and Israel avoided a showdown over the Israeli nuclear program.

The issue resurfaced when Israel responded to Egyptian saber-rattling over its newly imported ballistic missile capability by pursuing its own Jericho ballistic missiles which, in theory, could be suitable delivery vectors for nuclear warheads. The CIA delivered Kennedy a memo on the consequences of Israeli nuclearization in March 1963, which outlined the various destabilizing effects should Israel attain nuclear weapons.[41] A key line in this memo concerned Israel's strategy for pursuing nuclear weapons in the face of American nonproliferation efforts. It noted: "[Israel] would use all the means at its command to persuade the US to acquiesce in, and even to support, its possession of nuclear capability."[42] Shortly thereafter, in a meeting with Kennedy, then deputy defense minister Shimon Peres was asked point-blank about the nuclear program, to which he replied, "We will not introduce nuclear weapons to the region, and certainly will not be the first."[43] This single reply would form the basis of the American-Israel pirouette around Israel's nuclear weapons program until 1970, since it all turned on the definition of "introduce." Israel defined "introduce" as testing or publicly declaring a nuclear weapons capability; the United States wanted to define "introduce" as mere possession of an assembled nuclear weapon *or* its constituent parts. It would take until the Nixon administration to formally do so, but the United States would ultimately acquiesce to Israel's definition.

Before he was assassinated in November 1963, Kennedy struck an agreement with the new government of Levi Eshkol, who became prime minister after Ben Gurion's sudden resignation. The United States would be allowed periodic visits to Dimona, which was understood to be approximately semiannual, but the frequency was left vague after his assassination

41. "Memorandum from the Board of National Estimates, Central Intelligence Agency, to Director of Central Intelligence McCone," March 6, 1963, *FRUS, 1961–1963*, vol. XVIII, Near East, 1962–1963, https://history.state.gov/historicaldocuments/frus1961-63v18/d179.

42. Ibid.

43. Peres quoted in Cohen, *Israel and the Bomb*, 119.

and, indeed, the agreement began to crumble several years later.[44] Cohen notes that "Johnson and the CIA likely sensed what Israel was doing. They were probably not fooled by Israel's efforts to deceive the American scientists. They must have also concluded that any effort to stop Israel's nuclear weapons project was futile."[45] The only reason the United States made these visits was so that it could assure Arab states, particularly Egypt, that Dimona was strictly for peaceful purposes (though Israel opposed providing this reassurance, Eshkol ultimately relented).[46] The scripted visits in which the United States essentially engaged in willful ignorance about the progressing nuclear weapons program served that function. Israel would not allow "inspections," and the Johnson administration relented to the fiction of "scientific visits by friends" to avoid a "battle royal," write Cohen and Burr, who ultimately conclude that "as important as nonproliferation was to Johnson and his advisers, in practice they often found it necessary, as they did in this instance, to balance it against other, no-less-important political, diplomatic and security considerations."[47] America was doing nothing short of shielding Israel's nuclear program from the Arab world and their Soviet patron.

When Johnson took office, he approached nonproliferation with much less personal conviction than had Kennedy, despite taking office at a historically momentous time for nuclear proliferation. Within a year of his accession to power, a nuclear test by China triggered the Gilpatric Committee Report, which recommended tough measures against Israel should it develop nuclear weapons.[48] First, there was no appetite in Congress for such measures, since Israeli leaders had actively cultivated American domestic political support for the shelter they needed to pursue nuclear weapons.

44. It became increasingly clear that the Israelis were scripting the visits in order to obfuscate the scope and scale of the nuclear activity at Dimona. Ben Gurion's and Eshkol's Israel was being duplicitous with the American teams, though it is equally clear that at some level the American teams knew this. Cohen writes, "The teams did not discover the ongoing clandestine activity at Dimona, but they had been equipped with neither the political mandate nor the intelligence and technical means and time required to detect such activity" (ibid., 190).

45. Ibid., 193.

46. See ibid., 205.

47. Cohen and Burr, "How Israel Built a Nuclear Program Right under the Americans' Noses."

48. With respect to Israel, the Gilpatric Committee Report recommended: "As long as Israel remains a non-nuclear power, we should continue to give Israel assurances against being overrun by the UAR. We should make clear to Israel that these assurances would be withdrawn if she develops a nuclear weapon capability and that we would be prepared to consider other measures as well." See "Report by the Committee on Nuclear Proliferation," Johnson Library, National Security File, Committee File, Committee on Nuclear Proliferation, Report (Final, 12/21/65), box 8, Secret, January 21, 1965, https://history.state.gov/historicaldocuments/frus1964-68v11/d64.

Second, Johnson's attention on nonproliferation focused mostly on the MLF within NATO and the inchoate Nonproliferation Treaty, with the bilateral Israeli question languishing due to both a lack of bandwidth and the realization by 1965–66 "that the Israeli program was unstoppable."[49] The only pathway to contain the Israeli program at this point would be if it signed the NPT and put Dimona under IAEA safeguards, which was viewed as a herculean task in Washington and a nonstarter in Tel Aviv. As a strictly bilateral matter, America's efforts to get eyes on, and potentially contain, Israel's march toward nuclear weapons were failing. They were failing because Johnson and then Nixon were unwilling to use the significant coercive leverage at their disposal to stop Israel, and they were unwilling to offer the one thing that could have kept Israel an insurance hedger: a formal security guarantee and a nuclear umbrella. An unanswerable counterfactual is whether Israel would have had the immunity it required to attempt a sheltered pursuit strategy if Kennedy had not been assassinated.

Nevertheless, as would become the pattern during the Johnson and Nixon administrations, officials at State and Defense showed far more concern about the danger of proliferation, particularly in the case of proliferation by Israel, than the presidents themselves. Johnson would in fact set the precedent of delinking American conventional aid to Israel from the nuclear question. Avner Cohen writes that the "special deal" with Israel began to take shape in this period and to become an "established feature of U.S. policy": "U.S. tolerance of Israel's nuclear capability in return for Israeli opacity in its official nuclear posture."[50] More specifically, in a Memorandum of Understanding dated March 10, 1965, the United States "reaffirmed its concern for the maintenance of Israel's security" (read: arms sales, including, for the first time, combat aircraft) while Israel, for the first time in writing, pledged to "not be the first to introduce nuclear weapons into the Arab-Israel area."[51] As before, the entire understanding turned on the wide discrepancy between the American and Israeli definitions of "introduce."

This understanding allowed Johnson to begin the process of delinking American arms sales to Israel from the nuclear question. Nowhere was this more evident than in the sale of A-4 Skyhawk aircraft. While officials within

49. Avner Cohen, "Israel and the Evolution of U.S. Nonproliferation Policy: The Critical Decade (1958–1968)," *Nonproliferation Review* 5, no. 2 (Winter 1998): 14.

50. Ibid., 17.

51. Telegram, Embassy of Israel to the Department of State, "Text of Signed Memorandum of Understanding," March 11, 1965, *FRUS, 1964–1968*, vol. XVIII, Arab-Israeli Dispute, 1964–67, doc. 185, https://history.state.gov/historicaldocuments/frus1964-68v18/d185.

the administration debated how to explicitly link the request for combat aircraft to Dimona visits and the nuclear question, Johnson essentially shifted U.S. policy from trying to use arms as leverage, as Kennedy had meekly threatened, to using arms as the conventional edge to prevent Israel's "introduction" of nuclear weapons. That is, if Israel could maintain conventional superiority over its adversaries, overt breakout or "introduction" of its nuclear weapons capability could be forestalled and spare the United States and the region the resulting complications. On February 8, 1966, Deputy NSA Robert Komer wrote Johnson a memo capturing this shift:

> From 1948–61 we managed to avoid becoming a major arms supplier by indirectly subsidizing Israeli purchases in Europe. But the drying up of Israel's regular European sources (they just don't produce the right items any more—and Bonn opted out entirely) forced us to become direct suppliers—first Hawks and then tanks. Since our own deep commitment to Israel's security would almost force us to intervene if there were another major Arab-Israeli flareup, it is in our interest to help Israel maintain a sufficient deterrent edge to warn off Nasser and other eager beavers . . .
>
> *Can we use planes as a lever to keep Israel from going nuclear*? Desperation is what would most likely drive Israel to this choice, should it come to feel that the conventional balance was turning against it. So judicious US arms supply, aimed at maintaining a deterrent balance, is as good an inhibitor as we've got.[52]

Any links to the nuclear weapons program were now implicit; arms sales were not formally conditioned on Israel allowing inspectors to Dimona or otherwise adhering to anything but the formulation that it would not be the first to introduce nuclear weapons to the region. The Israelis exploited strong domestic sympathy for American arms sales to Israel to help cultivate this shelter, as administration officials were deeply worried about how they would explain to Congress and the American people any withholding of conventional arms to Israel.[53] The only language restricting the Skyhawk role was that they could not be used as "nuclear weapons carriers," which actually implicitly conceded that the United States knew that Israel would

52. "Memorandum from the President's Deputy Special Assistant for National Security Affairs (Komer) to President Johnson," February 8, 1966, *FRUS, 1964–1968*, vol. XVIII, Arab-Israeli Dispute, 1964–67, doc. 267, https://history.state.gov/historicaldocuments/frus1964-68v18/d267.

53. See Jackson, "The United States, the Israeli Nuclear Program, and Nonproliferation," 381–82.

likely possess nuclear weapons in the near future.[54] Secretary of State Rusk would report to Secretary of Defense Clifford that the president is "strongly opposed to twisting arms on the nuclear thing in connection with Phantoms. *Doesn't want them linked.*"[55] Indeed, at this point, Cohen writes that America's ambassador to Israel, Walworth Barbour, "was not interested in learning too much about Dimona, and he did not instruct the embassy personnel to do much about it. He believed that this attitude would best serve Johnson's interests and wishes. Barbour interpreted Johnson's interests and wishes correctly. The White House knew something, but also did not want to know too much."[56] All this dithering led U.S. officials to conclude during the Johnson administration: "All indications are toward Israeli acquisition of a nuclear capability . . . U.S. hesitation and delays . . . have led the Israelis to believe we are not serious" in opposing its pursuit of nuclear weapons.[57] Jackson concludes that Johnson's occasional statements in opposition to Israeli nuclear ambitions were performance theater. In a June 1964 conversation with Eshkol, Johnson "used tough language during his formal meeting with Eshkol to appease his subordinates and thereby neutralize them," Jackson comments.[58]

Several months later—and several months before the Six Day War—Israel crossed the threshold that Johnson assumed they inevitably would, probably conducting a cold test (a test without the fissile material) of a plutonium implosion nuclear weapons design on November 2, 1966.[59] Possessed of the necessary fissile material, Israel was likely just a proverbial screwdriver turn away from a nuclear weapon at this point. Unlike Ben Gurion, who stated to the Knesset that Dimona was only for peaceful purposes, Eshkol publicly stated, "Israel has no atomic weapons and will not be the first to introduce them into our region."[60] He did not say that Israel has no nuclear weapons program, and his carefully chosen words simply meant that Israel did not

54. Ibid.

55. Memorandum of Telephone Conversation, Secretary of State Rusk and Secretary of Defense Clifford, *FRUS, 1964–1968*, vol. XX, Arab-Israeli Dispute, 1967–68, doc. 299, November 1, 1968, https://history.state.gov/historicaldocuments/frus1964-68v20/d299, emphasis added.

56. Cohen, *Israel and the Bomb*, 214.

57. Memorandum from the Director of the Office of Near Eastern Affairs (Davies) to the Assistant Secretary of State for Near Eastern and South Asian Affairs (Talbot), *FRUS, 1964–1968*, vol. XVIII, Arab-Israeli Dispute, 1964–67, doc. 178, March 5, 1965, https://history.state.gov/historicaldocuments/frus1964-68v18/d178.

58. Jackson, "The United States, the Israeli Nuclear Program, and Nonproliferation."

59. Cohen, *Israel and the Bomb*, 232.

60. Eshkol speech to Knesset quoted in ibid., 233.

possess assembled nuclear weapons, which was almost certainly true at the time. However, during the Six Day War in June 1967, Avner Cohen claims Israel assembled at least two nuclear weapons in an improvised manner.[61] In crossing this critical threshold, even if they were disassembled after the war (as they almost surely were), Israel essentially culminated its attainment of nuclear weapons, though it was an extremely limited potential arsenal and thus still required American shelter and the grand bargain on "introduction" in order to survive.

After the Six Day War, the Johnson administration did not put any overt pressure on Israel regarding its nuclear program, nor did it do much more than continue to request that Israel consider signing what would eventually become the NPT, though it knew Israel would not do so (and eventually delinked arms sales from this request as well, making "no threat whatsoever, either direct or veiled," according to Cohen).[62] At the end of the Johnson administration, a heated series of crucial exchanges took place between Assistant Secretary of Defense Paul Warnke and then ambassador Yitzhak Rabin.[63] The issue about what "introducing" nuclear weapons meant in practice came to a head. Warnke insisted that mere possession of nuclear weapons or their component parts—"although part A may be in one room and part B in another room"—constituted "introduction of nuclear weapons."[64] Rabin refused to accept this definition and insisted that a nuclear weapon had not been "introduced" until it had been tested *or* publicly acknowledged.[65] The key part of the exchange came at the end of the meeting:

> Mr. Warnke said: "Then in your view, an unadvertised, untested nuclear device is not a nuclear weapon." Ambassador Rabin said: "Yes, that is correct." Mr. Warnke asked: "What about an advertised but untested nuclear device or weapon. Would that be introduction?" Ambassador Rabin said: "Yes, that would be introduction." Mr. Warnke said he would interpret mere physical presence in the area as constituting, in itself, "introduction."[66]

61. Avner Cohen, "Crossing the Threshold: The Untold Nuclear Dimension of the 1967 Arab-Israeli War and Its Contemporary Lessons," *Arms Control Today* 37, no. 5 (June 2007), https://www.armscontrol.org/act/2007_06/Cohen.

62. See Cohen, *Israel and the Bomb*, 316.

63. "Negotiations with Israel, F-4 and Advanced Weapons," Memorandum of Conversation, November 12, 1968, http://nsarchive.gwu.edu/NSAEBB/NSAEBB189/IN-03c.pdf.

64. Ibid., 2.

65. Ibid., 3.

66. Ibid., 4.

This exchange, and Rabin's insistence on rejecting the American definition of "introduce nuclear weapons," left Warnke and the U.S. government convinced—in 1968—that Israel already possessed nuclear weapons, albeit likely in a disassembled state but which could be rapidly constituted. In his memoirs, Dean Rusk wrote that, at this point, Israel was essentially "eight and three-fourths months pregnant and could produce nuclear weapons on very short notice," particularly after Israeli foreign minister Eban "gave [him] the usual assurance: 'We'll not be the first.' But as [Eban] was leaving [his] office, he turned and said, 'But we won't be the second!'"[67] But Johnson nevertheless insisted on de-linking the Phantom sale to Israel's nuclear program or to signing the NPT. Just before yielding office to Nixon, Johnson announced the sale of fifty F-4s to Israel and "the NPT issue was no longer mentioned."[68] Israel essentially attained a nuclear weapons capability under Johnson's watch, while the administration engaged in willful ignorance. It did not want to know any details that would make American nonproliferation policy appear inconsistent. Washington also worked to avoid triggering coercive action against a friendly state upon which American interests in a vital region depended. This amounted to a purposeful extension of immunity to the Israeli nuclear program.

This was the state of affairs when President Nixon took office in January 1969, followed shortly thereafter by Levi Eshkol's passing, giving way to the premiership of Golda Meir. The first several months of the Nixon administration saw a flurry of activity related to Israel's nuclear status. But even before taking office, in a transition meeting with Rabin, Henry Kissinger stated that "the Republican administration would be more relaxed on the nuclear issue."[69] The problem for Nixon and Kissinger would be officials at State and Defense who were more hawkish about stopping Israel from culminating weaponization—though unbeknownst to many of them, they were likely already too late. Secretary of Defense Laird went so far as to write that he was convinced Israel was pretty much at the point of weaponization and likely believed that Israel "may have both [redacted, but probably nuclear weapons and strategic missiles] this year . . . such developments were not in the United States' interest and should, if at all possible, be stopped."[70]

67. Dean Rusk and Tom Rusk, *As I Saw It* (New York: Penguin Books, 1991), 343.

68. Cohen, *Israel and the Bomb*, 319.

69. Kissinger quoted in ibid., 327.

70. Secretary of Defense Melvin Laird to Secretary of State et al., "Stopping the Introduction of Nuclear Weapons into the Middle East," March 17, 1969, http://nsarchive.gwu.edu/NSAEBB/NSAEBB189/IN-06.pdf.

Secretary of State William Rogers generally agreed with this assessment, which was at odds with Kissinger's view. This triggered an interagency study National Security Study Memorandum (NSSM) 40 on April 11, 1969.

The policy study following NSSM 40 was drafted on May 29, 1969, and probably delivered to Kissinger shortly thereafter. A declassified version of the document weighs the various policy options to address Israel's nuclear weapons capability.[71] In terms of sheltering the Israeli program from particularly the Soviets, the study interestingly concluded that "we believe that the Soviet Union is generally aware of Israel's nuclear weapons program, although we do not know to what extent. The fact that the Soviets have not made an issue with us on this subject may indicate that they feel that this is a U.S. problem."[72] In terms of how the U.S. government should deal with this particular situation, the Department of Defense was much more willing to threaten delaying F-4 deliveries than State, which advocated political "suasion rather than coercive tactics."[73] The Defense position was summarized by Deputy Secretary of Defense David Packard in a memo declaring that "the choice of decision before the President is to lean on the Israelis or not to lean on them. In my opinion, to not lean on them would, in effect, involve us in a *conspiracy with Israel* which would leave matters dangerous to our security in their hands."[74]

Kissinger's own memo to President Nixon after receiving the NSSM 40 policy study offered starkly different advice and analysis. Kissinger's memo ultimately formed the basis of Nixon's policy to even more aggressively shelter Israel's nuclear program.[75] He clearly identified the American objective at that point: "What this means is that, while we might ideally like to halt actual Israeli possession, what we really want at a minimum may be just to keep Israeli possession [of nuclear weapons] from becoming an established international fact."[76] Furthermore, "for our own internal purposes, we would decide that we could tolerate Israeli activity short of assembly of a completed

71. "Israeli Nuclear Weapons Program—Issues and Courses of Action," from NEA Roger P. Davies to Dr. Henry Kissinger, National Security Study Memorandum, May 29, 1969.

72. Ibid., Annex, 3.

73. Ibid., 10.

74. "Israeli Nuclear Program," Memorandum for the Secretary of Defense from Deputy Secretary of Defense David Packard, June 27, 1969, emphasis added.

75. "Israeli Nuclear Program," Memorandum for the President from National Security Advisor Henry Kissinger to President Nixon, July 19, 1969, http://nsarchive.gwu.edu/nukevault/ebb485/docs/Doc%2010%207-19-69%20circa.pdf.

76. Ibid., 2.

nuclear device."[77] In terms of how to approach the impending F-4 deliveries, Kissinger writes: "There is the danger that we will become accomplices . . . we might look as if we acquiesced, especially if we talked and then delivered the Phantoms—a nuclear weapons carrier—anyway. Even if we get what we want and the Israelis violate their pledge, we might look like accomplices. There could be an argument for acting in *pretended ignorance*."[78] In presenting the downside to delivering the Phantoms, which were clearly suitable for nuclear delivery, Kissinger continued: "We would accept complicity in Israel's possession of nuclear weapons by saying in effect: We know what Israel has, but we will close our eyes to it—and deliver the Phantoms—provided the Israelis promise not to announce what they have. . . . It puts the Israelis in a position—with our acquiescence—to let the world know indirectly but unmistakably what it has without violating any pledge to us."[79]

Kissinger ran through the pros and cons of delaying F-4s until the United States and Israel reached an understanding on "its plans for its nuclear weapons program"[80] for the president. At one point, Kissinger again reiterated the basic conundrum:

> Saying that we want to keep Israel's possession of nuclear weapons from becoming an established international fact may come very close to describing what we really want in this case. Our interest is in preventing Israeli possession of nuclear weapons. But since we cannot—and may not want to try to—control the state of Israel's nuclear program and since Israel may already have nuclear weapons, the one objective we might achieve is to persuade them to keep what they have secret. This would meet our objective because the international implications of an Israeli program are not triggered until it becomes public knowledge. . . . It leaves us highly vulnerable to the charge of acquiescing in the proliferation of nuclear weapons—and even of abetting it by delivering the Phantom, a nuclear weapons carrier.[81]

Nixon would take all this into consideration over the next couple months in the run-up to his one-on-one meeting with Golda Meir on September 26, 1969. He would decide not to delay the F-4s or to condition American aid or arms on Israel accepting the Warnke definition of "introducing nuclear

77. Ibid., 3.
78. Ibid., Tab A, 5, emphasis added.
79. Ibid., Tab A, 10.
80. Ibid., Tab A, 17.
81. Ibid., Tab A, 10–11.

weapons." He would in fact follow a course of action that Kissinger described as acquiescing and even abetting proliferation, and what Packard described as a conspiracy to allow Israel to achieve and retain a nuclear weapons capability. In that monumental meeting, of which there is no declassified record to date, Avner Cohen writes:

> Meir almost certainly confided in Nixon that Israel already was in possession of a bomb, with the bomb assembled or otherwise . . . President Nixon, who had accepted that America could not—and should not—exert pressure on Israel, received a firm commitment from the prime minister that Israel would not change its declaratory pledge not to be the first country to introduce nuclear weapons to the region . . . [Meir] pledged to keep them invisible, that is, untested and undeclared. In return, Nixon agreed to end the United States' annual visits to . . . Dimona and apparently agreed not to pressure Israel to sign the NPT. This practical agreement between the leaders became the foundation of the secret bilateral understanding of the issue.[82]

The basis of this understanding, which has persisted since that historic meeting, was that, as Cohen puts it, "as long as Israel kept the bomb in the basement, the United States could live with Israel's 'nonintroduction' pledge . . . Israelis understand the bargain as an American pledge to shield the Israeli nuclear program."[83] It has reportedly become tradition for new Israeli and American heads of state to reaffirm this secret pledge at their first meeting.[84] This concluded a decade-long Israeli strategy to acquire immunity for its nuclear program from the United States, who would not try to actively stop Israeli nuclearization and protected it from preventive attacks from the Soviets and Arabs by giving it both diplomatic cover in international forums and advanced conventional arms. While lower-level American officials—and perhaps even President Kennedy—may have wanted to stop the Israeli bomb, Presidents Eisenhower, Johnson, and Nixon largely tolerated the Israeli nuclear weapons program (as has each president since), so long as it did not test, because of the critical role Israel plays in American Middle East policy. Indeed, the U.S. government would go to great lengths to keep the mysterious 1979 Vela incident—a possible Israeli atmospheric nuclear test with South African assistance in the Indian Ocean—highly ambiguous

82. Cohen, *The Worst-Kept Secret*, 26.
83. Ibid., 32.
84. Ibid.

to maintain this bargain, despite a suspected Israeli violation of it, and continue to shelter the Israeli nuclear program.[85] This bargain is what ultimately enabled Israel to adopt a catalytic nuclear posture, as I have argued elsewhere, using the threat of public revelation or testing to compel the United States to come to its aid in moments of crisis, to ensure that Israel would keep its bomb in the "basement."[86]

The Israeli proliferation strategy from the moment Ben Gurion initiated an active nuclear weapons program due to Israel's acute security predicament was to cultivate the shelter of greater powers—at first France, but then critically the United States—to immunize the program against attacks from the Arabs and Soviets. Given its vulnerable geography and geopolitical situation, absent such a shelter, Israel faced a steep uphill battle to develop nuclear weapons. So, it made itself indispensable to its potential patrons, actively seeking and constructing that shelter. It did so first by participating in the Suez operation with France and using that leverage and coinciding interests to extract what it needed for a nuclear weapons program: a reactor and a reprocessing facility. Once that shelter began crumbling with

85. See, for example, Leonard Weiss, "Flash from the Past: Why an Apparent Israeli Nuclear Test in 1979 Matters Today," *Bulletin of the Atomic Scientists*, September 8, 2015, http://thebulletin.org/flash-past-why-apparent-israeli-nuclear-test-1979-matters-today8734; William Burr, Avner Cohen, and Richard Wolfson, "The Vela Flash: Forty Years Ago," National Security Archive, Briefing Book, no. 686, September 22, 2019, https://nsarchive.gwu.edu/briefing-book/nuclear-vault/2019-09-22/vela-flash-forty-years-ago; William Burr and Avner Cohen, "Revisiting the 1979 Vela Mystery: A Report on the Critical Oral History Conference," Wilson Center, August 31, 2020, https://www.wilsoncenter.org/blog-post/revisiting-1979-vela-mystery-report-critical-oral-history-conference; and Secretary Cyrus Vance, cable for U.S. Embassy Paris, "Press Panel Review of South Atlantic Event," February 7, 1980, in Kenneth Mokoena, ed., *South Africa and the United States: A Declassified History*, A National Security Archive Documents Reader (New York: New Press, 1993), doc. 25, p. 136. The CIA, for example, assessed the probability that the event was a nuclear detonation at 90 percent. South Africa is unlikely to have had enough fissile material for a test at this time, leaving Israel as the prime suspect. President Carter would later point the finger at Israel in his memoirs. Interestingly, however, the Ruina Panel, which was commissioned to analyze the event, concluded that it could have been non-nuclear, thereby shielding Israel and the bargain. Contrary to conventional wisdom, the Ruina Panel was not tasked with finding the most likely explanation, only with very narrowly determining if there were *any plausible* non-nuclear explanations for the event: "evaluat[ing] the possibility that the signal in question was a 'false alarm' resulting from technical malfunction" and "evaluat[ing] the possibility that the signal recorded by the satellite was of natural origin." The scientists on the panel, being the good scientists they were, assessed the probabilities of both of those possibilities as technically non-zero, allowing the panel's conclusions to be framed in a way that could exonerate the perpetrating party which, at that point, was increasingly feared in the U.S. government to be Israel since many (correctly) doubted that South Africa had the capability to conduct a full-blown test in September 1979.

86. See Narang, *Nuclear Strategy in the Modern Era*, chap. 7.

de Gaulle's arrival, Israeli leaders actively tried to foster American shelter. Leveraging the increasingly powerful diaspora in America, and the fact that it was the bulwark against socialist influence in the Middle East, Israel convinced American leaders that U.S. Middle East policy depended upon Israeli strength. It became an article of faith among members of Congress that Israel needed to be supported almost unquestionably, and that included conventional arms sales and delinking anything, particular the thorny problem of Israel's nuclear weapons program, that might threaten arms deliveries. Only Kennedy might have prioritized nonproliferation over the critical geopolitical value Israel provided. But his successors, Johnson and Nixon, increasingly accepted that they could not and would not hold the relationship hostage over Israel's nuclear weapons and tacitly, and then actively, accepted Israel as a nuclear weapons state. This was a strategic decision by Tel Aviv: to impress upon Washington the geopolitical value it provided the United States, a value that outstripped America's general nonproliferation objectives so long as Israel kept its bomb in the basement. Because the United States was not a formal ally, Israel needed more than an insurance hedge. It needed to develop nuclear weapons that were readily usable in the event it faced abandonment from the United States.

TESTING PROLIFERATION STRATEGY THEORY

My theory explains the active strategy of proliferation that Israel would choose. Once Ben Gurion decided to embark on an active nuclear weapons proliferation strategy in the mid-1950s, Israel's successful search for great power immunity to at least shelter the program against Arab and Soviet prevention yielded two sequential shelterers: France and then, most critically, the United States. Israel's goal was to weaponize its nuclear capabilities under that shelter as quickly as possible, in the event it disappeared. Indeed, Israel went full steam ahead under American shelter in the 1960s in order to weaponize. This is exactly what my theory predicts, given Israel's security threats, domestic consensus, and the arduous international counterproliferation environment. The relevant counterfactual to my theory's prediction that shelter is important is whether the Arab states and Soviet Union would have allowed a nuclear Israel absent American patronage, or whether they would have tried to prevent it by force if necessary. Counterfactuals are necessarily difficult to evaluate, but the prospect of a direct American-Soviet conflict over Israel's nuclear program—as was almost foreshadowed in the 1973 Yom Kippur War when both superpowers went on nuclear alert—would have likely given the Soviets and its client states pause in ways that Israel defending itself and infrastructure alone may not have.

Even standard structural realist theories would have a hard time predicting that Israel would select sheltered pursuit in the period it did, when the patrons it was seeking were initially lukewarm at best. If realism has a determinate prediction for how Israel might develop nuclear weapons, it would most likely be a hiding strategy, particularly given the stated nonproliferation goals of the United States that could potentially coerce Israel into rolling back its program by threatening to withhold military aid. It was not a foregone conclusion that Israel could successfully cultivate American immunity. Instead, Israeli leaders, particularly Ben Gurion and Eshkol, believed that garnering some American protection—even if they were less than forthcoming about the advanced state of the nuclear weapons program—was better than hiding it outright and being caught and coerced into giving the program up. This is not what the self-help theories derived from structural realism would necessarily predict.

Furthermore, contrary to the predictions of technological determinism, Israel declined to conduct an underground test in the late 1960s despite having the ability and technical incentive to do so. This was a deliberate choice in order to preserve U.S. shelter. Even assuming that the 1979 Vela incident was in fact an Israeli test—a possibility the U.S. government almost certainly downplayed once Israel emerged as a likely perpetrator, searching for almost *any other* (im)plausible explanation besides a nuclear test to explain the satellite readings—Israel had delayed performing any tests until a decade after it was in a position to conduct them. Indeed, Israel has not conducted an underground test to this day, potentially accepting technical constraints on the character of its nuclear arsenal (e.g., thermonuclear designs) in order to retain shelter. Furthermore, a technological determinism explanation for Israeli proliferation strategy could have equally predicted that it would attempt to select a uranium enrichment pathway that might be easier to hide, obviating the need to cultivate superpower immunity. However, Israeli politicians wanted the plutonium pathway so it could develop missile-mateable warheads and selected a sheltering strategy so it could choose that pathway—with Dimona being a visible signature to everyone from Cairo to Moscow. It was a strategic decision to select this path, which would best suit Israel's security needs; Israel had the choice and opted for plutonium under shelter.

Finally, Israel pursued nuclear weapons just as the Nonproliferation Treaty was taking shape on the heels of the Chinese nuclear test in 1964.

It was one of the key "second generation" proliferators that the NPT was trying to freeze along with India, Sweden, and Pakistan. Again, if the emerging nonproliferation regime was driving Israel's strategy of proliferation, it should have chosen hiding to avoid complete detection from the prying eyes of the international community and the IAEA. Instead, remarkably, Israel was able to cultivate so much shelter from the United States for its program that both Johnson and Nixon dropped signing the NPT as a condition for arms sales, knowing full well that Israel could not and would not sign—much to the consternation of many within their administrations. The country perhaps most responsible for shaping the NPT, the United States, was making a colossal exception from the outset by knowingly allowing Israel to stay out of it—allowing others to infer what they would about the state of Israel's nuclear program and America's knowledge and complicity in it. While other states such as Sweden and Switzerland were turning away from their nuclear weapons pursuit to champion nonproliferation, Israel remained unmoved and, indeed, managed to nurture so much shelter in Washington that it received an unprecedented license to stay out of the nonproliferation regime entirely.

Proliferation Strategy Theory explains Israel's search for shelter, calculating that if it could exploit its position as a bulwark against socialist expansion in the Middle East, it could extract protection for nuclear weapons. A strategy of sheltered pursuit established a level of implausible deniability to the United States but masked Israel's advances to the rest of the world, allowing it to select the technology—plutonium—that it believed was more strategically useful. At first, France would provide temporary shelter. But it would be the United States that would extend the greatest protection owing to the confluence of strategic utility and strong domestic political support for Israel in America. And it was ultimately with Nixon's blessing that Israel attained the possession of nuclear weapons.

Pakistan: The Goat Shed at Kahuta

Hard Hedging: 1954–71
Hiding: 1971–80
Sheltered Pursuit: 1980–90

Almost twenty years later, the United States would essentially make the same Nixon-Meir bargain with Pakistan. Unlike Israel, which was a crucial—but informal—friend of the United States and which enjoyed tremendous domestic political support in the United States, Pakistan suddenly found itself transformed from a virtual pariah to the frontline state in the American struggle against the Soviet Union, first when there was a 1978 communist coup in Afghanistan, but most critically a year later following the December 25, 1979, Christmas invasion by the USSR. This event forced the United States to prioritize the war in Afghanistan—and the crucial conduit Pakistan provided to it—over its nonproliferation objectives, allowing Pakistan to build nuclear weapons with a sheltered pursuit strategy. Pakistan used the shelter to redouble its uranium enrichment program and weapons design efforts while enjoying immunity from the United States.

Indeed, prior to the Soviet invasion, as mandated by the Glenn and Symington amendments, the Carter administration had essentially cut Pakistan off from everything but agricultural aid due to its continued pursuit of reprocessing technology from France (French nuclear assistance to so many proliferators of concern requires an entirely separate book), as well as evidence of a hidden Pakistani enrichment program. Relations between the United States and Pakistan following a November 21, 1979, mob attack on the U.S. embassy in Islamabad that killed four people and destroyed the embassy were, according to NSC member Thomas Thornton, "about as bad as with any country in the world, except perhaps Albania or North Korea."[87] The Carter administration, which had come down hard on Pakistan for not only General Muhammad Zia-ul-Haq's military coup and execution of Prime Minister Zulfikar Ali Bhutto but also its nuclear program, would be forced to do a full about-turn "overnight, literally," and provide Pakistan shelter to develop nuclear weapons.[88] The Carter administration tried to be "aboveboard," seeking the congressional waivers necessary to provide aid despite Pakistan's nuclear activity, tacitly indicating that Washington was fully aware of Islamabad's sordid nuclear activities.

This sheltering pattern would only intensify during the Reagan administration. The United States looked the other way on Pakistan's advancing nuclear weapons program and, ironically, ended up flipping the script and using Shimon Peres's definition of "introduction of nuclear weapons" as a full-blown nuclear test in order to sustain American aid to Pakistan. Islamabad, in turn, was more than happy to use its newfound leverage to steadily march to the bomb, persistently calling the Reagan administration's bluffs and thumbing its nose at American nonproliferation threats. The Pakistan

87. Thornton quoted in Dennis Kux, *The United States and Pakistan, 1947–2000: Disenchanted Allies* (Baltimore: Johns Hopkins University Press, 2001), 245.

88. Ibid.

case illustrates that hiding is not the only pathway to the bomb in the post-NPT, and post–American sanctions legislation, era. If a state somehow finds itself sheltered by—that is, geopolitically useful to—a great power, it can exploit that shelter to pursue nuclear weapons. Had the Soviet Union not invaded Afghanistan in 1979 and the United States not provided Pakistan shelter for its nuclear program as a result, it is unlikely that Pakistan would have successfully built nuclear weapons. Either America alone or America and India would have been in a good position to destroy the program militarily or through sanctions. Instead, Pakistan took advantage of the American shelter extended after the Soviet invasion to accelerate its nuclear weapons efforts and essentially weaponized under American sanctuary.

Pakistan's active—initially hidden—nuclear weapons program officially began in January 1972 at the Multan meeting, in which Prime Minister Bhutto instructed his scientists to develop nuclear weapons by any means necessary in order to avoid a repetition of the disastrous 1971 war with India, which saw Pakistan bisected and humiliated, birthing Bangladesh from Pakistan's erstwhile eastern flank.[89] Through various civil nuclear deals, Pakistan had already constructed a 5 MW research reactor at the PINSTECH facility near Islamabad (PARR-1) and in 1972 added a CANDU reactor known as KANUPP in Karachi. Prior to the 1971 loss, Pakistani leaders such as Ayub Khan, according to Feroz Hassan Khan's definitive work on the program, "never explicitly rejected the bomb option. He simply decided not to decide."[90] There was some hard hedging at this point, with Bhutto as early as 1965 calling for a Pakistani nuclear weapons program, famously saying that Pakistanis will "eat grass" if they have to, but they must possess nuclear weapons if India does so. But Pakistan's acute security predicament significantly intensified after the humiliating loss in 1971—all previous wars with India could be optimistically counted as draws—in whose aftermath Bhutto came to power. Confronting a clearly acute security threat that posed an existential threat to Pakistan, Bhutto essentially ordered Pakistan's Atomic Energy Commission (PAEC) to "deliver" a nuclear weapon, installing a new head, Munir Ahmad Khan, to direct the program on January 20, 1972.[91]

89. For work on Pakistan's nuclear weapons program, see Khan, *Eating Grass*; and George Perkovich, "Could Anything Be Done to Stop Them? Lessons from Pakistan's Proliferating Past," in *Pakistan's Nuclear Future: Worries beyond War*, ed. Henry D. Sokolski (Carlisle, PA: Strategic Studies Institute, 2008), 59–84; also see Samina Ahmed, "Pakistan's Nuclear Weapons Program," *International Security* 23, no. 4 (Spring 1999): 178–204.

90. Khan, *Eating Grass*, 65.

91. Ibid., 87.

When India tested its peaceful nuclear explosion (PNE) in May 1974, no one in Pakistan believed it was peaceful and, according to Khan, the test "turned Pakistan's policy option into an imperative," further catalyzing its quest for nuclear weapons and steeling Bhutto's resolve.[92]

The problem for Pakistan was that the Indian PNE triggered a tightening of export controls. The international community tried to close loopholes that allowed states to exploit the civilian energy market to develop nuclear weapons. This forced Pakistan to try every possible pathway to weapons-grade fissile material, both uranium enrichment and plutonium reprocessing.[93] Munir Ahmad Khan developed an initial plan that "started looking at both routes."[94] As a nonsignatory of the NPT, Pakistan had to essentially hide its true purpose in seeking enrichment or reprocessing technologies, or hide its acquisitions altogether, otherwise it risked significant coercive pressure from the international community and especially the United States. At the last minute, Canada and West Germany halted shipments of a nuclear fuel fabrication plant and a heavy water production plant, respectively, for this reason.[95] In December 1976, Canada cut off all supplies and assistance to the KANUPP reactor.[96] The French firm Saint Gobain provided Pakistan with hope for a reprocessing facility that would facilitate the plutonium route to a bomb. After the Indian PNE, France insisted that the reprocessing facility be placed under IAEA safeguards, which Pakistan initially acceded to on the hope that it could obtain detailed designs of the plant and build it indigenously. In February 1978, under strong pressure from the Carter administration, the French suggested modifying the plant to produce mixed oxide fuel rather than plutonium.[97] Then-president Zia rejected that proposal, at which point the French were "convinced Pakistan wanted the bomb" and terminated its sale of the reprocessing plant.[98] The plutonium route, attempting to exploit dual-use technologies on the open market, was (only temporarily) shunted.

However, the uranium enrichment pathway was still possible because of the entrepreneurial activities of a URENCO (the European centrifuge

92. Ibid., 92.

93. Ibid., 100–101.

94. Munir Ahmad Khan quoted in ibid., 104.

95. Ibid., 105.

96. Ibid., 114.

97. See Kux, *Disenchanted Allies*, 236; and Khan, *Eating Grass*, 132.

98. French nuclear expert Andre Jacomet, who was involved in the proposal, quoted in Kux, *Disenchanted Allies*, 236.

consortium) employee named Abdul Qadeer (AQ) Khan. In a 1974 meeting with Bhutto, AQ Khan convinced the prime minister to finance a uranium enrichment facility. The key to Khan's plan was to circumvent export controls by leveraging suppliers of individual components for gas centrifuges, which were not on export control lists, rather than trying to import entire centrifuges.[99] AQ Khan was playing a "cat and mouse game" against suppliers, writes Feroz Khan, and managed to stay "one step ahead of [his] pursuers," leveraging his deep knowledge of the suppliers from his time at URENCO and using European middlemen to evade export control laws.[100] This strategy would allow Pakistan to hide the enrichment activity for as long as possible from the threat of American sanctions as well as Indian (and possibly Israeli) military prevention. As Feroz Khan notes, in this period, "Pakistan was extremely vulnerable and did not have any leverage of its own," making a hiding strategy the only viable option.[101]

But knowing that the network of suppliers was fragile and that foreign intelligence agencies would eventually piece together the ultimate purpose of these discrete purchases—Britain ultimately sniffed out the purpose of a Pakistani purchase of inverters in 1978[102]—Pakistan searched urgently for shelter from a great power. The first shelter Pakistan attempted to secure was its enduring "all weather" ally China, which envisioned encircling India and squeezing it with two nuclear powers. Indeed, Bhutto reportedly signed a wide-ranging agreement with China in 1976 that allegedly included nuclear assistance including UF_6 feed material, 50 kilograms of weapons-grade uranium, a workable uranium bomb design, and most importantly the hope of potential shelter—according to Dennis Kux, "its main security blanket"—against a potential Indian attack, despite the fact that Beijing had never come to Islamabad's aid in its previous wars against India.[103]

Although China could and would provide substantial nuclear assistance, it could not provide Pakistan immunity from an even greater power, the United States, which during the Carter administration was keying in on Pakistan's pursuit of nuclear weapons and was moving to cut off military and economic assistance as mandated by new congressional legislation. Although the Ford administration was aware of Pakistan's general interest in nuclear weapons—after India's PNE the entire world was aware—and

99. See Khan, *Eating Grass*, chap. 7.
100. Ibid., 164.
101. Ibid., 162.
102. Ibid., 169.
103. Ibid., 171; Kux, *Disenchanted Allies*, 224.

Kissinger was informed by Assistant Secretary of State Alfred Atherton in 1975 that Pakistan "is trying to develop an independent nuclear fuel cycle and the technical skills that would make a nuclear explosion option feasible,"[104] Ford was more hesitant to use sticks than was the Carter administration that would succeed him. In a meeting between President Ford and Prime Minister Bhutto on February 5, 1975, Kissinger made clear that the White House only needed ammunition against domestic critics. He told Bhutto: "If we could say to the Congress that we had discussed your nuclear program, that would help much. If we could say we achieved some nuclear restraint for some help in conventional arms, that really would defuse the opposition."[105] Bhutto replied, directly to Ford and Kissinger: "You know where we are on this—you have your people there. We have made some progress. We have some good people and it is within reach not like some Arab states. We come after India in capability. I am not enchanted by the grandiose notion that we must explode something, no matter how dirty, if our security needs are met. I want to spend the money on something else. We will have a nuclear program, but if our security is assured, we will be reasonable."[106] Kissinger was particularly reluctant to put pressure on the Pakistanis, instead offering conventional arms to alleviate their security concerns, due to his historically warm relations with Pakistan and the fact that they served as the conduit for his greatest foreign policy achievement: establishing formal relations with China.

Had the Republicans won in 1976, Pakistan might have enjoyed some shelter from the United States. In September 1976, Kissinger, trying to get Pakistan to take a conventional arms deal in exchange for canceling the French reprocessing deal, told Pakistan's ambassador to the United States, Yaqub Khan: "You (turning to Yaqub) and I know why you want the reprocessing plant. You also know why I don't want it. You understand the problem. It's whether you are prepared to pay the costs."[107] After Carter won the election several months later, Kissinger essentially telegraphed to Ambassador Khan that Pakistan was about to lose a friend and should be prepared

104. Alfred (Roy) Atherton Memo to Kissinger cited in Kux, *Disenchanted Allies*, 219.

105. Memorandum of Conversation, President Ford and Prime Minister Bhutto et al., February 5, 1975, *FRUS, 1969–1976*, vol. E-8, Documents on South Asia, 1973–1976, doc. 188, https://history.state.gov/historicaldocuments/frus1969-76ve08/d188.

106. Ibid.

107. Memorandum of Conversation, Kissinger and Amb Khan et al., September 11, 1976, *FRUS, 1969–1976*, vol. E-8, Documents on South Asia, 1973–1976, doc. 235, https://history.state.gov/historicaldocuments/frus1969-76ve08/d235.

for the hammer: "Early in January, it will be a new administration which was elected on a plank of nonproliferation. And I think I can assure you that it won't avail itself of escape clauses, or Symington Amendments."[108] Kissinger was trying to avoid the inevitable showdown between a Pakistan that was clearly in the nascent phases of an active nuclear weapons program and a Carter administration that ran on a platform of nonproliferation and democracy promotion—both of which would put Pakistan in Carter's crosshairs after Zia's coup in July 1977—and whose hands were going to be tied by much stronger congressional nonproliferation legislation. Kissinger was correct about the showdown, at least until December 1979.

The Carter administration lived up to its promise to take a harder line on nonproliferation, canceling the A-7 aircraft deal that Ford and Kissinger had put on the table. In September 1977, Joe Nye, who was then at the State Department, went to Pakistan, but Kux writes that "he brought only sticks after Washington had withdrawn the principal carrot," threatening a full aid cutoff (minus agricultural aid) due to the Glenn and Symington amendments if Pakistan did not cease and desist in its quest for reprocessing technology outside of the NPT.[109] In 1978, after British intelligence divined the purpose of AQ Khan's illicit procurement activities, the United States directly laid out to Zia what it knew about the secret enrichment program. He defiantly denied the allegations, claiming to American ambassador Hummel: "That's absolutely ridiculous."[110] In 1978 and 1979, the United States suspended aid to Pakistan because of its nuclear program, which Zia continued to insist was for peaceful purposes only, while simultaneously refusing to rule out the future possibility of a PNE, which, after India's test, was a nonstarter for the Carter administration.[111] Although AQ Khan had managed to set up manufacturing facilities for his centrifuge components, he was evidently feeling the pressure of American sanctions on the Pakistani program, saying, "The way they are after us, it looks as if we have killed their mother."[112]

There were some in Carter's administration, notably Peter Constable, the chargé d'affaires in the U.S. embassy in Islamabad, who advocated treating

108. Memorandum of Conversation, Kissinger and Amb Khan et al., December 17, 1976, *FRUS, 1969–1976*, vol. E-8, Documents on South Asia, 1973–1976, doc. 239, https://history.state.gov/historicaldocuments/frus1969-76ve08/d239.

109. Kux, *Disenchanted Allies*, 235.

110. Ambassador Hummel quoted in ibid., 236.

111. See ibid., 239.

112. AQ Khan quoted in Adrian Levy and Catherine Scott-Clark, *Deception: Pakistan, the United States, and the Secret Trade in Nuclear Weapons* (New York: Walker and Company, 2007), 67.

Pakistan as a "special case" because "we have [otherwise] come to a dead end in our bilateral and multilateral efforts to prevent the spread of nuclear weapons technology" to India and Pakistan.[113] He noted that "we believe that what Pakistan seeks is, in part, a full fuel cycle . . . and that the GOP [government of Pakistan] might be willing to hold its nuclear capability at a stage short of actual weapons development." Constable suggested that "actual weapons development" was where the Carter administration should draw the line in order to salvage its global nonproliferation agenda.[114] He further stated: "While we would be accepting an unfortunate reality . . . we might also be able then to look to our other strategic policy interests in the region."[115] In an analysis of Constable's proposal, Gerard Smith, ambassador at large for nonproliferation, wrote Carter a memo rejecting the notion: "It would be a mistake to acquiesce in Pakistan's acquiring unsafeguarded sensitive facilities, treating South Asia differently from the rest of the world as regards nonproliferation. We are already vulnerable to the charge of such behavior with respect to Israel. A second exception would drain most of the consistency out of your nonproliferation policy."[116] In the marginalia, Carter himself settled the matter, writing: "Agree. True."[117] True, indeed. Foreshadowing what was to come, Ambassador Pickering, in an interview with Or Rabinowitz, stated: "we thought we had an opportunity to stop the program short, so going on a non-testing agreement would seem to be implied permission to get up to that line but not beyond."[118] The fundamental problem is that Pakistan did not want to stop short—it wanted to develop and possess nuclear weapons. Several months later, U.S.-Pakistan relations would hit their Cold War nadir when the U.S. embassy was burned by a mob attack on November 21, 1979, and many in Washington blamed Zia's government for being either complicit or indifferent.[119]

113. Peter Constable, U.S. Department of State Cable 145139 to U.S. Embassy India [repeating cable sent to Embassy Pakistan], "Non-Proliferation in South [Asia]," excerpts, June 6, 1979, in William Burr, ed., *New Documents Spotlight Reagan-Era Tensions over Pakistani Nuclear Program*, NSA EBB 377, doc. 1, https://www.documentcloud.org/documents/347012-doc-1-6-6-79.html.

114. Ibid.

115. Ibid.

116. Gerard C. Smith, Special Representative of the President for Non-Proliferation Matters, to the President, "Nonproliferation in South Asia," June 8, 1979, in Burr, *The United States and Pakistan's Quest for the Bomb*, doc. 36, http://nsarchive.gwu.edu/nukevault/ebb333/doc36.pdf.

117. Ibid.

118. See Pickering quoted in Rabinowitz and Miller, "Keeping the Bombs in the Basement," 76.

119. See Kux, *Disenchanted Allies*, 244–45.

All of this would change on December 25, 1979, when the Soviet Red Army rolled into Afghanistan. Pakistan was now on the front lines of the Cold War fight against communism. Carter would now have to choose between his nonproliferation agenda and his anticommunism agenda. National Security Advisor Brzezinski's memo the very next day to Carter explicitly stated the required shift in policy: "To make [arming Afghan rebels] possible, we must both reassure Pakistan and encourage it to help the rebels. This will require a review of our policy toward Pakistan, more guarantees, more arms aid, and, alas, a decision that our security policy toward Pakistan *cannot be dictated by our nonproliferation policy*."[120] Brzezinski would later inform Secretary of State Cyrus Vance of President Carter's decision that the United States would "make clear the legislative restrictions" but would, "however, urge the Pakistanis to put the problem aside for solution later while we deal with the Soviet-Afghan problem."[121] Days later, on January 8, 1980, Defense Secretary Harold Brown, in a meeting with Chinese vice premier Deng Xiaoping, clearly stated which agenda took priority: "Our big problem with Pakistan was their attempts to get a nuclear program. Although we still object to their doing so, we will now set that aside for the time being and concentrate on strengthening Pakistan against potential Soviet action."[122] Deng, unsurprisingly, "applaud[ed] this decision."[123] At the end of the month, Carter himself instructed his team that the line should be testing a weapon, adopting the very Israeli line that the United States had previously rejected, telling them to simply "seek assurances that the Zia government will not test a nuclear device and to impress upon Zia how dangerous a test would be to Pakistan's security and to the new Western relationship we are seeking to develop."[124]

120. Zbigniew Brzezinski, "Reflections on Soviet Intervention in Afghanistan," Memorandum to the President, December 26, 1979, http://nsarchive.gwu.edu/NSAEBB/NSAEBB396/docs/1979-12-26%20Brzezinski%20to%20Carter%20on%20Afghanistan.pdf, emphasis added.

121. Zbigniew Brzezinski, "Presidential Decisions of Pakistan, Afghanistan, and India," Memorandum to Secretary of State Cyrus Vance, January 2, 1980, http://nsarchive.gwu.edu/NSAEBB/NSAEBB396/docs/1980-01-02%20Presidential%20Decisions%20on%20Pakistan%20-%20Afghanistan.pdf.

122. Secretary of Defense Harold Brown to Ambassador-at-Large Gerard C. Smith, January 31, 1980, enclosing excerpts from memoranda of conversations with Geng Biao and Deng Xiaoping, January 7 and 8, 1980, January 31, 1980, in William Burr, ed., *New Documents Spotlight Reagan-Era Tensions over Pakistani Nuclear Program*, NSA EBB 377, doc. 3, https://www.documentcloud.org/documents/347015-doc-3-1-31-80.html, emphasis added.

123. Deng Xiaoping quoted in ibid.

124. Memo from Jimmy Carter to Zbigniew Brzezinski and Warren Christopher, January 30, [1980], Document CO00459, CIA Covert Operations, 1977–2010 collection, DNSA, http://search.proquest.com/dnsa_co/docview/1679094917/36F1F7D35A2A4B8FPQ/1?accountid=12492.

This would essentially green-light Pakistan to develop nuclear weapons so long as they were not publicly revealed or tested.

The CIA very shortly thereafter assessed that Pakistan was quick to use its newfound shelter to accelerate its nuclear weapons pursuit, moving as quickly as possible in the event the Afghan war was short and the shelter suddenly evaporated. An April 30, 1980, CIA assessment noted: "The recently reported belief within the Pakistani government that the US is reconciled to a Pakistani nuclear weapons capability . . . could have had the effect of reinforcing Pakistani resolve to move ahead with its nuclear weapons program. Efforts to complete construction of the enrichment plant at Kahuta for production of weapons-useable uranium have not slackened."[125] A detailed assessment of the accelerated activity at Kahuta that had occurred in the previous four months follows and, though much is redacted, the context makes it clear that Pakistan was using its newfound immunity to accelerate its development of nuclear weapons—using its shelter wisely lest it evaporate quickly.

The conventional wisdom is that Reagan ushered in Pakistani immunity for its nuclear program when he took office in January 1981. There is no doubt that the Reagan administration strengthened Pakistan's immunity and would run strong interference against Congress to shelter both Pakistan and American efforts in Afghanistan. But the contours of that shelter emerged in the year before Reagan took office. It was the Carter administration that decided to tolerate Pakistani nuclear activity short of a test in its effort to enlist Zia's cooperation in America's covert supply of the Afghan mujahideen. Zia, understanding the leverage he suddenly enjoyed over the United States, played hard to get, even rejecting Carter's $400 million aid offer and famously deriding it as "peanuts" on the belief that he would get a better deal from Reagan (which he did).[126] The shift in American attitudes had nothing to do with differential views of proliferation between Democratic and Republican administrations but everything to do with the fact that Pakistan was now suddenly a critical frontline state against the Soviet Union after the Christmas invasion. Events forced Carter and Reagan to prioritize grand strategic objectives, and both administrations believed that they had to tolerate Pakistan's pursuit of a nuclear weapons capability, so long as it did not test, in order to successfully prosecute the war in Afghanistan.

125. "Warning Report—Nuclear Proliferation," Memorandum from Special Assistant for Nuclear Proliferation Intelligence to Director of Central Intelligence, April 30, 1980, http://nsarchive.gwu.edu/nukevault/ebb333/doc47.PDF.

126. See Kux, *Disenchanted Allies*, 249–51.

When the Reagan administration came to office in January 1981, it inherited the emerging shelter over Pakistan's nuclear program and would strengthen it. Jane Coon, who was deputy assistant secretary of state for Near Eastern and South Asian Affairs during the transition, stated: "there was, in effect, a tacit understanding that the Reagan administration could live with Pakistan's nuclear program so long as Islamabad did not explode a bomb."[127] The Reagan administration bought itself and Pakistan some breathing room in May 1981 when Congress granted a six-year waiver on sanctions for importing nuclear enrichment or reprocessing technologies outside of safeguards but added explicit amendments that would snap back sanctions if it tested a nuclear device. This made, according to Kux, the "tacit understanding . . . a legal requirement for U.S. aid."[128] Over the next couple of years, Pakistan would proceed as rapidly as it could with its enrichment program. By November 1982, Secretary of State George Schultz would note with alarm how advanced the Pakistani program had gotten under American shelter. In a memorandum to President Reagan, Schultz outlined Washington's dilemma and described the state of Pakistani activities, essentially advocating turning a blind eye to Pakistani nuclearization in the service of defeating the Soviets in Afghanistan:

> Pakistan is in the advanced stage of a nuclear weapons development program. In addition to programs to produce the necessary fissile material, Pakistan has been working on the design and development of the nuclear explosive triggering package, including sending designs for components of a relatively sophisticated nuclear weapon to purchasing agents in Europe for the purpose of having the components fabricated for Pakistan. More recently the Pakistanis have also sought to purchase specialized machines to permit indigenous fabrication of these components. . . .
>
> Last year we received assurances from Zia that Pakistan would not manufacture nuclear weapons, not transfer sensitive nuclear technology, and not "embarrass" us on the nuclear use while we are providing aid. (We both understood this clearly to mean that Pakistan would not test a nuclear device; it was left ambiguous as to what it meant short of a test). . . .
>
> The intelligence community on balance believes that if forced to choose between U.S. aid and a nuclear weapons capability, Zia will opt for the latter. (Others do not believe that is a foregone conclusion). Zia

127. Jane Coon cited in ibid., 257.
128. Ibid., 260.

> could well believe *that we will never pose that choice for him, and will bail him out if Congress moves to cut off aid as we previously did.* The intelligence community thinks it likely that in response further to U.S. warnings Zia will try to disguise the weapons program and will delay the more politically risky and detectable phases in order to preserve the U.S. supply relationship. Additionally, the Pakistanis have alleged that we have publicly ignored the Israeli nuclear program and that it has not affected in any way our military and economic aid to Israel. Zia may think he is offering us diplomatic cover: the Pakistanis will not acknowledge publicly when and if they acquire a nuclear capability. . . .
>
> Sustaining our new relationship with Pakistan bears directly on U.S. global, as well as regional interests. . . . A rupture of our relationship would call into question a central tenet of this Administration's foreign policy—strong support for our friends. . . . An aid cutoff would greatly damage our ability to realize those interests served by close ties to Pakistan.[129]

It also turned out that U.S. intelligence had earlier detected "new evidence of significant PRC assistance on at least the weapons design side," suggesting that the Reagan administration was well aware of just how far and fast Pakistan was progressing.[130] Nevertheless, the Reagan administration's strategy was to shield Pakistan from congressional nonproliferation pressure, even as it was well aware of this activity. Feroz Khan describes in great detail how the Pakistani nuclear program marched along knowing full well the leverage it believed it had against the United States.[131] Indeed, Khan writes that "Zia had the enrichment project *sped up* and increased security on the nuclear installations. . . . Pakistan was very vulnerable to its two nemeses [India and the Soviet Union] and the United States was its only recourse."[132] At this point, Arnold Kanter, acting assistant secretary of state, would note in 1984: "The Pakistanis are pressing forward to perfect

129. Secretary of State George Schultz to President Reagan, "How Do We Make Use of the Zia Visit to Protect Our Strategic Interests in the Face of Pakistan's Nuclear Weapons Activities," November 26, 1982, in William Burr, ed., *New Documents Spotlight Reagan-Era Tensions over Pakistani Nuclear Program*, NSA EBB 377, doc. 16, https://www.documentcloud.org/documents/347090-doc-16-11-26-82.html, emphasis added.

130. Note for [name excised] from [name excised], "State/INR Request for Update of Pak SNIE, and Assessment of Argentine Nuclear Program," excerpts, June 4, 1982, in William Burr, ed., *New Documents Spotlight Reagan-Era Tensions over Pakistani Nuclear Program*, NSA EBB 377, doc. 11, https://www.documentcloud.org/documents/347024-doc-11-6-4-82.html.

131. Khan, *Eating Grass*, 214.

132. Ibid., 214–15.

the design of a nuclear weapon, fabricate nuclear weapon components, and acquire the necessary nuclear material for such a device. . . . Recent progress in Pakistan's uranium enrichment program . . . [forces us to] confront a stark choice between (1) *acquiescing in Pakistan's nuclear activities . . . or (2) terminating the U.S.-Pakistan security relationship.*"[133]

The Reagan administration would essentially choose the first option, and would go to great lengths to ensure, on the one hand, that Congress would not cut off aid for Pakistan's activities and, on the other hand, that Pakistan would not go so far as to visibly assemble or test a nuclear weapon. Zia continued to assure the Reagan administration that Pakistan would not "embarrass" the United States with a nuclear test. But Zia did blow past a tacit agreement not to enrich uranium beyond 5 percent (recall the enrichment curve from figure 3.2: 5 percent enrichment is roughly 60 percent of the separative work to weapons-grade uranium) and only tenuously agreed to respect the testing red-line. Kenneth Adelman, director of the Arms Control and Disarmament Agency (ACDA), would write to White House: "We may eventually be forced to conclude that the 'least bad' alternative is to accept Pakistani enrichment while toughing it out with Congress on the aid relationship. . . . I assume we would not want to terminate aid, thereby damaging our Afghan interests."[134] Pakistan would continue to push the line, and the Reagan administration continued to acquiesce. Some in Congress, such as Senator Alan Cranston, were disgusted with the Reagan administration, publicly airing frustrations that the administration had "obscured, withheld or downright misrepresented the facts about the Pakistan nuclear program" in order to avoid invocation of sanctions.[135]

Zia was similarly undeterred from riskily pursuing foreign components for what was clearly a rapidly advancing nuclear weapons program. According to Kux:

133. Arnold Kanter, Acting Assistant Secretary of State for Politico-Military Affairs, and Richard Murphy, Assistant Secretary of State for Near East and South Asian Affairs, to Under Secretary of State for Political Affairs Michael Armacost, "Memo on Pakistan Nuclear Issue for the NSC," August 24, 1984, with enclosure, "Responding to Pakistan's Continuing Efforts to Acquire Nuclear Explosives," http://nsarchive.gwu.edu/nukevault/ebb531-U.S.-Pakistan-Nuclear-Relations,-1984-1985/documents/doc%204%208-24-84%20interagency%20memo.pdf, emphasis in original.

134. Kenneth Adelman, director, Arms Control and Disarmament Agency, to Assistant to the President for National Security Affairs, "Pakistan's Nuclear Weapons Programs and U.S. Security Assistance," June 16, 1986, Top Secret, https://www.documentcloud.org/documents/347039-doc-20-6-16-86.html.

135. Senator Alan Cranston quoted by Ambassador Hummel memorandum in Levy and Scott-Clark, *Deception*, 108.

> A shrewd judge of how far he could push the Americans on the nuclear issue, Zia calculated that occasional trouble over clandestine procurement of nuclear-related equipment—any link with the Pakistani government could be denied—and even enriching uranium to weapons grade, would not breach the "embarrassment" barrier. Zia assumed correctly that Washington would give the struggle against the Soviets in Afghanistan a higher priority than his country's nuclear program. As long as Pakistan did not explode a device, Zia believed, the Reagan administration would find some way to avoid undercutting the struggle against the Red Army by imposing nuclear sanctions against Pakistan.[136]

Confronted by administration officials in 1982 about Pakistani agents procuring sensitive technology abroad, Zia categorically denied any illegal activities, feigning insult to Ambassador Vernon Walters, who ultimately concluded: "[Zia] now knows we know and I believe he is intelligent enough to understand the consequences that could flow from that."[137] What Zia concluded was that although it might be difficult to hide Pakistan's activities from American intelligence, there would actually be few consequences for pursuing nuclear weapons in this period, given how critically the United States needed Pakistan for the war in Afghanistan.

Time and time again, the Reagan administration would reinforce this notion, continually running interference against congressional nonproliferation hawks as Pakistani agents and the state blatantly and defiantly crossed critical thresholds in its nuclear weapons program. The CIA evidently had excellent eyes on the Pakistani nuclear program, producing a twenty-two-page report in 1985 with apparently significant detail on personnel, activities, foreign procurements, and achievements that is still almost entirely redacted.[138] There was even some evidence, according to Richard Barlow, the CIA's top Pakistan nuclear analyst, that "the State Department had been sending detailed demarches tipping off contacts in the Pakistan government"

136. Kux, *Disenchanted Allies*, 278.

137. "US Embassy Pakistan Cable 10276 to State Department, 'My Final Meeting with President Zia,'" July 6, 1982, History and Public Policy Program Digital Archive, State Department Mandatory Declassification Review release, obtained and contributed by William Burr and included in NPIHP Research Update No. 6, http://digitalarchive.wilsoncenter.org/document/114253.

138. "Central Intelligence Agency, Directorate of Intelligence, Research Paper, 'Pakistan's Nuclear Weapons Program: Personnel and Organizations,'" November 1985, History and Public Policy Program Digital Archive, obtained and contributed by William Burr and included in NPIHP Research Update No. 11, http://digitalarchive.wilsoncenter.org/document/116903.

to impending raids on the procurement network.[139] For the Pakistanis, this was not a hiding strategy—they were sending agents to the United States to procure components for their nuclear program. Nazir Vaid tried to purchase krytrons in Houston in 1984 (useful primarily for detonation switches on nuclear weapons),[140] and Arshad Pervez was sent to acquire high-strength maraging steel from Philadelphia in 1987 (useful only for centrifuges).[141] Pakistan knew full well that this risky behavior would not trigger an aid cutoff because the Reagan government would go to great lengths to stop Congress from imposing sanctions—there were even allegations that the federal prosecutor in the Vaid case rewrote the indictment to whitewash it on administration orders.[142] This was the very definition of sheltered pursuit, exploiting American immunity to accelerate progress toward a nuclear weapons capability.

Indeed, the Vaid episode was one of the key catalysts for the 1985 Pressler Amendment, as Congress was increasingly convinced that both Zia and potentially the Reagan administration were lying to them. The Pressler Amendment would force the administration to certify every year that Pakistan did not "possess a nuclear explosive device" in order to sustain the aid program going forward.[143] But in reality, the Pressler Amendment bought the Reagan administration a significant reprieve because it dropped proposed language that the president certify that Pakistan was not pursuing or otherwise "developing" nuclear weapons or *its components*, that is, the "equipment or technology, covertly or overtly, for a nuclear device"[144]—which Reagan could not reasonably certify—and it failed to define at what point a state "possess[es] a nuclear explosive device," freeing the administration to define it how it wished: as a full-blown test.[145] So long as Pakistan continued to stay short of that line, Reagan could and would certify to Congress that Pakistan did not "possess" a nuclear device and thereby continued to shelter the program, permitting it to progress just short of that line. Congressman Stephen

139. Levy and Scott-Clark, *Deception*, 167.

140. See John Corry, "Buying the Bomb," *New York Times*, March 5, 1985, http://www.nytimes.com/1985/03/05/arts/a-look-at-investigative-journalism.html.

141. See Hedrick Smith, "A Bomb Ticks in Pakistan," *New York Times*, March 6, 1988, http://www.nytimes.com/1988/03/06/magazine/a-bomb-ticks-in-pakistan.html?pagewanted=all.

142. See Levy and Scott-Clark, *Deception*, 114–15.

143. Text of the Pressler Amendment, available in Richard N. Haass and Morton Halperin, *After the Tests: U.S. Policy toward India and Pakistan* (New York: Council on Foreign Relations Task Report, 1998), appendix, 19.

144. See Levy and Scott-Clark, *Deception*, 115.

145. See Rabinowitz, *Bargaining on Nuclear Tests*, 152; and Kux, *Disenchanted Allies*, 275–79.

Solarz was surprisingly frank with Indian prime minister Rajiv Gandhi about why Congress could not sanction Pakistan, which Solarz stated was "proceeding fast towards a capability to produce fissile material": if Congress were to sanction Pakistan, "there would be a major controversy around it . . . because it would complicate the US Afghan policy. The US has managed to induce Pak to not explode a device *so far*, but the US cannot stop them from collecting fissile material."[146] Similarly, Ambassador Teresita Schaffer, an old Pakistan hand at the State Department, told Or Rabinowitz: "Washington was willing to bargain with Pakistan to achieve non-testing and the Pressler amendment bought us a couple of years. . . . In the eyes of the Pakistani leaders the Pressler amendment was proof that there are ways to get past the nuclear problem—Afghanistan rules."[147] After the watered-down Pervez conviction in 1988, the theatrics would reach almost absurd levels when President Reagan was forced to invoke the Solarz Amendment but then proceeded to *waive it in the next paragraph*, writing that he "determine[d] . . . that the provision of assistance to Pakistan . . . is in the national interest of the United States and therefore waive[d] the prohibitions" he invoked in the preceding paragraph pursuant to the Solarz Amendment.[148] This was nothing short of active complicity in Pakistan's attainment of nuclear weapons—although it began under the Carter administration, it would reach new heights under the Reagan administration.

Furthermore, the United States provided active shelter against external threats to the Pakistani program, notably from India and, at least as far as the Pakistanis perceived, the Israelis as well. There are allegations that the Reagan administration deliberately downplayed Pakistan's progress on nuclear weapons, especially to the Israelis, claiming Pakistan was many years away from having enough fissile material for a single bomb to Tel Aviv while contemporaneous internal estimates predicted a much shorter timeline.[149] In 1984, sketchy intelligence that India had redeployed two squadrons of SEPECAT Jaguar attack aircraft, which Pakistan feared could be used for an

146. "Record of the Call Made by US Congressman Stephen Solarz on Prime Minister Rajiv Gandhi," May 28, 1986, New Delhi, Document 1106, in *India-Pakistan Relations 1947–2007, A Documentary Study, Vol. I–X, Published in Cooperation with Public Diplomacy Division, Ministry of External Affairs*, ed. Avatar Singh Bhasin (New Delhi: Geetika Publishers, 2012), 2948.

147. Ambassador Teresita Schaffer quoted in Rabinowitz, *Bargaining on Nuclear Tests*, 152.

148. "Presidential Determination No. 88-5 of January 15, 1988," January 5, 1988, History and Public Policy Program Digital Archive, Federal Register, vol. 83, no. 24, obtained and contributed by William Burr for NPIHP Research Update No. 24, http://digitalarchive.wilsoncenter.org/document/118596.

149. See Levy and Scott-Clark, *Deception*, 86.

attack on Kahuta, triggered alarm in both Washington and Pakistan. Ambassador Hinton told Pakistan that "if the United States were to see signs of an imminent Indian attack, Pakistan would be notified immediately."[150] Then-Vice Chief of Army Staff, General K. M. Arif, stated: "Our friends let us know what the Israelis and Indians intended to do so we let them know how we would respond."[151] This was more than a passive shelter; this was an active shelter against foreign preventive attacks.

The pattern would be repeated during the 1986–87 Brasstacks Crisis as well as the 1990 Kashmir Compound crisis, where the United States quietly and then very actively diffused crises on the Subcontinent in order to prevent Pakistan from crossing the "assembly" or "testing" thresholds in its nuclear program that would automatically trigger an aid cutoff and threaten the Afghan strategy.[152] Deep concern began mounting in the Reagan administration in 1987, shortly after the Brasstacks Crisis, that Zia's progress toward actual weapons "has approached a threshold which he cannot cross without blatantly violating his pledge not to embarrass the President."[153] The United States struggled to find ways to "convince Pakistan to 'rest on its oars' and avoid further *elaboration* of its nuclear capabilities" so as to not threaten its role in responding to "escalating Soviet pressure" in Afghanistan.[154] Indeed, it would finally be Pakistan's nuclear weapons–related activity in the 1990 Kashmir crisis—the intelligence that triggered the immediate dispatching of Deputy National Security Advisor Robert Gates to the region—that convinced Washington that Pakistan was undoubtedly a nuclear weapons state by any definition.

This development was several years in the making, with the Reagan and Bush administrations performing semantic gymnastics to avoid an aid cutoff in the waning years of the Afghan war. When Zia told *Time* magazine in 1987 that Pakistan could build a bomb "whenever it wishes," Pakistan's ambassador to the United States, Jamshed Marker, told Dennis Kux that the reaction

150. See Kanti Bajpai et al., *Brasstacks and Beyond: Perception and Management of Crisis* (New Delhi: Manohar Books, 1995), 56.

151. Arif quoted in Khan, *Eating Grass*, 220.

152. See Narang, *Nuclear Strategy in the Modern Era*, chap. 10.

153. "Fred McGoldrick to John Negroponte, 'Pakistan,' 9 April 1987, Secret, Enclosing Memo from Richard Murphy, Assistant Secretary for Near East and South Asian Affairs, 'Action Plan on Pakistan Nuclear and Security Problems,' to Secretary of State," April 9, 1987, p. 2, History and Public Policy Program Digital Archive, Mandatory Declassification Review Release, obtained and contributed by William Burr and included in NPIHP Research Update No. 6, http://digitalarchive.wilsoncenter.org/document/114319.

154. Ibid., emphasis added. Note concern on elaboration, not actual rollback.

in Washington "was what he regarded as 'an aye and a wink.'"[155] This was in the midst of Reagan having to certify, due to the Pressler Amendment, that Pakistan was not in possession of a nuclear device (which the administration continued to define as a fully assembled device that was actually tested). It was becoming harder and harder to run interference against Congress and certify that Pakistan did not "possess a nuclear explosive device." At this point, in fact, head of ACDA Kenneth Adelman recommended "against any certification now" that Pakistan did not possess a nuclear device, advocating for moving away from the "business-as-usual perception" operating in both countries.[156] Although Secretary of State Schultz and the president would grant the certification,[157] Adelman's letter indicated the increasing fissures at the highest levels of the administration about how to deal with a de facto nuclear Pakistan in the late 1980s.

Pakistan was on its final approach to nuclear weapons at this point, just as the war in Afghanistan was reaching its conclusion and as the Soviets announced their intention to withdraw. The Reagan and subsequently the Bush administrations would no longer have to make the unholy choice between anticommunism and nonproliferation in their Pakistan policy. In 1989, Brent Scowcroft would tell General Aslam Beg, Pakistan's army chief, directly: "You have to realize that the administration's hands are tied on the nuclear issue. President Bush [will] certify as long as he [can] under the Pressler amendment, but he [will] not lie. Pakistan [stands] very close to the line."[158] A similar message was delivered by Bush directly to Prime Minister Benazir Bhutto. But Pakistan, sensing that the end of the relationship was perhaps near, decided to take the final steps to develop nuclear weapons by manufacturing and machining uranium cores for nuclear weapons—likely during or shortly after the 1987 Brasstacks Crisis, a massive Indian military exercise that Pakistan feared was the pretext for an invasion. This step became apparent during the 1990 Kashmir crisis. When Deputy National Security Advisor Robert Gates

155. Quoted in Kux, *Disenchanted Allies*, 285.

156. "Arms Control and Disarmament Agency, Memorandum from Kenneth Adelman for the President, 'Certification on Pakistan,'" November 21, 1987, History and Public Policy Program Digital Archive, Department of State mandatory declassification review release, obtained and contributed by William Burr for NPIHP Research, Update No. 24, http://digitalarchive.wilsoncenter.org/document/118588.

157. "Letter, President Reagan to Speaker of the House, Enclosing Presidential Determination," December 17, 1987, History and Public Policy Program Digital Archive, Digital National Security Archive, obtained and contributed by William Burr for NPIHP Research, Update No. 24, http://digitalarchive.wilsoncenter.org/document/118592.

158. Brent Scowcroft interview with Kux, *Disenchanted Allies*, 299.

was dispatched to the region, he told Pakistan that unless it "melted down the bomb cores that it produced . . . Bush would not be able to issue the Pressler amendment certification needed to permit the continued flow of military and economic aid."[159] Pakistani foreign minister Yaqub Khan recalls Gates saying: "If it waddles like a duck, if it quacks like a duck, then maybe it is a duck."[160] Later that year, with the Afghan war over, Bush indeed refused to certify that Pakistan did not "possess" a nuclear weapon, and the Pressler Amendment came into force triggering a freeze in over $550 million in aid. The United States was now publicly admitting that Pakistan possessed nuclear weapons, which it had built, literally, under America's watch.

It is reasonable to believe that Pakistan would not have been able to attain a nuclear weapons capability as easily or quickly as it did without American shelter, which, in turn, depended on the Soviet Union invading Afghanistan. Had the Glenn and Symington sanctions remained in place, and had the United States acted with full force against AQ Khan's procurement network, it is unlikely that Pakistan would have been able to progress so rapidly to indigenously develop a nuclear weapons capability even with Chinese assistance (which the United States would likely have tried to coercively stop in the 1980s). Instead, Pakistan exploited the shelter it was given, knowing that the United States needed Pakistan at that particular moment. Indeed, Howard Schaffer indicates: "At the start of Reagan's term, the Pakistanis realized two things: first that America needs Pakistan more than Pakistan needs America. Second, when push comes to shove, the Afghan issue rules, and this fact will resolve the nuclear problems," meaning Pakistan could leverage American dependence to essentially go up to the line of not testing and the Reagan administration would effectively turn a blind eye.[161]

Zia continued to repeatedly lie to American officials about Pakistan's activities and its intentions, as well as the true purpose of Kahuta—"maybe it is a goat shed," he quipped.[162] However, even he could not truly believe that he was fooling anyone in Washington, particularly after Pakistani nationals with ties to the state were caught *on American soil* trying to buy components for the nuclear weapons program. He simply knew he could get away with it or, as Kenneth Adelman put it in 1986: "Still more words, without some action to back it up, will only reinforce Zia's belief that he can lie to us with

159. Ambassador Robert Oakley, U.S. ambassador to Pakistan, interview, in Kux, *Disenchanted Allies*, 307.

160. Yaqub Khan quoted in ibid.

161. Ambassador Howard Schaffer quoted in Rabinowitz, *Bargaining on Nuclear Tests*, 152.

162. Richelson, *Spying on the Bomb*, 342.

impunity."[163] Not only would the Reagan administration fail to take action against the program, but it actively ran interference against Congress—and India—in order to protect it. Action against Pakistan's nuclear activities would only come after the Afghan war ended and Pakistan's utility to American anticommunist efforts evaporated. But by then it was too late.

TESTING PROLIFERATION STRATEGY THEORY

My theory captures the sheltered pursuit proliferation strategy Pakistan would select, taking advantage of its newfound utility to the United States to develop nuclear weapons. After its defeat in the 1971 war at the hands of the Indians, which split the nation in two, Pakistani pursuit of nuclear weapons as a deterrent against Indian conventional power was essentially a foregone conclusion. The question is how it would go about doing so. According to my theory, at first, Pakistan would have no option but to pursue a hiding strategy because it was vulnerable not only to Indian (and potentially refueled Israeli) air power to destroy known facilities but also to American economic coercion. That was in fact the envisioned strategy when Bhutto initiated the program in January 1972. But circumstances and nuclear proliferation strategy changed when Pakistan could avail itself of American shelter and, to a lesser extent, Chinese assistance. Pakistan's utility to the United States fortuitously emerged due to the exogenous shock of the Soviet invasion of Afghanistan just as the Carter administration was determined to heavily, and likely cripplingly, sanction Pakistan for its nuclear weapons activity, particularly after discovering evidence of uranium enrichment development after France canceled the reprocessing deal. Almost instantaneously, the invasion transformed Pakistan from a pariah in Washington to a partner on the front line against Soviet expansion and Pakistan would be showered with military and economic aid as a result. However, the most impactful policy reversal was on the nuclear program: the Carter and then the Reagan administrations chose to shelve their nonproliferation agenda with respect to Pakistan on the fear that pursuing a freeze on Pakistan's nuclear program would threaten the supply routes to Afghanistan and therefore American strategy.

Although Rabinowitz and Miller are correct to say that the United States still insisted on a no-testing line, this allowed Pakistan to blow past all the

163. Kenneth Adelman, director, Arms Control and Disarmament Agency, to Assistant to the President for National Security Affairs, "Pakistan's Nuclear Weapons Programs and U.S. Security Assistance," June 16, 1986, Top Secret, pp. 2–3, https://www.documentcloud.org/documents/347039-doc-20-6-16-86.html.

other soft "pink lines" the United States set on enrichment, and eventually on even possession of component parts that could readily and rapidly be assembled into a "nuclear explosive device." It is also possible that the United States was aware of outright weapons assembly around or shortly after the 1987 Brasstacks Crisis with India but opted for willful ignorance so long as there was no actual test. According to Feroz Khan, Zia actually accelerated the nuclear program in these years. This fits with my theoretical expectations. In order to weaponize before the shelter might evaporate, which Islamabad clearly understood could disappear just as rapidly as it materialized, Pakistan needed to seize the opportunity. Islamabad may also have sought to extend this propitious period of superpower protection. Pakistan had long been accused of playing a double game with the United States in Afghanistan—simultaneously supplying the mujahideen as well as their local adversaries to bait and bleed both sides—in order to prolong the conflict to extract more aid and concessions from the United States. Such a diabolical strategy is risky but it is not irrational, since Pakistan benefited so much from the largesse the United States provided, including shelter for its nuclear program. Evidence for such a strategy is thin and would obviously be difficult to conclusively show, but it is certainly not implausible.

This is a relatively sophisticated realist explanation for Pakistan's nuclear weapons proliferation strategy. Proliferation Strategy Theory and structural realism generally dovetail in terms of predicting how Pakistan might go about developing nuclear weapons. Each of the operating variables in this case—acute security threat, domestic consensus (in this case, easily achieved given the severity of the threat from India after 1971), and availability of superpower immunity—was driven by structural variables: an acute threat from India and, eventually, external shelter from the United States. Most realist theories of proliferation, however, stop at the acute security threat. But the Pakistan case illustrates that security threats can motivate a variety of potential strategies. Pakistan chose a hiding strategy at first because, prior to the Soviet invasion of Afghanistan, the United States seemed determined to prevent Pakistan from achieving a nuclear weapons capability. The invasion, however, immediately reoriented America's priorities and, rather than being a threat to the Pakistani nuclear program, Washington would become its shield. Under American shelter, Pakistan accelerated its development of nuclear weapons, hoping to reach the finish line before shelter evaporated with the end of the Afghanistan war—which it succeeded in doing. My theory, in this case, therefore represents an improvement and a more sophisticated understanding of which structural variables might generate distinct *strategies* of nuclear proliferation.

Technological determinism does not provide a satisfactory account of the Pakistani sheltered pursuit strategy. It is either tautological—arguing that Pakistan nuclearized when and how it did because of the technology available to it, which is true but uninteresting—or wrong, assuming that there was no political direction to the technological choices Pakistan pursued. When Bhutto initiated the program in January 1972, he pushed on both plutonium and uranium pathways to see what offered Pakistan the best chance of achieving nuclear weapons. The genesis of the January 1972 decision was not the sudden availability of these technologies but rather an intensely political calculus motivated by the 1971 defeat. Bhutto ordered his scientists to go out and *develop* these pathways. At the time, Pakistani scientist Samar Mubarakmand thought Pakistan was decades behind India and it simply "didn't have the infrastructure for that kind of program. . . . But if you're playing political poker and have no cards, you have to go on betting."[164] Plutonium was more attractive for a variety of reasons, but it proved harder to hide, especially with tightening global export controls following India's 1974 PNE. AQ Khan assembled a veritable global supply network to develop the uranium pathway, but Pakistan never abandoned the plutonium pathway. Indeed, since plutonium is more desirable for weapons (higher yield-to-weight ratios, facilitating compact designs), Pakistan developed uranium bombs first to ensure its survival and then shifted to plutonium much later. Zia made a conscious political decision to go all-in on uranium enrichment since that offered the greatest prospect for success in the 1980s, and uranium enrichment was accelerated once American shelter materialized. It is also true, as Feroz Khan shows, that AQ Khan was simply more politically savvy in convincing Zia that his uranium enrichment pathway was farther along than his competitors' plutonium pathway at PAEC. This was naked lobbying and brutal politics motivated by a fierce rivalry between AQ Khan and Munir Ahmad Khan, not technological determinism.[165] Furthermore, Pakistan was in a position to culminate weaponization and perform a hot test as early as 1984, but Zia, according to Khan, "declined on the grounds that the time was not appropriate" and he did not want to "embarrass" the Reagan administration by violating his commitment not to test.[166] Zia controlled

164. Mubarakmand quoted in Levy and Scott-Clark, *Deception*, 19.

165. See Khan, *Eating Grass*, chaps. 7–9.

166. Ibid., 185.

the tempo of Pakistan's program—accelerating weaponization but delaying full-blown tests—for political and strategic reasons; the pace was not limited by the availability of technology.

The emerging global nonproliferation regime explains Pakistani nuclear proliferation strategy until December 25, 1979. The teeth of American sanctions, as legislated by the Glenn and Symington amendments following the Indian PNE, were just about to sink into Pakistan's economy. Export controls were tightening—even France would no longer supply reprocessing equipment for programs that were clearly not entirely peaceful. AQ Khan played a cat-and-mouse game—mostly succeeding until 1978—with these global export control laws in trying to develop the uranium enrichment program. Had the Soviet Union not invaded Afghanistan, the story of Pakistan's quest for nuclear weapons would have likely been about American sanctions and the James Bond-esque story of AQ Khan versus European export control laws and intelligence agencies. That all went by the wayside when Washington opted to prioritize the war in Afghanistan over its nonproliferation objectives. The Reagan administration sought and received a six-year waiver on the Glenn and Symington amendments and later played tenuous semantic gymnastics to certify under the Pressler Amendment that Pakistan did not "possess a nuclear explosive device." Afghanistan rules.

The unforeseen emergence of American shelter was the critical variable that explains Pakistan's shift away from a hiding strategy. In essence, the 1981 sanctions waiver was an American permission slip for Pakistan to become a nuclear weapons state, provided it was able to do so before the war in Afghanistan ended. Luckily for Pakistan, the war lasted almost a decade, several years more than Pakistan would need to develop nuclear weapons. Pakistan's nuclear development would likely have been stunted, or stymied, if not for American shelter and successive U.S. administrations turning a blind eye to its progress in the pursuit of what they believed to be higher-priority geopolitical goals.

The Curious Case of North Korea: The Furniture Factory at Yongbyon (1979–2006)

North Korea is a case of a state that had intense security motivations to pursue nuclear weapons, a series of dynastic personalist dictators committed to doing so, and a well-trained coterie of scientists and engineers to develop them. However, few academic theories of proliferation predicted it could successfully develop them—President Nixon once referred to it as a "fourth-rate . . . pipsqueak" power.[167] Jacques Hymans derides North Korea as the poster child for his inefficiency theory, an "ideal-typical case of neo-patrimonialism" and failure, capable of only "snail's pace" progress, at best, on its nuclear weapons program.[168] And yet, in October 2006, North Korea tested a purported fission device, becoming the world's tenth nuclear weapons power. One decade and five nuclear tests later, in 2017, it would become the first post–Cold War U.S. adversary to test an ICBM and an alleged thermonuclear weapon. Along the way, North Korea earned an additional distinction: the first non-nuclear weapons state to join and withdraw from the NPT and then attain a nuclear weapons capability.

How did North Korea defy the odds and build nuclear weapons? Data on North Korea's nuclear program and decision making are notoriously difficult to obtain. But North Korea's early success in developing a nuclear weapons program was largely due to the assistance it received from the Soviet Union but also, most critically, due to shelter from China after the end of the Cold War, which enabled North Korea to develop various routes to the bomb while Beijing ran interference against a West trying to stop and reverse it. The North Korean nuclear program centered on its nuclear reactor at the Yongbyon facility, which produces plutonium, and later a uranium enrichment capability both at Yongbyon and likely at several other undisclosed facilities elsewhere. Beijing calculated then, as it perhaps still does, that a nuclear-armed North Korea as a buffer state against the United States and South Korean alliance is preferable to a North Korea that collapses, on its border, under the weight of international sanctions. The Chinese shield allowed North Korea to obfuscate the true purpose of Yongbyon and to retain the reactor after the 1994 Agreed Framework, and further enabled North Korea to pursue a clandestine uranium enrichment capability—about which China was surely aware—while stalling on dismantling the nuclear reactor at Yongbyon.

Consistent with my theory, North Korea's success was largely due to its ability to adopt a sheltered pursuit strategy. Beijing tolerated North Korea's activities, and the Kims leveraged that protection especially over the plutonium route to then develop a sophisticated uranium enrichment capability initially hidden from the United States. China almost certainly looked the other way and perhaps facilitated Pakistan's assistance to North

167. See Nicholas L. Miller and Vipin Narang, "North Korea Defied the Theoretical Odds: What Can We Learn from Its Successful Nuclearization," *Texas National Security Review* 1, no. 2 (March 2018): 59–61.

168. Hymans, *Achieving Nuclear Ambitions*, 253–54.

Korea's centrifuge program: it is implausible that Beijing was unaware of Pakistani C-130s flying through Chinese military airspace, over the span of half a decade, with likely refueling stops in China, to deliver centrifuges to Pyongyang. North Korea engaged in tactical obfuscation to be sure, but its progress was *enabled* by the broader strategy of sheltered pursuit through the 2000s, culminating in the 2006 nuclear test when Kim Jong Il detonated a purported fission device at the underground Punggye-ri test site. North Korea's success further augments the empirical finding that a nuclear aspirant that is able to develop or select a sheltered pursuit strategy under the cover of a major power shield has a very strong chance of reaching the nuclear finish line. All four states that were able to pursue nuclear weapons under major power shelter for some period succeeded, but North Korea is perhaps the most important exemplar. Without Chinese shelter, it may have had little chance against a United States determined to prevent it from nuclearizing—even with Pyongyang's ability to conventionally hold Seoul at risk.

The origins of Chinese shelter of North Korea dates back to the 1950 Korean War. For China, North Korea serves as a buffer against Western imperial forces in South Korea, and it nominally shares a communist ideology. There is a formal Treaty of Friendship between China and North Korea, but unlike America's formal alliance instruments, Beijing has historically viewed its commitments to Pyongyang narrowly, and the treaty does not include formal extended deterrence guarantees. This eliminates the possibility of North Korea selecting insurance hedging as a strategy—if Pyongyang wanted nuclear defense, it had to develop its own deterrent. Indeed, even with a friendship treaty, Beijing's relationship with Pyongyang has been complicated and thorny—the nuclear program and particularly nuclear and missile tests are provocations that Beijing would prefer North Korea refrained from. It is in fact plausible that one goal of North Korea's nuclear weapons program and arsenal is to be able to establish greater independence from China by being more self-sufficient in its defense and foreign policy. China may never have welcomed North Korean proliferation, but it was willing to tolerate and even shield its program at times in order to maintain influence over a critical neighboring buffer state. Its overall attitude is encapsulated perhaps best by a seemingly resigned Chinese diplomat: even if "our mindset has changed . . . the length of our border has not."[169]

169. "Shades of Red: China's Debate over North Korea," Asia Report No. 179, International Crisis Group, November 2, 2009, https://d2071andvip0wj.cloudfront.net/179-shades-of-red-china-s-debate-over-north-korea.pdf, Executive Summary.

Although the Soviet Union initially provided nuclear technology and training to North Korea in the late 1950s, it would ultimately be Chinese diplomatic and political shelter that protected the program in the 1990s and 2000s, enabling North Korea to cheat and obfuscate on both plutonium production and its covert uranium enrichment capability.[170] As a detailed Congressional Research Service (CRS) report notes: "Beijing has stressed that a nuclear-free Korean peninsula is one of its priorities, but it also has supported North Korea as it has built, started, stopped, and restarted its nuclear plant."[171] It goes on to observe that "China appears casually tolerant of North Korea's erratic and unpredictable behavior, [and may be] why Beijing rarely criticizes North Korea for its provocations, and why Beijing has sided so often with the North Korean position in the Six Party Talks."[172] Whatever Beijing may say, its actions—undermining sanctions and providing diplomatic shielding at the United Nations at times through the 1990s and early 2000s—served the purpose of sheltering the North Korean nuclear program from external pressure.

The Yongbyon facility, which Jonathan Pollack notes that North Korean experts have colorfully labeled "the 'Furniture Factory,'" was the heart of North Korea's nuclear program, with a 5 MWe graphite reactor that became operational in 1986.[173] The reactor design was oriented for producing plutonium with minimal external assistance—relying on natural uranium fuel, graphite moderation, and gas cooling.[174] Although the Soviet Union intended the reactor to be for civilian purposes, Pollack notes that "Moscow's deep involvement in planning and construction at Yongbyon seems puzzling" for just a civilian program.[175] By 1985, American concern grew, leading the United States to request that Moscow pressure North Korea to accede to the NPT as a hands-tying and verification mechanism. Pyongyang ultimately joined the NPT but did not sign a safeguards agreement with the IAEA until 1992, by which time it was believed to have already extracted and reprocessed plutonium from the reactor's spent fuel rods.[176] American intelligence

170. Dick N. Nanto and Mark E. Manyin, "China-North Korea Relations," Congressional Research Service, December 28, 2010.

171. Ibid., 3.

172. Ibid., 4.

173. Jonathan D. Pollack, *No Exit: North Korea, Nuclear Weapons and International Security* (New York: Routledge, 2011), 51.

174. See Miller and Narang, "North Korea Defied the Theoretical Odds," 59–61.

175. Pollack, *No Exit*, 51.

176. See Ashton B. Carter and William J. Perry, *Preventive Defense: A New Security Strategy for America* (Washington, DC: Brookings Institution Press, 1999), 126.

was concerned about the reactor at Yongbyon in the late 1980s but concluded (erroneously, in hindsight) that "we have no evidence that North Korea is pursuing a nuclear weapons option."[177] Although North Korea and South Korea would sign a 1992 Joint Declaration on the Denuclearization of the Korean Peninsula following the withdrawal of American tactical nuclear weapons from the South at the end of the Cold War, the definition of "denuclearization" and of South Korea's and America's obligations were left intentionally ambiguous—a formula North Korea would exploit for decades to come to avoid "disarmament."

Shortly thereafter, the first North Korean nuclear crisis would come to a head when inconsistencies appeared between North Korea's declaration to the IAEA and what inspectors found on the ground, prompting suspicions that reprocessing had already begun at a partially completed hidden reprocessing facility.[178] As the newly installed Clinton administration contemplated military strikes, former president Jimmy Carter's visit to Pyongyang opened a diplomatic window that ultimately set the stage for the Agreed Framework. The Agreed Framework suspended operation of the 5 MWe reactor at Yongbyon, and all further construction of additional reactors and facilities at the complex, in exchange for light water reactors for energy production and a generous aid package. However, as would be the story for the next quarter century at least, North Korea would stall or obfuscate on implementing serious "denuclearization" steps and would often get just enough diplomatic cover from China to avoid sanctions or serious punishment.

China's calculation on North Korea is complicated, as was the United States' calculation with Pakistan. Neither particularly wanted their client states to attain or possess nuclear weapons. But they were both willing to tolerate it, if they had to, as the price of achieving higher-priority geopolitical goals. For China, the "traditionalist" view on North Korea is captured by an excellent International Crisis Group (ICG) report on the relationship between the two countries: it is "like lips and teeth" because of the blood shed together during the Korean War.[179] China "has a key interest in preventing international pressure that might lead to provocative actions by

177. CIA, "North Korea's Expanding Nuclear Efforts," May 3, 1988, in "North Korea and Nuclear Weapons: The Declassified U.S. Record," ed. Robert A. Wampler, National Security Archive Electronic Briefing Book, no. 87, Document 10, 2003, https://nsarchive2.gwu.edu/NSAEBB/NSAEBB87/nk10.pdf.

178. See Richelson, *Spying on the Bomb*; Reiss, *Bridled Ambition*; Joel S. Wit, Daniel B. Poneman, and Robert L. Gallucci, *Going Critical: The First North Korean Nuclear Crisis* (Washington, DC: Brookings Institution Press, 2004).

179. "Shades of Red," 7.

Pyongyang" and "must continue to provide aid in order to avert instability."[180] Most importantly North Korea—even, and maybe especially, a nuclear-armed North Korea—serves "as a buffer zone between the U.S. presence on the Korean peninsula and Chinese territory, is a strategic asset, not a strategic liability."[181] When push comes to shove, the analysis concludes, "for the time being China's overriding interest in peace and stability [and avoiding North Korean collapse] on the Korean peninsula continues to trump its interest in denuclearization and nonproliferation."[182] This view holds that peace and stability will lead to denuclearization rather than the reverse. It captures the essence of the sequencing disagreement between the United States and North Korea/China on North Korea's nuclear weapons program. This has led to a general policy that, despite perturbations and periodic optimism that China may change its approach to North Korea's nuclear weapons program, is fundamentally characterized as, according to the ICG analysis:

> China's overriding interest on the Korean peninsula remains peace and stability, with non-proliferation a secondary priority. Given its fear of regime implosion, or hundreds of thousands of North Korean refugees streaming across the border, or the strategic consequences of a precipitous reunification with South Korea, Beijing continues to act in ways that *shield* the DPRK from more punitive measures, including stronger economic sanctions.[183]

Few scholars and analysts would dispute that, at least until North Korea tested its first purported fission device in 2006, Beijing sheltered it from the most punitive measures—economic and military—that might have prevented North Korea from achieving nuclear weaponization but carried an attendant risk of chaos and collapse on China's borders.[184]

This was acutely evident as the Agreed Framework began to break down, notably after Kim Jong Il's North Korea provocatively tested a Taepodong-1 satellite launch vehicle (the basis of a long-range missile) over Japanese territory in August 1998. More concerning, perhaps, was growing evidence that North Korea was outflanking the Agreed Framework by developing a covert uranium enrichment capability, with likely assistance from Pakistan

180. Ibid.
181. Ibid.
182. Ibid., 8.
183. Ibid., 20, emphasis added.
184. See Pollack, *No Exit*, 143–44. Also Nanto and Manyin, "China-North Korea Relations," 11–12.

on advanced centrifuge designs and equipment.[185] There were suspicions that North Korea had already developed several nuclear weapons, but without a full-blown test it remained speculation.[186] The Clinton administration, embroiled in scandals at home, would essentially punt the North Korean problem to the subsequent George W. Bush administration, which, after 9/11, dubbed North Korea as a member of the "Axis of Evil." By the summer of 2002, it became clear to American intelligence that North Korea was proceeding full speed ahead with a hidden uranium enrichment pathway and that, given the size of at least one suspected facility, it might be able to enrich enough uranium to produce, writes Richelson, "two or more nuclear weapons a year when it became fully operational."[187] The broader international context is critical at this point: the Bush administration had all but explicitly committed to invading Iraq at this point, partly on the justification of terminating Saddam Hussein's suspected (but in fact no longer existent) clandestine nuclear weapons program. It had to choose between an Iraq that it was confident did not yet possess nuclear weapons and a North Korea that might, knowing the latter also had a Chinese patron that would not allow American forces to "liberate" Pyongyang. The Bush administration had little choice with North Korea at this point and, distracted by the preparations for Iraq, according to Pollack "pressed China to rein in the North. Beijing was deeply perturbed by North Korea's actions, but the Chinese were not prepared to undertake a highly coercive strategy . . . [China] also expressed open skepticism about US intelligence claims of an enrichment program and urged Washington to renew negotiations with the DPRK" even as Beijing ensured continuity of energy supplies to North Korea.[188]

China was actively sheltering North Korea and its nuclear activities at this point. It tolerated the collapse of the Agreed Framework—which included resumption of the 5 MWe reactor operation in 2003—and implausibly cast doubts over clear American evidence of a hidden uranium enrichment capability. Beijing was tacitly allowing, if not actively facilitating, the delivery of Pakistani centrifuges in exchange for North Korean missiles between 1997 and 2002. Not only were both stalwart Chinese client states, but Beijing had to allow the military transport aircraft to traverse the length of its vast military airspace (and likely refuel along the way) and must have been aware

185. Richelson, *Spying on the Bomb*, 529–30.

186. Ibid., 529.

187. Ibid., 530.

188. Pollack, *No Exit*, 132–33.

of the deliveries.[189] Even if China was unaware of the contents of the enrichment cargo being ferried to Pyongyang, at the very least, it chose not to find out. At best, Chinese authorities chose to willfully turn a blind eye to North Korea's development of an enrichment capability; at worst, they quietly but actively facilitated it by arranging the marriage with Pakistan. In December 2002, Richelson reports that American intelligence further determined that China had sold and delivered twenty tons of tributyl phosphate to North Korea which, given evidence of increased activity at Yongbyon, had likely but one purpose: to reprocess plutonium.[190]

Furthermore, even while it mediated the failed Six Party Talks, Beijing shielded North Korea through the 2000s from damaging sanctions by either diluting them at the United Nations Security Council itself or outright undermining them.[191] China, according to the CRS, "constitutes a large gap in the circle of countries that have approved UNSC Resolutions 1718 and 1874 and are expected to implement them. China takes a minimalist approach to implementing sanctions on North Korea. North Korea continues to use land and air routes through China with little risk of inspection, and luxury goods from China and from other countries through China continue to flow almost unabated to Pyongyang."[192] Indeed, China was often accused of duplicity on North Korea, nominally supporting more pressure with one hand and releasing that pressure with the other.

North Korea had its shelter and used it wisely. In contrast to Pakistan, however, it seems that Kim Jong Il was not hurrying because he feared abandonment from Beijing but rather because he wanted to attain nuclear weapons and demonstrate his capability before the Bush administration could turn from Iraq toward him. North Korean diplomats reportedly told their American counterparts several weeks after the United States invaded Iraq that "we've watched what you're doing in Iraq. . . . The lessons that we're getting out of that is that Iraq does not have weapons of mass destruction and you invaded them. So, we're going to reprocess the spent fuel rods, we're going to take them and create a nuclear deterrent so you cannot invade us."[193] Beijing's shelter and America's distraction in the Middle East allowed North

189. Khan, *Eating Grass*, 246–47.

190. Richelson, *Spying on the Bomb*, 531.

191. See Nanto and Manyin, "China-North Korea Relations," 11–19. Also see Chu Shulong and Lin Xinzhu, "The Six Party Talks: A Chinese Perspective," *Asian Perspective* 32, no. 4 (2008): 29–43.

192. Nanto and Manyin, "China-North Korea Relations," 18–19.

193. Quoted in Pollack, *No Exit*, 141.

Korea to join the nuclear club as its tenth member on October 9, 2006, with asterisks. There were persistent doubts about the success of the nuclear test, but the detonation did undoubtably try Beijing's patience: Kim gave Beijing only twenty minutes' advance notice of the blast. Whatever the technical status of the test, North Korea succeeded in immunizing itself from military attack by demonstrating enough of a capability to deter would-be regime changers, and it did so with the benefit—albeit in fits and starts—of Beijing's shield. North Korea provided the playbook for every aspiring proliferator going forward: find shelter, obfuscate under that shelter, and use the time to develop nuclear weapons before that shelter evaporates.

TESTING PROLIFERATION STRATEGY THEORY

North Korea faced an existential security threat from the United States-South Korea alliance on its border, with whom it has still technically been in a state of war since 1953, and which professes intent to reunite the Korean Peninsula through the use of force. Given the power asymmetry between North Korea and the U.S.-led alliance, North Korea had incredibly strong motivations to pursue nuclear weapons, particularly at the end of the Cold War when North Korea confronted an uncertain fate with its traditional allies, the Soviet Union and China. And as a personalist regime, domestic consensus for weaponization depends solely on the decision of the chairman. Despite this strong motivation and consensus for nuclear weapons however, without China's shelter of the North Korean nuclear program, it is highly unlikely North Korea would have been left undisturbed to build nuclear weapons, despite the deterrent threat posed by its ability to impose significant conventional damage on Seoul. China gave it space to pursue nuclear weapons, preferring stability and territorial buffer against the West over denuclearization, and facilitated the transfer of the very centrifuges that formed the basis for North Korea's successful uranium pathway. Very simply, Beijing preferred a nuclear North Korea to a collapsed North Korea. Certainly, the conventional threat posed by North Korea to the South is a deterrent to a military attack, but it is also true that the risk of triggering a major power war with China is equally a deterrent to American preventive action. Standard realist accounts of proliferation should argue that the power asymmetry between the United States and North Korea should have been sufficient to allow the United States to prevent North Korean nuclearization. But without accounting for Chinese shelter of the program through attaining nuclear weapons, these accounts would be incorrect and incomplete.

Technological determinism does have some purchase on North Korea's evolution as a nuclear weapons power. North Korea started off by availing itself of the technology that it could receive and absorb. It extracted plutonium from the Yongbyon reactor's spent fuel as soon as possible, before lawyering over the true purpose of Yongbyon. Knowing that it was vulnerable and could face preventive strikes if it continued to rely on a pathway concentrated at a single reactor, North Korea searched for a clandestine uranium enrichment program (hidden from the United States at least)—a strategic decision, but one that had significant technical constraints. North Korea had to seek centrifuge designs and technologies from Pakistan, and it took significant time for North Korea to absorb the technology and enrich uranium clandestinely.[194] There is no denying that technology—both acquiring and indigenizing it—was a significant bottleneck in North Korea's nuclear proliferation timeline and trajectory. But the shift from a dormant plutonium pathway to the uranium enrichment pathway was enabled by Chinese shelter, allowing North Korea the berth to seek and then receive advanced centrifuge designs from Pakistan, probably with China's help. Without China at least turning a blind eye to this transfer, there would have been no North Korean enrichment program.

North Korea showed no allegiance to the nonproliferation regime, nor to the NPT, remaining the only state to ever formally withdraw from the treaty and develop nuclear weapons. It acceded to the treaty under tremendous pressure from the Soviet Union in 1985 but never demonstrated any commitment to the spirit or the letter of the treaty, threatening to withdraw as soon as it signed the IAEA agreement. It then became the first state to formally withdraw in 2003, before declaring itself a nuclear weapons power several years later. North Korea made an open mockery of the NPT. China offered shelter in contravention of its nonproliferation obligations as well, just as it had done with Pakistan in the 1980s. Little about the nonproliferation regime constrained either North Korean or Chinese behavior. Instead, China prioritized North Korea as a buffer state—even if it meant allowing North Korea to build nuclear weapons—and sought to avoid a North Korean collapse above all. Chinese shelter and protection is the key variable in explaining how North Korea bucked the theoretical odds and developed nuclear weapons.

194. R. Scott Kemp, "The Nonproliferation Emperor Has No Clothes: The Gas Centrifuge, Supply-Side Controls, and the Future of Nuclear Proliferation," *International Security* 38, no. 4 (Spring 2014): 39–78.

Conclusion

This chapter has shown why sheltered pursuit is such an attractive proliferation strategy for states that can select it. Under the shelter of a major power, a state can redouble its efforts to develop nuclear weapons while the patron not only commits to tolerating its possession of nuclear weapons but deters other major powers from military, economic, or diplomatic action that might cripple or destroy the effort. Shelter can be actively cultivated, as in the case of Israel, or suddenly materialize, as in the case of Pakistan. It may also be extended for more durable strategic reasons, as in the case of China to North Korea. The goal of the proliferator is to take advantage of the temporary—or indefinite—shelter to build nuclear weapons, as all three sheltered pursuers did. The sheltered pursuer often tries to maintain plausible deniability, but the patron state in each of these cases—the United States with Israel and Pakistan, and China with North Korea—was well aware of their clients' nuclear weapons activity and chose to tolerate it for larger geopolitical reasons. Like the United States with Israel and Pakistan, China operated somewhere between tolerance and facilitation of North Korea's nuclearization in order to achieve more important goals like maintaining the regional balance of power. Under shelter, a state's prospects of successfully developing nuclear weapons are good. If North Korea could attain nuclear weapons under major power shelter, any state probably can—technology is not an insurmountable obstacle for states pursuing a 1940s capability in the twenty-first century.

This strategy is not easy to develop because it involves coordinating and achieving shelter at the right moment, when a state is poised to work quickly toward nuclear weapons. But for states with the ability, or fortune, to be able to create or select this strategy, it is a less risky strategy of proliferation than hiding and the likelihood of success is very high. Future potential proliferators, such as Saudi Arabia, may be able to cultivate shelter from the United States, which might tolerate Saudi nuclear weaponization in the event that Iran were to become a nuclear weapons state. However, patron states must guard against extending shelter to states that they do not want in the nuclear club in the future. In the case of Pakistan, for example, it is reasonable to ask whether extending shelter was truly necessary for the success of the Afghan strategy and, separately, whether the Afghan strategy was worth the price the world now pays for Pakistan's aggressive nuclear strategy and the risks of Pakistani loose nuclear weapons in a country beset by significant levels of domestic and international terrorism.[195] It is the sheltered pursuit strategy that gives rise to the reasonable charge that the major powers are hypocritical about horizontal proliferation: turning a blind eye to some of their friends, or to strategically useful client states (their frenemies), and not others. For nuclear aspirants seeking the bomb that do not have the luxury to sprint or the opportunity to adopt a sheltered pursuit strategy, however, only the riskiest strategy remains: hiding.

195. See Narang, *Nuclear Strategy in the Modern Era*, chap. 3.

6

The Hiders

IRAQ, TAIWAN, AND SOUTH AFRICA

This chapter examines hiding, the final, and most destabilizing, strategy of nuclear proliferation. Hiding is chosen by states that confront an underlying security threat alone and have generated domestic consensus, in whatever regime type they possess, for nuclear weaponization. However, lacking the ability to openly sprint or the availability of major power shelter, they face the possibility of coercive threats from more powerful states that could cripple the program itself, the state's economy, or the state altogether. The very threats that may motivate a hider's nuclear weapons pursuit force it underground to avoid detection and destruction. Hiders riskily attempt to keep their nuclear weapons activities clandestine. They hope to achieve a fait accompli before the program is discovered, thereby avoiding the duress most states face during the proliferation process and presenting adversaries with an established nuclear deterrent. If they are discovered, however, they can face the international political equivalent of murder.

Hiding can be inefficient. The need to maintain a small—ideally undetectable—footprint forces a state to pursue suboptimal technical pathways to nuclear weapons. This chapter will show that hiders have attempted to use both clandestine uranium and plutonium programs—I discuss Taiwan here, and then cover Syria's daring attempt to hide a nuclear reactor right under the world's nose as late as 2007 in the next chapter. Hiding is risky because if a hidden nuclear weapons program is discovered, there is often little doubt about the state's intentions to develop nuclear weapons, so it loses plausible deniability. This can potentially mobilize a broad coalition of states to economically or militarily terminate the program. But hiding remains attractive for states that believe they require nuclear weapons to deter significant security threats. If the state is able to present a fait accompli to adversaries, as South Africa succeeded in doing, it can fully avoid the window of volatility around proliferation in which proliferators have historically tended to be involved in more militarized disputes. If it fails, the failure can be spectacular. Although hiders rarely succeed, many states are tempted to try. Whether they succeed or not, hiders invariably disrupt the international system—success means another entrant into the nuclear club, and failure can often involve a violent fate.

This chapter explores cases of hiders across a range of regions, regime types, and power positions. Figure 6.1 depicts Proliferation Strategy Theory's hypothesized pathway to hiding. I begin with the important case of Iraq, which was forced into a hidden uranium enrichment pathway after Israel destroyed its potential plutonium pathway, bombing the Osirak reactor in 1981. The program was inefficient, but it made some headway in the late 1980s. When Saddam Hussein ill-advisedly invaded Kuwait in 1990 and provoked the American-led coalition to dislodge his forces, the international community—and the United States in particular—was stunned at the extent of the hidden nuclear program they discovered. A major problem for Saddam Hussein after the first Gulf War was that once he was caught as a hider, it was difficult to convince the world (especially some in the United States) that he had truly given up his desire for, and pursuit of, nuclear weapons and that he was not squirreling away an active nuclear weapons program. This largely conditioned American behavior over the next decade and ultimately contributed to President George W. Bush's 2003 decision to invade and overthrow Saddam Hussein. I turn next to Taiwan's hidden nuclear weapons program: a case where an abandoned American ally believed it needed nuclear weapons if it were forced to confront the People's Republic of China by itself. Even strong threats from the United States in the late 1970s were insufficient to compel Taiwan to terminate its program. Only a decade later, when Taiwan was caught red-handed for the second time doing experimental work on plutonium reprocessing, did Taipei cave to Washington's enormous pressure to finally terminate the program. I close with South Africa, which achieved every hider's dream: a clandestine indigenous uranium enrichment program that successfully produced nuclear weapons in the 1980s. South Africa's capabilities and nuclear weapons program ran far ahead of what either of the superpowers, both of which opposed South African nuclearization, knew.

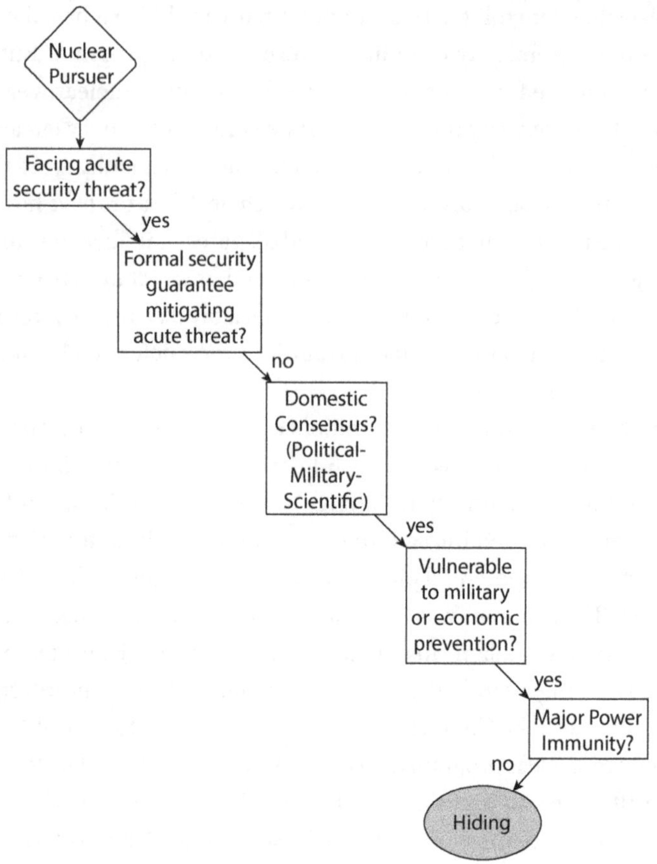

FIGURE 6.1. Proliferation Strategy Theory's pathway to the hiding strategy.

These three cases illustrate the conditions—consistent across a variety of regimes and states—that lead to a hiding strategy: an acute security threat, the absence of a formal security guarantee from a great power, domestic consensus in favor of seeking nuclear weapons, vulnerability to military or economic prevention, and the absence of major power shelter. A sophisticated realist assessment of the cases of Iraq, Taiwan, and South Africa would agree with Proliferation Strategy Theory and produce a prediction of hiding. However, my theory captures an important nuance: the necessity of domestic consensus in favor of nuclear weaponization. Multiple cases in this book have shown that political consensus is not epiphenomenal to the external threat environment. Hiding was only possible in Iraq, Taiwan, and South Africa because domestic consensus existed. If consensus had fractured, even in the exact same external environment, I predict that these states would have undertaken hard hedging. As in previous chapters, I describe the hiding behavior of the state in question and then I show how Proliferation Strategy Theory accounts for the proliferator's behavior and outperforms alternatives.

Iraq (1981–91): Sneaky Saddam

Perhaps no single failed pursuit of a nuclear weapons program has affected the international system as much as Saddam Hussein's Iraq. Iraq's pursuit of a potential nuclear weapons program prompted a 1981 Israeli strike on the Osirak reactor which, directly or indirectly, sparked Iraq's subsequent covert nuclear program and two ground wars in 1991 and 2003, the latter resulting in Saddam's removal and a power vacuum that has reordered the Middle East balance of power. Iraq had long-standing rivalries with Israel, Iran, and at times other neighbors including Saudi Arabia, Syria, and Egypt; its motivations for nuclear weapons in the hostile environment in which it resided were largely security driven. Whether Osirak was realistically intended as the basis for a nuclear weapons program is hard to definitively establish, but its destruction certainly galvanized Saddam's intent and resolve to pursue nuclear weapons and to do so covertly—Israel's attempt to prevent a nuclear weapons program may have counterproductively intensified Baghdad's demand for the bomb.

Once Osirak was publicly and humiliatingly destroyed, a hiding strategy was the only option available to Iraq: Israel had demonstrated the real vulnerability of Iraq's nuclear infrastructure to military prevention, so subsequent nuclear weapons efforts had to be siloed and indigenous to avoid detection and destruction. This generated inefficiencies that would plague the program until the two subsequent ground wars and effective regime change definitively terminated its efforts. On the one hand, Saddam was fairly successful at hiding the program until the first Gulf War, after which the international community seemed to be genuinely stunned at how they missed Iraq's covert efforts. On the other hand, the hiding strategy forced such inefficiencies in the program that, save for a crash program to extract HEU from IAEA-sealed reactor fuel, Iraq had made little progress toward a bomb by 1991. Absent Saddam's ill-advised invasion of Kuwait, slow progress might have been made through the 1990s, though whether Iraq would have ever succeeded in achieving a nuclear weapons capability undetected is an open question—red lights flash brighter as a program approaches completion.

Saddam's nuclear program went through several phases. The first involved the development of the Osirak reactor with (again) French assistance, which began in 1974. Although Saddam may have believed that Osirak would provide the basis for a sustained nuclear weapons program, Osirak's design and the fact that it was under IAEA safeguards limited the possibility of a plutonium route to nuclear weapons. There is quite a bit of evidence that senior officials at the Iraq Atomic Energy Commission (IAEC) nevertheless envisioned Osirak as the basis for a nuclear weapons program. Between 1976 and 1979, Iraq contracted with Italy for several hot cells for reprocessing plutonium on a pilot scale, as well as uranium extraction technologies, which could be useful for a future weapons program.[1] A key Iraqi scientist, Mahdi Obeidi, who would ultimately head the centrifuge project, was asked point-blank by the IAEC leadership: "will the reactor be able to fulfill its strategic requirements? . . . [which] indicated the government's desire to build nuclear weapons."[2] Saddam openly spoke of developing nuclear weapons to counter Israel's—his primary motivation it seems for nuclear weapons, though Iran certainly featured heavily as a potential existential threat given the 1980s war and Iraq's own large Shi'ia population—and that "without such deterrence, the Arab nation will continue to be threatened by the Zionist entity and Iraq will remain threatened."[3] In a public speech at Al-Bakr University in 1978, Saddam said: "Through all of this, we should generate the unusual capabilities of the Arab nation, including the capability to have a bomb, and that is no longer a monopolized science. The atom is a widespread and thorough science, and any country can produce the atomic bomb if it finds the central technical base for it. We do not have to be as advanced as France, for example, to use it. It is enough for us to be like India in order to have the atom and to have the ability to use it."[4] Jafar Dhia Jafar, who would be a key scientist in the program, was informed by Saddam's half brother during his brief detention in 1980 before Osirak was destroyed that once

1. See Braut-Hegghammer, *Unclear Physics*, 56–61.

2. Mahdi Obeidi and Kurt Pitzer, *The Bomb in My Garden: The Secrets of Saddam's Nuclear Mastermind* (Hoboken, NJ: Wiley and Sons, 2004), 48.

3. Saddam Hussein in Kevin M. Woods, David D. Palkki, and Mark E. Stout, *The Saddam Tapes: The Inner Workings of a Tyrant's Regime, 1978–2001* (Cambridge: Cambridge University Press, 2011), 226.

4. Saddam Hussein, "Transcript of a Speech Given by Saddam Hussein on 'The Role of the Iraqi Armed Forces in the Arab-Zionist Conflict' at Al-Bakr University" (Washington, DC: Conflict Records Research Center, June 3, 1978), 34–35, https://digitalarchive.wilsoncenter.org/document/116983.

he was released, "the President wants you to work on the bomb."[5] Osirak thus seemed to be a key piece of that plan in Saddam's mind. If Saddam envisioned Osirak as the basis of a nuclear weapons program, this phase was a more open quest for nuclear weapons than Iraq's later hiding strategy.

However, Osirak was under IAEA safeguards, limiting the ability to divert either unused or spent reactor fuel, and there was no viable plutonium reprocessing capability for a sustained nuclear weapons program. Furthermore, though the French-supplied reactor fuel was 93 percent enriched uranium,[6] which could theoretically be seized and fabricated to construct, at most, one or two uranium bombs in an emergency, this would not have been a sustainable nuclear weapons program either—and only 12.5 kilograms of the contracted 70 kilograms were ultimately delivered by France.[7] At best, it was a Hail Mary insurance scheme against regime change. From a purely technical standpoint, Obeidi writes, "When I stepped back to look at the larger picture, I saw a mismatch between the idea and reality. By purchasing the French reactor, the IAEC was possibly taking the first few steps on the road to a nuclear weapons program. The 40-megawatt reactor wouldn't contain enough uranium fuel to enrich for a weapon, however. And I was almost certain that the IAEC had no strategy for turning the fissile material into weapons even if the material could be produced."[8]

However, to guard against even the remote possibility that Iraq might leave the NPT and develop a reprocessing capability with Osirak, and thus a sustainable route to plutonium weapons, Menachem Begin's Israel took no chances and, on June 7, 1981, destroyed the reactor before it went critical in an audacious surgical strike, Operation Opera. Israeli Chief of the General Staff, General Rafael Eitan, wrote a letter to the South African defense minister delighting in the attack, saying: "Well, we did the deed with iron determination not to allow these crazy Arabs to possess nuclear weapons. Anyone who tries to say that the nuclear reactor in Iraq was only for research purposes is wicked, cynical and oil, not human blood, flows in his veins."[9]

5. Jafar Dhia Jafar and Numan Saadaldin al-Niaimi, unpublished English translation (2004) based on *Al-I'tiraf al-Akhir: Haqiqat al-Barnamaj al-Nawawi al-Iraqi* (The Last Confession: The Truth about the Iraqi Nuclear Program) (Beirut: Markaz Dirasat Al-Wahdah Al-Arabiya, 2005), 35.

6. The French tried to renegotiate the deal to provide so-called "caramel" fuel at 9 percent enrichment, but the IAEC rejected it on the grounds that it was not industrially proven. This may suggest the route the IAEC envisioned Osirak providing to nuclear weapons, if not plutonium.

7. See Målfrid Braut-Hegghammer, "Revisiting Osirak: Preventive Attacks and Nuclear Proliferation Risks," *International Security* 36, no. 1 (Summer 2011): 111–12.

8. Obeidi and Pitzer, *The Bomb in My Garden*, 48–49.

9. "Letter from Israeli General Rafael Eitan to South African Minister Magnus Malan on Israeli Airstrike on Iraqi Nuclear Reactor," June 10, 1981, History and Public Policy Program Digital

The destruction of Osirak seems to have had two effects on Saddam. First, it hardened his resolve that Iraq needed nuclear weapons, particularly to defend against Israel.[10] In a lengthy post-attack monologue released as part of the U.S. Department of Defense catalog of records seized in the 2003 invasion of Iraq, Saddam seems committed to rebuilding his nuclear weapons program to deter primarily Israel and goes on to essentially double down: "About Iraq I can say: there is no power that can prevent us from dealing with this subject matter or from possessing the forefront of the scientific and technical field in a sound and correct way that serves our national objectives. Moreover, I say about Iraq—that the lessons we have learned so far we have converted into programs. Let Begin hear this: we convert every lesson into a program; we do not say it just as words. Instead, we convert into a program."[11] Obviously Saddam's grandiose rhetoric, probably largely for domestic consumption, should be taken with appropriate skepticism. Nevertheless, Braut-Hegghammer reports that Jafar Dhia Jafar, who would be put in charge of the program, was told by Saddam "to work toward a nuclear deterrent. Without such a deterrent . . . Iraq would not be able to ward off future Israeli attacks."[12] Second, the preventive strike at Osirak conditioned *how* Jafar was to go about it. Withdrawing from the NPT to develop an unsafeguarded program was out of the question since it would arouse intense suspicion and invite further strikes. Instead, Iraq had no choice but to develop and hide a clandestine program. Saddam may have wished for nuclear weapons prior to the Israeli attack—the evidence suggests he did—but he explicitly ordered his scientists to accelerate and intensify their efforts to develop nuclear weapons after it, in September 1981.

Jafar and al-Niaimi write, in an unpublished translation of their memoirs, that the order to pursue nuclear weapons in September 1981 was "crystal clear," but "there was one debilitating caveat: we were not allowed to seek assistance from abroad" that might tip off foreign powers about Iraq's nuclear

Archive, South African Defence Forces Archive, MV 56/17, vol. 3, obtained and contributed by Sasha Polakow-Suransky, http://digitalarchive.wilsoncenter.org/document/116076.

10. See Hal Brands and David Palkki, "Saddam, Israel and the Bomb: Nuclear Alarmism Justified?" *International Security* 36, no. 1 (Summer 2011): 133–66; Braut-Hegghammer, "Revisiting Osirak"; Braut-Hegghammer, *Unclear Physics*, chap. 3; Hymans, *Achieving Nuclear Ambitions*, chap. 3; and Dan Reiter, "Preventive Attacks against Nuclear Programs and the 'Success' at Osiraq," *Nonproliferation Review* 12, no. 2 (July 2005): 355–71.

11. Saddam Hussein in "Meeting between Saddam Hussein and His Senior Advisors Following the Israeli Attack on Osirak" (Washington, DC: Conflict Records Research Center, circa 1981), 8; also see p. 5, https://digitalarchive.wilsoncenter.org/document/116987.

12. Jafar cited in Braut-Hegghammer, *Unclear Physics*, 77.

weapons activities and prompt an attempt to stop it.[13] Jafar and Obeidi suggest in their memoirs that Saddam's instructions were to develop a sustained nuclear weapons program without relying on foreign suppliers or on a large signature that might be detected and destroyed by either Israel or other major powers.[14] Braut-Hegghammer writes that "Saddam had *one* clear order for his nuclear scientists: avoid sensitive foreign assistance that could alert the outside world to the nuclear weapons program. The Iraqis were thus confined to a primarily indigenous route, unlike other developing states seeking nuclear weapons, despite lacking industrial resources similar to those in other large states that had produced nuclear weapons previously."[15] Jafar notes that "in [his] eyes, his order was to create the ability to enrich uranium on a large scale."[16] Furthermore, in addition to avoiding alerting foreign intelligence agencies through foreign supply, Braut-Hegghammer writes that "their key priority was to develop a program with a small signature," which obviously excluded a plutonium route that might require a reactor and reprocessing facilities but also meant avoiding large concentrated industrial uranium conversion or enrichment facilities that might also arouse suspicion.[17] Iraq was forced into a dispersed homegrown clandestine effort, generating inefficiencies that bought time—probably the most valuable commodity when trying to halt proliferation—for the international community to detect any covert program or for Saddam to make an unforced error that might reveal his clandestine efforts.

What did hiding force Iraq to do in practice? The need for secrecy forced Iraq's scientists to pursue suboptimal and largely obsolete uranium enrichment pathways like electromagnetic isotope separation (EMIS), gaseous diffusion through a hard-to-produce homemade diffusion barrier,[18] and ultimately gas centrifuges that it could manufacture *indigenously* (or buy

13. Jafar and al-Niaimi, unpublished translation, p. 39.

14. See, for example, Jafar Dhia Jafar, Numan Saadaldin al-Niaimi, and Lars Sigurd Sunnanå, *Oppdraget: Innsidehistorien om Saddams Atomvåpen* (Oslo: Spartacus Books, 2005); Obeidi and Pitzer, *The Bomb in My Garden*; Imad Khadduri, *Iraq's Nuclear Mirage: Memoirs and Delusions* (Richmond Hill, Ontario: Springhead Publishers, 2003); and Dhafir Selbi and Zuhair al-Chalabi, coauthored and edited by Imad Khadduri, *Unrevealed Milestones in the Iraqi National Nuclear Program, 1981–1991* (CreateSpace Independent Publishing Platform, 2011).

15. Braut-Hegghammer, *Unclear Physics*, 80, emphasis added.

16. Jafar cited in ibid., 77.

17. Braut-Hegghammer, "Revisiting Osirak," 118.

18. In addition, acquiring the number and strength of compressors required to scale up gaseous diffusion would make it impossible to, according to Obeidi, "keep such a large scale project secret from the eyes of the international community." See Obeidi and Pitzer, *The Bomb in My Garden*, 60.

from illegal private suppliers that would not tip off international intelligence agencies).[19] Scientists were further restricted by their access to information: they could only rely on literature that was unclassified and easily available. Braut-Hegghammer concludes that Iraqi scientists "could not pursue the optimal technological pathways for fear of detection."[20] Both Hymans and Braut-Hegghammer, in excellent and important studies on Iraq, focus on the domestic political inefficiencies of trying to develop a big science project like a nuclear weapons program in Saddam's Iraq, a neopatrimonial regime.[21] While there is no doubt that the autocratic nature of Saddam's regime mattered, the more important cause of Iraq's hiding nuclear proliferation strategy was its vulnerability to international coercion and military action. That lone constraint forced Iraqi scientists into inefficient enrichment pathways that they would not have otherwise had to select, even in a personalistic regime.

The first several years after the destruction of Osirak witnessed Iraqi scientists pushing on all possible doors for uranium enrichment, focusing primarily on EMIS and gaseous diffusion, while Saddam's attention was focused on the costly Iran-Iraq war. Jafar spearheaded the EMIS program, which uses large magnets to separate U-235 ions from U-238 ions and collects the enriched beam, and then repeats the cycle to further enrich U-235. EMIS was attractive because Iraq could acquire or develop the required equipment without arousing suspicion. Jafar started by focusing on the Penning Ionization Gauge (PIG) instead of calutrons (the magnets the United States used in the Manhattan Project but abandoned due to high power consumption) because it provided a smaller signature and some of his scientists had experience with PIG. Unfortunately for Jafar and his team, it did not work. Jafar switched to separators, or calutrons, by around 1987 but this proved difficult to install and scale up. By 1991, roughly a decade after the EMIS program had started, the IAEA estimates that only 640 grams of uranium with an average enrichment of 7.2 percent were produced at the Tuwaitha facility, and only 685 grams of uranium with an average enrichment of 3 percent were produced at al Tarmiya.[22] Even as a potential feed to another enrichment technique, EMIS had gotten pretty much nowhere; and

19. See Jafar and al-Niaimi, unpublished English translation, p. 60.

20. Braut-Hegghammer, *Unclear Physics*, 83.

21. See Hymans, *Achieving Nuclear Ambitions*, chap. 3; Braut-Hegghammer, *Unclear Physics*.

22. See International Atomic Energy Agency (IAEA), "Fourth Consolidated Report of the Director General of the International Atomic Energy Agency," October 8, 1997, part II, pp. 35–36, https://digitallibrary.un.org/record/244664?ln=en.

without another bulk enrichment technique, the Iraqi uranium enrichment program was likely a dead end.

In an internal power play, Hussein Kamel, Saddam's son-in-law, took charge of the nuclear weapons efforts in 1987. He established a dedicated group to "investigate an explosive device for the nuclear material" and championed the centrifuge program when Obeidi rightly pointed out that, if Iraq could domestically manufacture them, centrifuges were really the only viable option for a sustainable covert enrichment program.[23] The centrifuge program operated slowly as Obeidi and his team struggled to procure the components required to indigenously assemble and manufacture a centrifuge capable of greater than 50,000 rpm without exploding. Only extremely high-strength, precision-machined components can tolerate the stresses created in such centrifuges; acquiring them is complicated, and manufacturing them was beyond Iraq's industrial capability in the 1980s. Obeidi did not enjoy the luxury of a large private supplier network, as had AQ Khan—who actually approached the Iraqis as a potential client, but Saddam feared it might be a setup—but he was able to acquire some components from unscrupulous private German suppliers.[24]

On the eve of Saddam's risky and ill-advised invasion of Kuwait in 1990, Obeidi's team had developed a single working prototype centrifuge and had enriched exactly zero uranium (a test run's worth of UF_6 was blended back with the feed). He had enough components for, at most, 50 centrifuges—too few for a viable nuclear weapons program. Iraq also lacked an industrial-scale uranium conversion facility to produce the feed material for a centrifuge program. Iraq in the first Gulf War was certainly much further along than anyone knew in the research phase for gas centrifuges for a nuclear weapons program.[25] But even assuming no international constraints and even unrestricted access to foreign supply, the IAEA estimated that Iraq was still several years from being able to sustainably enrich uranium. Jafar's optimistic estimate was that if Iraq could erect a cascade of 1,000 continuously operating centrifuges—a big if given the production and procurement challenges for a program that only had enough parts for 50 centrifuges—it would be able to produce 10 kilograms of 93 percent highly enriched uranium (HEU) by the mid- to late 1990s, which was, at most, enough for just a single rudimentary bomb, if that. Perhaps Obeidi's team would have been able to get a

23. See Obeidi and Pitzer, *The Bomb in My Garden*, 65.

24. Ibid., 122–24.

25. See IAEA, "Fourth Consolidated Report."

cascade of 1,000 centrifuges running by the mid-1990s, but there were still significant obstacles in the way including an industrial-scale (and therefore detectable) uranium conversion facility,[26] a reliable set of cascades, machining cores, and actual weaponization work. Being forced into a hiding strategy significantly retarded Iraq's ability to develop a nuclear weapons program by pushing Iraq's scientists down inefficient pathways like EMIS, limiting foreign contact, and isolating horizontal communication to "force protect" the program if any one group was compromised. The addition of Saddam's terrifying rule, filtered through Hussein Kamel's ruthlessly unique management style of siloing and isolating the research groups to foster competition, certainly did not do anything to modulate those inefficiencies.

After Saddam's invasion of Kuwait in August 1990, but prior to the American-led Operation Desert Storm, Hussein Kamel ordered a "crash program" to rip the IAEA seals off of Iraq's enriched uranium reactor fuel and fabricate, at most, one or two uranium bombs. This was aimed at developing a limited rudimentary capability as an emergency measure to deter an American attempt at regime change. It was not a sustainable program but resurrected the original idea of how Osirak might be able to generate fissile material: using the reactor fuel to extract enriched uranium. Iraqi scientists were unable to extract any of the estimated 40 kilograms of HEU from the 175 elements of reactor fuel it had received from France and the Soviet Union—with an average enrichment level of 84 percent—before the American invasion, and the IAEA was able to account for all of it in its subsequent inspections.[27] Jafar's account includes only 27 kilograms of uranium in 106 fuel elements for the "crash program" because he does not include half the Soviet fuel elements that had been irradiated and from which extracting HEU may have been more difficult; this would have cut the available HEU from the fuel elements to barely enough for one unsophisticated bomb.[28] Even if Iraqi scientists had been able to extract the HEU from the reactor fuel and further enrich it to weapons-grade level, machining the uranium into metal cores and developing a workable weapons design—even a simple gun-type—would have taken a considerable amount of time. And it killed any possibility of a sustained weapons program. Once the IAEA caught Iraq

26. Jafar and al-Niaimi, unpublished English translation, 73.

27. See IAEA, "Fourth Consolidated Report," 48–52. Also see David Albright, "Iraq's Programs to Make Highly Enriched Uranium and Plutonium for Nuclear Weapons Prior to the Gulf War," Institute for Science and International Security (2001), https://www.isis-online.org/publications/iraq/iraqs_fm_history.html.

28. Jafar and al-Niaimi, unpublished English translation, 87–88.

diverting reactor fuel, the game would be up for Iraq's attempts to hide other facilities. It was an ill-conceived, rash judgment by Hussein Kamel that even Iraqi scientists knew was doomed to fail.[29]

Until the first Gulf War, Iraq's hiding strategy mostly succeeded in deceiving the international community, particularly British, American, and Israeli intelligence agencies, about the extent of Saddam's efforts. Most intelligence agencies recognized that Saddam was motivated to pursue and develop nuclear weapons but underestimated both Iraq's efforts and progress through the 1980s. In September 1985, a National Intelligence Council report on potential proliferators grouped Iraq in the category that had previously "shown interest in developing the kinds of capabilities that, if they succeed, might eventually bring them to the technological level where they could create an explosive device. But . . . there is virtually *no chance* any of them could reach that level in the next 10 years."[30] In 1988, the CIA noted that the Iran-Iraq war, especially Iranian chemical weapons use and the potential for Iranian nuclearization, had probably motivated Saddam to "place a high priority on developing a nuclear weapons capability."[31] The Agency highlighted "reports in the press . . . during the last two years claiming the existence of secret nuclear projects at Tuwaitha." But the CIA struck a neutral note in its bottom-line assessment. It judged that "economic constraints during the war have impeded progress on the Iraqi nuclear program." The CIA, it seems, dismissed the possibility that Iraq was actively attempting to assemble a uranium enrichment capability using centrifuges.[32]

On the eve of the Gulf War, the CIA conceded that Iraq might have strong security motivations to develop nuclear weapons. "We believe Iraq's activities, especially its covert nuclear procurement, strongly suggest a weapons program exists," they wrote. But the CIA also said it lacked concrete evidence of progress: "We have not identified a formal, coordinated nuclear weapons program."[33] The CIA judged in 1990 that "Iraq is at least five years from enriched uranium production on a small scale."[34] In an assessment prior

29. See Obeidi and Pitzer, *The Bomb in My Garden*, 135–40.

30. National Intelligence Council, NIC M 85-10001, "The Dynamics of Nuclear Proliferation: Balance of Incentives and Constraints," September 1985, Secret, excised copy, p. 9, http://nsarchive.gwu.edu/nukevault/ebb451/docs/8.pdf, emphasis added.

31. Central Intelligence Agency, "Iraq's National Security Goals," December 1988, CIA Electronic Reading Room, p. iv, http://nsarchive.gwu.edu/NSAEBB/NSAEBB80/wmd02.pdf.

32. Ibid., 2.

33. Central Intelligence Agency, "Iraqi Ballistic Missile Developments," July 1990, CIA Electronic Reading Room, p. 14, http://nsarchive.gwu.edu/NSAEBB/NSAEBB80/wmd03.pdf.

34. Ibid.

to Operation Desert Storm—when the intelligence community would have devoted every resource at its disposal to be accurate—the CIA estimated that:

> Iraq probably has the technical competence, when combined with clandestinely obtained foreign technology or assistance, to develop a nuclear weapon by the *late 1990s* using indigenously produced fissile material. Other worst case and much less likely scenarios exist in which Iraq could develop a nuclear explosive in as little as a few months after a decision to do so. These scenarios involve the use of a clandestine source of nuclear material—[redacted]—or the diversion and processing of safeguarded research reactor fuels into material suitable for a crash nuclear explosives program.
>
> Even though Iraq probably could develop a nuclear device by the end of the decade if its nuclear infrastructure remained intact, fitting the device into a missile's warhead will not be a simple task . . . [redacted] . . . Iraq could face two or more years' delay in fielding a nuclear weapon.[35]

These judgments were probably not far off the mark based on the capabilities Iraq had on the eve of the Gulf War. But the CIA would subsequently be stunned by what they missed when inspectors finally got eyes on the Iraqi uranium enrichment efforts. While they had an inkling of Saddam's incentive to continue to pursue nuclear weapons, they missed the activity outside of Tuwaitha and the progress Obeidi's team had made on developing prototype centrifuges for a weapons program. Iraq's surprising progress suggests that a motivated hider may be able to successfully cover its tracks early in a program from even the most sophisticated intelligence agencies, which are calibrated to look for "blinking red" signatures—those that often emerge closer to the finish line—to make firm conclusions about a nuclear weapons program. Assessments are notoriously difficult and fraught with uncertainty early in a program, especially against a strategic adversary attempting to hide its activities.

Just how close was Iraq's covert program to a nuclear weapons program by 1991? Certainly the United States and the IAEA were alarmed by the

35. Central Intelligence Agency, "Prewar Status of Iraq's Weapons of Mass Destruction," March 1991, CIA Electronic Reading Room, p. iv, http://nsarchive.gwu.edu/NSAEBB/NSAEBB80/wmd04.pdf, emphasis added. Most of the section on nuclear weapons in the body of the report is redacted, as is, interestingly, what is likely the CIA's guess above about a potential foreign clandestine source of fissile material.

clandestine efforts they had discovered that had gone undetected.[36] Peter Zimmerman's disquieting 1993 Congressional Research Service (CRS) report on the Iraqi nuclear program expresses the shock among experts, noting that Iraq was "alone among states" party to the NPT to "have advanced to the threshold of nuclear weapons production *while still being a member in good standing of the NPT regime, and while continuing to receive clean bills of health from inspectors of the IAEA*."[37] The degree of successful hiding shocked and dismayed inspectors and experts around the world. Leaving the crash program for a single or two nuclear bombs aside, since it was not a sustainable program and would have been detected by the IAEA at their next visit, scholars diverge on their assessment of where Iraq lay in 1991. Some claim the effort was hopeless, while others argue it was on the brink of success. Hymans avers: "Even if the Gulf War had not intervened the Iraqi nuclear weapons project would probably have been no more successful in the 1990s than it had been in the 1980s. Indeed, it would likely have run definitively into the ditch."[38] Braut-Hegghammer equally strongly claims that "by 1991, in contrast, the Iraqis had all of the necessary resources to develop nuclear weapons and were making rapid progress toward developing the overall capability to do so."[39] She concludes: "Despite making virtually every possible mistake, the Iraqis stood at the threshold of a nuclear weapons capability by early 1991."[40]

As usual, the truth probably lies somewhere in the middle. Although Iraq may have made progress toward a nuclear weapons capability had it not placed a noose around its neck with the Kuwait invasion, it was still years away from a sustainable enrichment program, lacking a proper large-scale uranium conversion facility as well as the ability to reliably and consistently manufacture enough centrifuges for large cascades. Zimmerman's somewhat alarmist CRS report estimated that in terms of fissile material, Iraq was "at about the stage of the American program in mid-1944," and in terms of

36. See IAEA, "Fourth Consolidated Report"; Robert E. Kelley, "The Iraqi and South African Nuclear Weapons Program: The Importance of Management," *Security Dialogue* 27, no. 1 (1996): 27–38; and Charles Duelfer, "Comprehensive Report of the Special Advisor to the DCI on Iraq's WMD," September 30, 2004, https://www.govinfo.gov/app/details/GPO-DUELFERREPORT.

37. Peter D. Zimmerman, "Iraq's Nuclear Achievements: Components, Sources, and Stature," Congressional Research Service Report, February 18, 1993, p. 1, emphasis in original.

38. Hymans, *Achieving Nuclear Ambitions*, 115.

39. Braut-Hegghammer, "Revisiting Osirak," 128.

40. Ibid., 130.

weaponization "at about the stage of Los Alamos in January 1945."[41] That is likely an overestimate. The Iraqi potential to actually produce weapons-grade enriched uranium was much farther behind than that. Nevertheless, he goes on to say that "in all respects it appears that the Iraqi program—although sophisticated and competently managed—is decades behind that of all five of the nuclear weapon states."[42] Even if one accepts that Iraq was at the same place as the Manhattan Project in 1944/1945, it would be a mistake to extrapolate linearly and assume that it would have developed the bomb in months or years. The program was inefficient. It enjoyed nowhere near the sanctuary or resources that any of the nuclear weapons states had—let alone the United States. Even absent the Gulf War, Iraqi scientists would have still faced significant hurdles, with the Iraqi program likely muddling along, constrained by its necessity to maintain a small undetectable footprint and avoid large foreign suppliers. The lack of a uranium conversion facility for feed material[43] and the lack of the proper components, and an inconsistent ability to manufacture them, for a large cascade of centrifuges were very real constraints on the Iraqi program that would have continued through the 1990s.

These constraints were not simply a matter of management style. The necessity of a hiding strategy shunted Iraq into inefficiency. Although both Hymans and Braut-Hegghammer offer compelling unit-level, bottom-up explanations for the character of Iraq's nuclear program, they understate the fact that it was forced into this condition—into being siloed, firewalled, inefficient, and suboptimal—due to Iraq's vulnerability to preventive action. Saddam could not micromanage it because doing so would likely tip off foreign intelligence agencies, since he had to assume he was being surveilled and tapped. As Braut-Hegghammer herself writes, the one directive Saddam had was to develop a program with no signature or footprint in order to maintain clandestineness. This was a top-down pressure—structurally determined, and filtered through Saddam. But the inefficiency of having to go down suboptimal enrichment pathways, born of the necessity of a hiding strategy, carried consequences. Iraq's ultra-secret pursuit generated a decade-long window either for Saddam to make a mistake and get caught or for intelligence agencies to put the pieces together that Iraq had a covert program. Saddam's impulsive decision to invade Kuwait in 1990 was just

41. Zimmerman, "Iraq's Nuclear Achievements," 27.

42. Ibid., 28.

43. See IAEA, "Fourth Consolidated Report," 18.

such a mistake—a colossal one at that. The sheikdom was driving down global oil prices, thereby impoverishing cash-strapped, debt-ridden Iraq. But Saddam's rash decision for war prompted an international response that ultimately exposed his covert program. It provided a broad international coalition with adequate justification to halt Iraq's nuclear activities. But for the war and associated international attention, Iraq might have continued to make clandestine progress through the 1990s, and with some luck and maybe if it had a bit more breathing room, it might have attained a nuclear weapons capability. But the structural conditions that forced Iraq into a hiding strategy would have persisted—and constraints became even tighter after the war—which meant that Saddam would not have been able to suddenly reorient the management or technical pathways to nuclear weapons. Developing states that are forced to pursue covert nuclear weapons programs with limited indigenous capacity—and thus need ample time to realize their ambitions—are ill-advised to draw the attention of superpowers. By invading and occupying Kuwait, Iraq failed to follow this prime directive.

When the war was over and the IAEA discovered the swath of facilities dedicated to uranium enrichment—from Tuwaitha to al-Atheer to Rashidiya, which was later found to be scrubbed of all centrifuge activity—as well as the crash program after Hussein Kamel's defection to Jordan, it put Iraq under a cloud of suspicion that would ultimately set the stage for the 2003 invasion: American decision makers such as Cheney and Rumsfeld presumed that Iraq, once a hider, would always be a hider.[44] The extent to which Saddam played hide-and-seek with inspectors through the 1990s, as the slow trickle of information got pieced together, boosted by Hussein Kamel's defection, generated a presumption of, at best, continued intent to reconstitute a covert nuclear weapons program and, at worst, an ongoing clandestine program that was unknown to inspectors. Saddam indeed professed his intention to restart his nuclear program internally, and may have even believed that he would be able to reconstitute it if given enough breathing room.[45] In an undated meeting, Hussein Kamel would say to Saddam: "Sir . . . do we have to reveal everything, or do we continue with the silence? Sir, if the meeting took this line, I must say that it is in our interest not to reveal anything . . .

44. See Målfrid Braut-Hegghammer, "The Cheater's Dilemma: Iraq, Weapons of Mass Destruction, and the Path to War," *International Security* 45, no. 1 (Summer 2020): 51–89.

45. See, for example, Woods, Palkki, and Stout, *The Saddam Tapes*, 240–42. Also see "Cabinet Meeting with Saddam Hussein and the Atomic Energy Committee," Conflict Records Research Center, Washington, DC, undated [post–Gulf War], http://crrc.dodlive.mil/files/2013/06/SH-SHTP-A-001-492.pdf.

not only out of fear of revealing the scientific technology we have acquired, or concealing it for some future action."[46] Tariq Aziz would say at one point, referring to the illegal programs, "we are cheating and we continue to cheat," with Saddam replying, "We need to know how to cheat."[47]

But Iraqi scientists would get pretty much nowhere after the first Gulf War due to the noose placed around them by international inspectors and their inability to leverage even shady illegal private suppliers as Obeidi had been able to do in the late 1980s. For the most part, despite whatever Saddam may have believed he might be able to do if given a free run, Iraq's nuclear program was essentially dead in the years following the first Gulf War.

The risk of a hiding strategy is if one is caught, as Iraq was after the first Gulf War, the cloud of suspicion may be almost impossible to remove.[48] Without relitigating the basis for the 2003 invasion, it is clear that the United States and United Kingdom had an "ingrained belief that Saddam Hussein's regime . . . was determined to preserve and if possible enhance its capabilities, including at some point in the future a nuclear capability, and was pursuing an active policy of deception and concealment."[49] As the U.K.'s Chilcot Report notes: "The judgements about Iraq's capabilities and intentions relied heavily on Iraq's past behavior being a reliable indicator of its current and future actions."[50] The retention of some nuclear scientific expertise combined with limited attempts to acquire dual-use equipment that *could* be used for centrifuges (e.g., very high-strength aluminum tubes) fed into confirmation bias that Saddam had never abandoned his hiding strategy for attaining nuclear weapons. There is likely little Saddam could have done in this period to convince the principals in the George W. Bush administration that he was not pursuing (or intent on) a hiding strategy of nuclear proliferation.[51] Robert Jervis writes, "For all groups, it did not make

46. Hussein Kamel in "Meeting between Saddam and His Security Council Regarding Iraqi Biological and Nuclear Weapons Program," February 5, 1995, Conflict Records Research Center, Washington, DC, p. 6, https://digitalarchive.wilsoncenter.org/document/116997.

47. "Meeting between Saddam Hussein and the Revolutionary Council Regarding the Sanctions Placed on Iraq and Tariq Aziz's Trip to the UN Security Council," circa November 8, 1995–December 28 1995, Conflict Records Research Center, Washington, DC, p. 7.

48. See Braut-Hegghammer, "The Cheater's Dilemma."

49. "The Report of the Iraq Inquiry: Executive Summary," *Report of the Privy Counsellors* (London: Crown, 2016), 69, http://www.iraqinquiry.org.uk/media/246416/the-report-of-the-iraq-inquiry_executive-summary.pdf.

50. Ibid., 75.

51. See Robert Jervis, *Why Intelligence Fails: Lessons from the Iranian Revolution and the Iraq War* (Ithaca: Cornell University Press, 2010), esp. 146–53.

sense that Saddam had nothing to hide."[52] Given Saddam's past behavior and the slow drip of previously undisclosed WMD-related capabilities and facilities through the 1990s that he had earlier "failed" to reveal, there was an unshakable suspicion that he continued to conceal a dormant, if not active, nuclear weapons program and intended to reactivate it or reconstitute it as soon as he had the space to do so. As such, the Bush administration believed the only definitive way it could terminate Iraq's pursuit of nuclear weapons was to eliminate Saddam altogether, which it did in the 2003 invasion.

Pursuing nuclear weapons clandestinely requires patience because it forces inefficiencies in the process, as the Iraqi case clearly demonstrates. Perhaps luckily for the international community, patience was a commodity in short supply in Saddam's decision-making cycle. It is impossible to know if Saddam's program would have succeeded if not discovered in 1991. What we *can* say with confidence is that Saddam's decision to invade Kuwait led to the—perhaps slow—death of the Iraqi nuclear weapons program. And the shock awaiting international weapons inspectors about just how far Iraqi scientists had gotten cast a suspicion that would, ultimately and literally, tighten the noose around Saddam through the 2003 U.S.-led invasion of Iraq.

TESTING PROLIFERATION STRATEGY THEORY

My theory correctly predicts that Iraq would choose hiding as a nuclear proliferation strategy. Saddam's motivations for nuclear weapons were overdetermined—from a nuclear Israel to a hostile Iran unafraid to unleash weapons of mass destruction against it, to an uneasy relationship with Saudi Arabia, no intelligence agency or analyst was surprised that Saddam might be interested in nuclear weapons. Saddam's ascension to power and consolidation of power as a personalist dictator generated the domestic consensus necessary for initiating an active nuclear weapons program if he so desired, which he desperately did. Whether Osirak would have provided the potential for a sustainable nuclear weapons program is debatable, but Israel took no chances and destroyed it, consistent with its de facto policy of not allowing any other nuclear reactors in its neighborhood. This evident and dramatic vulnerability of Iraqi nuclear infrastructure left Saddam with little option but to push his nuclear weapons effort underground and attempt a clandestine pathway to the bomb. My theory correctly predicts that Saddam would choose a hiding strategy after the attack on Osirak. He could not

52. Ibid., 147.

openly sprint, nor did he have a great power patron willing to immunize his program for a sheltered pursuit strategy. Thus, hiding was his only option.

My prediction dovetails with a nuanced realist prediction for how Iraq might go about developing nuclear weapons after the attack on the Osirak reactor. While generally silent about the "how" question, realists would find it unsurprising that a nuclear-aspirant Iraq would have no choice but to build underground: the prospect of nuclear Iraq terrified most of its more powerful neighbors as well as the superpowers who worried that Saddam might use it as a shield behind which to establish regional hegemony. My theory and a more sophisticated realist account should make similar predictions in cases where a state goes underground due to the very real fear of military coercion or prevention—or in Iraq's case, an object lesson in military prevention. Recall, however, that even Debs and Monteiro's realist theory would predict that states should rarely attempt to hide because they should be deterred from even initiating nuclear weapons pursuit by the threat of murder. Yet we nevertheless see many hiders—states like Iraq which are tempted to clandestinely try to develop nuclear weapons despite a small prospect of success.

Technological determinism is clearly wrong in the Iraqi case. After the Osirak attack, it is clear from the historical records and the memoirs of Jafar, Khadduri, and Obeidi that Saddam gave a single strategic direction: do not be detected. Iraqi scientists made technical compromises to keep the signature of the program extremely small, avoid foreign suppliers and foreign intelligence traps, and work in isolation to avoid horizontal communication that could foster leaks. Inefficient and obsolete uranium enrichment technologies were the only options that fit these parameters. No competent scientist in the 1980s would have selected EMIS or gaseous diffusion to enrich uranium if their primary directive was to maximize the chances of success. But these were the only technologies that could be hidden, so Iraqi scientists had little choice in the matter. Better technologies were available and could have been absorbed by the Iraqi scientific establishment, but it would have been too risky for Iraqi scientists to try to pursue them. Plutonium was excluded not because Iraqi scientists lacked competence with plutonium science—they would have loved nothing more than something larger than a pilot reprocessing facility for their research reactor—but because it would be easily detected. The strategy of hiding was chosen first, and (inefficient) uranium enrichment pathways followed. As in other cases where technological determinist theories highlight a program's use of antiquated or suboptimal technology, Iraq knowingly and purposefully avoided more propitious options.

Finally, international nonproliferation norms and the NPT had only a nominal impact in determining Iraqi *proliferation strategy*. It is certainly the case that the tighter export control list in the 1980s made it difficult for Iraqi scientists to acquire necessary components for advanced centrifuges. But when Obeidi was directed to switch to centrifuges in 1987, within a couple of years, he managed to leverage loopholes and unscrupulous European suppliers to acquire limited components for relatively advanced centrifuges to enrich uranium. Restrictions made a hiding strategy harder to pull off, but they did not change Iraq's strategic calculus. Moreover, the conditioning variable that forced Iraq into hiding was not a fear of being shamed as an NPT member in violation of its agreements but the very real kinetic coercion by the Israelis and Americans. Iraq was forced into hiding for power politics and military reasons, not because of entrenched or evolving nonproliferation norms. Saddam displayed open contempt for the nonproliferation regime. Military threat drove Saddam's nuclear program underground.

Taiwan: Hidden Holes

Insurance Hedging: 1967–74
Hiding: 1974–88

Since Chiang Kai-Shek retreated to Taiwan in 1950 after being driven out of mainland China, the People's Republic of China (PRC) has maintained that the Republic of China (ROC) is an integral part of the mainland and is committed to reclaiming it. As such, Taiwan faces perhaps one of the most significant existential threats in the world. The United States formally committed to the defense of Taiwan with the 1954 Mutual Defense Treaty. Despite the brutal dictatorship of the Kuomintang (KMT) under Chiang, the defense of Taiwan enjoyed substantial domestic support in the United States.[53] The United States would erect the Taiwan Defense Command, which would coordinate with Pacific Command on conventional operations. Declassified American records reveal that "beginning in January 1958, U.S. nuclear-armed Matador cruise missiles were deployed on Taiwan, less than 200 miles from mainland China."[54] The Matadors were removed in mid-1962, but the United States also stored nuclear bombs for American fighter-bombers, including F-4s, at Tainan Air Base. Norris, Arkin, and Burr write that "two

53. See Richard C. Bush, *At Cross Purposes: U.S.-Taiwan Relations since 1942* (Armonk, NY: M. E. Sharpe, 2004).

54. Robert S. Norris, William M. Arkin, and William Burr, "Where They Were," *Bulletin of the Atomic Scientists* 55, no. 6 (October 1999): 30.

to four of them [were placed] on 24-hour quick reaction alert," in the same fashion as American aircraft in West Germany during the 1950s.[55] Taiwan enjoyed a formal defense pact and extended nuclear deterrence from the United States from 1954 through the 1960s.

Given its underlying acute security threat from the behemoth PRC across the Taiwan Strait, mitigated by a formal defense pact with the United States, my theory predicts that Taiwan would—in this period—select an insurance hedging strategy to guard against a deterioration in its security environment due to either a shift in the threat level it faced from the PRC or U.S. abandonment of Taiwan. There is substantial evidence that this is what Taiwan selected.

Efforts at a viable insurance hedge against American abandonment began even before China's first nuclear test in 1964. In 1963, Chiang Kai-Shek sent permanent secretary of the Ministry of Defense Tang Junbo to attend the IAEA General Conference in Vienna on behalf of Taiwan, with orders to make contact with the head of the Israeli Atomic Energy Commission, Professor Ernst David Bergmann, and invite him on a secret visit to Taiwan. Chiang hoped that Israel could assist in setting up the foundations for Taiwan's independent nuclear weapons program, which was needed because Taiwan could not "completely rely on the Americans" in the face of a Chinese atomic attack.[56] This was a decision to lay the groundwork for a nuclear weapons program, not a political decision to pursue weaponization. Chiang found U.S. formal security guarantees dubious from the outset. The crucial difference between this period and the later period of U.S. abandonment is that at this point, Taiwan's mistrust of U.S. guarantees was limited to questions about whether the United States would respond to a nuclear attack by the PRC. Only later in the 1970s was Taiwan concerned about outright abandonment by the United States. This conditionality is what distinguishes the insurance hedging strategy of this period—breakout upon abandonment—from the hiding strategy in later years.

The Chinese nuclear test in 1964 tightened Taiwan's security constraints. Chiang Kai-Shek publicly went on the hunt for a heavy water reactor—ultimately sourced from Canada—to supplement the research reactor it had built in 1956 at National Tsinghua University. He acquired a 40 MWth reactor similar to the Canadian-supplied reactor India used to generate the fissile material for its 1974 peaceful nuclear explosion.[57] Construction began in 1969 and operations would begin in April 1973. U.S. State Department cables

55. Ibid., 34.

56. Yitzhak Shichor, "The Importance of Being Ernst: Ernst David Bergmann and Israel's Role in Taiwan's Defense," *Asia Paper 2* (2016): 4.

57. See Albright and Gay, "Taiwan: Nuclear Nightmare Averted," 57.

indicate that it believed that these efforts were designed to lay the technical foundation for a nuclear weapons program: "At the direction of President Chiang, the GRC [Government of the Republic of China] Defense Ministry continues to try to develop an atomic weapon and delivery systems, according to a source close to the effort."[58] The impetus behind this initial program was likely Chiang Kai-Shek's son, Chiang Ching-Kuo, who wanted to initiate a nuclear weapons program, code-named the Hsin Chu Project, very early on after the Chinese nuclear tests. However, Chiang Kai-Shek would table a decision about actual weaponization at this point because of a study by one of his scientific advisors, Professor Ta-You Wu, which pointed out the difficulties and cost—the military-run Chungshan Institute of Science and Technology had floated a $140 million proposal to lay the foundation for a weapons program.[59] Taiwan nevertheless openly purchased the Canadian reactor, christened the Taiwan Research Reactor (TRR), and heavy water from the United States itself. Taiwan's search on the international market for nuclear technology was not hidden, and it did not acquire any large-scale reprocessing equipment. Perhaps this search was designed to compel the United States to maintain its nuclear deployments in Taiwan, which it did. But before a strategy could really take shape, a seismic geopolitical event would force Taiwan to shift its proliferation strategy entirely.

After the Sino-Soviet split in the 1960s, punctuated by the Ussuri River clashes in 1969, it may have been inevitable that the United States would reorient its strategy to try to peel China away from the Soviet communist bloc. The casualty in any such reorientation would clearly be Taiwan. Just as Taiwan was constructing the TRR, President Nixon and Henry Kissinger were engineering the opening to China. Nixon would essentially abandon the basis of the 1954 Mutual Defense Treaty when he told Premier Zhou Enlai: "Principle one. There is one China, and Taiwan is a part of China. There will be no more statements made—if I can control our bureaucracy—to the effect that the status of Taiwan is undetermined. Second, we have not and will not support any Taiwan independence movement . . . we seek normalization of relations with the People's Republic."[60] Nixon further committed to removing

58. U.S. Embassy Taipei, Airgram 1037, June 20, 1966, "Indications GRC Continues to Pursue Atomic Weaponry," Subject-Numeric 1964–66, DEF 12-1 Chinat, http://nsarchive.gwu.edu/NSAEBB/NSAEBB20/docs/doc18.pdf.

59. Albright and Gay, "Taiwan: Nuclear Nightmare Averted," 55.

60. Memorandum of Conversation, President Richard Nixon and Prime Minister Zhou Enlai et al., February 22, 1972, 2.10–6 p.m., Great Hall of the People, Beijing, p. 5, National Archives, Nixon Presidential Materials Project, White House Special Files, President's Office Files, box 87,

American forces from Taiwan: "Two-thirds of our present forces on Taiwan are related to the support of our forces in Southeast Asia [Vietnam]. These forces . . . will be removed as the situation in Southeast Asia is resolved. I have made that decision. And the reduction of the remaining third of our military presence on Taiwan will go forward as progress is made on the peaceful resolution of the problem."[61] In a subsequent conversation, Nixon would say: "Now if someone asks me when I return, do you have a deal with the Prime Minister that you are going to withdraw all American forces from Taiwan, I will say 'no.' But I am telling the Prime Minister that it is my plan."[62] This was wholesale abandonment of Taiwan. Nixon was literally pledging directly to Zhou that he would throw Taipei under the bus in order to normalize relations with Beijing. Furthermore, if American conventional forces would be removed from Taiwan, so too would American nuclear weapons from Tainan Air Base; records suggest these were removed by 1974.[63]

Although it would take almost a decade for the abandonment of Taiwan to be codified through a series of communiqués between Washington and Beijing, formal normalization in 1979, and the Taiwan Relations Act, the writing was on the wall for Taipei with Nixon's trip to China. America's eroding commitment was exacerbated by international isolation—Taiwan was replaced by the PRC at the UN in late 1971. Although Congress would express policy intention with the Taiwan Relations Act, scholar Richard Pious notes that "in operational terms, the United States has no real commitment to the security of Taiwan . . . what it has, according to the terms of the Act itself, is a process by which the United States may recognize and act upon its own security interests. That is all the Taiwan Relations Act requires."[64] The Act lacks the binding force of the Mutual Defense Treaty—it is therefore not a security commitment. Furthermore, Beijing was increasingly disturbed by any American arms sales to Taiwan and would pressure Washington to restrain its conventional supply to Taiwan. Not only did the United States remove

---

Memoranda for the President Beginning February 20, 1972, http://nsarchive.gwu.edu/NSAEBB/NSAEBB106/NZ-1.pdf.

61. Ibid., 5–6.

62. Memorandum of Conversation, President Richard Nixon and Prime Minister Zhou Enlai et al., February 24, 1972, 5.15–8.05 p.m., Great Hall of the People, Beijing, pp. 11–12, National Archives, Nixon Presidential Materials Project, White House Special Files, President's Office Files, box 87, Memoranda for the President Beginning February 20, 1972, http://nsarchive.gwu.edu/NSAEBB/NSAEBB106/NZ-3.pdf.

63. Memorandum of Conversation, Ambassador Leonard Unger and Secretary of Defense James Schlesinger, April 3, 1974, http://nsarchive.gwu.edu/news/19991020/01-01.htm.

64. Pious quoted in Bush, *At Cross Purposes*, 155.

its foreign nuclear deployments at Tainan Air Base, but its commitment to strengthening Taiwan's conventional defenses against Beijing was tenuous.

Taiwan was thus left to face its primary security threat, China, alone. Furthermore, if it were to attempt an overt nuclear proliferation strategy, military prevention from China would almost certainly follow. Additionally, in order to avoid disrupting normalization with China—certainly trying to avoid a military strike on any Taiwanese nuclear facilities—the United States would attempt to use its considerable coercive leverage *against* a vulnerable Taiwanese economy to prevent it from pursuing nuclear weapons, not shelter it. Indeed, China back-channeled to American officials that "the PRC would hold the US responsible in the event Taiwan acquired nuclear weapons."[65] Faced with potential coercion from two major powers—one militarily and one diplomatically and potentially economically[66]—my theory predicts Taiwan would have no choice but to select a hiding strategy if it wanted to pursue nuclear weapons. That is what we observe. Alan Chang, who has written an excellent dissertation on Taiwan's nuclear program in part using Taiwanese-language sources and memoirs, writes that after Nixon's trip to China, "Chiang Ching-Kuo . . . began focusing even more intently on the secret weapons development program. In addition to nuclear weapons, a delivery system was also a priority."[67] As the United States was reorienting toward Beijing, the 1972 Special National Intelligence Estimate noted: "We estimate that the GRC [Government of the Republic of China] will continue to work toward the capability to design and produce nuclear weapons . . . when Taiwan may be alone and facing great risks. We believe, however, that Taipei will take pains to conceal its intentions, and will cover activities which are necessarily overt by associating them with research in the generation of nuclear power for peaceful uses."[68] The problem was, how to hide such a program, since the United States was keyed in on the possibility that Taiwan might attempt a hidden nuclear weapons program, and Taiwan lacks the real estate to disperse and effectively hide infrastructure.

65. Memorandum from Burton Levin, Office of Republic of China Affairs, to Oscar Armstrong, Deputy Assistant Secretary for East Asian Affairs, "PRCLO Comment on Taiwan Nuclear Development," October 12, 1976, http://nsarchive.gwu.edu/NSAEBB/NSAEBB20/docs/doc13.pdf.

66. See Miller, "The Secret Success of Nonproliferation Sanctions," 931–33.

67. Alan K. Chang, "Crisis Avoided: The Past, Present and Future of Taiwan's Nuclear Weapons Program" (master's thesis, Hawaii Pacific University, 2011), 31, http://www.hpu.edu/CHSS/History/GraduateDegree/MADMSTheses/files/alanchang.pdf.

68. Special National Intelligence Estimate 43-1-72, "Taipei's Capabilities and Intentions Regarding Nuclear Weapons Development," November 16, 1972, Secret, p. 5, http://nsarchive.gwu.edu/nukevault/ebb221/T-1a.pdf.

American government officials recognized the dilemma that seized Taiwan and knew that they would have to hide a nuclear weapons program if they were to try to pursue one. At one point, State Department officials quite accurately observed:

> Given the ROC's strategic/political vulnerability, the temptations to examine the possibility of acquiring a nuclear weapons capacity have to be assumed. There are, of course, many factors which would argue against such an effort in collective [GRC] thinking, e.g., relative ineffectiveness vis-à-vis PRC, heightened danger of a PRC preemptive strike if the ROC seemed to have such a capacity . . . economically disastrous cutoff of peaceful nuclear supplies from the U.S. We do not know definitively that any fundamental decision has in fact been taken. CCK has assured us emphatically and categorically in the negative. Admittedly, he could be expected to do this, if he saw his country's essential interests as requiring the achievement of nuclear weapons capacity. Clearly, if the ROC were to move in this direction, *they would have to conceal their effort from us at all costs*.[69]

This memo lays out several key facts: it would not surprise anyone if Taiwanese leaders after the U.S. normalization with the PRC would be interested in nuclear weapons. But given the vulnerability to both China and the United States if it were to do so openly, its only hope would be a hiding strategy. Thus the United States needed to be vigilant for any evidence that Taiwan might be hiding an active nuclear weapons program.

Was Taiwan pursuing a hidden nuclear weapons program? Almost certainly. There is strong evidence that Taiwan was trying to develop an indigenous plutonium reprocessing capability through the 1970s, and probably through 1988, using diverted fuel rods from its reactors to provide the basis for a nuclear weapons program under Chiang Ching-Kuo's direction. Taiwan was caught at one point with a hidden exit hole it had cut out from the spent fuel pond at the TRR.[70] The TRR was an obvious candidate to provide the basis for a nuclear weapons program. As a heavy water reactor, the CIA estimated that it was capable of producing 10 kilograms of plutonium per year at full operation.[71] Although it was under IAEA safeguards

69. U.S. Embassy Taiwan cable 6351 to State Department, "Proposed Assignment of U.S. Nuclear Scientists to ROC," September 18, 1978, Secret Nodis, excised copy, p. 2, http://nsarchive.gwu.edu/nukevault/ebb221/T-21e.pdf, emphasis added.

70. See Albright and Gay, "Taiwan: Nuclear Nightmare Averted," 58.

71. Special National Intelligence Estimate No. 43-1-72, "Taipei's Capabilities and Intentions Regarding Nuclear Weapons Development," Central Intelligence Agency, November 1972, p. 3, http://nsarchive.gwu.edu/nukevault/ebb221/T-1a.pdf.

at the time, the CIA worried that "the future of such inspections is in doubt because [Beijing] has demanded that the IAEA sever all ties to Taiwan, and the Canadians do not have a bilateral safeguards agreement with the GRC to serve as a fallback. Since Canada no longer officially recognizes the GRC, the chances that a bilateral safeguards agreement will be negotiated are essentially nil. Thus, assuming that unsafeguarded supplies of natural uranium and heavy water can be purchased from foreign sources, the GRC may be able to operate this reactor entirely free of safeguard restrictions."[72] The geopolitical earthquake of normalization with China created all sorts of legal problems including IAEA safeguards; the United States would ultimately serve as the guarantor of Taiwan's adherence to NPT guidelines in a trilateral agreement between the two countries and the IAEA. Interestingly, and relatedly, Mark Fitzpatrick notes the legal gymnastics Taiwan deployed to claim that it was not bound by the NPT as a non–nuclear weapons state to refrain from nuclear weapons activities: "Its logic was that the NPT authorized weapons possession by the states that had exploded them prior to the treaty entry into force, as Beijing had done in 1964, and since the Kuomintang government considered itself the legitimate government of all of China," it could legally possess nuclear weapons.[73] The 1972 and 1974 Special National Intelligence Estimates clearly indicated that the U.S. intelligence community believed Taiwan was pursuing nuclear weapons, with the 1974 NIE stating: "Taipei conducts its small nuclear program with a weapon option clearly in mind, and it will be in a position to fabricate a nuclear device after five years or so."[74]

There were basically two pathways to a hidden nuclear weapons capability with the Taiwan Research Reactor. Either Taiwan could try to enrich uranium for weapons from fresh reactor fuel elements (TRR was fueled by natural uranium), or it could reprocess spent fuel from the TRR to extract plutonium. There is sketchy evidence that Taiwan tried to develop a laser enrichment capability for uranium, perhaps in 1978[75] and then again jointly

72. Ibid.

73. Mark Fitzpatrick, *Asia's Latent Nuclear Powers: Japan, South Korea, and Taiwan* (London: Routledge, 2016), 128.

74. Special National Intelligence Estimate 4-1-74, "Prospects for Further Proliferation of Nuclear Weapons," August 23, 1974, Top Secret, excised copy, p. 4, http://nsarchive.gwu.edu/NSAEBB/NSAEBB240/snie.pdf.

75. See William Burr, "The Taiwanese Nuclear Case: Lessons for Today," Carnegie Endowment for International Peace, August 9, 2007, http://carnegieendowment.org/2007/08/09/taiwanese-nuclear-case-lessons-for-today.

with South Africa later in the 1980s,[76] from which it also purchased over 162 tons of natural uranium between 1972 and 1974.[77] However, it seems that most of the clandestine activity centered on attempting to develop a hidden reprocessing capability through either hot cells, which allowed for small-scale chemical separation, or a larger chemical reprocessing facility, which would be harder to hide. The Taiwanese strategy of attempting to develop a hidden plutonium pathway to nuclear weapons—as with Syria—suggests that hiders are not just restricted to uranium enrichment.

The timeline on Taiwan's attempt to develop a clandestine plutonium reprocessing capability is murky but initially centered on trying to procure sensitive reprocessing equipment from abroad in the mid-1970s. At first, Taiwanese authorities were not particularly savvy cheaters. In 1972, Taiwan approached several potential European suppliers, reportedly French and Belgian,[78] to purchase a large-scale reprocessing facility outright.[79] The United States was informed of these approaches and put pressure on both Taipei and the suppliers to not go forward with the sales. There was concern over a reactor for ostensibly research purposes but which was in fact unattached to any research program, and was under military control.[80] However, on October 12, 1973, "we [the U.S. government] learned to our surprise that a Belgian engineering company (Comprime, protect) had been told that the reprocessing project was still alive and that a French firm (Saint Gobain Nucleaire, protect) had been chosen as architect engineer for the project . . . despite ROC disclaimers, we have reason to believe they are still interested in developing a capacity to manufacture nuclear weapons."[81] Saint Gobain apparently seconded one of its employees to Taiwan on a long-term assignment to circumvent French laws to complete the Plutonium Fuel Chemistry Laboratory. The lab was capable of "producing plutonium metal . . . [which]

76. Chang, "Crisis Avoided," 82. Chang cites a memoir by General Pei-tsun Hau, Chief of the General Staff of the Taiwan military, where he claims there were efforts to enrich uranium throughout this period.

77. Interagency Intelligence Memorandum, "Prospects for Arms Production and Development in the Republic of China," May 1976, p. 9, https://www.cia.gov/readingroom/docs/DOC_0000917050.pdf; also see Albright and Gay, "Taiwan: Nuclear Nightmare Averted," 57.

78. See Burr, "The Taiwanese Nuclear Case."

79. See Roger Sullivan to Assistant Secretary of State for Far East and Pacific Affairs Arthur W. Hummel Jr., "Nuclear Study Group Visit to Taiwan," October 29, 1973, Secret, http://nsarchive.gwu.edu/nukevault/ebb221/T-2b.pdf.

80. Embassy Taipei to State Department, "Chung Shan Nuclear Research Institute," cable 1197, February 24, 1973, Source: Subject-Numeric 1970–73, FSE 13 Chinat, pp. 1–2, http://nsarchive.gwu.edu/NSAEBB/NSAEBB20/docs/doc09.pdf.

81. Sullivan to Hummel, 1–2.

is rarely if ever used in civilian programs."[82] Albright and Gay estimate that about .675 kilograms of weapons-grade plutonium was separated at this facility in 1975 or 1976 (roughly ten times that amount is required for a simple fission bomb).[83] In the midst of these attempts to develop a reprocessing capability, the United States was withdrawing not only its conventional forces but also its nuclear weapons from Taiwan. In the spring of 1976, the CIA concluded that "the ROC is attempting to develop the capability to fabricate nuclear devices," estimating that if it violated safeguards Taiwan could develop a crude device in three to four years.[84] The study indicated that detecting any cheating and halting Taiwan's ability to reprocess plutonium were of paramount importance because "sanctions would not materially affect the weapons program, because the ROC already has enough fuel for the research reactor for many years."[85]

The discovery of this limited reprocessing capability led to a confrontation between American officials and Taiwanese foreign minister Shen, in which Shen reiterated Premier Chiang Ching-Kuo's commitment to not make nuclear weapons and categorically denied that Taiwan was developing nuclear weapons. In September 1976, Chiang Ching-Kuo personally told American officials that "ROC would never manufacture nuclear weapons" and that "all reprocessing research, peaceful or otherwise, will be terminated."[86] Shen tried to blame overly enthusiastic scientists, saying the reprocessing activity was unsanctioned by the government and, in any case, it was such a small quantity that it would only produce one nuclear weapon "every 430 years."[87] Nevertheless, as Nicholas Miller shows, the American demarche was harsh and was backed by forthcoming congressional legislation—the Glenn and Symington amendments.[88] Chiang Ching-

82. Albright and Gay, "Taiwan: Nuclear Nightmare Averted," 57.

83. Ibid.; also see David Albright and Andrea Stricker, *Taiwan's Former Nuclear Weapons Program: Nuclear Weapons On-Demand* (Washington, DC: Institute for Science and International Security, 2018), 58–59.

84. Interagency Intelligence Memorandum, "Prospects for Arms Production and Development in the Republic of China," May 1976, p. 2, https://www.cia.gov/library/readingroom/docs/DOC_0000917050.pdf.

85. Ibid., 8.

86. U.S. Embassy Taiwan cable 6272 to State Department, "ROC's Nuclear Intentions: Conversation with Premier Chiang Ching-kuo," September 15, 1976, Secret Nodis, pp. 68, 70, http://nsarchive.gwu.edu/nukevault/ebb221/T-7a.pdf.

87. U.S. Embassy Taiwan cable 6100 to State Department, "Demarche on ROC's Nuclear Intentions," September 9, 1976, Secret Exdis, p. 2, http://nsarchive.gwu.edu/nukevault/ebb221/T-6b.pdf.

88. See Miller, *Stopping the Bomb*, chap. 6.

Kuo was, however, lying to American officials. Unlike Israeli and Pakistani leaders, who artfully obfuscated but never outright lied about the strategic intentions they had to American officials, Chiang Ching-Kuo never had any intention to halt Taiwan's reprocessing research.

In the months after Chiang Ching-Kuo's personal assurances to American officials, evidence continued to emerge that Taiwan not only had continued its reprocessing activity but was looking to expand it. The United States had compelling intelligence that, despite Chiang's pledge, Taiwan was continuing to contract with the European firm Comprimo to import equipment for further reprocessing.[89] What irked the State Department was "conclusive evidence that [Taiwan] is continuing its clandestine efforts to acquire reprocessing technology and equipment from COMPRIMO notwithstanding [the ambassador's] May 27 approach to the premier."[90] Fred Chien, vice minister at the Ministry of Foreign Affairs, was berated by American officials but denied any knowledge of this ongoing reprocessing activity, seeming "bewildered"—he either had no clue what Taiwan's Institute of Nuclear Energy Research (INER) was up to, which would suggest siloing the program to reduce the possibility of detection, or was "a better actor than we realize."[91] This led American technical teams and State Department officials to categorically conclude in 1977 that activities at the INER were "implementing the apparent [GRC] decision to acquire the capability to produce a nuclear explosive device."[92] In the next few months, inspectors made a startling discovery at TRR: a hidden exit hole was found in the spent fuel pond through which nuclear fuel rods could be diverted, cut, and reprocessed in the hot cells constructed at the plutonium laboratory. U.S. State Department officials noted that the original TRR design "does not show pond exit port" despite the ROC's defense to the contrary.[93] Inspectors believed that the condition of the port strongly suggested that "the port

89. State Department cable 4532 to Embassy Taiwan, "Taiwan's Continued Interest in Reprocessing," January 8, 1977, Secret Exdis, p. 1, http://nsarchive.gwu.edu/nukevault/ebb221/T-10b.pdf.

90. State Department cable 91733 to Embassy Taiwan, "ROC's Nuclear Intentions," September 4, 1976, Secret Exdis, p. 2, http://nsarchive.gwu.edu/nukevault/ebb221/T-6a.pdf.

91. U.S. Embassy Taiwan cable 209 to State Department, "Taiwan's Continued Interest in Reprocessing," January 8, 1977, Secret Exdis, p. 2, http://nsarchive.gwu.edu/nukevault/ebb221/T-10c.pdf.

92. U.S. Embassy Taiwan cable 332 to State Department, "US Nuclear Team Conclusions and Recommendations," February 17, 1977, Secret Nodis, p. 1, http://nsarchive.gwu.edu/nukevault/ebb221/T-10g.pdf.

93. U.S. Embassy Japan cable 3212 to State Department, "ROC/IAEA Safeguards," March 8, 1977, Secret Nodis, excised copy, pp. 1–2, http://nsarchive.gwu.edu/nukevault/ebb221/T-12.pdf.

cover had been removed sometime since construction"[94] and that discrepancies in fuel accounts suggested only one thing: Taiwan had almost certainly clandestinely diverted spent fuel for reprocessing. And it had been caught red-handed doing it.

American officials in the Carter administration were furious. American diplomats were instructed to read Taiwanese officials the riot act and demand "far-reaching action" to halt the covert nuclear weapons program.[95] Those demands included that Taiwan temporarily shut down the reactor so that a full inventory of the fuel elements could be conducted by American scientists—the reactor could and would be restarted after this accounting, under certain conditions. As Albright and Stricker write, "Chien ingeniously asked 'what penalties' a noncompliant nation would face? Levin stated that 'sanctions would not be confined to nuclear matters but would also affect a wide range of relations, including military cooperation' . . . Deputy Defense Minister Admiral Feng Chi-tsung . . . commented about the inherent difficulty of separating civilian and military nuclear programs."[96] American officials were unmoved. Under the threat of far-reaching sanctions, now backed by legislative teeth, Taiwan complied. This exercise provided a baseline to detect future diversions of reactor fuel. But it could not account for past discrepancies and it remained unclear how much fuel Taiwan had cut and diverted from the spent fuel pond, and where it had gone.[97] For all intents and purposes, the United States believed that this accounting shut down Taiwan's clandestine pursuit of nuclear weapons through reprocessing.

Apparently it did not. Despite Chiang Ching-Kuo's assurances that the 1977 episode would be the end of Taiwan's nuclear weapons-related activities, suspicion remained. Gerard Smith, President Carter's ambassador at large for nonproliferation, would note a couple of years later: "There is lingering suspicion, not entirely without foundation, that bomb-related work may be continuing on Taiwan (HE [high explosive] testing, laser isotope separation experiments, etc.). It seems clear that some of this work *could* be related to weapons efforts, but it is not clear that it is intended to be so

94. Ibid., 1.

95. State Department cable 67316 to Embassy Taiwan, "Nuclear Representation to the ROC," March 26, 1977, Secret Nodis, p. 1, http://nsarchive.gwu.edu/nukevault/ebb221/T-13a.pdf.

96. Albright and Stricker, *Taiwan's Former Nuclear Weapons Program*, 70.

97. See Albright and Gay, "Taiwan: Nuclear Nightmare Averted," 59; also Derek J. Mitchell, "Taiwan's Hsin Chu Program: Deterrence, Abandonment, and Honor," in *The Nuclear Tipping Point: Why States Reconsider Their Nuclear Choices*, ed. Kurt Campbell, Robert J. Einhorn, and Mitchell B. Reiss (Washington, DC: Brookings Institution Press, 2004), 299–300.

related. And if it is, it is not clear whether or not such work goes on with government sanction, or merely represents the enthusiasm of individual scientists or labs."[98] Smith highlights the possibility that Taiwan continued—or shifted to—covert uranium enrichment once it was unable to successfully hide its reprocessing efforts from the United States and IAEA. The extent of this uranium enrichment program is, to date, unknown in the public record. The American embassy noted with alarm that a member of the National Defense Committee openly advocated a secret nuclear weapons program, quoted as saying, "although Taiwan and other countries signed the convention not to develop nuclear weapons, many other countries have succeeded in developing their nuclear weapons secretly and that 'we need not keep the promise strictly and suffer.'"[99] Nevertheless, the embassy would characterize these debates as Taiwan's effort to "[keep] its options open to enhance its chances of adequate security guarantees from the U.S. after the expiration of the Mutual Defense Treaty."[100] That is, some in the U.S. government continued to erroneously believe that Taiwan was an insurance hedger and did not take seriously the possibility that Taiwan had already perceived American abandonment and might seek a nuclear weapons capability clandestinely as a hider. Continued suspicions would lead to another demarche to Chiang Ching-Kuo, and another categorical denial that Taiwan was engaged in any covert enrichment or reprocessing activity. Subsequent visits by American technical teams would satisfy the Carter administration that they could not detect any "gray area" research related to a potential nuclear weapons program.[101]

It would not be for another decade, until a defector from INER, Chang Hsien-Yi, revealed extensive ongoing reprocessing and uranium enrichment work to the CIA that the degree to which the United States had been in the dark about Taiwan's subsequent hidden nuclear program became apparent. After the 1977–78 confrontation over Taiwan's interest in enrichment and reprocessing technology, there is substantial evidence that Taiwan did not cease its covert pursuit of a potential nuclear weapons capability. Despite the

98. Memorandum, Gerard Smith to Allen, March 10, [1978?], with response by AL, n.d., unclassified, http://nsarchive.gwu.edu/nukevault/ebb221/T-19.pdf.

99. U.S. Embassy Taiwan cable 182 to Department of State, "The Nuclear Option Again," January 10, 1979, Confidential, p. 1, http://nsarchive.gwu.edu/nukevault/ebb221/T-25.pdf.

100. Ibid.

101. American Institute in Taiwan cable 372 to American Institute in Taiwan, Washington, "U.S. Nuclear Technical Visit Team," May 11, 1979, Secret Exdis, http://nsarchive.gwu.edu/nukevault/ebb221/T-26.pdf.

apparent lull after American warnings in 1977, it was short-lived in the wake of the Carter administration's termination of the Mutual Defense Treaty in 1978—the final nail in the coffin of U.S. abandonment of Taiwan. According to subsequent interviews with Chang Hsien-Yi by Albright and Stricker, the pace of sensitive nuclear weapons picked back up by 1981, and personnel who were previously moved out of the INER returned.[102] Hau Pie-tsun, the Chief of the General Staff, was put in charge of monitoring the nuclear weapons program and firmly believed that sensitive research was consistent with Taiwan's 1977 commitment so long as it did not *produce* nuclear weapons.[103] Harsh American pressure served to only push Taiwan's activities deeper into the clandestine realm, as it continued to pursue a hiding strategy. Indeed, Chang Hsien-Yi provides details about efforts to keep things hidden: he was made deputy director of the INER in 1984, and part of his job was to develop civilian cover stories for research related to the nuclear weapons program. If one could not be found, INER would not pursue the project.[104]

General Hau, who was Chief of the General Staff, notes that uranium enrichment was actively pursued through the 1980s. Alan Chang translated Hau's diary and writes that "on January 26, 1984, Hau wrote that the INER had achieved preliminary breakthrough on uranium enrichment by chemical method," which allowed Taiwan to enrich to 3 percent U-235.[105] Enriching to 3 percent represents over half the separative work—albeit with centrifuges—required to enrich to weapons grade (recall the curve in figure 3.2). Furthermore, Taiwan continued to have an interest in cruise missiles and other surface-to-surface missiles that could provide the basis for a delivery capability for nuclear weapons.[106] In 1986, General Hau ordered INER to be able to produce nuclear weapons within three to six months of an order to do so, writing in his diary that "maintaining the capability to make nuclear weapons is exactly INER's task."[107] The overall logic driving Taiwan's hiding strategy, to present a nuclear fait accompli to both the United States and China, is described by Albright and Stricker: "Taiwan's apparent calculation was that it could build its first weapon in secret and emerge with a nuclear weapon or weapons before the PRC or the United States would learn about it. The longer-term goal would have apparently been to rapidly build several

102. Albright and Stricker, *Taiwan's Former Nuclear Weapons Program*, 125.

103. Ibid., 127.

104. Ibid., 123.

105. Chang, "Crisis Avoided," 85.

106. Ibid., 87.

107. Hau quoted in Albright and Stricker, *Taiwan's Former Nuclear Weapons Program*, 144.

more, according to Chang."[108] This was not an insurance hedging strategy, nor sheltered pursuit. This was an active and remarkably brazen clandestine nuclear weapons program—hidden from both the United States and China, the latter of which might have resorted to military prevention if it was aware of the program's true extent.

Finally, in 1988, the defection of Chang Hsien-Yi to the United States revealed the existence of an active reprocessing capability through multiple hot cells that were clandestinely constructed in prior years, in direct violation of Taiwan's 1976 commitments. Much is still unsurprisingly classified about this episode, but Chang allegedly provided evidence that "Taiwan had achieved a major breakthrough in its nuclear research. Furthermore, Taiwan intended to avoid U.S. scrutiny and moved its nuclear weapons development from the experimental stage to the completion stage."[109] According to Mitchell, Chang "smuggled . . . classified documents that extensively detailed Taiwan's plans to produce a nuclear bomb."[110] It is possible that Chang Hsien-Yi embellished Taiwan's activities since he was a defector looking for protection. But he provided enough proof to convince the United States not only that Taiwan was cheating and hiding a nuclear weapons program but that, as Albright and Gay write, "the decision to build this reprocessing facility was taken by Chiang Ching-Kuo" directly—this was not scientific freelancing.[111] Even though Chiang Ching-Kuo died in January 1988, Albright and Gay note that "construction continued under his successor, Lee Teng-hui, although one official said that Lee probably did not know about it."[112] Mitchell reports that although the hot cells were not yet operational, their size led "U.S. intelligence officials [to] estimate that Taiwan was within a year or two of developing a nuclear bomb."[113] The United States, write Albright and Stricker, was stunned at the extent to which Taiwan "hid active programs aimed at being capable of rapidly making nuclear weapons and maintaining a well-rehearsed nuclear readiness to build them on short notice."[114]

If not for Chang Hsien-Yi's defection, it is entirely possible that Taiwan would have succeeded in building nuclear weapons through a hiding strategy. Nonetheless, Chang Hsien-Yi's defection spelled the end of Taiwan's

108. Ibid., 146.
109. Chang, "Crisis Avoided," 95.
110. Mitchell, "Taiwan's Hsin Chu Program," 300.
111. Albright and Gay, "Taiwan: Nuclear Nightmare Averted," 59.
112. Ibid.
113. Mitchell, "Taiwan's Hsin Chu Program," 300.
114. Albright and Stricker, *Taiwan's Former Nuclear Weapons Program*, preface.

hidden nuclear weapons program. With a regime change after Chiang Ching-Kuo's death, Lee Teng-hui at least had plausible deniability, even if he may have been aware of the covert activities. The Reagan administration—which had no problem turning a blind eye to Pakistan—was beyond furious because of the implications for U.S. relations with China. Under tremendous pressure and threat of sanctions, Taiwan was forced to permanently shut down the Taiwan Research Reactor and accede to conditions to convert it to a more proliferation-resistant light water reactor if it ever wished to restart it. The proposal to convert it to a light water reactor was greenlighted in 1988. President Reagan extracted a written guarantee from Lee Teng-hui that "Taiwan would end its nuclear program."[115] In the 1990s, Taiwan would accept stringent IAEA inspections and became the first "substantial" program to subject itself to the additional protocol, which would make it much more difficult for Taiwan to cheat again.[116] Nevertheless, Taiwan is a case of a very advanced hider—one who attempted clandestine proliferation through both the uranium and, more daringly, the plutonium pathways—which moved slowly and determinedly despite both the United States and China monitoring its activities. On the one hand, Taiwan again shows that inefficiencies induced by having to hide a nuclear weapons effort pry open the window in which a program can be detected. On the other hand, it also shows that it still requires a lucky break—a defector—to sometimes catch motivated and skilled hiders. It is perhaps ironic that, in the 1980s, Pakistan enjoyed greater sanctuary from American nonproliferation coercion than its purported ally, Taiwan.

TESTING PROLIFERATION STRATEGY THEORY

My typology and theory capture the character and motivations for Taiwan's nuclear proliferation strategy. Taiwan was not pursuing nuclear weapons capabilities to extract concessions from the United States. Insurance hedging requires threatening nuclear breakout to compel greater commitments from a formal ally. Perhaps early in its program, this was the strategy that Taiwan envisioned, and there is some evidence to support that. But before it could settle on a definitive insurance hedging strategy, Taiwan faced outright abandonment by the United States when the Nixon administration began the process of normalizing relations with China—at Taiwan's great peril. This

115. Mitchell, "Taiwan's Hsin Chu Program," 300.
116. Ibid., 302.

forced Taiwan into a hiding strategy—achieving the domestic consensus for weaponization was relatively simple due to the nature of the KMT regime: once the small group of relevant leaders supported the program, it could proceed. Taiwan's motivation for nuclear weapons increased post-abandonment, but its path to develop them became equally more difficult since it faced almost certain preventive motivations from both China and the United States if it ever tried to openly pursue nuclear weapons. U.S. preventive action likely would have taken the form of economic sanctions, rather than military action. Taiwan's aim was to therefore develop nuclear weapons covertly to present a fait accompli to both the United States and China, thereby avoiding a preventive military strike during the proliferation process. This is essentially what we observe in the Taiwanese case: repeated attempts to clandestinely develop nuclear weapons, going so far as to install hidden doors in spent fuel ponds to divert otherwise safeguarded fuel rods. When caught, Taiwan denied it was cheating but persisted in its strategy. If not for Chang Hsien-Yi's defection in 1988, Taiwan's renewed effort to hide a nuclear weapons program might have succeeded. As with other hiders, this essentially mirrors a sophisticated realist explanation for nuclear proliferation strategy.

Technological determinism does not provide an adequate explanation for Taiwan's nuclear proliferation strategy. Taiwan—along with Syria—is a hider that attempted to develop nuclear weapons using a clandestine plutonium reprocessing facility, which meant having to divert safeguarded spent fuel from a large-signature reactor and then use small hot cells to very slowly accumulate weapons-grade plutonium. It is probably not the most efficient way to hide. Uranium enrichment might have been easier to hide—and it appears Taiwan also attempted to develop this pathway especially after getting caught red-handed with the hot cells and hidden spent fuel pond exit door in the late 1970s. But Taiwan's inability to succeed in achieving a plutonium reprocessing pathway or uranium enrichment had nothing to do with available supply or skills. Instead it was driven by the overarching strategic requirement of having no visible footprint, while operating on an island roughly the size of Maryland over which the United States intelligence community had substantial collection capabilities. Taiwanese scientists found a frankly ingenious way to cheat the IAEA safeguard, managing techniques such as hidden doors, leveraging willfully ignorant European suppliers (again, like many nuclear pursuers), imperceptibly diverting spent fuel, and clandestinely developing small hot cells to reprocess plutonium. Continuing this activity without detection for over a decade after the 1976 incident suggests real technical ingenuity—even more so given that the clandestine activity remained hidden despite intense scrutiny from the Americans and Chinese. But the restrictions of having to hide the program generated inefficiency and languid progress. A long, slow program provides ample opportunities for bad luck—like a defector who reveals the program to the Americans.

Taiwan significantly violated nonproliferation norms, as well as its legal obligations, in its hidden quest for nuclear weapons. As the Chinese representative at the NPT negotiations, it had signed the treaty in 1968. But the flux introduced by normalization with Beijing meant that Taiwan had to negotiate a trilateral safeguards agreement with the United States and the IAEA. Taipei viewed itself as the sole representative of all of China and believed it had the right to nuclear weapons under the NPT—an interpretation held only in Taipei, and nowhere else. It was legal gymnastics designed to justify its cheating internally perhaps, since if it were true there would be no need to hide. Despite tremendous international pressure against horizontal nuclear proliferation, Taiwan persisted in its clandestine pursuit of nuclear weapons. It was not a normative concern—concern over its reputation or for the sustenance of the nonproliferation regime—that pushed Taiwan into hiding but a strategic one. The documentary evidence clearly suggests that Taiwan was not necessarily worried about international opprobrium but about sanctions and a military strike by the People's Republic of China. It was therefore the precarious security situation in which Taiwan found itself, particularly after the Sino-U.S. rapprochement, which forced Taiwan into a hiding nuclear strategy. Taipei was under the impression that the United States was abandoning it entirely. If China were ever to attempt to take Taiwan by force, perhaps only a nuclear deterrent could save it. But open pursuit would become a self-fulfilling prophecy and trigger the very invasion nuclear proliferation was designed to deter. Thus, Taiwan had no choice but to pursue a hiding strategy in an attempt to present a fait accompli to both the United States and China. The Taiwanese case is fascinating in its own right, but it also gives some insight into how, for example, South Korea, which similarly fears abandonment from the United States might pursue nuclear weapons in the future.

South Africa (1974–79): The Hider's Dream

South Africa's pursuit of nuclear weapons is unique for several reasons.[117] First, it is the only state that has ever indigenously developed a nuclear weapons capability—six completed gun-type uranium devices deliverable by

117. For previous work on South Africa's nuclear program, see Narang, *Nuclear Strategy in the Modern Era*, chap. 8; Hannes Steyn, Richardt van der Walt, and Jan van Loggerenberg, *Nuclear Armament and Disarmament: South Africa's Nuclear Experience* (Lincoln, NE: iUniverse, 2007); Liberman, "The Rise and Fall of the South African Bomb"; David Albright, "South Africa and

Buccaneer aircraft or as glidebombs and a seventh under construction—and then voluntarily dismantled it. When President F. W. de Klerk announced to a stunned world in 1993 that apartheid South Africa had indeed developed nuclear weapons between 1979 and 1991, he commissioned an official history of the program and submitted a full accounting to the IAEA. As scholars, we thus have a relatively good retrospective sense of what South Africa did, when, and why—though the record will perhaps always remain incomplete due to the high levels of secrecy that surrounded the program and due to motivated biases to spin Pretoria's preferred narrative. Comparing internal records of South Africa's progress and intent to the contemporaneous perceptions of outside powers, especially the United States, is particularly instructive: South Africa provides hints about what the externally visible signatures of successful hiders might be in the future. Second, South Africa is a hider that succeeded, and is important because successful hiders are rare. Taiwan never really came close because it was forced into such small-scale activity and got caught twice. Iraq might have eventually succeeded had Saddam Hussein not invaded Kuwait in 1991, but we will never know. South Africa actually did succeed in developing nuclear weapons under the nose of both the United States and Soviet Union—who colluded in 1977 to prevent what they believed was an imminent South African test in the Kalahari Desert, thinking they had stopped the program. They were wrong. In fact, Prime Minister Botha covertly redoubled South Africa's efforts to weaponize its capabilities after that episode.

---

the Affordable Bomb," *Bulletin of the Atomic Scientists* 50, no. 4 (August 1994): 37–47; Waldo Stumpf, "South Africa's Nuclear Weapons Program: From Deterrence to Dismantlement," *Arms Control Today* 25, no. 10 (December 1995): 3–8; Waldo Stumpf, "South Africa's Nuclear Weapons Programme," in *Weapons of Mass Destruction: Costs versus Benefits*, ed. Kathleen C. Bailey (Delhi: Manohar, 1994), 63–81; Reiss, *Bridled Ambition*, 7–44; David Albright and Mark Hibbs, "South Africa: The ANC and the Atom Bomb," *Bulletin of the Atomic Scientists* 49, no. 3 (April 1993): 32–37; David Albright and Tom Zamora, "South Africa Flirts with the NPT," *Bulletin of the Atomic Scientists* 47, no. 1 (February 1991): 27–31; J. W. de Villiers, Roger Jardine, and Mitchell Reiss, "Why South Africa Gave Up the Bomb," *Foreign Affairs* 72, no. 5 (November/December 1993): 98–109; Peter Liberman, "Israel and the South African Bomb," *Nonproliferation Review* 11, no. 2 (Summer 2004): 46–80; Stephen F. Burgess, "South Africa's Nuclear Weapons Policies," *Nonproliferation Review* 13, no. 3 (November 2006): 519–26; Verne Harris, Sello Hatang, and Peter Liberman, "Unveiling South Africa's Nuclear Past," *Journal of Southern African Studies* 30, no. 3 (September 2004): 457–75; Terence McNamee, "The Afrikaner Bomb: Nuclear Proliferation and Rollback in South Africa," in Avner Cohen and Terence McNamee, *Why Do States Want Nuclear Weapons? The Cases of Israel and South Africa* (Oslo: Norwegian Institute for Defence Studies, 2005), 13–23; Helen E. Purkitt and Stephen F. Burgess, *South Africa's Weapons of Mass Destruction* (Bloomington: Indiana University Press, 2005); and Richelson, *Spying on the Bomb*, chaps. 6 and 9.

Unlike the cases of Pakistan and Israel, where the United States was complicit in the development of nuclear weapons insofar as it determinedly looked the other way, the United States was always playing catch-up on the hidden South African nuclear program. Washington would have likely opposed South African activities, but the intelligence community determined South Africa possessed nuclear weapons only after the fact. South Africa attained a nuclear weapons capability before its potential coercers knew enough to try to prevent it, putting it in the enviable position of being able to present a fait accompli to the international community and avoid rollback efforts.

South Africa had an early interest in nuclear power, since it was endowed with a vast reserve of uranium deposits, which it could use to fuel nuclear reactors if it developed an indigenous uranium enrichment program. Taking advantage of President Eisenhower's Atoms for Peace program, South Africa constructed the 20 MW Safari-1 reactor in the early 1960s that was initially fueled by American-supplied enriched uranium.[118] However, to become self-sufficient in its then peaceful nuclear program, Prime Minister John Vorster initiated research on indigenous uranium enrichment technology to fuel the reactor. By 1969, Waldo Stumpf, who led South Africa's Atomic Energy Commission under de Klerk and performed the official study of the program, writes that South Africa had achieved promising results using a novel "stationary wall vortex tube" process.[119] Although in principle similar to the German Becker nozzle process, the so-called modified Helikon process developed by the South Africans was indigenously developed and did not require the powerful compressors that most countries—including South Africa—had difficulty acquiring and building.[120] South Africa was not party to the NPT, so Vorster had some leeway on safeguards, which he exploited on the Y Plant (and later the larger Z Plant) at Valindaba (which literally means "we don't talk about this at all" in Zulu)[121] on the grounds that he had to protect the proprietary nature of South Africa's vortex enrichment process.[122] Vorster stated to parliament that "South Africa will not run the risk of details of the new process leaking out as a result of the safeguards

118. See Purkitt and Burgess, *South Africa's Weapons of Mass Destruction*, 38.

119. Stumpf, "South Africa's Nuclear Weapons Programme," 64.

120. Director of Central Intelligence, Interagency Intelligence Memorandum, *South Africa's Nuclear Options and Decisionmaking Structures*, date illegible but circa July 1978, Top Secret, p. 3, http://nsarchive.gwu.edu/nukevault/ebb451/docs/2.pdf.

121. See Purkitt and Burgess, *South Africa's Weapons of Mass Destruction*, 39.

122. Stumpf, "South Africa's Nuclear Weapons Programme," 65.

system."[123] Y Plant was fully operational only by March 1977, and Stumpf notes that due to the time it took to establish the full enrichment gradient of the plant, it only started producing 80 percent HEU in January 1978.[124] Although the nominal rationale for Y Plant was to provide enriched uranium fuel for Safari-1 in the event of a fuel cutoff—which was a reasonable concern in 1976—it also had the potential to enrich uranium for nuclear weapons. And since there were no eyes on Y Plant, there was little preventing South Africa from enriching to weapons-grade. But very few in the outside world were aware of just how early South Africa's interest in nuclear explosives began.

As early as 1971, Vorster approved a secret program in the Ministry of Mines to study the possibility of peaceful nuclear explosives.[125] At the time, many developing countries such as India were studying the theoretical possibility of using so-called peaceful nuclear explosions (PNEs) for development projects such as dam construction. Stumpf writes that "no serious development work was carried out during this phase. Only three engineers were involved in conducting elementary research on gun type devices."[126] But in 1974, Vorster secretly "approved the development of a nuclear explosive capability for peaceful applications and also approved the budget for the development of a testing site for an underground test."[127] At this point, South Africa's official history begins to get vague as to when a dedicated nuclear weapons program was initiated. In his 1993 speech to parliament on the nuclear weapons program, however, President de Klerk stated: "The decision to develop this limited capability was taken as early as 1974, against the background of a Soviet expansionist threat in southern Africa, as well as prevailing uncertainty concerning the designs of the Warsaw Pact members. The build-up of Cuban forces in Angola from 1975 onwards reinforced the perception that a deterrent was necessary—as did South Africa's relative international isolation and the fact that it could not rely on outside assistance, should it be attacked."[128] This is about as definitive a statement and rationale as a head of government can give.

Just as South Africa's regional security situation was deteriorating, with Afrikaner fears of a "total communist onslaught" emanating from

123. Ibid.

124. Ibid.

125. Ibid., 66.

126. Ibid.

127. Ibid.

128. "Speech by South African President F. W. De Klerk to a Joint Session of Parliament on Accession to the Non-Proliferation Treaty," March 24, 1993, p. 3, History and Public Policy Program Digital Archive, Archives.un.org, contributed by Jo-Ansie van Wyk, obtained and contributed by Jo-Ansie van Wyk, http://digitalarchive.wilsoncenter.org/document/116789.

Mozambique and Angola to its north, and then eventually Namibia to its northwest, Western powers including the United States and the United Kingdom were increasingly isolating South Africa due to its apartheid policies. The fear of being left alone against potential Soviet expansion in southern Africa fueled South African paranoia, despite its significant conventional superiority. Stumpf writes that fifty thousand Cuban forces in Angola coupled with "increasing restrictions on the supply of conventional arms by the international community to South Africa added to the sense of vulnerability . . . the country virtually had no alternative but to develop its own nuclear deterrent."[129] Whether the security situation justified the pursuit of nuclear weapons is admittedly more difficult to defend in this case. Nevertheless, the sense of Afrikaner paranoia with regard to all threats external and internal, and especially about Western powers that might abandon South Africa against Soviet-backed forces, intensified the acuteness of the threat.[130]

Domestic consensus for a nuclear weapons program was relatively easy to achieve, since the South African prime minister enjoyed near dictatorial rule in national security matters and was able to assemble a cabinet of like-minded individuals. The CIA judged in an assessment of South Africa that "Vorster, unlike prime ministers in other industrial non-Communist states, need not consult or accommodate a wide variety of constituencies on nuclear matters. . . . this clearly gives Vorster at least the internal political flexibility to initiate, change, or terminate a nuclear program without broad accountability to the South African people. It also enhances the chances of maintaining secrecy about such matters."[131]

Perceiving an increasingly acute threat and with the broad autonomy to pursue nuclear capabilities, Vorster initiated an active nuclear program with a strong intent toward nuclear weapons as early as 1974, although it appears that the decision was preliminary. Work on weapons design proceeded in this period, with the first cold test of a gun-type device using a tungsten projectile secretly performed in May 1974 and a second covertly conducted in 1976 using a natural uranium projectile, according to key South African nuclear scientists.[132] Further evidence that this was intended to be a nuclear weapons program was retrospectively noted by the CIA, which mentioned

129. Stumpf, "South Africa's Nuclear Weapons Programme," 67.

130. McNamee, "The Afrikaner Bomb."

131. Director of Central Intelligence, Interagency Intelligence Memorandum, *South Africa's Nuclear Options and Decisionmaking Structures*, 14.

132. See Nic von Wielligh and Lydia von Wielligh-Steyn, *The Bomb: South Africa's Nuclear Weapons Programme* (Pretoria: Litera Publications, 2015), 134–35.

(in a footnote!) with interest a press release by the South African Air Force: "In 1976, the South African Air Force issued a public release describing practice toss bombing by Buccaneer (Hawker-Siddely) jets, a bombing technique normally associated with nuclear weapons delivery. This was an isolated piece of evidence [at the time], however."[133] This evidence was thus dismissed. However, retrospectively, it does appear to be credible based on de Klerk's parliamentary speech, and the fact that the South African Air Force was already thinking about delivery options suggests that South Africa was certainly actively pursuing nuclear weapons after 1975.

How did South Africa go about this? Completely clandestinely. Unsurprisingly, sensing abandonment and international isolation already due to its apartheid policies, South Africa feared there would be tremendous pressure against it—and potentially Soviet military prevention—if it was caught developing nuclear weapons. Already facing heavy apartheid sanctions, South Africa could have found itself in an existential crisis if additional sanctions were levied due to nuclear weapons activity or if the Soviets threatened to destroy the program outright. In this period, the only ally South Africa believed it had was Israel, which was in no position to offer protection against superpower coercion.[134] Indeed, much of the relationship between Israel and South Africa was also secret, since both believed that they faced widespread international opposition. Therefore Vorster's 1974 directive was made in secret. The 1993 IAEA account of South Africa's nuclear program concluded that, for the next several years, work on nuclear weapons was theoretical and largely able to be done clandestinely, as Y Plant was being made operational: "In the ensuing years, up to 1977, the AEC developed computer programmes (internal ballistic and neutronic codes), carried out experiments to determine equations-of-state of materials, designed and constructed a critical facility and carried out work with gun propellants. This phase of the programme resulted in the production, in mid-1977, of a gun-assembled device, without the HEU core."[135] It was reportedly almost a 3,500-kilogram device, 2.79 meters in length.[136] This work was largely undetected.

133. Director of Central Intelligence, Interagency Intelligence Memorandum, *South Africa's Nuclear Options and Decisionmaking Structures*, 16, footnote.

134. See Sasha Polakow-Suransky, *The Unspoken Alliance: Israel's Secret Relationship with Apartheid South Africa* (New York: Pantheon Books, 2010).

135. "Report, Director General of the International Atomic Energy Agency, 'The Agency's Verification Activities in South Africa,'" September 23, 1993, p. 5, History and Public Policy Program Digital Archive, IAEA Archives, contributed by Sasha Polakow-Suransky, http://digitalarchive.wilsoncenter.org/document/116790.

136. Von Wielligh and von Wielligh-Steyn, *The Bomb*, 135.

The turning point for the South African nuclear weapons program was Vorster's decision to allow ARMSCOR, the organization responsible for weapons design and construction, to potentially conduct a cold test of the gun-type device with a depleted uranium core in 1977 (there was not yet enough HEU from Y Plant to conduct a full-blown test at this time).[137] David Albright writes that the cold test was planned for August 1977 at one of two test shafts that had been dug at the Vastrap military facility in the remote Kalahari Desert and would be a "fully instrumented underground test with a dummy core. Its major purpose was to test the logistical plans for an actual detonation."[138] The South Africans tried to generate a plausible cover for the activity at the site by simultaneously testing a truck-mounted multiple rocket launch system.[139] Unfortunately for South Africa, preparations at the test site were detected by the Soviet Union, most likely with satellites, who then informed the Carter administration.[140]

Indeed, in an interesting example of Soviet-American Cold War collusion on nonproliferation,[141] Premier Brezhnev wrote to President Carter directly about the Soviet detection in early August 1977. In response to that letter, Warren Christopher would acknowledge that "we have no evidence that would lead us to believe that the Republic of South Africa is developing or preparing to test a nuclear weapon" and asked the Soviet Union to assist in American intelligence collection on the site by providing the United States with "geographic coordinates, size, configuration and exact nature of the facility" to help the U.S. government form "an independent judgment as to the probability of a test explosion."[142] Subsequent intelligence reports would suggest the United States was truly caught unaware by the news of a South African nuclear program. About a week later, Secretary of State Vance wrote to his South African counterpart, Pik Botha, that the U.S. government

137. See Purkitt and Burgess, *South Africa's Weapons of Mass Destruction*, 44; David Albright, "South Africa's Secret Nuclear Weapons Program," Institute for Science and International Security Report, May 1994, https://isis-online.org/isis-reports/detail/south-africas-secret-nuclear-weapons/13.

138. Albright, "South Africa's Secret Nuclear Weapons Program."

139. Richelson, *Spying on the Bomb*, 277.

140. See ibid., 278–80.

141. See Andrew J. Coe and Jane Vaynman, "Collusion and the Nuclear Nonproliferation Regime," *Journal of Politics* 77, no. 4 (August 2015): 983–97.

142. "Letter, Warren Christopher to William Hyland, 'Response to Soviet Message on South Africa,'" August 10, 1977, History and Public Policy Program Digital Archive, National Archives, Record Group 59, Department of State Records, Records of Warren Christopher, box 16, Memos to White House 1977, pp. 1–2, obtained and contributed by William Burr for NPIHP Research Update No. 25, http://digitalarchive.wilsoncenter.org/document/119249.

had concluded that the Vastrap test site was most likely for the purpose of "conduct[ing] underground tests of nuclear explosive devices."[143] The American ambassador piled onto Botha, writing that any detonation, peaceful or otherwise, or any "further steps to acquire or develop a nuclear explosive capability would have the most serious consequences for *all* aspects of our relations and would be considered by us as a serious threat to the peace."[144] The South African embassy in Washington cabled home to Pretoria that "the U.S. government—in concert with the British, French, West Germans and Russians—has been putting terrific heat [on us] . . . [they] pushed very hard in private."[145] Prime Minister Vorster had clearly discerned that both superpowers were vehemently pressuring him not to test and further mobilizing other erstwhile friendlier states, particularly France, to threaten to break diplomatic relations and cut all aid—nuclear, arms, and otherwise.[146] Under this pressure, Stumpf writes that Vorster abandoned the test sites: "Upon direct instruction from the Head of Government, the site was abandoned in August 1977, and not revisited until 1987."[147] André Buys, an ARMSCOR director, says that "the government decided to deny it—in the media, everywhere, they said it wasn't a nuclear test site, we don't have a program for nuclear explosives, they just flatly denied everything. What came down to us was the message to clear up that site—immediately."[148] President Carter would publicly announce Vorster's commitment to not develop or test nuclear explosive devices, "either peaceful or as a weapon," and implied that it was pressure from his administration that led South Africa to abandon a test at Vastrap.[149]

143. "Letter, US Secretary of State Vance to South African Foreign Minister Botha," August 19, 1977, History and Public Policy Program Digital Archive, South African Foreign Affairs Archives, Brand Fourie, Atomic Energy, File 2/5/2/1, Vol. 1, Vol. 2, obtained and contributed by Anna-Mart van Wyk, Monash South Africa, http://digitalarchive.wilsoncenter.org/document/114153.

144. "Letter, US Ambassador Bowlder to South African Foreign Minister Botha," August 18, 1977, History and Public Policy Program Digital Archive, South African Foreign Affairs Archives, Brand Fourie, Atomic Energy, File 2/5/2/1, Vol. 1, Vol. 2, obtained and contributed by Anna-Mart van Wyk, Monash South Africa, http://digitalarchive.wilsoncenter.org/document/114150.

145. "Telegram from South African Embassy in the US on President Carter's Press Conference on the Kalahari Nuclear Test Site," August 23, 1977, History and Public Policy Program Digital Archive, South African Foreign Affairs Archives, Brand Fourie, Atomic Energy, File 2/5/2/1 Vol. 1, Vol. 2, obtained and contributed by Anna-Mart van Wyk, http://digitalarchive.wilsoncenter.org/document/116609.

146. See Richelson, *Spying on the Bomb*, 281.

147. Stumpf, "South Africa's Nuclear Weapons Programme," 69.

148. André Buys, interview by Mark S. Bell and Noel Anderson, Pretoria, July 1, 2014.

149. "Telegram from South African Embassy in the US on President Carter's Press Conference on the Kalahari Nuclear Test Site," August 23, 1977, History and Public Policy Program Digital Archive, South African Foreign Affairs Archives, Brand Fourie, Atomic Energy, File 2/5/2/1 Vol. 1,

Vorster was furious at President Carter's statement. In parliament the next day, he remained defiant regarding the Vastrap Incident, as it would be known. In the first place, he could plausibly deny that South Africa was planning to test a full-blown *nuclear* device, peaceful or otherwise. The intended test was a cold test with, at most, a depleted uranium core. There would have been no nuclear yield. South Africa, at that point, did not have any enriched uranium suitable for a fissile core in a nuclear device. So Vorster and Botha were not technically lying when they categorically denied to American officials, and the world, that the site was intended for a nuclear explosive test.[150] But Vorster was certainly stretching the truth when he stated, in the same parliamentary speech, that South Africa's program was "solely for peaceful purposes" and that it was only a technicality that prevented South Africa from placing Y Plant under international safeguards.[151] He launched into a full-blown attack on the superpowers for not living up to their disarmament bargains on Article VI of the NPT, the fact that South Africa was thrown off the IAEA's board of governors, replaced by Egypt, because of its apartheid policies, and smarted at the unilateral American cutoff of fuel to Safari-1 the previous year (and the fact that South Africa had paid for the fuel but had yet to be reimbursed).[152] He proceeded to blast France for not yet acceding to or ratifying the NPT, colorfully (and accurately) pointing out in the speech, "may I pause here for a moment and say 'et tu Brute.'"[153] Highlighting the hypocrisy and "double standards" of the nuclear superpowers pressuring South Africa, Vorster closed with: "If these things continue and don't stop, the time will arrive when South Africa will have no option, small as it is, to say to the world: So far and no further, do your damndest if you so wish (loud applause)."[154]

The Vastrap Incident may have steeled South Africa's resolve to develop nuclear weapons, and do so clandestinely, as it illuminated just how isolated Pretoria was. This was reinforced by the imposition of a United Nations arms embargo with UNSCR 418 several months later. Interest in and work on

---

Vol. 2, obtained and contributed by Anna-Mart van Wyk, http://digitalarchive.wilsoncenter.org/document/116609.

150. "Extract from Speech by the South African Prime Minister at Congress of the National Party of Cape Province," August 24, 1977, History and Public Policy Program Digital Archive, UK National Archives, FCO45-2131, obtained and contributed by Anna-Mart van Wyk, http://digitalarchive.wilsoncenter.org/document/116617.

151. Ibid., 2–3.

152. Ibid., 3.

153. Ibid., 4.

154. Ibid., 5.

weapons clearly existed prior to the episode but accelerated afterward. J. W. de Villiers, who was chairman of South Africa's Atomic Energy Commission, writes, along with Roger Jardine and Mitchell Reiss, that "after the discovery of the Kalahari testing site, the character of South Africa's nuclear program started to change toward acquiring a nuclear deterrent" more aggressively and more covertly, and "Prime Minister Vorster convened his senior officials to consider the program's future, ordering that a document be drafted to articulate the country's nuclear strategy."[155] In the meantime, Vorster was forced to resign due to a domestic political scandal, but his successor, P. W. Botha, formally approved the military program under ARMSCOR's direction and authorized final weaponization in October 1978. That three-stage "catalytic nuclear strategy" envisioned the use of nuclear weapons to compel Western, particularly American, intervention in the event South Africa ever faced an existential threat, identifying three discrete stages from private disclosure to a nuclear test.[156] At this meeting, Botha approved the target development of seven nuclear weapons for the arsenal. Stumpf is quoted as saying that this was due to the fact the designs were untested and, after Vastrap, likely to continue to be untested: "ARMSCOR said at that stage that if you have an untested device you need two devices in reserve in case the first one does not work and then you need to double it—that is where the number [seven] came from."[157]

More importantly, the Vastrap Incident pushed the program entirely into hiding. Helen Purkitt and Stephen Burgess write that insiders involved with the test learned several lessons from it. To begin with, "there was a general recognition that it was not possible to conduct secret nuclear tests. This recognition led to research to 'reduce the size and yield of the devices such that it could be shipped to the site and detonated in a very short period of time.'"[158] André Buys, one of the most important scientists involved in the weaponization process at ARMSCOR, says he was instructed by the political leadership: "We unfortunately have to do this in secret, because the international community will not believe us that we are doing this for peaceful purposes. The moment it becomes known that we are working on nuclear explosives, we're going to be accused of developing a nuclear weapon. And

155. De Villiers, Jardine, and Reiss, "Why South Africa Gave Up the Bomb," 100.

156. See Narang, *Nuclear Strategy in the Modern Era*, chap. 8; Stumpf, "South Africa's Nuclear Weapons Programme," 69.

157. Stumpf quoted in Rabinowitz, *Bargaining on Nuclear Tests*, 123.

158. Purkitt and Burgess, *South Africa's Weapons of Mass Destruction*, 44. Also see von Wielligh and von Wielligh-Steyn, *The Bomb*, 149.

then we're going to suffer all the negative consequences of that, when in fact we're innocent. It's unfortunate, it's not really necessary, but because South Africa was becoming more and more isolated internationally, it has to be a secret project."[159] In particular, the Vastrap Incident led to further political pressure that Buys and his team pursue their work completely clandestinely, being told: "If we want to continue with this project as a deterrent, we must do it in absolute secrecy—we don't want an incident like this again. If you can do it in absolute secrecy, then you can carry on."[160] But there was no doubt about Vorster's, and eventually Botha's, purpose after Vastrap. Buys reports: "We [told them we] could probably do it in secret, but their main question is what you mean by deterrent strategy. Do you have nuclear weapons in mind, or is just the ability to demonstrate that we have this knowledge sufficient . . . very soon the answer came back, firmly: nuclear weapons."[161] Waldo Stumpf bluntly states, "South Africa's political situation made it necessary for us, if we wanted to go ahead with such a program, to keep it secret."[162]

South Africa was able to successfully maintain secrecy over its program due to the lack of safeguards at Y Plant, using the cover rationale of producing indigenous reactor fuel, the compartmentalization of the program—beyond the heads of state and relevant ministers and the technical teams involved in the project, very few people were aware of it—and active concealment efforts to disguise facilities and activity. Purkitt and Burgess write that "sensitive facilities were also camouflaged to protect against discovery by satellite or air reconnaissance and hardened against sabotage attacks or natural events such as earthquakes."[163] In a wide-ranging 1978 analysis of the program by the CIA, the U.S. intelligence community's best assessment was: "we are still far from certain what the South Africans are up to. We do not know precisely what their capabilities are, *or how they got there*."[164] It goes on to say that "a veil of secrecy has continued to surround the Valindaba uranium enrichment plant since Vorster's announcement in 1970, and,

159. Buys, interview.

160. Ibid.

161. Ibid.

162. Waldo Stumpf, interview by Mark S. Bell and Noel Anderson, Pretoria, June 11, 2014.

163. Purkitt and Burgess, *South Africa's Weapons of Mass Destruction*, 65.

164. Director of Central Intelligence, Interagency Intelligence Memorandum, *South Africa's Nuclear Options and Decisionmaking Structures*, p. ii; also see Leslie H. Gelb, Memorandum for Secretary Cyrus Vance, "Your Meeting with Gromyko: South African Nuclear Issue," September 21, 1977, in *South Africa and the United States: A Declassified History*, A National Security Archive Documents Reader, ed. Kenneth Mokoena (New York: New Press, 1993), doc. 23, pp. 127–28.

aside from one open paper and several published photographs, information concerning the technical details of the plant has been very tightly held."[165]

It was clear that the CIA was playing catch-up and had little idea about where the South Africans were with enrichment or nuclear weapons: "In sum, it appears that South Africa has intended from the outset—the late 1960s—to translate its uranium enrichment technology into not only a commercial advantage but also a nuclear weapons option. Substantial quantities of weapons grade uranium may become available in the near future or may already exist. . . . The present operational status of the plant is unclear. Thus, while the South Africans apparently wish to produce highly enriched uranium at Valindaba, their capability to do so is not yet clear."[166] It notes that the U.S. intelligence community was in the dark after the Vastrap Incident and the consequent South African decision to go underground. "We do not know where the South Africans are along the [technical] continuum," the CIA admitted. "While we suspect that South Africa was preparing for nuclear tests until mid-1977, we do not know its current intentions."[167] The analysis closed with a prescient concern about South African proliferation strategy: "[A clandestine] strategy is an attractive one for South Africa, particularly because its leaders feel that their actions are under intense scrutiny from abroad. Clandestine development would avoid the heavy political repercussions that a test would bring on, would be relatively easy to deny plausibly, and would give the South Africans the capability which we believe they seek."[168] Noting that it could hide budgetary activity and work at the weapons-related facilities, the CIA predicted that "once a stockpile of weapons grade uranium is in hand, South Africa probably would attempt to pursue a covert weapons program separate from the facilities under safeguards."[169] It could not definitively assess whether South Africa was already a nuclear weapons state.

In an attempt to get the Reagan administration—which was much less harsh toward South Africa than the Carter administration—to allow France to restart fuel shipments for South Africa's Koeberg nuclear power plant, Pik Botha says he elliptically told President Reagan and Secretary of State Haig that South Africa was a de facto nuclear weapons state in a May 15, 1981, meeting, where he hoped a promise not to test would be enough to get the

165. Director of Central Intelligence, Interagency Intelligence Memorandum, *South Africa's Nuclear Options and Decisionmaking Structures*, 4.

166. Ibid., 5.

167. Ibid., 18.

168. Ibid., 21–22.

169. Ibid., 23–24.

fuel shipments.[170] An alarmed—reportedly almost angry—Haig tried to cut off the conversation, saying "[we] cannot be remotely associated with this at all. We cannot be associated with any nuclear matters, the whole world suspects they are producing a bomb." When Reagan reportedly asked Botha if this was true, Botha recalls saying "well, Mr. President, we have the capacity to do so," but he promised not to test any devices without first informing Washington.[171] Reagan does seem to have accepted this disclosure but Haig's account remains silent about it.[172] By then, however, it was too late—South Africa had already become a de facto nuclear weapons state by any measure. Botha was essentially presenting a fait accompli to Reagan. But the U.S. intelligence community would still be playing catch-up. In 1983, a CIA memo noted that it judged that "the resulting international uproar [after Vastrap] reportedly caused Prime Minister Vorster to order a halt to further nuclear weapons development. We have no direct indication of any subsequent activities in the weapons program. We believe, however, that South Africa already either possesses nuclear devices or has all the components necessary to assemble such devices on very short notice."[173] In other words, the CIA thought the program was dormant—which it most certainly was not—but it guessed the enrichment at Y Plant might have produced enough enriched uranium for weapons, even though it had no direct evidence. The next year, the CIA could only say that "it is possible that South Africa has leapfrogged the testing phase and is concentrating on the weaponizing and delivery of its nuclear explosives devices." By then it was assumed by the American intelligence community that South Africa had long become a nuclear weapons state.[174]

The CIA's 1984 report was a remarkably accurate assessment of the South African program and its probable proliferation strategy, but the CIA arrived

170. "Notes on Meeting between South African Minister of Foreign Affairs R. F. Botha and US President Reagan," May 15, 1981, History and Public Policy Program Digital Archive, South African Foreign Affairs Archive, File 137/10/02 Vol. 9, doc. no. 82214/006772, obtained and contributed by Or Rabinowitz, http://digitalarchive.wilsoncenter.org/document/116764. Also see Rabinowitz, *Bargaining on Nuclear Tests*, 120.

171. Botha interviewed by Rabinowitz, in Rabinowitz, *Bargaining on Nuclear Tests*, 120. Also see von Wielligh and von Wielligh-Steyn, *The Bomb*, 170, for a similar recounting.

172. See Rabinowitz and Miller, "Keeping the Bombs in the Basement," 69.

173. Central Intelligence Agency, "New Information on South Africa's Nuclear Program and South African-Israeli Nuclear and Military Cooperation," March 30, 1983, p. 1, Secret, http://nsarchive.gwu.edu/NSAEBB/NSAEBB181/sa26.pdf.

174. Central Intelligence Agency, "Trends in South Africa's Nuclear Security Policies and Programs," October 5, 1984, Top Secret, p. 16, http://nsarchive.gwu.edu/NSAEBB/NSAEBB181/sa27.pdf.

at that assessment with very little hard evidence. Despite all its assets and capabilities and despite South Africa being under the spotlight after the Vastrap Incident, the American intelligence community was largely in the dark about exactly what South Africa was doing or where it was with the nuclear program. Though South Africa was ultimately successful, it is still worth noting that its hiding strategy did force South Africa to make some inefficient choices. Producing enriched uranium turned out to be a slower process than anticipated due to unforeseen accidents and slowdowns at Y Plant. The IAEA report provides the following timeline, retrospectively: "by the second half of 1979 [Y Plant] had produced sufficient HEU material for the first nuclear device. This device was completed by the AEC in November 1979[175] and was designed in such a way that, if the need arose, it could be rapidly deployed for an underground test to demonstrate South Africa's nuclear weapons capability. Its purpose remained that of a demonstration device throughout the programme; it was never converted to a [reliably] deliverable device."[176] In an emergency, however, it could have possibly been delivered off of a cargo plane. This was a complete device, and reportedly maintained in this state for several years, code-named Video and then changed to Melba.[177] For all intents and purposes, South Africa attained a rudimentary nuclear weapons capability then at the very end of 1979. There was interest in this time in potentially using tritium to boost the uranium fission devices, and, in fact, in a secret deal with Israel, South Africa imported 30 grams of tritium in exchange for uranium shipped to Israel. It is possible that some boosted designs were attempted, but "the IAEA team was informed that no tritium was actually used in this work."[178]

South Africa developed its second device—the first it converted into a deliverable weapon—only in 1982, code-named Hobo and then changed to

175. This timeline makes it virtually impossible for the so-called Vela Incident in September 1979 to have been a South African nuclear weapon. If the event was indeed a nuclear device, it had to almost certainly be Israeli, since it seems highly unlikely South Africa would risk wasting the limited HEU it had at the time on a test. This does not mean that South Africa might not have benefited from the data if it was in fact a nuclear test, however, although Israeli weapons were plutonium-based and South Africa's were uranium-based.

176. "Report, Director General of the International Atomic Energy Agency, 'The Agency's Verification Activities in South Africa,'" September 23, 1993, p. 6, History and Public Policy Program Digital Archive, IAEA Archives, contributed by Sasha Polakow-Suransky, http://digitalarchive.wilsoncenter.org/document/116790.

177. See von Wielligh and von Wielligh-Steyn, *The Bomb*, 170–72.

178. "Report, Director General of the International Atomic Energy Agency, 'The Agency's Verification Activities in South Africa,'" September 23, 1993, p. 7.

Cabot before being assigned the production number 306.[179] Due to delays in safety and reliability issues, this device was not "fully qualified" for serial production until August 1987. In a pivotal private meeting chaired by then-president Botha in September 1985, the decision was made to limit the arsenal size to seven uranium gun-type devices and terminate all research on plutonium designs and boosted fission or thermonuclear weapons.[180] This strategic decision limiting the scope of the arsenal helped maintain the shroud of secrecy around it. After that, South Africa produced "four further qualified deliverable gun-assembled devices" through 1989, the 500-series Hamerkop glidebomb weapons, which were maintained in disassembled state to ensure safety.[181] That was a total of six by 1989 (Melba, the gravity bomb 306, 501, 502, 503, and 504),[182] and then a seventh was under construction when—after Botha's resignation due to health issues—President F. W. de Klerk issued a written order on February 26, 1990, to cease production of nuclear weapons and dismantle the six and a half nuclear completed weapons,[183] following the Tripartite Accord that ended the war in Angola at the conclusion of the Cold War.[184] One weapon was to be deliverable by Buccaneer bomber if necessary, and the rest were constructed for air-to-surface glidebomb delivery.[185]

Even as the program was dismantled, the United States was unaware of how far South Africa had gotten or precisely what its arsenal looked like. South Africa successfully built nuclear weapons clandestinely, even though the 1977 Vastrap Incident tipped off a previously unaware United States that South Africa might have a nuclear weapons program. The reasons for South Africa's disarmament in 1990 and 1991 are interesting in their own right but beyond the scope of this book. De Klerk identified the evaporation of South Africa's perceived external threats and wanted to "make this country once again a respected member of the international community . . . and we will have to terminate this program, turn it around and accede to the

179. See von Wielligh and von Wielligh-Steyn, *The Bomb*, 172.

180. Ibid., 183–84.

181. "Report, Director General of the International Atomic Energy Agency, 'The Agency's Verification Activities in South Africa,'" September 23, 1993, p. 7.

182. See von Wielligh and von Wielligh-Steyn, *The Bomb*, 173.

183. "Report, Director General of the International Atomic Energy Agency, 'The Agency's Verification Activities in South Africa,'" September 23, 1993, p. 7.

184. "Speech by South African President F. W. De Klerk to a Joint Session of Parliament on Accession to the Non-Proliferation Treaty," March 24, 1993, p. 4.

185. Purkitt and Burgess, *South Africa's Weapons of Mass Destruction*, 64.

Nuclear Nonproliferation Treaty."[186] Scholars of South Africa note that it was a remarkable turnaround for a die-hard conservative Afrikaner.[187] That may certainly be the case, but it is also the case that de Klerk foresaw the end of apartheid and the electoral reality that the African National Congress would almost certainly govern the country one day—and he did not want them to inherit nuclear weapons, though few would ever admit it (Director of Intelligence Neil Barnard would).[188]

Whatever the reasons, de Klerk's South Africa acceded to the NPT in July 1991, but it did not declare its past nuclear weapons activities. Stumpf writes that "there was no requirement to include projects or programs of the past which had been fully terminated before accession to the NPT."[189] He notes that public acknowledgment was considered very seriously in 1991 but rejected due to the "internal political situation" and because the IAEA had just caught Iraq hiding red-handed after the first Gulf War.[190] Great effort was made to scrub Y Plant of any traces of weapons-grade uranium, and according to a member of the AEC, "much thought had been given to different possible ways of hiding the abandoned weapons program from future international inspections."[191] Initially, the strategy was to hide the proliferation and rollback of the arsenal—as if it never existed. It would not be until de Klerk's 1993 parliamentary speech that South Africa would openly disclose the fact that it once was a nuclear weapons power, that it had successfully hidden a program to produce weapons-grade uranium and half a dozen actual nuclear weapons. It was a remarkable admission unprecedented in the nuclear era.

How was South Africa able to succeed in covertly attaining nuclear weapons? There are many reasons that contributed to its ultimate success. First, it had large reserves of natural uranium, so it did not depend on foreign supply of the basic input into fissile material. Second, it had a very advanced technical base and world-class scientists. These scientists were able to indigenously develop the Helikon vortex enrichment system that South Africa used to enrich weapons-grade uranium, freeing it from dependence on foreign suppliers that could be embargoed. If Iraq's scientists had had this capability, they might have succeeded as well. Third, it had legitimate grounds

186. De Klerk quoted to J. W. de Villiers and Waldo Stumpf, in ibid., 124.

187. Ibid.

188. See von Wielligh and von Wielligh-Steyn, *The Bomb*, 266, 276–78.

189. Stumpf, "South Africa's Nuclear Weapons Programme," 74.

190. Ibid.

191. Von Wielligh and von Wielligh-Steyn, *The Bomb*, 217.

for pursuing indigenous uranium enrichment technology, so it could be self-sufficient in fueling its nuclear power industry. Fourth, South Africa engaged in active efforts at concealment and deception in its facilities. Fifth, South Africa settled on gun-type devices for its uranium weapons that did not necessarily need to be fully tested, since the designs are clean, simple, and predictable—they will almost certainly go boom. Finally, the United States and Soviet Union were simply preoccupied elsewhere—for instance, the United States was dealing with cheaters in Pakistan, Taiwan, and potentially Iraq at the time. South Africa was just a lower priority which, given its location in the Southern Hemisphere, also escaped dedicated satellite monitoring that would have had to be specifically tasked. As Sasha Polakow-Suransky writes in his excellent study of the Israeli-South African alliance: "Outside the CIA—and even within it—few people cared about Pretoria's budding arsenal. South Africa was not on the agency's nonproliferation A-list, according to Bob Campbell, a CIA veteran . . . by the early 1980s, halting South Africa's nuclear program was a secondary objective, and Israel's was accepted as a fait accompli."[192] Thus, South Africa did not have to do much to hide its program. Though overt activity such as a potential test at Vastrap, as in 1977, would mobilize coercive pressure against it, South Africa could conceal the rest of its activity. Thus, while South Africa was forced into hiding, a confluence of factors allowed it to succeed in ways that Iraq and Taiwan could not. But it that does not mean it is not replicable by other potential determined hiders.

TESTING PROLIFERATION STRATEGY THEORY

Proliferation Strategy Theory offers a compelling explanation for South Africa's choice of a hiding strategy. Facing what it believed to be an acute threat on its borders with the ramp up of communist forces in Angola through the mid-1970s, South Africa was at the same time increasingly isolated because of its apartheid policies. The official histories, and de Klerk's own 1993 speech describing the motivations for its program, illuminate South Africa's threat perception in substantial detail. But what strategy of proliferation would my theory predict? While nuclear weaponization was largely theoretical between 1974 and 1977, the Vastrap Incident demonstrated the level of coercion South Africa could face if it openly attempted to build nuclear weapons. It also revealed that there would be no potential shelter

192. Polakow-Suransky, *The Unspoken Alliance*, 142.

from the United States, since the Carter administration explicitly showed that it prioritized nonproliferation and opposition to apartheid over South Africa's role in the struggle against communism in southern Africa. These twin revelations from the Vastrap Incident convinced South Africa that it had to adopt an even more covert hiding strategy than the one Vorster had envisioned earlier—which was already largely clandestine. This meant no overt signatures, and probably no full-blown tests. South Africa likely chose to focus on gun-type designs—and abandoned the plutonium pathway—so that their scientists could live with the no-testing stricture. Other active pursuit pathways were closed by South Africa's relative power and isolation. In contrast to Israel and Pakistan, it enjoyed no patron willing to shelter it. Unlike the early nuclear weapons states, it feared coercion and could not openly sprint for a nuclear weapons program. Domestic consensus for weaponization existed almost by definition in this case, because Vorster possessed the freedom as a strong prime minister to essentially dictate national security policy. In combination, these variables pushed South Africa into an active nuclear weapons pursuit, specifically via hiding.

This story, as with that of most hiders, largely dovetails with a sophisticated realist explanation for South Africa's choice of nuclear proliferation. Realists have had a difficult time explaining why South Africa pursued nuclear weapons in the first place, since its threat perception was largely fueled by a deep Afrikaner paranoia.[193] However, conditional on the choice to pursue a nuclear weapons program at all, realism might largely predict hiding. South Africa's isolation and the pressure of a global arms and economic embargo further isolating it and crippling its economy would make Afrikaner rule even more difficult to sustain. Without any superpower shelter—and indeed facing explicit collusion against it in the 1977 Vastrap Incident—South Africa had little choice but to try to pursue nuclear weapons in hiding. The remarkable feature of this story is that the United States, even after 1977, was unable to get eyes on the South African nuclear program, which it should have assumed continued after the Vastrap Incident despite Vorster's and Botha's denials. Nevertheless, structural realism and my theory largely overlap in the South African case.

Technological determinism does fare reasonably well in explaining South Africa's nuclear proliferation strategy. The uranium enrichment pathway largely arose out of a preexisting need to be self-sufficient in fuel supplies for the Safari-1 and Koeberg reactors. South African scientists innovatively

193. See Liberman, "The Rise and Fall of the South African Bomb."

modified the principle of the German Becker nozzle principle—many were trained in Germany—to develop a unique stationary wall vortex system that they could develop and manufacture indigenously. Once this technology was developed, and given South Africa's extensive uranium deposits, applications beyond fuel supplies were considered—including PNEs—which were not out of the ordinary in the early 1970s. The study of PNEs naturally raised the possibility of whether nuclear explosive devices for military purposes could be constructed and needed. This coincided with an escalating South African threat perception. The evidence makes it difficult to disentangle whether the deteriorating security situation was used as a convenient rationale for pursuing nuclear weapons when the opportunity presented itself, or whether it was truly the cause of South Africa's pursuit of nuclear weapons. Stumpf and de Klerk identify the latter mechanism, which is more consistent with my theory and structural realism, and less so technological determinism. Where my theory (and structural realism) outperforms technological determinism is that a concerted strategic decision to focus on hiding as a strategy was made after the 1977 Vastrap Incident. The fact that South Africa had pursued uranium enrichment from the get-go made it easier, but it was also important that Y Plant was not under safeguards. The implication of my theory is that if pursuing different technical pathways made hiding more likely to succeed, South Africa would have pursued those, since hiding was a strategic decision after the coercive pressure brought to bear on Pretoria in 1977. As it was, uranium enrichment was available and the type of technology the South Africans were employing lent itself almost perfectly to a hiding strategy. It is true that difficulty in operations at Y Plant slowed South Africa down in producing the first fissile cores, but since the program was successfully hidden, South African scientists could recover from their mistakes and had the luxury to take their time.

Nonproliferation norms and the tightening of the NPT regime in the late 1970s did condition the coercive pressure South Africa faced to push it into hiding. As noted earlier, the Vastrap Incident was an illuminating, and unusual, instance of superpower collusion on nonproliferation. The Soviets detected the activity at Vastrap and informed the United States, expecting it to police the noncommunist bloc on nonproliferation. Whether the United States was genuinely caught by surprise or feigned it, the evidence shared by Brezhnev mobilized the Carter administration to threaten even further sanctions against South Africa—not just for apartheid but for proliferation, as the Glenn and Symington amendments were just taking effect. They even mobilized the proliferation-happy French ("et tu Brute," as Vorster would say) to threaten diplomatic, economic, and arms cutoff against Pretoria. But much of this pressure was driven by outrage at South Africa's apartheid policies, and its pursuit of nuclear weapons was simply an additional charge in the indictment. Nevertheless, perhaps unable to withstand additional sanctions, the threat of coercion flowing from the collusive efforts of the nuclear weapons states drove South Africa into hiding. It was not due to normative reasons, however, like its apartheid policies but a rational calculation. Indeed, Vorster stood in public defiance against the hypocrisy of the nuclear weapons states the day after the Vastrap flap ended. He carved out the right of South Africa to develop nuclear weapons, but the teeth of potential coercion from all azimuths drove him to order the program deep underground.

South Africa is thus a case where both my theory and some of the alternative explanations capture parts of the logic that led Pretoria to pursue a hiding strategy. But only Proliferation Strategy Theory provides a complete account of why South Africa selected an active weaponization strategy and that it would ultimately choose to hide due to the potential coercive pressure that was revealed in the 1977 Vastrap episode. It provides the alternatives that South Africa could have selected—sheltered pursuit and sprinting—and why, after Vastrap, neither were viable possibilities. South Africa thus had no choice but to hide its nuclear proliferation. Unlike the other cases in this chapter, however, it succeeded in developing nuclear weapons and became the seventh nuclear weapons state in the nuclear era. But for a variety of external and internal reasons, it also became the first to voluntarily relinquish those weapons.

Conclusion

This chapter has demonstrated the risks and rewards of the hiding strategy, which, along with sheltered pursuit for those who can choose it, are the strategies most likely to dominate the current and future nuclear landscape. Many states in the system left to seek nuclear weapons are those the major powers least want to possess them. They pursue nuclear weapons not only in the face of a stronger major power opposition but also monitored by ever more robust U.S. intelligence and more accurate military capabilities that can credibly sabotage or threaten preventive strikes on nuclear infrastructure. The very threats that motivate many states to pursue nuclear weapons today drive them into hiding. Hiding is risky, as Iraq and Taiwan discovered. Being caught casts a pall of suspicion over the hider's behavior that may be impossible to remove, setting the groundwork for significant future volatility and a violent fate. But the strategy has substantial upsides if it succeeds, as the South African case illustrates. If a state is able to present a nuclear weapons capability as a fait accompli before being detected by major powers, it can bypass the duress a nuclear aspirant tends to face during pursuit of the ultimate deterrent. This prospect alone—the small chance of attaining the most powerful deterrent in international politics—will likely continue to motivate many hiders to keep rolling the dice, hoping to roll sixes. If they are caught or fail, however, the outcome can often involve significant instability, including war.

7

The Consequences for Nuclear Proliferation and Conflict

HALTING HEDGERS AND HANDLING HIDERS (LIBYA, SYRIA, AND IRAN)

This chapter will outline why strategies of proliferation *matter* to international politics, particularly to the nuclear landscape. Each chapter has, thus far, focused on moving "down" the Proliferation Strategy Theory decision tree to a particular strategy of proliferation. Here, I analyze the prospects for future proliferation and identify the levers that the United States and others can pull to stop or reverse states from developing nuclear weapons. This chapter shows how Proliferation Strategy Theory can help us understand how and why states might *stop*, or be stopped, along the road to nuclear weapons. Perhaps more importantly, it also shows what variables might be manipulated to induce states to *reverse* direction—that is, to go from an active weapons program to some form of hedging or to terminate a program outright. Special attention is paid to the most dangerous type of proliferator in the contemporary and future landscapes: hiders.

Identifying the reasons why states choose either a variety of hedging or a particular active strategy of nuclear proliferation is critical to understanding how to stop them from fully attaining nuclear weapons. The first part of this chapter focuses on what Proliferation Strategy Theory tells us about how to stop states from weaponizing—which variables, if changed, may inhibit further proliferation or provoke outright abandonment of a nuclear program. Some hedgers, for example, have eventually opted for active weaponization programs and built the bomb. India and France, which were hard and insurance hedgers, respectively, shifted to active sprints and developed nuclear weapons. Other hard hedgers such as Sweden, Switzerland, and Brazil opted to effectively abandon any nuclear weapons program once domestic political debate forced the governments to forswear future weaponization. Still other hedgers such as Japan persist with insurance hedging, with clear conditions for switching to active weaponization: a shift in its security environment or fears of American abandonment, or some combination of the two.

I also argue that, although sprinters almost always succeed in attaining nuclear weapons, the historical sequencing of nuclear weapons proliferation and the strategic acquisition of sophisticated counterproliferation capabilities (intelligence, sanctions, military capabilities) to deter and stop proliferation have limited the number of sprinters left in the pool of potential proliferators—save perhaps powerful countries such as Australia and Japan. Going forward, hiding and sheltered pursuit are the most relevant active strategies of proliferation, and the policy options to address them are distinct. Sheltered pursuers are those states that the major powers—usually the United States but sometimes China or Russia—elect to shield from counterproliferation efforts, both their own and from others, due to higher-priority geopolitical goals. Sheltered pursuers, like sprinters, almost always succeed in developing nuclear weapons—Pakistan, Israel, and North Korea all successfully developed nuclear weapons under great power shelter. Future proliferators such as Saudi Arabia may be able to adopt sheltered pursuit, seeking to develop nuclear weapons if a patron, in this case the United States, decides it will tolerate it. Extending shelter is a strategic decision, and the sheltering power accepts that its tolerance of the pursuer will likely result in a new member of the nuclear club. In some cases, such as Israeli nuclearization, the consequences may be manageable. But in others, such as Pakistan or perhaps North Korea, the risks of allowing a sheltered pursuer to achieve its nuclear ambitions are non-trivial.

Hiders are the most disruptive proliferators in the international system, both when they are caught, potentially triggering conflict or the international political equivalent of murder, and when they succeed and present a fait accompli nuclear deterrent to the world. A robust nonproliferation regime and the threat of sanctions certainly dissuades some states from trying to hide a nuclear weapons program,[1] so those that embark on a clandestine nuclear weapons program are thus likely to be the most resolute pursuers and therefore the hardest states to stop. These are countries that have priced in the threat of force or sanctions but are nevertheless determined to build the bomb. If they succeed, they are likely to be the types of states that the world least wants to possess nuclear weapons—the Syrias and Libyas of the world. Detecting hiders can be difficult, even with advanced and sophisticated intelligence, and stopping them even after they are caught can involve crippling economic sanctions or war. Whether successful or terminated, hiding is the most consequential proliferation strategy and the one most likely to dominate in the future given the pool of likely proliferators and the suite of nonproliferation and counterproliferation measures presently available to the great powers. This chapter explores various counterproliferation strategies—such as exploiting inefficiency as in the Libyan case, surgical strikes as in the Syrian case, and retarding progress as in the Iranian case—to stop hiders in their tracks. All rely upon exploiting the slow pace—or attempting to even further slow the pace—of the hiding strategy to detect the program before it is too far advanced, and then focus on applying effective coercive pressure through either sanctions or the implicit or explicit use of force. Buying and exploiting time is the best weapon against hiders, increasing the chance they make a mistake and get caught. Unfortunately, it also almost always requires a little luck.

The second part of the chapter goes beyond how Proliferation Strategy Theory illuminates policies for *stopping* states from progressing toward nuclear weapons: it focuses on the idea of nuclear *reversal,* or pushing an active proliferator back to hedging or outright abandonment. This is distinct from the notion of rollback, or forcing nuclear states to disarm. South Africa is the only case where a state with an independent nuclear weapons arsenal surrendered it, although the post-Soviet states Ukraine, Belarus, and Kazakhstan returned nuclear weapons to Russia after inheriting them from the breakup of the Soviet Union.[2] Reversal refers to a state which is actively pursuing nuclear weapons—but not yet at the finish line—reversing direction to either a nuclear hedge or abandonment. I focus extensively on the case of Iran as a critical success story for nuclear reversal under the 2015 Joint Comprehensive Plan of Action (JCPOA). Especially given the

1. See Miller, "The Secret Success of Nonproliferation Sanctions"; and Debs and Monteiro, *Nuclear Politics.*

2. See Levite, "Never Say Never Again"; and Rupal N. Mehta, *Delaying Doomsday: The Politics of Nuclear Reversal* (New York: Oxford University Press, 2020).

potential disruption posed by hiders—who generate the so-called "cheater's dilemma," which in part led the United States to invade Iraq in 2003 for example[3]—the Iranian case is one where an exceptionally sophisticated and advanced hider, one whose progress stunned even the United States, was pushed back to hard hedging. It was pushed back by a combination of sanctions that fractured domestic political consensus for nuclear weapons and the offer of the JCPOA, which attempted to lock in that fractured consensus by trying to empower moderates within Iran through economic inducements.[4]

Importantly, the architects of the JCPOA recognized that Iran could not and would not fully relinquish the technical basis for a nuclear weapons program, and did not demand the impossible: full surrender of Iran's nuclear technology. Instead, they were satisfied with pushing it back to hard hedging—extending Iran's so-called "breakout time" to detect and punish clandestine activity and relying on the belief that a fractured domestic political consensus for weaponization in which the moderates might be empowered would disincentivize any attempt to cheat. The JCPOA did not fully eliminate Iran's intent to potentially pursue nuclear weapons in the future—nor could it have—but it attempted to dissuade Iran from *acting* on that intent and established a mechanism to detect and punish cheating. Proliferation Strategy Theory highlights the critical variable that enabled Iran's nuclear reversal under the JCPOA: fractured domestic political consensus for nuclear weapons. The agreement exploited the division between Iran's moderates, who were willing to verifiably put the nuclear weapons program on ice, and the hard-liners, who still perhaps wanted a bomb. Iran, which had a full-fledged advanced nuclear weapons program until 2003 under the AMAD Plan, is an important example of how Proliferation Strategy Theory can illuminate the pathway to nuclear *reversal* as well as nuclear proliferation.

Halting Hedgers: What Strategies of Proliferation Tell Us

I will first highlight the insights strategies of proliferation provide on how to contain various hedgers—technical, insurance, and hard hedgers—before turning to the active proliferation strategies—sprinting, sheltered pursuit, and hiding. Hedgers have essentially three options over time. First, they

3. See Braut-Hegghammer, "The Cheater's Dilemma."

4. See Miller, *Stopping the Bomb*, chap. 9; and Reid B. C. Pauly, "Stop or I'll Shoot, Comply and I Won't: Coercive Assurance in International Politics" (PhD diss., Massachusetts Institute of Technology, 2019), chaps. 5 and 6.

can shift to an active weaponization strategy and attempt to exercise their nuclear option. Second, they can decide to openly forswear that option and publicly abandon any intent to retain a nuclear weapons option. Third, they can persist with hedging, maintaining a nuclear weapons option indefinitely. Hedgers are not failed proliferators. They have chosen to intentionally stop short of an active weaponization strategy, and incentivizing them not to reconsider active pursuit should be the primary objective of nonproliferation policies—hedging is better than active pursuit and easier to incentivize than abandonment. Recall that the empirical success rate of active weaponization strategies is over 50 percent. Stopping hedgers from actively pursuing nuclear weapons is the single most important way to prevent nuclear proliferation, generally speaking. By disaggregating nuclear hedging into three theoretically and empirically exhaustive types, strategies of proliferation can help identify the key variables that regulate a given hedger's future trajectory.

TECHNICAL HEDGERS

Technical hedgers are the closest category to "nuclear latency," where a state may have a civilian nuclear program that forms the basis for a potential future nuclear weapons program but does not possess the capability to produce weapons-suitable fissile material—either domestic uranium enrichment or reprocessing plutonium. There is no centralized intent to explore a weapons option, though there may be fringe groups or individuals interested in doing so. How does one keep a technical hedger from pursuing an active weaponization strategy? The theory and the evidence explored in chapter 3 suggest there are at least three points of leverage to stop technical hedgers.

First, technical hedgers often do not perceive an acute security threat. Without the emergence of an acute security threat, it is unlikely that a technical hedger would ever consider exercising its nuclear weapons option. Second, even in the face of an acute security threat, technical hedgers can still be stopped if they find a formal ally that can satisfy their security needs. Indeed, after India lost the 1962 war to China and witnessed China's 1964 nuclear test, its first strategy was to seek an informal nuclear umbrella—either the United States or Soviet Union—to shift to insurance hedging.[5] Implicit statements from the U.S. government and the Soviet Union led the Indian government to briefly, according to Andrew Kennedy, "believe that the moment there is a Chinese attack then inevitably the other nuclear

5. Kennedy, "India's Nuclear Odyssey."

powers would rush to India's aid even if India did not ask for it."[6] Of course, these perceived umbrellas were incredibly leaky and no such promise of extended deterrence was forthcoming from either the United States or the Soviet Union to India. However, had it been the case, it is possible that India could have become an insurance hedger and emplaced itself under an extended deterrent umbrella with the emergence of the Chinese threat. It is a fascinating counterfactual. Nevertheless, theoretically, extended deterrence provides a mechanism to prevent a technical hedger from an active weaponization program if a perceived security threat emerges.

Finally, in terms of nonproliferation mechanisms to keep technical hedgers in their box, export control arrangements such as the Nuclear Suppliers Group (NSG) and verification mechanisms such as the IAEA's Additional Protocol are critical to verifying that no fringe elements are abusing a state's technical hedge for anything beyond civilian purposes. A state that refuses to sign an Additional Protocol now raises suspicion about how "fringe" its technical hedge might be. Nevertheless, strengthening export control regimes is an important mechanism for the international community to monitor technical hedgers and stay ahead of the cat-and-mouse games nuclear weapons aspirants may play to evade them.

INSURANCE HEDGERS

Insurance hedgers forego an independent nuclear weapons program by relying on a superpower patron, usually the United States, for extended deterrence to meet their security needs. Insurance hedgers are pushed off their perch if their underlying security threat becomes so severe that the state believes that extended deterrence is inadequate, or if the superpower patron abandons them. Insurance hedging can, and often does, persist indefinitely as it has in much of Western Europe under NATO, as well as Japan and South Korea in East Asia, which all continue to enjoy American extended deterrence commitments. Although the appetite for reassurance by allies is often infinite, the United States in particular has so far been able to assure its allies of its commitment and capability to extend nuclear deterrence except for one major case: France. Because de Gaulle doubted America's willingness to trade "New York for Paris" after the advent of Soviet ICBMs, France rejected even extensive NATO stockpile-sharing offers and concluded that no level of reassurance could substitute for an independent French nuclear deterrent.

6. Ibid., 130.

Although France has historically been the only case of an insurance hedger opting for an independent deterrent, there is no guarantee it will be the last. Under President Trump's leadership, significant doubts about America's commitment to both Europe and East Asia led to growing concerns that the United States may not indefinitely remain a reliable and credible provider of extended deterrence—concerns that may remain long after the Trump administration as allies fear abandonment temptations could one day return to the White House. Burden-sharing disputes with NATO, Japan, and South Korea, and efforts to reduce America's conventional footprint—a key indicator of its commitment to its allies—have led to questions in Germany[7] about whether it requires a substitute to American extended deterrence, and similar discussions at least privately in Japan[8] and South Korea[9] among some domestic constituencies. Doubts about the reliability of America's commitment to extended deterrence came to a boil under President Trump, who was at times perceived by allies such as South Korea as being willing to throw partners under the bus in pursuit of his own policy objectives, such as a deal with North Korea's Kim Jong Un. The experience has the potential to revive debates about independent deterrents in America's long-time allies—and not just for instrumental reasons to elicit stronger reassurance from Washington to hedge against future incarnations of Trumpism that seek to retrench America's commitments back home.

Even if these states fear abandonment from the United States, however, an active weaponization strategy is not a foregone conclusion. Some current hedgers, particularly Japan as discussed in chapter 3, may face difficulty in generating a domestic political consensus for nuclear weapons. Germany would similarly have to overcome opposition from environmental groups, normative aversion to possessing independent nuclear weapons, and a public and large swath of the opposition that is skeptical of their utility. In both cases, domestic political processes might buy time or create opportunities to prevent a rapid weaponization process. Other hedgers, such as South Korea where historical support for an independent nuclear deterrent has hovered between 60–70 percent of the public, might have an easier time generating domestic political consensus for nuclear weapons, especially if led by a conservative government. South Korea, though, is farther from

7. See Ulrich Kuhn, Tristan Volpe, and Bert Thompson, "Tracking the German Nuclear Debate," Carnegie Endowment for International Peace, March 5, 2020, https://carnegieendowment.org/2017/09/07/tracking-german-nuclear-debate-pub-72884.

8. Mark Fitzpatrick, "How Japan Could Go Nuclear," *Foreign Affairs*, October 3, 2019, https://www.foreignaffairs.com/articles/asia/2019-10-03/how-japan-could-go-nuclear.

9. Lee, "Don't Be Surprised When South Korea Wants Nuclear Weapons."

being able to produce weapons-grade fissile material than either Japan or Germany. Proliferation Strategy Theory identifies not only the variable—reliability of the superpower patron to satisfy the insurance hedger's security needs—that can maintain insurance hedging[10] but also the extent of the next hurdle, generating domestic consensus for a bomb, that an insurance hedger would have to clear in order to actively pursue nuclear weapons. My framework suggests that South Korea, among U.S. allies currently protected by formal extended deterrence guarantees, is the greatest risk for switching from insurance hedging to active pursuit. Nevertheless, there is some truth to the argument that, with allies, credible extended deterrence guarantees are one of the most powerful nonproliferation tools available. Allied fear of potential abandonment risks a cascade of proliferation among Washington's friends, with attendant risks of more weapons and more uncertainty in the system as additional nuclear nodes emerge, each with the independent ability to start or escalate a nuclear conflict.

HARD HEDGERS

Hard hedgers are in the most precarious state of any of the hedgers—often only one leadership decision away from either actively pursuing nuclear weapons or, sometimes, forswearing them altogether. By bringing the nuclear question to a head at the top of the leadership, whether autocratic or democratic, a state is confronted with one of the most important security decisions it may ever face: should it pursue nuclear weapons or not? An answer in the affirmative pushes a state to an active nuclear weapons strategy, as in the case of India. An answer in the negative can lead to nuclear abandonment entirely, as in the cases of Switzerland, Sweden, Argentina, and Brazil, who all decided—when the time came to generate consensus—that their futures were better-off without nuclear weapons.

What are the policy options to keep a hard hedger from pursuing an active strategy? Much depends on the specifics of the time and case. I have noted that a generalizable theory of how and when domestic consensus for nuclear weapons congeals or fractures is almost impossible to assemble across time and regime type—presidential democracies have different constituencies than parliamentary democracies, both of which are different from party totalitarian states and personalist dictatorships. The individuals and constituents required to form "consensus" in each of the different configurations vary

10. See Susan J. Koch, "Extended Deterrence and the Future of the Nonproliferation Treaty," *Comparative Strategy* 39, no. 3 (April 2020): 239–49.

considerably. The extent of the group required to form a "policy consensus" varies from case to case and must be analyzed in a bespoke fashion—in the Soviet Union the last dominoes to fall were essentially Stalin and his trusted circle of Beria and Molotov, while in Sweden it was Erlander and the parliament, while in India a strong prime minister such as Rajiv Gandhi was alone necessary and sufficient to achieve consensus for weaponization. This case-by-case analysis matters because keeping domestic political consensus for weaponization fractured is one way to keep hard hedgers from shifting to active strategies. A deep and sophisticated understanding of the domestic politics of all potential nuclear aspirants—something to which realists are often allergic—is required to possibly forestall them.

In some cases, a hard hedger might be willing to accede to an extended deterrence agreement with a nuclear power. If not, the key is determining how to empower domestic opponents of weaponization. There is no one tool kit for this. Miller has shown how the threat of effective sanctions, which grew enforcement teeth after 1976, can sometimes act on domestic consensus.[11] Solingen shows that outward-looking proliferators, who are more vulnerable to the threat and then inducement of removing sanctions, are easier to halt by empowering moderates.[12] There may be no one-size-fits-all approach, but the notion of empowering those who oppose the bomb to keep domestic consensus for a bomb from congealing offers at least a broad strategy the international community can pursue to stop hard hedgers. In some cases this may be a long-term project. In other cases, those who oppose the bomb may—as in Switzerland and Sweden—carry the political day without external nudging and forever forswear the bomb option. One key insight from strategies of proliferation, one neglected by the recent "security above all" turn in the proliferation literature,[13] is that no state can pursue nuclear weapons without domestic political consensus for a bomb, whatever form consensus takes in that particular regime.

Stopping Active Proliferators

States choose strategies of proliferation purposefully, seeking either to maximize their security without fully developing their nuclear capability or to maximize their chance of attaining nuclear weapons given the particular constraints and opportunities they face. Because states choose strategies with

11. Miller, *Stopping the Bomb*.
12. Solingen, *Nuclear Logics*.
13. See Debs and Monteiro, *Nuclear Politics*.

purpose, and with an eye toward their particular situation, it is hard to say which strategy is optimal or most likely to succeed in a vacuum.[14] In general, states are in fact selecting the strategy that they believe is optimized for their particular hedging objectives or for an active pursuit of nuclear weapons that maximizes their prospects of achieving the bomb. Thus far, 10 of 19 active proliferators—over half—have succeeded in developing nuclear weapons, a far higher success rate than is generally appreciated. Conditional on an actual attempt to develop weapons, attaining nuclear weapons is not a particularly rare feat—a 50/50 proposition. While it is difficult to say which strategy is intrinsically better than the rest, the empirical record of the nuclear age shows distinct variations in success rates across different strategies—choice of strategy is, after all, related to a state's underlying power position, and being stronger is usually better in international politics. Success is heavily skewed toward sprinters and sheltered pursuers, but many states—half the attempted active proliferators—try hiding anyway. They rarely succeed, and their failures are often violent. But the rarity of success has thus far failed to deter many determined hiders to nevertheless roll the dice against the very threats that often motivate their nuclear pursuit.

So far, every sprinter has been able to attain nuclear weapons, as have, perhaps surprisingly, the three main sheltered pursuers—Israel, Pakistan, and North Korea. However, hiders pose the biggest challenge to the nonproliferation regime and for counterproliferation efforts. Though few—South Africa, and perhaps nearly Iran—succeed, the number of states that have ignored the threat of being caught and attempted to hide and cheat as members of the NPT is concerningly high. Hiders are especially disruptive to the international system as major powers attempt to discover and stop them—potentially through sanctions, which can carry significant human costs for the target population, or through the use of force, which can be exceptionally bloody. What do strategies of proliferation tell us about how states that are actively weaponizing might be stopped?

SPRINTERS

Nuclear aspirants choose to sprint when they have calculated that no one can stop them. For the first generation of proliferators—the Soviet Union, France, China, the United Kingdom—three things worked in favor of sprinting as a

14. See Vipin Narang, "The Use and Abuse of Large-n Methods in Nuclear Security," in "What We Talk about When We Talk about Nuclear Weapons," ed. James McAllister and Diane Labrosse, H-Diplo ISSF Forum, no. 2 (2014): 91–97, http://issforum.org/ISSF/PDF/ISSF-Forum-2.pdf.

strategy. First, these were the major powers who possessed the industrial and scientific resources and capability to efficiently develop nuclear weapons programs, as well as the military capability or territory to effectively avoid or deter preventive attempts on their programs. Second, counterproliferation intelligence to accurately characterize and military capabilities to precisely destroy nuclear programs were technologically limited in this first period of proliferation. At best, a preventive attack might delay these early proliferators by several years. At worst, a preventive attack would spark a major power war without even achieving delay. For example, not only was the United States' understanding of both the Soviet and Chinese programs exceptionally poor in retrospect, but mounting a preventive military strike into the Soviet or Chinese hinterland was a herculean task that even the Curtis LeMays of the world would consider practically impossible. This made it easier for sprinters to sprint. Third, nonproliferation was not a high-priority policy objective for the United States until after Chinese nuclearization in 1964 and, more importantly, the 1974 Indian peaceful nuclear explosion, which exposed the risks of states exploiting nuclear assistance for military programs.[15] It was only after the Indian PNE that the United States passed legislation to give sanctions teeth, while intelligence resources were deliberately developed and improved to provide higher resolution on the activities of potential proliferators. This gave the early proliferators wide berth to pursue nuclear weapons openly and essentially without fear of prevention.

Some states such as India, and in the future potentially Japan, are able to adopt sprinting strategies in the final stage of their weaponization strategies only after making substantial progress as hard hedgers. And there are still potential states in the international system—such as Australia, whose economy would be hard to punish and whose vast interior territory would complicate military prevention—that may be able to select sprinting strategies from start to finish if they choose to pursue nuclear weapons. What can be done to stop a determined sprinter, which correctly calculates that it is unlikely to be stopped in its pursuit of nuclear weapons? Not much. The good news is that the pool of potential sprinters left in the system is incredibly small. The bad news is that should any of those states experience a shift in their security situation and be unwilling to accept extended deterrence arrangements, they will probably choose to sprint to a bomb and become nuclear weapons powers.

15. See Miller, *Stopping the Bomb*.

SHELTERED PURSUERS

One of the most surprising findings from the book is the frequency and success of sheltered pursuit, which is a strategy that depends on both a state determined to develop nuclear weapons *and* a great power—historically the United States as well as China—willing to *shield* that state from external efforts to stop it. The shelterer elects not to punish the proliferator and shields it from external coercion by, for example, undermining or weakening sanctions or raising the risk that an attack on the proliferator may draw in the shelterer and spark a major power war. Israel and Pakistan were able to successfully develop nuclear weapons while the United States willfully turned a blind eye to their efforts—both pretended to not have active nuclear weapons programs and Washington pretended to believe them. Israel succeeded in making itself indispensable to the United States as a foothold in the Middle East, and Washington was limited in what it was willing and able to do to stop Israel from weaponizing due to strong congressional and White House opposition to, for instance, conditioning arms sales on nonproliferation. Israel took advantage of that shelter to develop and keep nuclear weapons in 1967 and thereafter.

In the Pakistani case, it is entirely plausible that the American sanctions that had begun taking shape during the Carter administration might have prevented Pakistan from attaining nuclear weapons if not for the Soviet invasion of Afghanistan on Christmas Day, 1979. But, whereas Israel made itself indispensable by carefully cultivating key stakeholders in the United States, Pakistan found itself indispensable by sheer luck, finding fortune in Afghanistan's misfortune. The United States needed to funnel arms and money through the Pakistan military and intelligence services to wage the mujahideen war in Afghanistan. Any sanctions over Pakistan's nuclear weapons program would have threatened that relationship, and the White House and CIA went to extraordinary lengths—in some cases outright lying to Congress—to shield Islamabad from American congressional pressure, on the belief that a nuclear Pakistan was an acceptable price to pay to defeat the Soviet Union in Afghanistan. Once shelter was extended to Pakistan, it accelerated its program and was able to take greater risks to acquire foreign components, knowing it enjoyed immunity from the United States, in order to develop nuclear weapons before the shelter evaporated. Absent American shelter, Pakistan may have still succeeded in weaponizing but would probably have taken longer as it would have been forced into a more inefficient hiding strategy. In any case, it would have certainly been costlier for the

Pakistani economy, given the harsh sanctions that likely would have been imposed on Islamabad.

North Korea benefited from China's shield, after China calculated that a nuclear North Korea was preferable to a weak and desperate North Korea that sent millions of refugees across the border and that no longer served as a buffer against the United States and South Korea. As in the Israel and Pakistan cases of sheltered pursuit, China calculated that other geopolitical objectives were higher priority than nonproliferation. While previous generalizable theories have a difficult time accounting for how North Korea—a fourth-rate pipsqueak power, as Nixon once derided it—developed nuclear weapons, Proliferation Strategy Theory offers the answer: Chinese shelter, which both undermined international sanctions efforts and served as a deterrent against significant American military action against North Korea by introducing the small, but non-zero, risk that such an attack might spark a major power conflict with China.

Sheltered pursuit is a strategy that depends on two actors: a determined proliferator and a major power willing to shield the program. Its frequency over time is consistent: about one per decade, and nothing about the contemporary era makes it less likely to happen. Some candidates for sheltered pursuit include Saudi Arabia, which has declared that it would develop nuclear weapons if Iran does so, and would certainly be a candidate for shelter from the United States under some American administrations, owing to its role as key oil producer and friend of the United States.[16] Saudi Crown Prince Mohammed bin Salman declared in a March 2018 interview: "Saudi Arabia does not want to acquire any nuclear bomb, but without a doubt if Iran developed a nuclear bomb, we will follow suit as soon as possible."[17] In August 2020, it was reported that Saudi Arabia had procured equipment from China for extracting uranium yellowcake from uranium ore and that the knowledge of this procurement "has been tightly held within [the] U.S."—suggesting Washington is aware of these efforts, which do not technically

16. Kim Obergfaell, "U.S.-Saudi Nuclear Cooperation under Scrutiny," International Institute for Strategic Studies, March 4, 2019, https://www.iiss.org/blogs/analysis/2019/03/us-saudi-nuclear-cooperation; Timothy Gardner, "U.S. Should Keep Congress Informed about Nuclear Talks with Saudi: GAO," Reuters, May 4, 2020, https://www.reuters.com/article/us-usa-saudi-nuclearpower/u-s-should-keep-congress-informed-about-nuclear-talks-with-saudis-gao-idUSKBN22G2XV.

17. Mohammed bin Salman, "Saudi Crown Prince: If Iran Develops Nuclear Bomb, So Will We," *60 Minutes*, CBS News, March 15, 2018, https://www.cbsnews.com/news/saudi-crown-prince-mohammed-bin-salman-iran-nuclear-bomb-saudi-arabia/.

have to be declared to the IAEA, but is keeping quiet.[18] The United States was also in discussions to conclude a 123 Agreement for the sale of reactors to Saudi Arabia, despite Saudi reluctance to sign the IAEA's Additional Protocol to stringently monitor its nuclear program. Saudi Arabia does not have any publicly known enrichment capabilities, or reactors, yet. However, with the 2020 revelations of uranium milling activity and foreign procurements, the *New York Times* reported: "At the White House, Trump administration officials seem relatively unperturbed by the Saudi effort. They say that until the Iranian nuclear program is permanently terminated, the Saudis will most likely keep the option open to produce their own fuel, leaving open a pathway to a weapon. But now the administration is in the uncomfortable position of declaring it could not tolerate any nuclear production ability in Iran, while seeming to remain silent about its close allies, the Saudis, for whom it has forgiven human rights abuses and military adventurism."[19] As such, Saudi Arabia is a leading candidate to pursue a sheltered pursuit strategy in the future under an American shield, particularly if Iran is perceived to be developing, or succeeds in developing, nuclear weapons. The combination of Chinese assistance—Beijing is much more relaxed about horizontal proliferation—and American shelter was a winning formula for Pakistan that could be modeled by Saudi Arabia. It is also possible, as unlikely as it may sound today, that Turkey could emerge as a sheltered pursuer under the right configuration, and receive shelter from, say, perhaps Russia, as a geopolitically critical state at the crossroads of Asia and Europe and as the price for a NATO exit one day.

How does one stop sheltered pursuers? Major powers make a decision to extend shelter, pricing in the tolerance of the pursuer's nuclear weapons program to the cost of their broader geopolitical goals. A smart sheltered pursuer—and nuclear aspirants are usually quite smart—will attempt to exploit the shelter to weaponize its nuclear capabilities as quickly as possible, before the shelter potentially disappears. Short of convincing a sheltered pursuer that they do not want or need nuclear weapons after all, the only way to stop sheltered pursuers is to eliminate their shelter from sanctions or military attempts at prevention. In some cases, shelter might evaporate

18. Warren P. Strobel, Michael R. Gordon, and Felicia Schwartz, "Saudi Arabia, with China's Help, Expands Its Nuclear Program," *Wall Street Journal*, August 4, 2020, https://www.wsj.com/articles/saudi-arabia-with-chinas-help-expands-its-nuclear-program-11596575671.

19. Mark Mazzetti, David E. Sanger, and William J. Broad, "U.S. Examines Whether Saudi Nuclear Program Could Lead to Bomb Effort," *New York Times*, August 5, 2020, p. A1, https://www.nytimes.com/2020/08/05/us/politics/us-examines-saudi-nuclear-program.html.

because the patron state independently decides that the nuclear aspirant they are sheltering is no longer worth the hassle or that the price of their future entry into the nuclear club is too steep to bear. This is what Pakistan feared when it benefited from U.S. shelter to develop nuclear weapons in the 1980s. Islamabad understood that U.S. forbearance depended on the continuation of the war in Afghanistan. Without the war, the United States would have had less need for Pakistan and therefore less willingness to protect their nuclear program. It is in fact plausible that Pakistan played a double-game with the United States and attempted to prolong the Afghanistan war in order to extend the shelter and largesse it was receiving from Washington for as long as possible. The United States was a willing participant in this game, however. This was a strategic—and not an inevitable—choice, one the United States could have reversed at any time.

If shelter does not evaporate on its own, other major powers might engage the patron state (rather than the nuclear aspirant) to convince them to stop protecting the proliferator. This is the strategy the United States attempted with China over North Korea's nuclear program during the Six Party Talks—seeking to get Beijing's buy-in on stopping North Korean proliferation. China was fundamentally unpersuaded and continued to shield Pyongyang and issue denials about its progress while simultaneously appearing to support—but slow-roll—diplomacy and effective sanctions. There are no cases where a third party has successfully coerced or cajoled a patron state to stop protecting a "sheltered pursuer," but driving a wedge between the nuclear pursuer and its patron if no wedge appears naturally remains the only logical option to reverse a sheltered pursuit strategy. If that can be achieved, the erstwhile sheltered pursuer would be exposed in two ways. First, the existence of a nuclear program would now be implausibly deniable and, second, the proliferator could now be vulnerable to economic or military coercion. But the difficulty of peeling off another major power's shelter for a proliferator should not be understated, as it would be no easy task, and likely priced in by the shelterer prior to extending protection to the proliferator. Major powers have—both under the bipolar Cold War configuration and after—decided that nuclear proliferation is tolerable in pursuit of other geopolitical priorities. It is likely to occur again, and identifying where it might be possible provides insight into the future nuclear landscape, as a sheltered pursuit strategy—if it can be selected—has a high probability of leading to a nuclear weapons capability. As such, states like Saudi Arabia and Turkey (American frenemies) that may be able to select this strategy have a high likelihood of becoming independent nuclear states if they ever choose to do so.

HIDERS

Early in the nuclear era, most states did not have to strategically hide their intentions to pursue nuclear weapons. But the rise of nonproliferation as a general policy objective, backstopped by a stronger sanctions regime, export control regimes such as the Nuclear Suppliers Group (NSG) in parallel to the NPT, and both more sophisticated counterproliferation intelligence and better military capabilities have pushed—and will continue to push—a large number of the remaining pool of potential proliferators into hiding. Certainly, there are a handful of potential sprinters and sheltered pursuers, but the overwhelming number of states left in the system who have the motivation for an active weapons program will have little choice but to hide. Hiding is a high-risk, high-reward proliferation strategy, and all outcomes are disruptive. Either the system births a new nuclear weapons state, usually an unwelcome addition to the club, or catching a hider prompts an international political crisis, mobilization of long-term and potentially crippling economic sanctions, and, at worst, the use of military force. The destabilizing consequences of a hidden nuclear weapons program have long half-lives even after a hider is caught: whatever the Bush administration's multiple motivations for the 2003 Iraq invasion, there was certainly a belief that Saddam Hussein would never surrender his nuclear ambitions unless he was removed from power—the "cheater's dilemma." This was one of the most disruptive wars in the twenty-first century and cannot be viewed independently of Iraq's earlier hidden nuclear weapons program and the belief that Saddam would reconstitute it if he could. Many of the future potential proliferators—both allies and adversaries, friends and foes, of the United States—are likely to be hiders.

Unlike hiders in the past who had not ratified the NPT, future hiders will likely try to cheat and develop clandestine programs while being members of the NPT and under IAEA safeguards. Iran succeeded in doing this until at least 2003, the same year North Korea withdrew from the NPT after cheating on the treaty for years. Until the end of the Cold War, opting out of the NPT or delaying ratification was a pretty clear signal of a state's potential intent to keep the bomb option open. This is no longer the case: all states in the system except for South Sudan have either acceded to the NPT or already possess nuclear weapons. Modern nuclear proliferators cheat, developing clandestine programs while pretending to be members of the NPT in good standing. Most hiders fail, but many have come dangerously close in the past half century: Iraq, Libya, Iran, Taiwan, and Syria, for example, had sustained interest and made substantial progress toward nuclear weapons before they were caught. The seduction of presenting the world a nuclear fait accompli may be exceptionally tempting for states that believe they may be in another state's—especially a major power's—crosshairs. They may be willing to risk preventive attack or sanctions in order to attain the one capability that can essentially indefinitely insure their regime or country. The low success rate of hiding should not provide much comfort: hiding will continue to be an attractive strategy for nuclear aspirants in the future, and hidden pursuit of nuclear weapons is geopolitically disruptive whether it succeeds or fails.

Short of sanctions and war,[20] how does one stop hiders? Time is the world's best weapon against hiders. One advantage of pushing states into hiding is that it induces inefficiencies into the proliferation process. Hiding forces states to disperse and silo their programs in order to maintain a small footprint, thereby slowing progress and increasing the amount of time available for a hider to potentially slip up or be detected. And the concerted development of sophisticated intelligence capabilities across the spectrum of platforms—imagery, electronic, signals, and human intelligence—means it is increasingly difficult to completely and indefinitely hide a nuclear program from a powerful global intelligence apparatus, particularly from the collection tools of the United States and its partners.[21] It is certainly possible, however, to hide early work on a nuclear weapons program, and the red lights flash much brighter as a program progresses and approaches the finish line. The key is detecting a hidden nuclear program before it is too far advanced, before the hider is fully invested in the program, and before terminating the program becomes infeasible. If a hidden program is detected early enough, there are several options to delay or eliminate it.

The primary risk with any of the following options—especially those that involve sabotage or military action—is that they may harden a hider's resolve to clandestinely pursue nuclear weapons and, if they do not fully eliminate or induce sufficient delay in its capability, may backfire and only serve to accelerate the pace and commitment of a hidden program. This is why hiders invariably disrupt the international system, whether they succeed in attaining nuclear weapons or whether they are punished or killed for trying.

20. See Miller, *Stopping the Bomb*.

21. See Amy Zegart, "Understanding Nuclear Threats: The Past and Future of American Intelligence," in *The Fragile Balance of Terror: Deterrence in the New Nuclear Age*, ed. Vipin Narang and Scott D. Sagan (draft manuscript); also Cullen G. Nutt, "Proof of the Bomb: The Influence of Previous Failure on Intelligence Judgments of Nuclear Programs," *Security Studies* 28, no. 2 (2019): 321–59.

Exploiting Inefficiences and a Little Luck: Libya

Terminating Libya's nuclear dreams in 2003 is an example of good luck: catching a hider that is in the infancy of its weapons development or is technically incompetent. Libyan dictator Muammar Gaddafi had a decades-long interest in developing nuclear weapons or acquiring them from abroad.[22] But due to Libyan technical incompetence, Gaddafi struggled to develop an indigenous nuclear weapons program and instead went shopping for the bomb—first with some comical attempts to buy nuclear weapons from both China and India in the 1970s.[23] Libya was never able to develop, according to Braut-Hegghammer, "the actual experience in operating these technologies and the necessary numbers of scientists, engineers, and technicians" to absorb nuclear technology, whether reactor-based or for uranium enrichment.[24] Three years after the 1986 American strike on Tripoli—retaliation for Gaddafi's sponsorship of terrorism—Libya approached the AQ Khan network for off-the-shelf centrifuges for a clandestine uranium enrichment pathway to nuclear weapons.[25] In 1995, Libya placed an order, delivered beginning in 1997, for 20 assembled first-generation Pakistani (P-1/L-1) centrifuges and parts for 200 more.[26] Literally ordering out of the AQ Khan catalogue, the Libyans purchased the deluxe turnkey package, complete with the Chinese CHIC-4 missile mateable warhead design and a whole kit of centrifuges, and even 1.7 tons of UF_6 feed material by 2001.[27]

There was one small problem: Libyan scientists and engineers apparently had little knowledge of or experience in what to do with all this material. They could not manage sensitive and precise centrifuge operations effectively and made no progress despite starting from an off-the-shelf kit replete with manuals, warhead designs, and raw material. Before Libya could think about reverse engineering a nuclear weapon, it had to figure out how to enrich uranium. It never could, and even Libyan officials would

22. See Braut-Hegghammer, *Unclear Physics*, chaps. 5–8.

23. Nuclear Threat Initiative Country Profile, "Libya," January 2015, https://www.nti.org/learn/countries/libya/nuclear/; also see Braut-Hegghammer, *Unclear Physics*, 159.

24. Braut-Hegghammer, *Unclear Physics*, 183.

25. Ibid., 201.

26. Nuclear Threat Initiative Country Profile, "Libya"; also see Board of Governors, International Atomic Energy Agency, "Implementation of the NPT Safeguards Agreement of the Socialist People's Libyan Arab Jamahiriya," GOV/2004/59, August 30, 2004, https://fas.org/nuke/guide/libya/iaea0804.pdf; Gordon Corera, *Shopping for Bombs: Nuclear Proliferation, Global Insecurity, and the Rise and Fall of the A. Q. Khan Network* (Oxford: Oxford University Press, 2006), chap. 5.

27. Braut-Hegghammer, *Unclear Physics*, 204.

later "dismiss the nuclear project as not much of a program at all."[28] This incompetence was lucky for the region and world because neither the United States nor Britain (nor, it would turn out, Israel, which had Libya high on its regional watchlist) was fully aware at the time of how much weapons-related equipment and designs Libya had procured from the Khan network.[29]

Although it is tempting to correlate the timing of Libya's eventual surrender of its nuclear program in 2003 with the Iraq war, Gaddafi, perhaps realizing how far away Libya was from being able to make a clandestine program succeed, in fact offered to surrender the program as early as May 1999 in exchange for sanctions relief from the United States.[30] The Clinton administration was more focused on Libya's support for terrorism, believing, according to Ambassador Martin Indyk, that Libya's nuclear program "barely existed." This was not terribly far from the truth in terms of indigenous progress, but the United States was still only beginning to understand how much the Khan network had transferred before Libya made the offer.[31] After 9/11, there was renewed interest in Khan's activities and customers, and the discovery that Libya was a major customer took Washington and London by surprise.[32] British prime minister Tony Blair convinced President Bush to revisit Gaddafi's offer of trading the WMD program in exchange for American sanctions relief. As negotiations were ongoing, officials "discovered" an AQ Khan shipment bound for Libya in the Italian port of Taranto on the German-flagged ship the *BBC China*. Whether this was a convenient justification for Gaddafi to surrender his program after being "caught," or whether this helped accelerate negotiations, or whether this was a Libyan tip to help unravel the AQ Khan network is publicly unknown.[33] Nevertheless, in December 2003, Libya reached an agreement with the United States and Britain to surrender its clandestine WMD programs in exchange for sanctions relief. The United States quite literally picked up the unassembled and inoperative centrifuges sitting in Libya and transported them on a C-130 military aircraft to Oak Ridge, Tennessee. A full accounting to the IAEA in 2004 revealed the extent to which Libya was involved in clandestine

28. Libyan diplomat paraphrased in ibid., 208.

29. See Nutt, "Proof of the Bomb," 338–39.

30. Miller, *Stopping the Bomb*, 146.

31. Indyk quoted in Braut-Hegghammer, *Unclear Physics*, 211.

32. Nutt, "Proof of the Bomb," 338–39.

33. William Tobey, "Cooperation in the Libya WMD Disarmament Case," *Studies in Intelligence* 61, no. 4 (December 2017): 33–34, https://www.cia.gov/static/c134fac60c8d3634a28629e6082d19eb/Cooperation-in-Libya-WMD.pdf.

purchases of nuclear material and technology in violation of its NPT and IAEA obligations.[34]

What does the Libya case tell us about levers to stop hiders? A combination of sanctions, intelligence, and luck unraveled the Khan network. Gaddafi himself admitted that he had a low probability of successfully developing nuclear weapons due to technical incompetence—an inability to even make minimal progress despite being handed a turnkey kit. This realization was perhaps accelerated by the implicit threat of force after 9/11. As such, the Libyan experience may be difficult, but perhaps not impossible, to replicate. Gaddafi would (perhaps self-servingly) explain that he surrendered the program because: "Libya [had] risked becoming involved in producing weapons at an inappropriate level. This [was] because such weapons need a solid base, great technological expertise, and vectors. Moreover, in which field could such weapons be used, in which theater of combat? I believe that this question faces all countries producing nuclear weapons. . . . So the best decision, the most courageous decision, was to dismantle it."[35]

It is hard to overstate the importance of technological incompetence in Libya's failure to develop nuclear weapons before they were caught.[36] Adding these technical difficulties to the inefficiencies that are induced by hiding seems to have opened a window in which Libya was interested in a trade. After substantial effort, it was hopelessly nowhere near achieving a nuclear deterrent, with little chance to get there, and Gaddafi came to find other policy objectives like sanctions relief more attractive. Hiders are driven into inefficiency, buying time for intelligence to detect and unravel the program—this is critical to enable detection before the program fully gets off the ground. The counterproliferator's job, in this regard, gets easier when the hider is slow for reasons that have little to do with secrecy. This might be important going forward: the remaining pool of potential hiders may look technically more like Libya than South Africa. Though Libya was an odd case of hiding, it still shows that effective pressure, for example through sanctions, and a little luck can combine to defang a hider.

34. See Board of Governors, International Atomic Energy Agency, "Implementation of the NPT Safeguards Agreement of the Socialist People's Libyan Arab Jamahiriya," GOV/2004/59, August 30, 2004.

35. Gaddafi quoted in Braut-Hegghammer, *Unclear Physics*, 215–16.

36. See R. Scott Kemp, "The Nonproliferation Emperor Has No Clothes."

Surgical Strike: Syria

The Libya episode was a major embarrassment for Israel, which kept close tabs on Gaddafi given his stated interest in weapons of mass destruction, his support for international terrorism, his erratic (to put it mildly) leadership style, and Libya's status as a regional adversary. That Libya imported a turnkey program without even the faintest Israeli knowledge represented a major "intelligence failure . . . Israel didn't have [any] idea about this program," according to General Shlomo Brom, a former IDF military intelligence officer.[37] After missing Libya's program in the early 2000s, Israel took no chances of letting Syria's program survive. It was particularly concerned about a curious structure known as al Kibar that ended up being a brazen attempt by Bashar al-Assad to develop a clandestine plutonium nuclear reactor in a remote region in northern Syrian. While the United States hesitated, fearing a broader war in the Middle East, Israel unilaterally destroyed the structure in September 2007. It appears the strike came just in the nick of time: al Kibar was reportedly scheduled to become operational mere weeks later, and striking an operational plutonium reactor would have caused cataclysmic environmental fallout.

The Syrian example provides a second pathway to stopping a hider in its tracks: a surgical military strike that significantly cripples the program. Twice, Israel has destroyed suspicious nuclear reactors before they went operational: in Iraq (1981) and Syria (2007). Whether the reactors were to be the basis of a hidden plutonium route for Iraq and Syria was merely an academic question to Israel: Tel Aviv saw no benefit in waiting to find out.[38] I discussed the Osirak strike at length in chapter 6. But the curious case of the Syrian strike in 2007 is highly instructive. Cullen Nutt's accounting of the strike is one of the most comprehensive available, reporting that "sometime in 2006, the Israelis identified a building in northeastern Syria that they suspected might relate to a nuclear program. . . . the United States was also aware of this building. As in the United States, Israeli intelligence harbored doubts. How could Assad be so obtuse?"[39] That is, would Assad—after the American invasion of Iraq, after the Israeli strike on Osirak—really be so brazen as to attempt a hidden plutonium pathway for nuclear weapons, in plain sight? It turns out, he was.

37. Shlomo Brom quoted in Nutt, "Proof of the Bomb," 337.

38. Ibid.

39. Ibid., 345.

In March 2007, the Mossad discreetly copied files from the laptop of Ibrahim Othman, the head of the Syrian Atomic Energy Agency, from his Vienna apartment while he was visiting the IAEA.[40] What they discovered was stunning, according to investigative reporting by David Makovsky in the *New Yorker*: "three dozen color photographs taken from inside the Syrian building, indicating that it was a top-secret plutonium nuclear reactor. The reactor, called Al Kibar, was nine hundred yards from the Euphrates River," a backup water source for cooling the reactor.[41] The pictures included selfies with "workers from North Korea at the site, which was far from Syria's biggest cities. The sole purpose of this kind of plutonium reactor, in the Mossad's analysis, was to produce an atomic bomb. Inside, the reactor had many of the same engineering elements as the North Korean graphite-moderated gas-cooled reactor in Yongbyon—a model that no one but the North Koreans had built in the past thirty-five years."[42] A key Yongbyon nuclear scientist, Chon Chibu, was photographed at the facility with Othman. The Syrians were constructing a replica of the North Korean Yongbyon nuclear reactor whose only purpose, with no evidence that it was going to produce electricity for the Syrian power grid, was to produce plutonium for nuclear weapons—and North Korea was helping it. Until this Mossad operation in Vienna, neither the United States nor Israel had definitive evidence that one of the world's biggest sponsors of terrorism, a state high on the watchlist for nuclear proliferation, was *clandestinely* building a nuclear *reactor* with assistance from one of the world's worst proliferators, North Korea.

For years, the U.S. intelligence community had harbored suspicions about the structure, but according to senior American officials, "It's hard to figure out looking at that building what its purpose is. And it certainly didn't have any observable, externally observable characteristics that would say 'Oh, yeah you got yourself a nuclear reactor here—things like massive electrical supply system, massive ventilation, and most importantly a cooling system.'"[43] The Syrians had learned how to obfuscate. They avoided installing dead-giveaway signatures like a heavy perimeter or deploying defenses anywhere near the facility that might scream that something on the site was worth defending.[44]

40. Makovsky, "The Silent Strike."

41. Ibid.

42. Ibid.

43. "Background Briefing with Senior U.S. Officials on Syria's Covert Nuclear Reactor and North Korea's Involvement," April 24, 2008, p. 2, https://www.dni.gov/files/documents/Newsroom/Speeches%20and%20Interviews/20080424_interview.pdf.

44. Nutt, "Proof of the Bomb," 344.

The Syrians also built a superstructure over the reactor that made it look like an ordinary cube, littered construction debris around the compound, and avoided obvious traffic patterns that might suggest the presence of anything of high—let alone of the highest—value. Knowing Israeli and American satellites were watching overhead, the Syrians appear to have made the "box" look like nothing more than one of many neglected buildings in the Syrian hinterland, demonstrating that one could potentially hide a plutonium pathway to nuclear weapons as recently as 2007. The United States was stunned at the revelations, with Secretary of Defense Robert Gates writing, "Syria for years had been a high-priority intelligence target for the United States. . . . nuclear weapons in particular. Early detection of a large nuclear reactor under construction in a place like Syria is supposedly the kind of intelligence collection the United States does superbly well. Yet by the time the Israelis informed us about the site, the reactor construction was already well advanced. This was a significant failure on the part of the U.S. intelligence agencies."[45]

Once the Mossad operation obtained photographs of the inside of al Kibar, U.S. intelligence also quickly concluded "this non-descript-looking building in al Wadi, near the Euphrates River in eastern Syria was indeed a covert nuclear reactor. . . . The reactor inside that building was clearly not configured to produce electricity. We saw no way and there are no power lines coming out of it, none of all the switching facilities that you would need."[46] Syria was clearly trying to hide the reactor: "Features of the facility and its location indicate Syria attempted to maintain its secrecy."[47] But the internal replica of Yongbyon—and undeniable evidence of North Koreans bizarrely roaming around the Syrian hinterland—left little doubt as to the purpose of the facility: to produce plutonium for a nuclear weapons program. At this point, however, U.S. intelligence curiously had a "low confidence" judgment about the existence of a dedicated nuclear weapons program, since they saw no evidence of a reprocessing facility: "To go with the question you're asking—weapons—we said, we believe it. There's no other reason for it. But our confidence level that it's [a weapons program] is low at this point. We believe it, but it's low based on the physical evidence."[48] President Bush writes in his memoirs that CIA director Michael Hayden reported that the Agency "had high confidence the plant housed a nuclear

45. Robert M. Gates, *Duty: Memoirs of a Secretary at War* (New York: Knopf, 2014), 171.

46. "Background Briefing with Senior U.S. Officials on Syria's Covert Nuclear Reactor and North Korea's Involvement," 2.

47. Ibid., 4.

48. Ibid., 11.

reactor. But because they could not confirm the location of the facilities necessary to turn the plutonium into a weapon, they had only low confidence of a Syrian nuclear weapons program."[49]

The Israelis did not care for the American hesitation or rhetorical gymnastics on "confidence" levels: Tel Aviv would not allow an adversarial state in the region to operate a reactor that had the sole logical purpose of generating plutonium for a nuclear weapon.[50] Through the summer, President Bush attempted to stall Prime Minister Olmert, who wanted the United States to execute a preventive strike on the reactor before it was loaded with uranium fuel rods. If the United States did not act, Olmert implied that he would. Bush wanted diplomacy, and Secretary of State Condoleezza Rice feared an Israeli strike would spark a regional war.[51] Olmert was disappointed that the United States would not lead the attack, but President Bush promised him there would be "no leaks" that might sabotage any action the Israelis were unilaterally contemplating.[52] Makovsky reports that an Israeli general told him: "Olmert said he did not ask Bush for a green light, but Bush did not give Olmert a red light . . . Olmert saw it as green."[53]

In August 2007, a pumphouse was constructed at the Euphrates presumably as part of an external or backup cooling system, but uranium fuel had not been loaded into the reactor as far as anyone knew. The new structure induced urgency in Tel Aviv: with the pumphouse built there would be no other external indicators if the reactor went "hot." The Israelis feared that the reactor could go operational within weeks, after which a strike was out of the question due to the environmental catastrophe that could result (though evidently Ehud Barak argued that should not stop Israel). A covert option with special forces was debated, but destroying the reactor in a ground operation would have been difficult even leaving aside the concern that an operation gone awry could result in Israeli operatives caught in a firefight or captured deep in Syrian territory. A single airstrike with significant redundancy was selected, an option that would certainly destroy the reactor but risked escalation if the Syrians retaliated.[54] Olmert's government decided to strike just after midnight on September 6, 2007. Four F-15s and four F-16s jammed Syrian air defense and dropped seventeen tons of ordnance on al Kibar,

49. George W. Bush, *Decision Points* (New York: Crown, 2010), 421.
50. Nutt, "Proof of the Bomb," 352.
51. Makovsky, "The Silent Strike."
52. Ibid.
53. Ibid.
54. Harel and Benn, "No Longer a Secret."

flattening the structure and the reactor.[55] The Israelis did not take a public victory lap, and the Syrians simply reported that Israeli aircraft had been repelled by Syrian air defense with no acknowledgment of any incident at al Kibar. The Israelis gambled that Assad would not react and risk a broader war after being caught red-handed, and they gambled correctly, though it was certainly not a foregone conclusion. For his part, Assad bet big that he could hide the reactor—in plain sight to no doubt confuse the United States and Israel—before it went hot, and his credit ran out likely weeks before he would have succeeded.

The Syrians moved quickly to sanitize the site so there was no evidence of a reactor. But in 2011, the IAEA concluded that "based on all the information available to the Agency and its technical evaluation of that information, the Agency assesses that it is very likely that the building destroyed at the Dair Alzour [al Kibar] site was a nuclear reactor which should have been declared to the Agency," and that it was essentially a replica of North Korea's Yongbyon reactor constructed clandestinely with North Korean assistance.[56] This is IAEA-speak for: Syria was cheating on the NPT and we had no idea. It is remarkable, in retrospect, that the reactor was caught just before it went hot, enabling Israel to fully destroy it in a single surgical attack with no resulting escalation. This is another possible way to stop a hider, who is caught and whose infrastructure is vulnerable to such prevention. But the Syrian case shows how important time and luck are in detecting the program. And a surgical strike can be risky, since any unilateral or multilateral use of force always runs the risk of retaliation, escalation, or failure. It also risks, as the Iraqi case illustrates, accelerating the development of a more clandestine effort. Assad now finds himself in the "cheater's dilemma": having been caught red-handed once trying to develop nuclear weapons secretly, what would it take to convince the world that he is not still trying?

Sabotage: Retarding Progress and Buying Time

Once Syria was caught, destroying the basis of its nuclear weapons program—a single aboveground reactor—was a relatively easy task. However, some of the more concerning hiders have more complicated programs and have learned from these examples, developing multiple facilities—hardened,

55. Makovsky, "The Silent Strike."

56. Board of Governors, International Atomic Energy Agency, "Implementation of the NPT Safeguards Agreement in the Syrian Arab Republic," GOV/2011/30, May 24, 2011, pp. 8–9.

hidden, and dispersed across various sites—that make a Libyan-style surrender unlikely and a Syrian-style surgical strike that can completely destroy a program in a single sterile strike infeasible. What options are available in these cases? One time-honored strategy—the United States used it against the nascent Nazi bomb program even before the Manhattan Project was complete—is broadly described as "buying time." It involves a variety of measures like direct sabotage, supply-chain pollution, assassination of scientists, and introduction of misinformation to slow down the program by delaying breakthroughs or impeding weaponization efforts at suspected or known facilities. A former Mossad chief described time-buying efforts—both Israeli and global—against Iraq and Iran as seeking "delay, delay, delay . . . because you never know what might happen in the interim."[57] Even a two-year delay of a nuclear program buys time for a fortuitous change—domestic political change, external regime change, a change in circumstance or calculation—that may result in the termination of the program.

The destruction of the Osirak reactor in 1981, for example, may have pushed Saddam's nuclear program underground, but it also bought some time for the region and the world if Osirak was planned to ever supply fissile material for a nuclear weapons program, forcing Iraq to abandon the plutonium pathway. Since the end of the George W. Bush administration, the "sabotage" model has gained greater prominence with the famous Stuxnet attack on Iran's Natanz enrichment facility, part of President Bush's Olympic Games program, which was accelerated by President Obama.[58] I will discuss Iran's reversal from hiding to hard hedging in greater detail below, but one critical tool in addressing Iran's nuclear program, one that may have helped bring Tehran to the negotiating table, was buying time through sabotage. Much of this activity is obviously classified, but the broad scope of the program is relatively clear. Before he left office, President Bush, according to David Sanger, "authorized a covert plan to undermine electrical systems, computer systems, and other networks on which Iran relies, in hopes of delaying the day that Iran could produce a workable nuclear weapon."[59] The pièce de résistance of this campaign was the Stuxnet worm, a sophisticated "man-in-the-middle" attack specifically designed for the control software

57. Author discussion with retired chief of the Mossad, Tel Aviv, May 2019.

58. David E. Sanger, "Obama Order Sped Up Wave of Cyberattacks on Iran," *New York Times*, June 1, 2012, https://www.nytimes.com/2012/06/01/world/middleeast/obama-ordered-wave-of-cyberattacks-against-iran.html.

59. David E. Sanger, *The Perfect Weapon: War, Sabotage, and Fear in the Cyber Age* (New York: Crown Books, 2018), 22.

being used at Natanz—and tested on the centrifuges that the United States had boosted from Libya earlier in the decade, since the Iranian centrifuges were the same Pakistani model. Israeli cooperation was also critical, particularly for planting the worm into the air-gapped Natanz facility. The Stuxnet bug destroyed the delicately calibrated centrifuges by varying the speed of rotation without showing corresponding fluctuations on the control interface. Unmonitored changes in speed caused the highly precise centrifuges to explode or tip over. Several thousand centrifuges were apparently destroyed by Stuxnet, and some estimate that it pushed the Iranian enrichment program back eighteen to twenty-four months as it was forced to disassemble cascades, clean debris, and manufacture and install replacement centrifuges.[60] Stuxnet did not stop Iran, but it likely bought time.

Meir Dagan, a former chief of the Mossad, described the challenge that Iran posed—a technically competent, smart, and potentially determined hider—and why repeated sabotage, rather than overt kinetic strikes that might accelerate Iran's nuclear pursuit, were an attractive option:

> "Bombing would be the stupidest thing we could do," Dagan told me. This was not like striking Iraq's Osiraq nuclear reactor in 1981 or Syria's reactor in 2007. He believed Iran's program was simply too sprawling: they were not about to repeat their neighbors' mistakes. So while an air attack on Iran's facilities "might make me feel good," Dagan said . . . it would provide an illusory solution. The satellite photographs, he said, would show Iran's facilities flattened, and everyone would cheer. But within months, he predicted, those facilities would be rebuilt so deep as to be impermeable to a second strike. . . . It was fine to try to slow down Iran's progress, said Dagan. But if Israel attempted to destroy the country's nuclear facilities in an overt attack, it would ensure a nuclear Iran.[61]

Against a hider like Iran, then, an attempted surgical strike might provoke the very outcome that the world is trying to avoid. An attractive strategy is therefore to try to slow its progress, while remaining below the threshold of escalation. This was the logic behind Olympic Games, which reportedly included cyberattacks, sabotaging the supply chain for critical parts required for Iran's missile and nuclear program (so-called "left of launch" efforts),[62]

60. Sanger, "Obama Order Sped Up Wave of Cyberattacks on Iran."

61. Sanger, *The Perfect Weapon*, 28.

62. David E. Sanger and William J. Broad, "U.S. Revives Secret Program to Sabotage Iranian Missiles and Rockets," *New York Times*, February 13, 2019, https://www.nytimes.com/2019/02/13/us/politics/iran-missile-launch-failures.html.

and suspected Israeli assassination of Iranian nuclear scientists to set back the program.[63] There are reports that the United States sabotaged the highly precise parts for centrifuges—such as vacuum pumps, motors, and rotors—and planted them in the front companies Iran used to source parts for its enrichment program.[64] It has similarly attempted to this with North Korea over the years as well.[65]

The goal of cyberattacks, sabotage, and assassinations is to delay progress, which creates more opportunities for non-kinetic efforts to stop a country's nuclear pursuit. Setting a program back by eighteen to twenty-four months, like the United States did to Iran's program with Stuxnet, buys eighteen to twenty-four more months for intelligence gathering and diplomacy. It also forces political leaders of the nuclear aspirant to hold together a domestic coalition (potentially a fragile one) for eighteen to twenty-four months longer. In short, delay tactics buy time in which external or internal events, either intentional or coincidental, can derail a nuclear program more definitively. Going forward, the "buying time" model may be the most frequent suite of options employed against hiders.

There are potential downsides of course. Hiders will learn, and the sabotage efforts will have to get increasingly sophisticated and penetrative as hiders go deeper underground, literally and figuratively. Some may backfire and actually harden a hider's resolve to accelerate its clandestine efforts. Some may create unintended collateral damage: Stuxnet, for example, crippled banks and hospitals around the world. Some may trigger escalation, particularly if they involve assassinations or are otherwise viewed as crossing a line of casus belli. However, given the likely infrequency of the Libya model and the low likelihood that a future hider will provide as ripe a target as al Kibar in Syria, the cat-and-mouse game of a "buying time" strategy is perhaps the most likely approach that the international community—especially the United States given its will and capability to sustain such covert programs—will have to take with hiders. In the Iranian case, it is possible that buying even a crucial couple of years in 2010 opened the door for one of the most

63. Josh Levs, "Who's Killing Iranian Nuclear Scientists?" CNN, January 11, 2012, https://www.cnn.com/2012/01/11/world/meast/iran-who-kills-scientists/index.html.

64. Mike Shuster, "Inside the United States' Secret Sabotage of Iran," National Public Radio (NPR), May 9, 2011, https://www.npr.org/2011/05/09/135854490/inside-the-united-states-secret-sabotage-of-iran.

65. David E. Sanger and William J. Broad, "U.S. Strategy to Hobble North Korea Was Hidden in Plain Sight," *New York Times*, March 4, 2017, https://www.nytimes.com/2017/03/04/world/asia/left-of-launch-missile-defense.html.

important nuclear reversals in contemporary proliferation history, pushing Iran back from a nuclear hider to a hard hedger. The case of nuclear reversal is what I turn to now, and how strategies of proliferation can help us understand it and provide a template for future reversals.

Reversing Hiding: Iran and the JCPOA

Iran is a crucial case where the typology and theory I lay out in this book provide some leverage on *nuclear reversal*. For decades beginning in the mid-1980s, Iran was a nuclear hider, with an active clandestine nuclear weapons program, officially known as the AMAD Plan. Although formally halted in 2003, Iran's clandestine enrichment activity and potential work on "filling the gaps" in its nuclear weapons program—including work on neutron initiation, potential implosion simulations, and maintaining an enrichment capability to produce weapons-grade uranium if necessary—continued at least until 2009, and the technology and knowledge base persists.[66] Based on later IAEA assessments on the possible military dimensions of the Iranian nuclear program, Iran made much more progress before 2003 than the United States knew. After 2003, external pressure such as crippling economic sanctions and the growing threat of military action by the United States, Israel, or both eventually brought relatively more moderate politicians—such as President Hassan Rouhani—to power and began to fracture Iran's domestic consensus for active weaponization. The Obama administration exploited these internal changes to ink a historic agreement with Iran, the Joint Comprehensive Plan of Action (JCPOA). This multilateral agreement offered sanctions relief in exchange for limits on the technical capabilities of Iran's nuclear program and allowed for unprecedented IAEA access to monitor and verify those limits.

The JCPOA reversed Iran's nuclear proliferation strategy from *hiding* to *hard hedging*, taking advantage of the elevation of Iranian moderates who were willing to accept limits on the nuclear program in exchange for an opportunity to reengage with the global economy and institute domestic reforms. The sequencing of domestic political changes was important: the

66. Board of Governors, International Atomic Energy Agency (IAEA), "Implementation of the NPT Safeguards Agreement and Relevant Provisions of Security Council Resolutions in the Islamic Republic of Iran," GOV/2011/65, November 8, 2011, Annex: Possible Military Dimensions to Iran's Nuclear Programme; Board of Governors, International Atomic Energy Agency (IAEA), "Final Assessment on Past and Present Outstanding Issues Regarding Iran's Nuclear Programme," GOV/2015/68, December 2, 2015.

negotiations that ultimately led to the JCPOA would have been dead on arrival without the elevation of moderates in the Iranian government in the 2013 presidential election but, at the same time, the success of Iranian moderates in selling the JCPOA at home was partly due to adroit diplomacy by the P5 + 1 negotiators, who offered inducements that further fractured the domestic coalition for active weaponization. The JCPOA did not attempt to fully eliminate Iran's possible intent to weaponize in the future—as my theory describes, this intent depends on Iran's external security environment and domestic politics. What it did instead was reduce Iran's *incentive* to actively pursue weapons, establish a mechanism to *detect* if it cheated, and created a vehicle—snap-back sanctions and the threat of military force looming in the background—to *punish* it severely if it did so. By exploiting and deepening fractures in Iran's domestic consensus for weaponization, the JCPOA pushed Iran back from hiding to hard hedging. The agreement shows how Proliferation Strategy Theory can help us understand and craft nuclear reversal. Short of eliminating the Iranian regime or nuclear program in what would surely be a costly and catastrophic war, the JCPOA represents the best-case scenario for nuclear reversal, as well as an enormous success in global nonproliferation policy.

The biggest threat to the success of the JCPOA proved to be not domestic politics in Iran but domestic politics in the United States. Egged on by congressional opponents of the agreement who believed that it did not go far enough in limiting Iran's missile activity or support for regional terrorism, President Trump withdrew from the JCPOA in 2018, though America's European partners, plus Russia and China, and Iran remained party to the agreement. Although Iran slowly nibbled away at the enrichment limits imposed by the JCPOA after Trump's withdrawal, it did not fully abrogate the JCPOA, hoping that a subsequent American administration may return to it.[67] But even if that is the case, future Iranian negotiators may seek protections or concessions to hedge against American unreliability, specifically the chance that a future president may again rip up the nuclear agreement—which is possible because the JCPOA is an executive agreement and not a Senate-ratified treaty. In the worst case, the Trump administration's withdrawal may succeed in slowly unraveling this historic success by reconsolidating Iranian domestic consensus in favor of nuclear weapons:

67. Kingston Reif, Thomas Countryman, and Daryl Kimball, "Iran Takes Another Step Away from Compliance with JCPOA," *Arms Control Association*, September 15, 2019, https://www.armscontrol.org/pressroom/2019-09/iran-takes-another-step-away-compliance-jcpoa-experts-available.

convincing Iran's leadership that the United States cannot be trusted and that it must therefore resume its clandestine nuclear program. The resumption of a suspected dedicated clandestine nuclear weapons program would at the very least trigger a dangerous cat-and-mouse game between Iran and the IAEA and Western intelligence services, and could set the United States on a collision course to a war with Iran. Nevertheless, pushing Iran from being an active hider to a hard hedger was a nonproliferation success and provides a template for nuclear reversal by leveraging the drivers of strategies of proliferation.

FROM HIDING TO HARD HEDGING

Although Iran's nuclear energy program dates back to an American-supported program during the Shah's regime, its active, clandestine, nuclear weapons program took shape in the 1980s under the Islamic Republic. The decade-long war with Iraq, which included Iraqi chemical weapons use against Iran, led Ayatollah Khomeini to revisit Iran's interest in nuclear technology. The program included a search for international assistance to complete the Bushehr nuclear reactor, gas centrifuge–based uranium enrichment technology from the AQ Khan network in 1987, and experiments on plutonium reprocessing.[68] Iran's clandestine nuclear weapons program was motivated by at least three potential adversaries: Iraq, Israel, and the United States.

Although suspicions continued to grow about Iran's hidden nuclear weapons program, there was significant uncertainty among Western intelligence agencies about how far along Iran was through the 1990s. Iran was a party to the NPT, but there was substantial concern that civilian infrastructure provided cover for certain weapons-related activities, while clandestine facilities spread across and underneath a sprawling geography might focus on enrichment or reprocessing in violation of Iran's NPT obligations.[69] In 1992, the United States became alarmed at Iran's "suspicious procurement pattern" and suspected "Iran of having a similar clandestine nuclear weapons program but so far has produced 'no smoking gun.'"[70] The CIA director

68. See Gary Samore, ed., *Iran's Strategic Weapons Systems: A Net Assessment* (London: IISS, 2005), 12.

69. Richelson, *Spying on the Bomb*, 503–5.

70. Steve Coll, "U.S. Halted Nuclear Bid by Iran," *Washington Post*, November 17, 1992, https://www.washingtonpost.com/archive/politics/1992/11/17/us-halted-nuclear-bid-by-iran/0e215f24-43b2-4791-b24a-ea23b46b5a28/.

at the time, Robert Gates, testified to Congress that "Iran was seeking a nuclear bomb and could have one by 2000."[71] The United States intelligence community must have had some suspicion of the AQ Khan contacts that transferred centrifuge technology, and possibly weapons designs, to Iran. Its overall picture and penetration of the Iranian program, however, were poor. Suspicions persisted and Iranian contacts with Russian nuclear scientists, in particular, sparked alarm, though much of the intelligence seemed nonspecific. In January 1995, senior American and Israeli officials told the *New York Times* that "Iran is much closer to producing nuclear weapons than previously thought, and could be less than five years away from having an atomic bomb."[72] Much of this was based on observed procurement effort, however: "If the Iranians maintain this intensive effort to get everything they need, they could have all their components in two years. Then it will be just a matter of technology and research. If Iran is not interrupted in this program by some foreign power, it will have the device in more or less five years."[73] But there was still no smoking gun, even by 1999, as Iran's efforts to hide its most sensitive weapons-related activity were relatively successful.[74]

By 2003, however, American intelligence believed it had discovered a smoking gun with the apparent assistance of an Iranian dissident group. First, they found suspicious activity at a facility known as Natanz, whose true purpose was suspected to be related to enrichment, and second, activity at a complex related to heavy water production at Arak, along with a reactor for a potential plutonium pathway. The CIA stated: "The United States remains convinced that Tehran has been pursuing a clandestine nuclear weapons program, in violation of its obligations as a party to the Nuclear Nonproliferation Treaty (NPT)."[75] Although suspicions about Natanz had lingered for some time, Arak was a surprise and had not been, writes Richelson, "flagged as being nuclear related because from above it looked like a common factory."[76] Iran's ability to hide the true purpose of Arak and also bury and harden facilities at Natanz set off alarm bells, as it had in Iraq—what else was Iran hiding, and how far along was it? Finally confronted,

71. Ibid.

72. Chris Hedges, "Iran May Be Able to Build an Atomic Bomb in 5 Years, U.S. and Israeli Officials Fear," *New York Times*, January 5, 1995, p. A10, https://www.nytimes.com/1995/01/05/world/iran-may-be-able-build-atomic-bomb-5-years-us-israeli-officials-fear.html.

73. Ibid.

74. Richelson, *Spying on the Bomb*, 510.

75. Quoted in ibid., 511–12.

76. Ibid., 512.

Iran admitted to a hidden enrichment facility at Natanz and the heavy water production activity at Arak but would continue to claim that they were solely for peaceful purposes.[77]

After the discovery of Natanz and Arak, Iran sought a nuclear "grand bargain" with the United States as American forces sat parked in neighboring Iraq and Afghanistan, poised to—Tehran might have feared—turn toward Iran if those wars were won quickly (they were not).[78] For the next three years the United States and its European partners pressured Iran to come clean on its nuclear program, while the United States attempted to construct a better picture of Iran's past and present nuclear activities by attempting to inspect Natanz and other facilities such as Parchin through the IAEA, with whom Iran continued to be evasive.[79] Although a 2005 American National Intelligence Estimate assessed "with high confidence that Iran currently is determined to develop nuclear weapons," a crucial 2007 U.S. National Intelligence Assessment judged with "high confidence that in fall 2003, Tehran halted its nuclear weapons program," though it also assessed "with moderate-to-high confidence that Tehran at a minimum is keeping the option open to develop nuclear weapons."[80] Two things are noteworthy in this language. First, Iran "halted" but did not "terminate" its nuclear weapons program in 2003 according to the 2007 NIE and second, it maintained the technical basis to keep the option open in some form of hedge but "had not restarted its nuclear weapons program as of mid-2007."[81]

This was not entirely true. In 2009, despite overtures from newly elected president Obama, Iran was still hiding enrichment facilities and may have been continuing to engage in some weapons-related activity under the leadership of the hard-line president Mahmoud Ahmadinejad—who declared in 2006 that America "cannot do a damned thing" to stop Iran's nuclear program.[82] Indeed, Iran then admitted the existence of a new, previously concealed gas centrifuge enrichment facility at Fordow that had been under construction since 2006. Iran told the IAEA—belatedly according to the IAEA—that it intended to operate almost 3,000 centrifuges at Fordow

77. Ibid., 513. Also see Board of Governors, International Atomic Energy Agency (IAEA), "Implementation of the NPT Safeguards Agreement in the Islamic Republic of Iran," GOV/2003/40, June 6, 2003.

78. See Miller, *Stopping the Bomb*, 231.

79. Ibid., 232–33.

80. National Intelligence Council, "Iran: Nuclear Intentions and Capabilities," National Intelligence Estimate, November 2007.

81. Ibid.

82. Miller, *Stopping the Bomb*, 233.

arrayed in 16 cascades, enough to potentially enrich uranium for a couple of bombs a year.[83] Fordow was built to hide and survive—buried deep underground and reinforced. Only the United States possesses large enough conventional weapons capable of potentially destroying it, and even then it may require multiple direct hits and significant redundancy. If Israel possessed the capability to unilaterally destroy Fordow, it might have attempted to do so despite tremendous pressure from both Presidents Bush and Obama to refrain from unilateral military strikes against Iran.[84] Iran misleadingly claimed that it was under no obligation to report Fordow until six months prior to nuclear material being introduced to the facility, but in 2003 it had actually agreed to notify the IAEA of any construction of such facilities—which it had failed to do, further stoking suspicions about the scope of Iran's clandestine activity.[85] Although one can litigate whether Fordow was part of an active weaponization decision at this time, it was clearly part of an ongoing effort to hide enrichment and reprocessing facilities that could be used for a weapons program.

The discovery of Fordow triggered great consternation within the Obama administration. A front-page story in the *New York Times* reported: "After reviewing new documents that have leaked out of Iran and debriefing defectors lured to the West, Mr. Obama's advisers say they believe the work on weapons design is continuing on a smaller scale—the same assessment reached by Britain, France, Germany and Israel."[86] A month later, Iran announced that it was enriching uranium up to 20 percent levels at Natanz—a hop, skip, and a jump away from weapons grade given the nature of enrichment curves (see figure 3.2).[87] Ahmadinejad reiterated his taunt that Iran would continue its nuclear work and could not be stopped.[88] The United States and Israel certainly tried, however, attempting to assassinate Iranian nuclear scientists[89] and unleashing the specifically tailored Stuxnet

83. See Wyn Q. Bowen and Jonathan Brewer, "Iran's Nuclear Challenge: Nine Years and Counting," *International Affairs* 87, no. 4 (2011): 927.

84. See Pauly, "Stop or I'll Shoot," chap. 6.

85. Ibid., 928.

86. David Sanger and William Broad, "U.S. Sees an Opportunity to Press Iran on Nuclear Fuel," *New York Times*, January 2, 2010, p. A1, https://www.nytimes.com/2010/01/03/world/middleeast/03iran.html.

87. Bowen and Brewer, "Iran's Nuclear Challenge: Nine Years and Counting," 926.

88. "Ahmadinejad: Iran Is Now a 'Nuclear State,'" Associated Press, February 11, 2010, http://www.nbcnews.com/id/35343465/ns/world_news-mideast_n_africa/t/ahmadinejad-iran-now-nuclear-state/.

89. Levs, "Who's Killing Iranian Nuclear Scientists."

cyberweapon to destroy centrifuges at Natanz.[90] As noted above, Israel has had a long-standing strategy of inducing delay, buying time, wherever it can in the region—whether Iraq, Syria, or Iran—based on the theory that inducing a series of delays in an adversary's nuclear program can buy time for events like regime changes to intervene and trigger reversal or outright abandonment. The United States was now a fully invested partner in attempting to sabotage Iran's nuclear efforts. Nevertheless, these were mostly delay tactics, designed to make life more difficult for Iran because, while these efforts might slow Iran down, they could not fully stop a determined state with indigenous design and production capability from weaponizing. But these delays, as noted earlier, may have bought crucial time to open the diplomatic window. Iran's continued enrichment activities triggered even tighter United Nations sanctions by the P5 + 1 (the United States, United Kingdom, France, Russia, China, and Germany), getting even Russia and China on board. These began to have a crippling effect on Iran's economy, but elements of the nuclear program still persisted.

In November 2011, in a routine quarterly safeguard compliance report, the IAEA released a bombshell annex on which it had been working for years with member states, innocuously titled "Possible Military Dimensions to Iran's Nuclear Programme," colloquially known as the PMD.[91] It was a comprehensive and stunning account of how far Iran's hidden nuclear program had actually progressed through at least 2003, and possibly beyond. It details the extent of uranium enrichment and reactor technology it had procured since the 1980s and that "Iran had used undeclared nuclear material for testing and experimentation in several uranium conversion, enrichment, fabrication, and irradiation activities, including the separation of plutonium, at undeclared locations and facilities" for decades.[92] The PMD Annex describes the extensive organization and coordination of a state-directed nuclear weapons program, called the AMAD Plan. Procurement activities included "high speed electronic switches and spark gaps (useful for triggering and firing detonators); high speed cameras (useful in experimental diagnostics); neutron sources (useful for calibrating neutron measuring equipment)," and so on.[93] Iran had sought "a source of uranium suitable for use in an undisclosed enrichment programme, the product of which would be converted

90. Kim Zetter, *Countdown to Zero: Stuxnet and the Launch of the World's First Digital Weapon* (New York: Crown, 2014).

91. IAEA, GOV/2011/65.

92. Ibid., Annex, 1.

93. Ibid., Annex, 6.

into metal for use in the new warhead which was the subject of the missile re-entry vehicle studies."[94] It had received centrifuge assistance and "nuclear explosive design information . . . more advanced design information than the information identified in 2004 as having been provided to Libya" by members of the AQ Khan network.[95] Furthermore, it had received "information on the design concept of a multipoint initiation system that can be used to initiate effectively and simultaneously a high explosive charge over its surface."[96] Iran had further "manufactured simulated nuclear explosive components using . . . tungsten."[97] It had built a large explosive containment vessel for hydrodynamic tests at Parchin. It had also worked on a neutron initiator to kick off the nuclear explosion, and the IAEA was not convinced this work terminated in 2003.[98]

What does all this mean? Translating IAEA-speak into English: Iran had received the blueprints and design information for advanced centrifuges and was manufacturing them. It had received blueprints and design information for an advanced and compact missile-mateable uranium implosion warhead and had not only improved them but likely conducted cold tests using tungsten that would leave no trace of radioactive material. This was not Iraq's jury-rigged nuclear weapons program of the 1980s. This was a full-fledged clandestine nuclear weapons program that was organized and capable, one that was stunningly advanced and sophisticated—far more than the United States or any nation outside Iran fully appreciated by 2003. Iran had learned how to hide and obfuscate and bury its "smoking guns."

So what happened in 2003? The PMD Annex reports:

> Owing to growing concerns about the international security situation in Iraq and neighboring countries at that time, work on the AMAD Plan was stopped rather abruptly pursuant to a "halt order" instruction issued late in 2003 by senior Iranian officials. According to that information, however, staff remained in place to record and document the achievements of their respective projects . . . some activities previously carried out under the AMAD Plan were resumed later. . . . The agency is concerned because some of the activities undertaken after 2003 would be highly relevant to a nuclear weapons programme.[99]

94. Ibid., Annex, 7.
95. Ibid., Annex, 8.
96. Ibid., Annex, 8–9.
97. Ibid., Annex, 9.
98. Ibid., Annex, 11.
99. Ibid., Annex, 6.

Consistent with the 2007 NIE, the IAEA judged that Iran "halted," but did not fully terminate, its hidden nuclear weapons program in 2003, likely due to fears of an American attack should it defeat Iraq and Afghanistan quickly. After all, Iran was labeled as part of Bush's "Axis of Evil" and was a prime sponsor of terrorism against the United States, particularly since the 1979 Islamic Revolution. The "halt order" importantly included sanitizing the program and disbanding as much as possible to cover its traces. The PMD Annex reports that "subsequently, equipment and work places were either cleaned or disposed of so that there would be little to identify the sensitive nature of the work which had been undertaken."[100]

The IAEA was also aware of activity that continued after 2003—at Fordow and Parchin, for example, along with work on neutron initiation, detonators, modeling implosion—as well as efforts to retain the documentation and tacit knowledge to reconstitute the program if necessary in the so-called "nuclear archive," which was partially recovered by Israel in a 2018 covert operation.[101] In a 2015 final update to the PMD report, the IAEA notes that "extensive activities undertaken by Iran since February 2012 at [Parchin] seriously undermined the Agency's ability to conduct effective verification" and that Iran "conducted computer modelling of a nuclear explosive device prior to 2004 and between 2005 and 2009."[102] But it concludes—whether plausibly or implausibly—that its overall assessment "is that a range of activities relevant to the development of a nuclear explosive device were conducted in Iran prior to the end of 2003 as a coordinated effort, and some activities took place after 2003 . . . [but] these activities did not advance beyond feasibility and scientific studies, and the acquisition of certain relevant technical competences and capabilities. The Agency has no credible indications of activities in Iran relevant to the development of a nuclear explosive device after 2009."[103]

Independent examination of Iran's "nuclear archive" revealed some interesting tidbits, most notably that the AMAD Plan intended to—at first at least—produce five nuclear weapons and conduct a test.[104] It also adds some

100. Ibid.

101. See IAEA, GOV/2015/68.

102. Ibid., 14.

103. Ibid.

104. See Aaron Arnold, Matthew Bunn, Caitlin Chase, Steven E. Miller, Rolf Mowatt-Larssen, and William H. Toby, *The Iran Nuclear Archive: Impressions and Implications* (Cambridge, MA: Belfer Center for Science and International Affairs, Harvard Kennedy School, April 2019), 4, https://www.belfercenter.org/sites/default/files/files/publication/The%20Iran%20Nuclear%20Archive_0.pdf.

color to the IAEA report to the "halt order," which even the IAEA notes did not stop all work on the nuclear program through 2009. The Harvard Belfer Center team that examined portions of the archive notes that it suggests that "when the decision was taken to stop work on large identifiable facilities, in a series of meetings, the program's leaders decided to continue research to fill in some technical gaps they still believed needed work. They divided these continuing efforts into two parts—efforts that would be conducted openly under civilian rationales [such as neutron work] and other efforts that would be carried out covertly, because they had no plausible civilian rationale," such as presumably computer modeling of nuclear implosion.[105] There is no evidence Iran conducted any of this work after 2009, though it is impossible to prove the negative—since theoretical and small-scale work can be conducted entirely clandestinely.

Consistent with the IAEA PMD Annex, the picture that emerges from the archive is that Iran was poised to develop nuclear weapons in 2003, and was just missing weapons-grade uranium, as Natanz was not yet operational. At the same time, the U.S. invasion of neighboring Iraq heightened Iranian fears of a preventive strike against their nuclear program, or worse, an invasion of Iran that used the yet-unfinished AMAD Plan as pretext. Indeed, Iran was in the middle of the window of volatility at this point: it had an active nuclear weapons program that was enough pretext for Washington to attack it, but it did not have the nuclear weapons to deter it. The program was officially disbanded, but theoretical and experimental work that could be done in secret likely—and it should be assumed—did continue, so that Iran could maintain an ability to revive the program quickly if necessary. If Iran was hiding before 2003, increasingly acute concerns about military prevention led it to adopt a super-hiding strategy from 2003 forward, intentionally halting any major detectable activity and slowing any work to a snail's pace. This was an incredibly successful clandestine nuclear weapons program. It was in clear violation of Iran's NPT obligations—the IAEA and the world had suspicions but were unaware of the scale, scope, and sophistication of Iran's activities even in an era where national intelligence capabilities were highly penetrative. Indeed, it often took tips from dissident groups or defectors to confirm intelligence about Iran's activities (or launder it) to the United States and its partners.

So how did Iran avoid the fate of Iraq, at least so far? In 2013 with the election of the moderate president Hassan Rouhani—facilitated in large part

105. Ibid., 5.

by the crippling effect sanctions were having on an Iranian economy that contracted 6.6 percent in 2012—Iran signaled that it was willing to reverse its nuclear program in exchange for comprehensive sanctions relief from the P5 + 1.[106] As President Obama would later say: "Sanctions alone could not stop Iran's nuclear program. But they did help bring Iran to the negotiating table."[107] Colin Kahl, Vice President Biden's national security advisor and an official intimately involved with the construction of the JCPOA, says that "Rouhani's election provided a window of opportunity after Ahmadinejad to test if the moderates were serious about limiting the nuclear program."[108] Very quickly after Rouhani's election, the United States began back-channel diplomacy with Iran in Oman, but the extent of Iran's previous clandestine activity posed a challenge to any deal. Iran did not fully come clean and cannot, and will not, likely admit to how far it had gone while under IAEA safeguards and as a member of the NPT. Iran's account of its previous secret activity as documented in the 2011 and 2015 PMD was largely obfuscation and understatement—a fiction to enable diplomacy without forcing Iran to admit it was lying to the IAEA, and to partially allow the IAEA and member states to save face as well.[109] However, as Secretary of State John Kerry would later explain, the deal was enabled by moving on: "We're not fixated on Iran specifically accounting for what they did at one point in time or another. We know what they did. We have no doubt. We have absolute knowledge with respect to the certain military activities they were engaged in. What we're concerned about is going forward. It's critical to us to know that going forward, those activities have been stopped, and that we can account for that in a legitimate way."[110]

An interim deal, the Joint Plan of Action (JPOA), was quickly reached in November 2013 that capped Iranian uranium enrichment at 5 percent, downblended the 20 percent enriched uranium, capped its total stockpile of

106. See Miller, *Stopping the Bomb*, 237.

107. President Barack Obama, "Statement by the President on the Framework to Prevent Iran from Acquiring a Nuclear Weapon," The White House, Office of the Press Secretary, April 2, 2015, https://obamawhitehouse.archives.gov/the-press-office/2015/04/02/statement-president-framework-prevent-iran-obtaining-nuclear-weapon.

108. Colin Kahl, interview by the author, July 22, 2020.

109. See Austin Carson, *Secret Wars: Covert Conflict in International Politics* (Princeton: Princeton University Press, 2018).

110. Secretary of State John Kerry quoted in Louis Charbonneau, "U.S. 'Not Fixated' on Iran Answering Queries on Atomic Work," Reuters, June 16, 2015, https://www.reuters.com/article/iran-nuclear-usa/u-s-not-fixated-on-iran-answering-queries-on-atomic-work-kerry-idINKBN0OW2CE20150616.

low enriched uranium to 300 kilograms, and limited the number of operational centrifuges in exchange for almost $7 billion in sanctions relief.[111] This would form the basis for the 2015 JCPOA, which further capped Iranian enrichment at 3.67 percent, further decreased its total uranium stockpile, resulted in the uninstalling of nearly two-thirds of its centrifuges, including all advanced centrifuges, and eliminated all uranium enrichment at Fordow (which was restricted to the production of medical isotopes). It also shut off the plutonium pathway by proposing to redesign the Arak reactor core, shipping out the spent fuel for the life of the reactor, and prohibiting any reprocessing. In exchange, Iran received comprehensive P5 + 1 sanctions relief.[112] Critically, Iran accepted unprecedented and exceptionally stringent IAEA monitoring and verification provisions, including a fourteen-day deadline on a demand to inspect any facility the IAEA issued. This detection and monitoring architecture was backed by a credible snapback capability that would enable the P5 + 1 to quickly and severely punish Iran through the UN Security Council if it violated the terms of the JCPOA.[113] The agreement would have various sunsets, lasting out to fifteen years on enrichment limits and up to twenty-five years on mining and milling.[114]

The idea behind the JCPOA was to close off the plutonium pathway entirely and cap enrichment capability to extend out Iran's so-called breakout time—the time it would take to enrich enough weapons-grade uranium for a single bomb—from several months to one year. The notion of "breakout time" is admittedly odd given that a state can do little with a single bomb, but it is useful as a standardized metric for how far a state is from a nuclear weapons capability. To extend "breakout time," the JCPOA put caps on Iran's uranium stockpile, the number of centrifuges it could operate, and the level of enrichment it could achieve on those centrifuges, while imposing a monitoring and verification mechanism that ensured compliance. Kahl notes that "President Obama often said that you cannot get Iran to 'zero' so long as they have competent scientists and the ability to design and manufacture centrifuges. But you can push them farther away from a bomb, and a year was not only a good round number, but provided the time necessary

111. Ibid., 237–38.

112. Ibid., 238. Also see "Text of the Joint Comprehensive Plan of Action," July 14, 2015, https://2009-2017.state.gov/e/eb/tfs/spi/iran/jcpoa/index.htm.

113. Also see the role of "coercive assurances" in Pauly, "Stop or I'll Shoot," chaps. 5 and 6.

114. See Kelsey Davenport, "The Joint Comprehensive Plan of Action at a Glance," Arms Control Association Fact Sheet, May 2018, https://www.armscontrol.org/factsheets/JCPOA-at-a-glance.

to detect any suspicious activity—with a built-in buffer—and then act if necessary diplomatically, all of which takes time."[115] As President Obama described it in his Rose Garden statement: "International inspectors will have unprecedented access not only to Iranian nuclear facilities, but to the entire supply chain that supports Iran's nuclear program—from uranium mills that provide the raw materials, to the centrifuge production and storage facilities that support the program. If Iran cheats, the world will know it. If we see something suspicious, we will inspect it."[116]

The JCPOA was the mechanism that pushed Iran from hiding to what I classify as hard hedging: Iran maintains the technical capability and organizational capacity to develop nuclear weapons if it chooses to do so, and still faces an acute threat from the United States. But crucially, the JCPOA took advantage of a fractured domestic political consensus for active weaponization and hiding by offering a package to further strengthen the domestic political position of *moderates* in Iran who valued economic growth and reform over nuclear weapons, provided there was some implicit assurance that the United States would not attack it.[117] President Obama outlined this theory explicitly in explaining the motivation for the deal, while noting that even if the moderates were not empowered in the long term, the deal was still better than no deal:

> I think there are hard-liners inside of Iran that think it is the right thing to do to oppose us, to seek to destroy Israel, to cause havoc in places like Syria or Yemen or Lebanon. And then I think there are others inside Iran who think that this is counterproductive. And it is possible that if we sign this nuclear deal, we strengthen the hand of those more moderate forces inside of Iran. But . . . the deal is not dependent on anticipating those changes. If they don't change at all, we're still better off having the deal.[118]

115. Kahl, interview.

116. Obama, "Statement by the President on the Framework to Prevent Iran from Acquiring a Nuclear Weapon."

117. See Ariane Tabatabai, "Negotiating the 'Iran Talks' in Tehran: The Iranian Drivers That Shaped the Joint Comprehensive Plan of Action," *Nonproliferation Review* 24, no. 3–4 (2017): 225–42; and Ariane Tabatabai, "Nuclear Decisionmaking in Iran: Implications for U.S. Nonproliferation Efforts" (Columbia University, Center on Global Energy Policy, August 2020), 22–29, https://www.energypolicy.columbia.edu/sites/default/files/file-uploads/IranNuclear_CGEP-Report_080520.pdf.

118. President Barack Obama, "Transcript: President Obama's Full NPR Interview on Iran Nuclear Deal," National Public Radio, April 7, 2015, https://www.npr.org/2015/04/07/397933577/transcript-president-obamas-full-npr-interview-on-iran-nuclear-deal.

Richard Nephew, a key State Department official involved with the deal, similarly writes that one of the key theories undergirding the JCPOA was to "enable more conciliatory elements to have greater influence on government policy. The logic of this strategy flows from the conviction that people do not prefer to be repressed and will test the limits of their repression to the extent possible. Greater financial resources and enhanced access to the outside world will enable such forces as exist in Iran to win power and influence in the country's complicated politics. . . . And the administration is hoping that, from a position of greater comfort and security, Iran will be induced to take a more constructive approach to regional politics."[119] Although the JCPOA was criticized for not addressing Iran's ballistic missile or terrorist activities and for having sunset provisions, one rationale driving the initiative was to try to empower Iranian moderates—fracturing previous hard-line consensus for nuclear weapons[120]—so that Iran would not only choose to refrain from pursuing a hidden nuclear weapons program but also integrate with the world economically and reform within so that its nefarious activities would ultimately cease anyway out of choice, not coercion. This is one reason the United States could not insist on "zero enrichment" or elimination of Iran's ballistic missiles—it would not be accepted by Rouhani and Zarif, who still had to save face, and such demands would only embolden the hard-liners. The JCPOA did not fully eliminate Iran's intent or capability to develop nuclear weapons. What it attempted to do was to disincentivize moderates to *act* on that intent, and establish a mechanism to detect if Iran was cheating and a method to punish it severely if it did so. If it managed to permanently fracture domestic consensus for a clandestine nuclear program, great. If it did not, it was still an important deal that pushed Iran back in the proliferation process.

In the framework of strategies of proliferation, the JCPOA is a rare and herculean feat. It is a critical example of how strategies of proliferation can provide a blueprint for nuclear reversal. The bulk of this book has focused on states going down the proliferation strategy tree. But each variable can change and allow for *reversals* as well—at least before an active weaponizer attains a nuclear weapons capability, after which it is highly unlikely to surrender its weapons. In the Iranian case, Proliferation Strategy Theory offers unique insight into the key variable that underpinned the rationale of the

119. Richard Nephew, "What the Nuclear Deal Means for Moderates in Iranian Politics," *Markaz*, Brookings Institution, February 16, 2016, https://www.brookings.edu/blog/markaz/2016/02/16/what-the-nuclear-deal-means-for-moderates-in-iranian-politics/.

120. See Tabatabai, "Nuclear Decisionmaking in Iran," 26–28.

JCPOA: fracturing domestic consensus within Iran for nuclear weapons by offering incentives that empower moderates to voluntarily accept verifiable limits on the program. There is no doubt that sanctions were a powerful tool to manipulate these incentives, but belying realist-inspired predictions about proliferation, such as that of Debs and Monteiro, there was no change in Iran's security situation in 2009 or 2013 when it opted to reverse from hiding to hard hedging. Indeed, after a decade of war in Iraq and Afghanistan, Iran was in a relatively stronger position vis-à-vis the United States in 2013 than it was in 2003. But sanctions allowed the international community to fracture Iran's domestic consensus for a nuclear weapon and induce nuclear reversal, for now.[121]

This theory also gives important insight into the conditions under which Iran might resume its clandestine nuclear program. On May 8, 2018, President Trump announced the American withdrawal from the JCPOA, calling it "defective at its core" because it did not attenuate Iran's missile developments or destabilizing regional activity and allowed Iran to retain some enrichment capability—which is legally allowed under its NPT and IAEA obligations.[122] Nowhere did he say that Iran was violating the terms of the JCPOA—because it was not. The IAEA had not found any violations prior to the American withdrawal. Furthermore, members of the Trump administration concurred, with Secretary of Defense Mattis testifying that Iran was "fundamentally in compliance" with the deal months prior to American withdrawal,[123] and Dan Coats, Director of National Intelligence, confirming that Iran was still in compliance with its JCPOA obligations as late as January 2019.[124] In 2019, however, Iran began taking a series of reversible steps to nibble away at its JCPOA caps by reactivating centrifuges at Fordow, increasing its stockpile of enriched uranium, and enriching beyond 3.67 percent.[125] Iranian foreign minister Javed

121. See Miller, *Stopping the Bomb*, chap. 9.

122. President Donald Trump, "Remarks by President Trump on the Joint Comprehensive Plan of Action," White House, Office of the Press Secretary, May 8, 2018, https://trumpwhitehouse.archives.gov/briefings-statements/remarks-president-trump-joint-comprehensive-plan-action/.

123. "Mattis Says Iran 'Fundamentally' in Compliance with Iran Deal," Reuters, October 3, 2017, https://www.reuters.com/article/us-usa-iran-nuclear/mattis-says-iran-fundamentally-in-compliance-with-nuclear-deal-idUSKCN1C82GK.

124. Daniel R. Coats, "Worldwide Threat Assessment of the US Intelligence Community," Statement for the Record, Senate Select Committee on Intelligence, January 29, 2019, p. 10, https://www.dni.gov/files/ODNI/documents/2019-ATA-SFR---SSCI.pdf.

125. Laurence Norman and Michael R. Gordon, "Iran's Stockpile of Enriched Uranium Has Jumped, U.N. Atomic Agency Says," *Wall Street Journal*, March 3, 2020, https://www.wsj.com/articles/irans-stockpile-of-enriched-uranium-has-jumped-u-n-atomic-agency-says-11583243861. Also see Board of Governors, "Verification and Monitoring in the Islamic Republic of Iran in Light

Zarif made it clear that these were all reversible, and aimed at pressuring the United States to return to the JCPOA.[126] The American assassination of Quds force head Major General Qassem Soleimani in January 2020 and the presumed Israeli assassination of Iran's most senior nuclear scientist, Mohsin Fakhrizadeh, in November 2020, coupled with a series of unexplained—but obviously suspicious—explosions at facilities including Natanz through 2020, potentially hardened Iranian consensus against the United States. Moderates may have a difficult time in the future defending themselves against hard-liners who claimed the Great Satan could never be trusted.

It remains to be seen whether the post-Trump United States returns to something akin to the JCPOA, which, given the crumbling state of the Iranian economy, Iran may be open to as well. The technical conditions are more difficult, though. Since the Trump administration withdrew from the JCPOA, Iran's "breakout" time had compressed from one year in January 2019 to less than two months when he departed office in January 2021, though the critical variable—domestic consensus to resume an active clandestine nuclear weapons program—does not yet seem to have congealed so long as moderates such as Rouhani and Zarif remain in power.[127] But Iran may demand some insurance against a future U.S. administration that similarly withdraws from the agreement. It remains to be seen if the historic reversal success of the JCPOA can be fully recovered given the approach of the Trump administration and changes in Iran's domestic political configuration following the June 2021 presidential elections.

Conclusion

This chapter has attempted to outline how the strategies of proliferation typology and Proliferation Strategy Theory *matter* for the politics and policy of nuclear proliferation and nonproliferation, and how they can help illuminate and manage the new and emerging nuclear landscape. It has identified how to slow or reverse proliferators depending on the strategies they adopt, arguing that nonproliferation and counterproliferation efforts should pay

---

of United Nations Security Council Resolution 2231 (2015)," IAEA, GOV/2020/26, June 5, 2020, https://www.iaea.org/sites/default/files/20/06/gov2020-26.pdf.

126. See Foreign Minister Javed Zarif, Twitter, January 5, 2020, https://twitter.com/JZarif/status/1213900666164432900.

127. David Albright and Sarah Burkhard, "Iranian Breakout Estimates and Enriched Uranium Stocks," *Institute for Science and International Security*, April 21, 2020, https://isis-online.org/isis-reports/detail/iranian-breakout-estimates-and-enriched-uranium-stocks.

close attention to hard hedgers and especially hiders, since they are invariably destabilizing to international security.

Hedgers face multiple obstacles to active pursuit. Most importantly, perhaps, fractured domestic political consensus is the last hurdle a state has to overcome before it can embark on an active weaponization program. This is a variable that existing theories of proliferation and nuclear politics neglect but has historically been powerful in inducing delay or outright abandonment in nuclear weaponization. The time to stop proliferators is before they commence an active weaponization strategy. Active proliferators select into weaponization pathways that they believe will optimize their chances for success, making them the hardest cases to stop. Sprinters and sheltered pursuers select these strategies when they are available and they are very difficult to stop—sprinters because they are essentially immune from prevention and sheltered pursuers because they are externally immunized from prevention. Many of the major powers who can select sprinting have already done so, leaving only a small remaining pool of potential sprinters, such as Australia and perhaps Germany and Japan. Sheltered pursuit depends on the willingness of a major power to shield a proliferator due to higher geopolitical priorities. The conditions that have enabled sheltered pursuit strategies in the past persist to this day, particularly in states such as Saudi Arabia and Turkey. Stopping a sheltered pursuer would largely depend on the shelterer opting to remove the shield before the proliferator attains the bomb.

The most dynamic strategy of proliferation remaining—both due to sequencing and because of the global export control, nonproliferation, and sanctions regimes—is hiding. The pool of potential proliferators consists overwhelmingly of the states in the international system that the major powers least want to possess nuclear weapons—otherwise sheltered pursuit might be an option. Most will have little option but to attempt to seek nuclear weapons clandestinely. A state that attempts to hide a nuclear weapons program has already priced in the threat of sanctions or the use of force but persists anyway. It is likely to disrupt the international system in one of two ways. If it succeeds, a state of concern has joined the nuclear weapons club. If it fails, it likely means that the hider was caught and had to be coerced—either economically or militarily—to terminate its illicit and clandestine program, sometimes violently.

This chapter has identified several options to address hiders, all of which exploit the fact that hiding introduces inefficiencies in a state's nuclear program, thereby buying time for external powers to detect and stop it. Once detected, and depending on how far along the program is and its configuration (e.g., overground reactor versus sprawling underground clandestine enrichment facilities), options short of war range from inducing abandonment as in Libya, surgical strikes as in Syria, or simply trying to buy time through covert sabotage as in some periods in Iran and North Korea. There is no escaping the reality that each of these counterproliferation strategies depends on some lucky breaks, but the inefficiency of hiding a nuclear program widens the window of opportunity for the hider to slip up or for intelligence agencies to detect the program. Simply put, time is the most valuable commodity to detect and stop hiders, who are forced to pace their programs in ways to avoid getting caught. Extended timelines make hiders vulnerable by increasing the likelihood of mistakes and giving external powers more opportunities to discover the hidden program.

This chapter has also highlighted the important case of nuclear reversal: pushing Iran back from hiding to hard hedging. The JCPOA pushed Iran further away from a nuclear weapons capability by giving the moderates in power leverage against proponents of nuclear weapons in Tehran, thereby fracturing domestic consensus for the bomb. This logic of the JCPOA is predicted by Proliferation Strategy Theory and shows that these categories matter—they can provide a template and a pathway to not only stop states but also reverse them. It remains to be seen whether the United States can sustain the nonproliferation success that it achieved with the stunning reversal of Iran's nuclear program. Reversal is important because it helps regulate a potential nuclear aspirant's *intent* to weaponize and its ability to act on it. Reversal is, however, unfortunately rare and, as the roller-coaster ride of the JCPOA suggests, difficult to sustain. Absent reversal mechanisms, then, the world must attempt to indefinitely monitor, retard, and halt hiders, a process that—as the 2003 Iraq war demonstrates—rarely ends well.

8

Conclusion

This book has developed the first rigorous analysis of strategies of nuclear proliferation. It makes three important contributions. It shows that there are in fact distinct strategies of proliferation, that a parsimonious strategic logic—generalizable across regime types, historical periods, and regions of the world—determines which strategy a nuclear aspirant will adopt, and that the variation among the strategies matters to the nuclear landscape and to international politics and conflict.

First, the book identifies a *variety* of strategies of nuclear proliferation. Not all states seek a nuclear weapon as quickly as possible or undertake open marches to nuclear weapons, as the existing literature overwhelmingly assumes. Some states seek only a bomb option, hedging on whether they will seek a nuclear weapons capability in the future. And even among hedgers, substantial, important variation exists. Some hedge because they simply have an underlying technical capacity that may one day be suitable for nuclear weapons, others hedge because they have emplaced themselves under extended nuclear deterrence umbrellas and must prepare for potential abandonment or the day that their security environment demands an independent nuclear capability, while yet others hedge because of domestic political ambivalence: despite external security threats they cannot decide whether they require, and can sustain, a nuclear weapons program. Hedging is an important strategy of proliferation, one likely to be particularly frequent as states continue to see value in developing a bomb option to be potentially exercised if conditions demand it. It is a pivotal pit stop on the long road to nuclear weapons and proliferation for many states. Locating hedging on the proliferation continuum is crucial to understanding which hedgers might continue on the journey to nuclear weapons and which may turn around and abandon it.

For those that seek to attain a nuclear weapons capability, I show that, contrary to the portrait of a world full of nuclear sprinters, the majority of nuclear weapons aspirants adopt creative and heretofore understudied strategies such as sheltered pursuit—pursuing nuclear weapons under the shield of a great power that tolerates its nuclear proliferation—or hiding, pursuing nuclear weapons clandestinely due to fear of economic or military prevention. These two strategies, in particular, are likely to dominate the interaction between active nuclear aspirants and major powers in the coming decades. This book is the first effort to disaggregate nuclear pursuers on the observation that there are *different*, strategically selected pathways to the bomb that can be usefully separated for analytical and practical policy-making purposes.

Second, the book offers a comprehensive theory, Proliferation Strategy Theory, that outperforms alternative explanations in explaining and predicting *why* states select the strategies of proliferation they do. The theory highlights the critical role of, of course, security in driving a state's interest in nuclear weapons capability and determining the strategy they select to pursue it. But perhaps the biggest insight from the theory is the role of domestic political consensus in regulating whether a state shifts from considering a future bomb option—hedging—to an active weaponization strategy in the immediate term. For hard hedgers debating whether to actively pursue nuclear weapons, it is domestic political consensus—sometimes the decision of an apex leader, sometimes consensus among key constituencies depending on the configuration and regime type of the state—that is the crucial determinant of whether and when they decide to pursue nuclear weapons. This is an important revision to a number of studies on nuclear proliferation, some of which argue that nuclear pursuit is driven entirely by regime type[1] and others which argue that it is exclusively determined by security considerations.[2] I argue that both are important, but are relevant in a clear sequence: security provides motivation to consider weaponization, but it is domestic political consensus that ultimately regulates whether a state acts on that motivation. Once domestic political consensus congeals, the role of

1. See Hymans, *Achieving Nuclear Ambitions.*
2. See Debs and Monteiro, *Nuclear Politics.*

external coercion decides *how* a state might pursue nuclear weapons. Those who can, sprint. Those who can proliferate under a major power shield select sheltered pursuit. And those who can do neither hide.

Third, the book shows that variation in strategies of proliferation matters practically to the nuclear landscape and to international politics, because the different strategies vary in their destabilizing potential, their historical record of success, and the policy tools that can be used to confront them. One key practical insight from strategies of proliferation is that a large number of states that have flirted with nuclear weapons pursuit have been hedgers, some of which still persist but many of which have forsworn the nuclear option at some point. All three types of hedging are likely to exist in the future and may increase in frequency if the international security environment deteriorates or as the United States' extended deterrence commitments continue—or not—to emplace allies under its nuclear umbrella. The theory provides insight into, for example, insurance hedgers that may increasingly consider escaping the extended deterrence barn, as it were, for fear that the credibility and reliability of the United States as an extended deterrence provider might be crumbling. It suggests focusing efforts to keep domestic consensus for active weaponization from congealing in states that might be considering it.

For states that select an active weaponization strategy, not all have equal chances of attaining the bomb. Even though states strategically select into their proliferation pathways, some are more likely to successfully attain nuclear weapons than others. Sprinting—for those that can adopt this strategy—almost never fails. Some possible nuclear weapons pursuers, including Australia, Japan, and possibly Germany, have the capability to openly and quickly sprint to a bomb in the future. Others could follow the template of India: hard hedging over a long period such that their final sprint is short, should it ever occur. Sheltered pursuit is a surprisingly successful strategy for those that can select it and critically depends on a major power shielding the state's pursuit of nuclear weapons, essentially ensuring that it has the buffer and protection to succeed. Not only has sheltered pursuit been empirically successful, but the conditions that enable its selection and its success persist—countries such as Saudi Arabia may enjoy a future American shield for proliferation if, for example, Iran were to achieve nuclear weapons. Major powers offering shelter to a proliferator should consider their choices carefully, as it will likely have to live with that state as a new member of the nuclear family.

The most common, and destabilizing, proliferation strategy going forward is likely to be hiding. There is no escaping the observation that the remaining pool of potential proliferators consists of many states that, my theory predicts, have no option but to select hiding as a proliferation strategy. These are states in volatile regions such as the Middle East or East Asia, they may be led by personalist regimes with dangerous pathologies, and they may lack the organizational and domestic political capabilities to safely and securely manage nuclear weapons once they possess them.[3] Even though hiders seldom succeed, the temptation to try will remain strong: a successful hider clandestinely develops international politics' most powerful insurance policy against regime change and invasion. Clandestine pursuit of nuclear weapons is disruptive to the international system whether it succeeds or fails. Given that the likely pool of states that must pursue nuclear weapons clandestinely often includes precisely those the major powers least want to possess nuclear weapons (otherwise they may offer shelter), success can lead to dangerous outcomes such as nuclear emboldenment.[4] And failure is usually a significant disturbance to global security. Catching a hider triggers significant turbulence in the international system, as some states attempt to assemble economic coercive leverage with sanctions or even consider launching preventive wars. Both options impose great humanitarian costs on civilians. The emerging nuclear era is likely to be exceptionally unstable for successful and unsuccessful pursuers alike, and, unfortunately, for bystander states as well.

The Findings and Their Implications

This book corrects the scholarly record on nuclear proliferation, showing that few nuclear aspirants in history fit the proliferation archetype of the United States or Soviet Union—or even China or France—sprinting to complete the bomb as quickly as possible. Instead, the typical nuclear pursuit has looked—and will continue to look—like India, Japan, North Korea, Pakistan, Syria, and Iran. What are the key ways in which they vary?

First, there are the hedgers: those that want a bomb option, not necessarily a bomb. But even within hedging there is critical and important variation. Technical hedgers most closely resemble what the literature refers to as nuclear latent states—states with the technical foundation for a military capability but no development of key weaponization features,

3. See Vipin Narang and Scott D. Sagan, eds., *The Fragile Balance of Terror: Deterrence in the New Nuclear Age* (Ithaca, NY: Cornell University Press, forthcoming).

4. See Mark S. Bell, *Nuclear Reactions: How Nuclear-Armed States Behave* (Ithaca: Cornell University Press, 2021); also see Narang and Sagan, *Fragile Balance of Terror*.

such as enrichment or reprocessing, and no centralized intent to explore such options.

Insurance hedgers are states that enjoy a formal extended deterrence guarantee, historically from the United States, though other states could be guarantors going forward. Insurance hedgers develop the technical foundations of a nuclear weapons program to keep their options open, driven by fear that extended deterrence may be rescinded or decay in the future, or that existing guarantees will fail to remain adequate as threats evolve. South Korea, Japan, and much of Western Europe have been content with insurance hedging—so far. France should have remained an indefinite insurance hedger according to my theory, but after a series of perceived betrayals from Washington in the 1950s, it concluded that no American president would trade Pittsburgh for Paris and therefore that France could not rely on the United States for nuclear deterrence. France is unlikely to be the last insurance hedger to reach this conclusion. The United States during the Trump administration showed how quickly it could cultivate the perception that it was an unreliable and reluctant extended deterrence provider.

Hard hedgers are the most interesting hedging category because they face an external security threat alone and at least some serious domestic constituencies believe that nuclear weapons could be an effective security tool against that threat. Hard hedgers remain hedging because the relevant veto players in national leadership have not, for whatever reason, agreed unanimously that nuclear weapons are possible or the ideal solution to that security threat. Hard hedgers are states that *need* nuclear weapons according to realist theories but do not want them. My typology is the first to identify hard hedging—the result of this tension—as a distinct strategy. It has actually been quite common throughout the nuclear era—and it describes some of the most important hedgers from Sweden and Switzerland to India. Identifying hard hedging also shows that technical and insurance hedgers will not automatically weaponize in response to changing security situations: they still have to cross significant domestic political hurdles, as Japan would certainly have to if it ever opted for a nuclear weapons capability. Hedgers are not failed proliferators. Hedgers have made the conscious decision to stop short of weaponization for strategic and political reasons. Policymakers' goal should be to prevent them from deciding to move forward.

Only states that have both security motivation and the domestic political will for a nuclear weapons capability become active weaponizers. These are the states that have already priced the possible risk of external coercion into their determination to pursue nuclear weapons. But that threat of external coercion—whether economic or military—shapes *how* they seek nuclear weapons once a decision to do so has been made. Early in the nuclear age, the states who had the motivation for nuclear weapons were almost exclusively major powers who could operate with near impunity from prevention and were weaponizing before the nonproliferation regime—and the intelligence and institutions designed to support it—existed. They could almost all sprint, at least until China's nuclearization in 1964. Sprinting is still possible in theory—Australia could probably sprint from start to finish, Japan and Germany if they shifted from insurance hedging could likely do so as well. But the pool of states that are strong enough to openly sprint is now quite small.

Instead, the vast majority of remaining active proliferators have two options to creatively pursue nuclear weapons. The first, one that maximizes chances of success, is seeking or cultivating major power shelter that can shield the proliferator from outside attempts at coercion—both from the shelterer itself, which looks the other way and tolerates the state's proliferation in service of higher geopolitical goals, and from other major powers—by providing a veneer of (im)plausible deniability about the state's proliferation activities, undermining sanctions, or introducing the risk of direct major power war if another state tries to attack the client state. Israel and North Korea cultivated or otherwise enjoyed shelter from a major power and exploited it to pursue nuclear weapons. The United States was well aware of Israel's proliferation activities but looked the other way. China, too, shielded the North Korean program, and even facilitated it by allowing Pakistan Air Force C-130s to overfly Chinese airspace to deliver repeated shipments of centrifuges for North Korea's uranium enrichment program, all the while consistently gaslighting American suspicions of North Korean clandestine procurements. Pakistan's shelter arrived unexpectedly with the Soviet Christmas Day invasion of Afghanistan in 1979. A Carter administration that had intended to bring the hammer down on Pakistan for its suspected reprocessing acquisitions and enrichment imports found its hands suddenly tied by the need to funnel money and guns through Pakistan to wage a proxy war against the Soviet Union. The Reagan administration would continue to shield the Pakistani nuclear program from not only India but also the U.S. Congress—sometimes engaging in outright lies to prevent sanctions or military assistance cutoffs that would threaten the supply conduit through Pakistan. The United States chose to prioritize the Cold War battle in Afghanistan over trying to stop Pakistani nuclearization and turned a blind eye to the program. This choice has had enduring consequences for international security and the nuclear landscape. Not only has the AQ Khan network fueled subsequent proliferation attempts in states like Libya and North Korea, Pakistan's risky nuclear behavior has also been persistent cause for concern—provoking India and deterring retaliation with a forward-leaning nuclear strategy that includes a variety of battlefield nuclear systems.[5]

The conditions for sheltered pursuit to materialize or be cultivated still exist. It is entirely possible that an American administration chooses—if Iran were to ever nuclearize or threaten to do so—to shield a Saudi program. Saudi Arabia's Crown Prince Mohammed bin Salman has openly expressed intent to pursue nuclear weapons should Iran do so and is already laying the preliminary groundwork to potentially do so under an American shield. Taiwan could similarly consider sheltered pursuit under the right configuration—risky as it might be given Chinese incentives to prevent it—as the competition between the United States and China intensifies. A key insight from the book is that sheltered pursuit is remarkably successful for those who can select it. Major powers who extend shelter and tolerate nuclear proliferation must carefully consider the consequences of their largesse, because its effects are essentially irreversible.

States who pursue an active weaponization strategy without shelter will typically be hiders. These states have no option but to pursue a clandestine program in the hope that they can hide long enough to attain a sufficiently advanced capability to deter prevention. The very threats that motivate the pursuit of nuclear weapons drive these states' nuclear programs underground for fear of murder. If detected before they succeed, they risk potentially crippling economic sanctions, military strikes, and even regime change in extreme cases. States that pursue hiding strategies have already shown their risk tolerance and are likely to be hard to coerce or manipulate.[6] The vast majority of the remaining potential nuclear aspirants are potential hiders—the states the major powers in the system least want to possess nuclear weapons. All future potential hiders are presently members of the Nonproliferation Treaty, subject to export control regimes and a robust international counterproliferation intelligence network and precision military capabilities. Yet the seduction of possessing nuclear weapons motivates them to gamble on a clandestine proliferation strategy anyway. It is certainly the case that uranium enrichment programs are easier to disperse and hide underground, as Iran illustrates, for example. But as recently as 2007 Syria

5. Narang, *Nuclear Strategy in the Modern Era.*

6. Miller, "The Secret Success of Nonproliferation Sanctions."

attempted to hide an aboveground nuclear reactor, built with North Korean assistance, that would have fueled a plutonium pathway. Hiders are determined, creative, and smart, and their techniques continue to evolve along with the detection abilities of even the most sophisticated intelligence agencies. Hiders are not going away.

The proliferation literature has largely assumed that nuclear aspirants will all seek nuclear weapons as quickly as they possibly can. In reality, nuclear aspirants are much more diverse and creative because they are forced to optimize for a variety of considerations besides speed to the bomb. Some hedge, some hide, some seek shelter, some jog and then sprint. This variation is systematic and it is important.

The second major contribution in this book is developing a generalizable theory to help explain, and predict, which strategy a state might adopt. Proliferation Strategy Theory offers a testable and falsifiable decision-theoretic template for predicting which strategy a state might select based on a series of variables that are roughly measurable in real time, without waiting decades for declassification. The key contribution of the theory is identifying the sequence in which security and domestic variables intervene in the decision process, to produce a testable and a falsifiable theory for *how* states pursue nuclear weapons. The theory highlights the centrality of domestic political consensus for an active weaponization strategy, arguing that while security threats may motivate a nuclear weapons program, it is domestic political consensus that provides the drive and momentum to actively sustain one. Figure 8.1 reproduces Proliferation Strategy Theory and the variables, in sequence, that lead states to a specific proliferation strategy.

How does Proliferation Strategy Theory fare in identifying the proliferation strategy—or sequential strategies—of the 29 states that have considered pursuing nuclear weapons? In total, as table 8.1 shows, the theory correctly predicts 85 percent of the proliferation strategies chosen over time (40 of 46 strategies across 29 states), *for the hypothesized* reasons. That is, states that stalled at hard hedging all did so because of a lack of domestic consensus for weaponization, despite identifiable security threats. Those that shifted from hard hedging to an active weaponization strategy—India, for example—did so *because* domestic political consensus finally congealed. Providing higher resolution on the domestic political consensus variable—a generalizable way to measure and operationalize it—is an important avenue for future research.[7] The theory is not without significant mispredictions, however.

7. See Saunders, "The Domestic Politics of Nuclear Choices—A Review Essay."

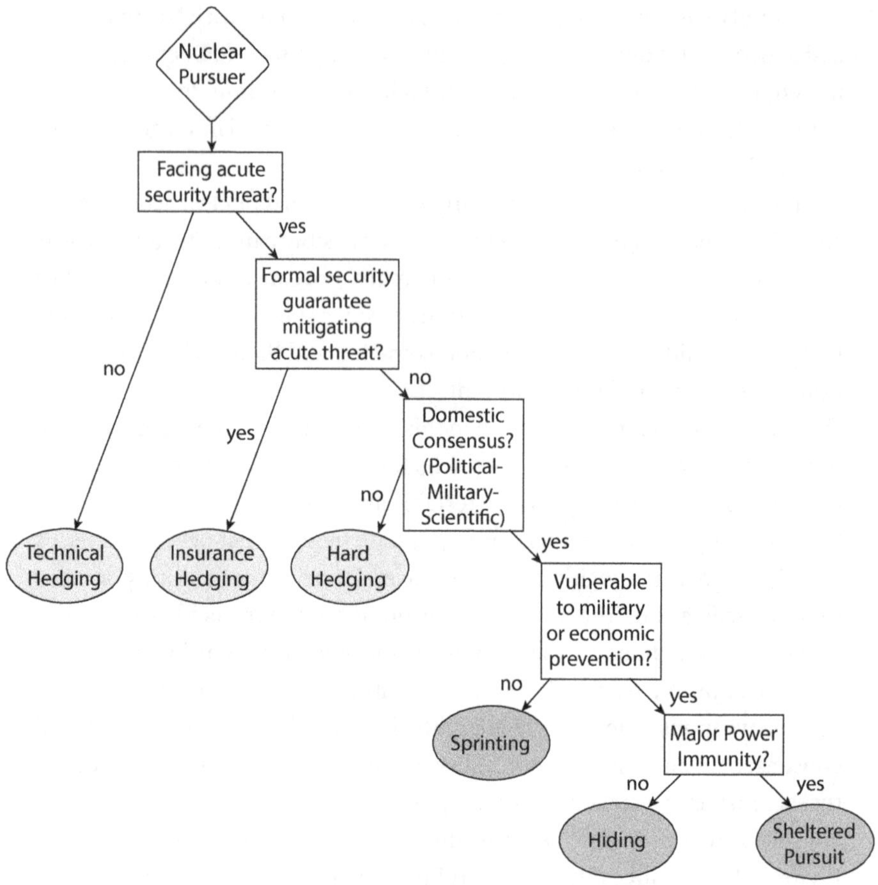

FIGURE 8.1. Proliferation Strategy Theory.

According to Proliferation Strategy Theory, France should have remained an insurance hedger and been content with NATO nuclear-sharing arrangements. Instead, France chose to break free of American extended deterrence and develop an independent deterrent—sprinting to one in the late 1950s. The theory is partially redeemed in that it would predict France to be a sprinter rather than a sheltered pursuer or hider, conditional on France deciding to actively pursue weapons. The misprediction of France is further instructive in that it suggests that perceptions, intentionally excluded from this theory to facilitate generalizable predictions, may matter at the margins. Insurance hedgers' fear of abandonment, for example, might be relevant in the future because it could lead other formal U.S. allies to one day pursue independent deterrents as well. And, to be fair, France defies most theories in international relations.

Throughout the book, I have tested Proliferation Strategy Theory on a variety of cases and compared its predictions against alternative explanations derived from a security model, technological determinism, and the nonproliferation regime. In some cases, certainly, alternative explanations fare well—the security model and technological determinism perform quite well with the sprinters, for example. The security model's biggest failings are underestimating the delay that can be induced independently by a lack of domestic political consensus in some cases and indeterminacy in explaining *how* a proliferator may actively pursue nuclear weapons, particularly sheltered pursuit or hiding. The global nonproliferation regime may have made it more difficult for states to proliferate, but by itself, it is not a very powerful theory of nuclear pursuit. States have not stopped attempting to develop nuclear weapons, and states after the advent of the nonproliferation regime are observed adopting all available strategies ranging from hedging in Japan's case, to sprinting in India's case, to sheltered pursuit in North Korea's case, to hiding in the cases of South Africa and Iran. Sprinting may be a less frequent strategy in the contemporary landscape, but that is largely because the major powers in the system with the ability to sprint have largely already done so, not necessarily because nonproliferation norms function independent of the distribution of power. Indeed, sheltered pursuers and hiders openly—or clandestinely—flout the norms of the nonproliferation regime, to which many previous and all future nuclear aspirants were legally party.

In the aggregate, Proliferation Strategy Theory offers a superior comprehensive theory of proliferation strategies. It shows that different security variables intervene at distinct points in a state's calculations and that states must overcome a significant domestic political hurdle at a key decision point—whether to retain the bomb option or whether to seek the bomb outright. It also, crucially, identifies the variables that might cause a state to *shift* strategies toward active pursuit of nuclear weapons. For example, if insurance hedger Japan decides that it requires an independent deterrent because U.S. extended deterrence commitments no longer satisfy Tokyo's perceived security requirements, it will still have to jump the nontrivial hurdle of generating domestic consensus for an independent deterrent in the face of a public that is largely anti-nuclear. Proliferation Strategy Theory provides the most comprehensive treatment of those that have pursued nuclear weapons in the past, but it also provides a crucial template for how to think about proliferation strategies in the future.

Finally, the book shows why identifying and understanding strategies of proliferation matters to international politics and to the future nuclear

TABLE 8.1. Empirical Codings of Strategies of Nuclear Proliferation

	Proliferation Strategy	Country (Approximate Years)
Hedging Strategies	*Technical Hedging*	Argentina (1968–1976)
		Brazil (1953–1976)
		Iran (1974–1978)*
		India (1948–1964)
		Libya (1970–1981)
		Norway (1946–1962)*
		South Africa (1969–1974)
	Insurance Hedging	Australia (1956–1973)
		France (1945–1954)
		Italy (1955–1959)
		Japan (1954–present)
		Romania (late 1960s–1989)
		South Korea (1975–present)
		Taiwan (1967–1974)
		West Germany/Germany (1956–present)
		Yugoslavia (1948–1960)*
	Hard Hedging	Argentina (1977–1990)
		Brazil (1977–1990)
		Egypt (1955–1980)
		India (1964–1989)
		Iran (2003–present)
		Iraq (1973–1981)
		Israel (1949–1955)
		Pakistan (1954–1971)
		Sweden (1945–1966)
		Switzerland (1945–1969)
Weaponization Strategies	*Sprinting*	**China** (1958–1964)
		France (1954–1960)*
		India (1989–1998)
		USSR (1945–1949)
		United Kingdom (1945–1952)
		United States (1940–1945)

TABLE 8.1. *(continued)*

	Proliferation Strategy	Country (Approximate Years)
	Sheltered Pursuit	China (1955–1958)
		Israel (1956–1967)
		North Korea (1979–2006)
		Pakistan (1980–1990)
	Hiding	Algeria (1986–1992)*
		Iran (1987–2003)
		Iraq (1981–1991)
		Libya (1981–2003)*
		Pakistan (1972–1979)
		South Africa (1974–1979)
		South Korea (1970–1974)
		Syria (2000–2007)
		Taiwan (1974–1988)
		Yugoslavia (1974–1987)

Note: Cases with an * denote cases Proliferation Strategy Theory mispredicts relative to alternative explanations (6 of 46 strategies, or a success rate of over 85 percent). Cases in bold successfully attained nuclear weapons.

landscape. Each strategy of proliferation poses different challenges and creates different opportunities in the current and emerging nuclear landscape. Chapter 7 discussed how hedgers and active proliferators can be stopped by focusing on the variables that prevent a state from moving "down" the tree. Security threats in the international system—either regionally or systemically as the polarity and configuration of international politics shift—will inevitably motivate states to continue to consider pursuing at least a nuclear weapons option, if not nuclear weapons outright. Various measures in the nonproliferation tool kit, including robust and credible extended deterrence commitments as well as the global export control regime, can keep hedgers from shifting to active weaponization strategies. Hard hedgers may require the most significant monitoring and inducements in order to keep domestic consensus for nuclear weapons fractured. Hedging is likely to be a frequent strategy in the future—many states have kept and will keep the option to develop nuclear weapons open, or their centrifuges warm, as it were. By directly locating hedging on the road to proliferation, this book helps us understand how to keep hedgers hedging and what might trigger them to shift to an active weaponization strategy.

The two active weaponization strategies that are likely to pose the most frequent and significant challenges to the world are sheltered pursuit and hiding. It is certainly possible that a major power will again decide that it is willing to tolerate nuclear proliferation from a "friend" (or "frenemy" like Pakistan) or client state in the service of what it believes to be higher geopolitical goals. However, such a tolerance for proliferation—as with Pakistan, for example—can have deleterious and durable consequences for global security. For major powers in the future that are considering nonproliferation forbearance or shelter for a nuclear program in order to pursue some more important political goal, it is worth interrogating the assumption that those priorities are mutually exclusive. Again returning to the example of Pakistan, there is a reasonable argument that the Reagan administration could have conditioned its generous military and economic assistance on Pakistan rolling back large pieces of its nuclear weapons program—after all, Pakistan's dependence on aid should have given the United States tremendous leverage. Given the surprising historic success of sheltered pursuit, potential shelterers in the future must seriously consider whether their geopolitical goals are worth the cost of indefinitely living with the client state's nuclear status. Whether major powers can justify extending shelter to future potential proliferators such as Saudi Arabia, the United Arab Emirates, or Turkey (who could seek it from Russia, for example) is a question that should be considered carefully.

The biggest challenge in the contemporary nuclear landscape is posed by hiders. The remaining pool of states that might consider active weaponization strategies is dominated by potential nuclear aspirants that have no choice but to pursue nuclear weapons clandestinely. And many hiders have been, and all future hiders will be, members of the NPT who have cheated on their nonproliferation obligations by pursuing clandestine nuclear weapons programs while potentially benefiting from access to safeguarded civilian nuclear technology. They have objectives that are at odds with the major powers, they often reside in hostile security environments, they are increasingly led by personalist dictators (for whom generating domestic consensus may be easier in some cases), and they may lack the domestic stability to safely and securely manage nuclear weapons. In the past, the export control regime, the inefficiencies induced by having to a hide a program, and technical limitations opened windows to detect hiders before they reached the finish line. In general, that is still the best playbook to stop hiders. Despite misses and missteps from intelligence agencies in Iraq, Iran, Libya, and Syria, they were all eventually detected—though at some point over time it is likely that a hider will sneak through.[8]

Although hiding may rarely succeed, it is always disruptive to the international system. A hider, such as South Africa, that succeeds is—quite literally—a seismic shock to the international system. The emergence of a new nuclear power, particularly one that the major powers least want to possess nuclear weapons, reshapes regional and global security orders. A hider such as Syria in 2007 or Iran that is caught, however, is equally disruptive because a major power (or several) mobilizes to stop the state—sometimes through crippling economic sanctions that destabilize the regime or people of the state or sometimes through war as in Iraq.

The inefficiency of a hiding strategy is still the best weapon the international community has to stop hiders—and various tactics can further slow progress and extend the time available to detect and stop a hider before it is too late. If the international community is lucky, it may catch a hider like Libya that cannot find its own way out of a centrifuge hall and can be coerced to surrender the program before it goes anywhere. It takes an equal amount of luck, but more force, to stop a hider like Syria. The best-case scenario is the Iranian case and the JCPOA, which took an active hider and pushed it back to hard hedging through a combination of security pressure, sabotage, and a major diplomatic initiative based precisely on the logic of Proliferation Strategy Theory: empower the moderate factions in the leadership who oppose nuclear weapons and thereby forestall or prevent the state from acting on any possible intent to resume a hidden nuclear program, while implementing an extensive monitoring and verification mechanism to catch it if it ever cheats. Hiders may seldom succeed, but the temptation to present their adversaries with the ultimate deterrent as a fait accompli will continue to motivate many to try. The mere attempt to hide often generates significant volatility for global security, irrespective of the final outcome.

Final Words

The world is entering a new nuclear era. The major nuclear powers—the United States, China, and Russia—are engaging in renewed arms races and nuclear modernization programs. The regional nuclear powers are expanding and modernizing their own arsenals and are increasingly tempted by the

8. See Jervis, *Why Intelligence Fails*; Nutt, "Proof of the Bomb"; and Zegart, "Understanding Nuclear Threats."

Cold War's most dangerous tendencies, such as counterforce and damage limitation strategies.[9] The prospects for further nuclear proliferation look even more grim thirty years after the end of the Cold War. Nuclear aspirants such as Iraq, Iran, Libya, Syria, North Korea, India, and Pakistan have dominated international political attention over the past three decades. Many have created substantial instability and are often states whose possession, or potential possession, of nuclear weapons poses grave risks to regional and global security. They include states led by personalist dictators or military regimes whose pathologies may lead them to engage in risky behavior, whose instabilities raise concerns about their ability to safely and securely manage nuclear weapons, and for whom the notion of "rational" cost-benefit deterrence may be swamped by concerns for personal survival or revenge.

So long as nuclear weapons exist and are perceived to be a valuable security and political tool, states will continue to seek them. Possible nuclear aspirants in the future do not just include American adversaries such as Iran and Syria but also "friends" such as Saudi Arabia. Even formal U.S. allies such as Japan, South Korea, Turkey, and even Germany may one day disrupt the East Asian and European security architectures by deciding that an independent nuclear weapons capability is preferable to depending on Washington's security commitments. There is a growing likelihood that the United States will have to confront proliferation attempts from not just foes but friends and frenemies as well.

Understanding which states may pursue nuclear weapons now and in the future, and how they may do so, is therefore critical to managing the contemporary and emerging proliferation landscape. Nuclear weapons remain the most destructive weapon a state can possess and are still believed to be the most effective insurance a state can buy against its adversaries. This is precisely why the most dangerous and destabilizing states in the world will continue to pursue them and attempt to break into the nuclear club. This book has identified the different ways those states might think about seeking nuclear weapons. It provides higher resolution on how we may be able to stop them from getting there and thereby hopefully helps reduce the risk that one day a nuclear weapon may be used accidentally or in anger.

9. See Christopher O. Clary and Vipin Narang, "India's Counterforce Temptations: Strategic Dilemmas, Doctrine, and Capabilities," *International Security* 43, no. 3 (Winter 2018–2019): 7–52.

BIBLIOGRAPHY

Abraham, Itty. "The Ambivalence of Nuclear Histories." *Osiris* 21 (2006): 49–65.

———. *The Making of the Indian Atomic Bomb: Science, Secrecy, and the Postcolonial State*. New York: St. Martin's Press, 1998.

"Ahmadinejad: Iran Is Now a 'Nuclear State.'" Associated Press, February 11, 2010. http://www.nbcnews.com/id/35343465/ns/world_news-mideast_n_africa/t/ahmadinejad-iran-now-nuclear-state/.

Ahmed, Samina. "Pakistan's Nuclear Weapons Program: Turning Points and Nuclear Choices." *International Security* 23, no. 4 (Spring 1999): 178–204.

Albright, David. "South Africa and the Affordable Bomb." *Bulletin of the Atomic Scientists* 50, no. 4 (August 1994): 37–47.

Albright, David, and Sarah Burkhard. "Iranian Breakout Estimates and Enriched Uranium Stocks." Institute for Science and International Security, April 21, 2020. https://isis-online.org/isis-reports/detail/iranian-breakout-estimates-and-enriched-uranium-stocks.

Albright, David, and Corey Gay. "Taiwan: Nuclear Nightmare Averted." *Bulletin of the Atomic Scientists* 54, no. 1 (February 1998): 54–60.

Albright, David, and Mark Hibbs. "South Africa: The ANC and the Atom Bomb." *Bulletin of the Atomic Scientists* 49, no. 3 (April 1993): 32–37.

Albright, David, and Andrea Stricker. *Taiwan's Former Nuclear Weapons Program: Nuclear Weapons On-Demand*. Washington, DC: Institute for Science and International Security, 2018.

Albright, David, and Tom Zamora. "South Africa Flirts with the NPT." *Bulletin of the Atomic Scientists* 47, no. 1 (February 1991): 27–31.

Arnold, Aaron, Matthew Bunn, Caitlin Chase, Steven E. Miller, Rolf Mowatt-Larssen, and William H. Toby. *The Iran Nuclear Archive: Impressions and Implications*. Cambridge, MA: Belfer Center for Science and International Affairs, Harvard Kennedy School, April 2019. https://www.belfercenter.org/sites/default/files/files/publication/The%20Iran%20Nuclear%20Archive_0.pdf.

"Background Briefing with Senior U.S. Officials on Syria's Covert Nuclear Reactor and North Korea's Involvement." April 24, 2008. https://www.dni.gov/files/documents/Newsroom/Speeches%20and%20Interviews/20080424interview.pdf.

Bajpai, Kanti, Sumit Ganguly, Stephen P. Cohen, Pervaiz Iqbal Cheema, P. R. Chari, Piper Hodson, and Chetan Kumar. *Brasstacks and Beyond: Perception and Management of Crisis*. New Delhi: Manohar Books, 1995.

Barletta, Michael. "The Military Nuclear Program in Brazil." Stanford CISAC Working Paper, August 1997. https://fsi-live.s3.us-west-1.amazonaws.com/s3fs-public/barletta.pdf.

Bas, Muhammet A., and Andrew J. Coe. "A Dynamic Theory of Nuclear Proliferation and Preventive War." *International Organization* 70, no. 4 (Fall 2016): 655–85.

Bass, Warren. *Support Any Friend: Kennedy's Middle East and the Making of the U.S.-Israel Alliance*. New York: Oxford University Press, 2003.

Bell, Mark S. "Beyond Emboldenment: How Acquiring Nuclear Weapons Can Change Foreign Policy." *International Security* 40, no. 1 (Summer 2015): 87–119.

———. "Examining Explanations for Nuclear Proliferation." *International Studies Quarterly* 60, no. 3 (September 2016): 520–29.

———. *Nuclear Reactions: How Nuclear-Armed States Behave.* Ithaca: Cornell University Press, 2021.

Berinsky, Adam J. "Assuming the Costs of War: Events, Elites, and American Public Support for Military Conflict." *Journal of Politics* 69, no. 4 (November 2007): 975–97.

Bleck, Mark E., and Paul R. Souder. "PAL Control of Theater Nuclear Weapons." Sandia National Laboratory, March 1984. https://www.cs.columbia.edu/~smb/nsam-160/Theater_Control/Theater_Control.pdf.

Bleek, Philipp C. "Does Proliferation Beget Proliferation?: Why Nuclear Dominoes Rarely Fall." PhD diss., Georgetown University, 2010. http://hdl.handle.net/10822/558060.

Bowen, Wyn Q., and Jonathan Brewer. "Iran's Nuclear Challenge: Nine Years and Counting." *International Affairs* 87, no. 4 (2011): 923–43.

Brands, Hal, and David Palkki. "Saddam, Israel and the Bomb: Nuclear Alarmism Justified?" *International Security* 36, no. 1 (Summer 2011): 133–66.

Braut-Hegghammer, Målfrid. "The Cheater's Dilemma: Iraq, Weapons of Mass Destruction, and the Path to War." *International Security* 45, no. 1 (Summer 2020): 51–89.

———. "Revisiting Osirak: Preventive Attacks and Nuclear Proliferation Risks." *International Security* 36, no. 1 (Summer 2011): 101–32.

———. *Unclear Physics: Why Iraq and Libya Failed to Build Nuclear Weapons.* Ithaca: Cornell University Press, 2016.

Brzezinski, Zbigniew. "Presidential Decisions of Pakistan, Afghanistan, and India." Memorandum to Secretary of State Cyrus Vance, January 2, 1980. http://nsarchive.gwu.edu/NSAEBB/NSAEBB396/docs/1980-01-02%20Presidential%20Decisions%20on%20Pakistan%20-%20Afghanistan.pdf.

———. "Reflections on Soviet Intervention in Afghanistan." Memorandum to the President, December 26, 1979. https://nsarchive2.gwu.edu//NSAEBB/NSAEBB396/docs/1979-12-26%20Brzezinski%20to%20Carter%20on%20Afghanistan.pdf.

Burgess, Stephen F. "South Africa's Nuclear Weapons Policies." *Nonproliferation Review* 13, no. 3 (November 2006): 519–26.

Burr, William, ed. "The Algerian Nuclear Problem, 1991: Controversy over the Es Salam Nuclear Reactor." National Security Archive, Electronic Briefing Book, no. 228, September 10, 2007. http://nsarchive.gwu.edu/nukevault/ebb228/.

———. "Japan's Plutonium Overhang." *Wilson Center NPIHP Research Updates*, June 8, 2017. https://www.wilsoncenter.org/publication/japans-plutonium-overhang.

———, ed. "Stopping Korea from Going Nuclear, Part I." National Security Archive, Briefing Book, no. 582, March 22, 2017. https://nsarchive.gwu.edu/briefing-book/henry-kissinger-nuclear-vault/2017-03-22/stopping-korea-going-nuclear-part-i.

———. "The Taiwanese Nuclear Case: Lessons for Today." Carnegie Endowment for International Peace, August 9, 2007. http://carnegieendowment.org/2007/08/09/taiwanese-nuclear-case-lessons-for-today.

Burr, William, and Avner Cohen. "Revisiting the 1979 Vela Mystery: A Report on the Critical Oral History Conference." Wilson Center, August 31, 2020. https://www.wilsoncenter.org/blog-post/revisiting-1979-vela-mystery-report-critical-oral-history-conference.

Burr, William, Avner Cohen, and Richard Wolfson. "The Vela Flash: Forty Years Ago." National Security Archive, Briefing Book, no. 686, September 22, 2019. https://nsarchive.gwu.edu/briefing-book/nuclear-vault/2019-09-22/vela-flash-forty-years-ago.

Burr, William, and Jeffrey T. Richelson. "Whether to 'Strangle the Baby in the Cradle': The United States and the Chinese Nuclear Program, 1960–64." *International Security* 25, no. 3 (Winter 2000/2001): 54–99.

Bush, George W. *Decision Points*. New York: Crown, 2010.

Bush, Richard C. *At Cross Purposes: U.S.-Taiwan Relations since 1942*. Armonk, NY: M. E. Sharpe, 2004.

"Cabinet Meeting with Saddam Hussein and the Atomic Energy Committee." Conflict Records Research Center. Washington, DC, undated [post–Gulf War]. https://conflictrecords.files.wordpress.com/2013/06/sh-shtp-a-001-492.pdf.

Campbell, Kurt, and Tsuyoshi Sunohara. "Japan: Thinking the Unthinkable." In *The Nuclear Tipping Point: Why States Reconsider Their Nuclear Choices*, edited by Kurt Campbell, Robert J. Einhorn, and Mitchell Reiss, 218–53. Washington, DC: Brookings Institution Press, 2004.

Carnegie, Allison, and Austin Carson. "The Spotlight's Harsh Glare: Rethinking Publicity and International Order." *International Organization* 72, no. 3 (Summer 2018): 627–57.

Carson, Austin. *Secret Wars: Covert Conflict in International Politics*. Princeton: Princeton University Press, 2018.

Carter, Ashton B., and William J. Perry. *Preventive Defense: A New Security Strategy for America*. Washington, DC: Brookings Institution Press, 1999.

Cavanna, Thomas P. "Geopolitics over Proliferation: The Origins of US Grand Strategy and Their Implications for the Spread of Nuclear Weapons in South Asia." *Journal of Strategic Studies* 41, no. 4 (2018): 576–603.

Central Intelligence Agency (CIA). "Iraqi Ballistic Missile Developments." July 1990. CIA Electronic Reading Room. http://nsarchive.gwu.edu/NSAEBB/NSAEBB80/wmd03.pdf.

———. "Iraq's National Security Goals." December 1988. CIA Electronic Reading Room. http://nsarchive.gwu.edu/NSAEBB/NSAEBB80/wmd02.pdf.

———. "New Information on South Africa's Nuclear Program and South African-Israeli Nuclear and Military Cooperation." March 30, 1983. Secret. http://nsarchive.gwu.edu/NSAEBB/NSAEBB181/sa26.pdf.

———. "North Korea's Expanding Nuclear Efforts." May 3, 1988. In "North Korea and Nuclear Weapons: The Declassified U.S. Record," edited by Robert A. Wampler, National Security Archive Electronic Briefing Book, no. 87, Document 10, 2003. https://nsarchive2.gwu.edu/NSAEBB/NSAEBB87/nk10.pdf.

———. "Prewar Status of Iraq's Weapons of Mass Destruction." March 1991. CIA Electronic Reading Room. http://nsarchive.gwu.edu/NSAEBB/NSAEBB80/wmd04.pdf.

———. "Trends in South Africa's Nuclear Security Policies and Programs." October 5, 1984. Top Secret. http://nsarchive.gwu.edu/NSAEBB/NSAEBB181/sa27.pdf.

Central Intelligence Agency, Directorate of Intelligence, Research Paper. "Pakistan's Nuclear Weapons Program: Personnel and Organizations." November 1985. History and Public Policy Program Digital Archive, Obtained and contributed by William Burr and included in NPIHP Research Update No. 11. http://digitalarchive.wilsoncenter.org/document/116903.

Chang, Alan K. "Crisis Avoided: The Past, Present and Future of Taiwan's Nuclear Weapons Program." Master's thesis, Hawaii Pacific University, 2011.

Charbonneau, Louis. "U.S. 'Not Fixated' on Iran Answering Queries on Atomic Work." Reuters, June 16, 2015. https://www.reuters.com/article/iran-nuclear-usa/u-s-not-fixated-on-iran-answering-queries-on-atomic-work-kerry-idINKBN0OW2CE20150616.

Chengappa, Raj. *Weapons of Peace: The Secret Story of India's Quest to Be a Nuclear Power*. Delhi: Harper Collins, 2000.

Clary, Christopher O., and Vipin Narang. "India's Counterforce Temptations: Strategic Dilemmas, Doctrine, and Capabilities." *International Security* 43, no. 3 (Winter 2018/2019): 7–52.

Coats, Daniel R. "Worldwide Threat Assessment of the US Intelligence Community." Statement for the Record, Senate Select Committee on Intelligence, January 29, 2019. https://www.dni.gov/files/ODNI/documents/2019-ATA-SFR---SSCI.pdf.

Coe, Andrew J., and Jane Vaynman. "Collusion and the Nuclear Nonproliferation Regime." *Journal of Politics* 77, no. 4 (August 2015): 983–97.

Cohen, Avner. "Crossing the Threshold: The Untold Nuclear Dimension of the 1967 Arab-Israeli War and Its Contemporary Lessons." *Arms Control Today* 37, no. 5 (June 2007). https://www.armscontrol.org/act/2007_06/Cohen.

———. *Israel and the Bomb*. New York: Columbia University Press, 1998.

———. "Israel and the Evolution of U.S. Nonproliferation Policy: The Critical Decade (1958–1968)." *Nonproliferation Review* 5, no. 2 (Winter 1998): 1–19.

———. *The Worst-Kept Secret: Israel's Bargain with the Bomb*. New York: Columbia University Press, 2010.

Cohen, Avner, and William Burr. "The Eisenhower Administration and the Discovery of Dimona: March 1958–January 1961." National Security Archive Electronic Briefing Book, no. 510, April 15, 2015. https://nsarchive2.gwu.edu/nukevault/ebb510/.

———. "How Israel Built a Nuclear Program Right under the Americans' Noses." *Haaretz.com*, January 17, 2021. https://www.haaretz.com/israel-news/.premium.MAGAZINE-how-israel-built-a-nuclear-program-right-under-the-americans-noses-1.9445510.

Cohen, Avner, and Benjamin Frankel. "Opaque Nuclear Proliferation." *Journal of Strategic Studies* 13, no. 3 (1990): 14–44.

Cole, Paul. "Atomic Bombast: Nuclear Weapon Decisionmaking in Sweden, 1945–1972." Henry L. Stimson Center Occasional Paper, no. 26, April 1996. https://www.stimson.org/wp-content/files/file-attachments/Occasional%20Paper%20No.%2026%20April%201996.pdf.

Coll, Steve. "U.S. Halted Nuclear Bid by Iran." *Washington Post*, November 17, 1992. https://www.washingtonpost.com/archive/politics/1992/11/17/us-halted-nuclear-bid-by-iran/0e215f24-43b2-4791-b24a-ea23b46b5a28/.

Constable, Peter. "U.S. Department of State Cable 145139 to U.S. Embassy India [Repeating Cable Sent to Embassy Pakistan], 'Non-Proliferation in South [Asia],' Excerpts." June 6, 1979. In *New Documents Spotlight Reagan-Era Tensions over Pakistani Nuclear Program*, edited by William Burr, Document 1. National Security Archive Electronic Briefing Book, no. 377, 2012. https://www.documentcloud.org/documents/347012-doc-1-6-6-79.html.

Corera, Gordon. *Shopping for Bombs: Nuclear Proliferation, Global Insecurity, and the Rise and Fall of the A. Q. Khan Network*. Oxford: Oxford University Press, 2006.

Corry, John. "Buying the Bomb." *New York Times*, March 5, 1985. http://www.nytimes.com/1985/03/05/arts/a-look-at-investigative-journalism.html.

Craig, Campbell, and Sergey Radchenko. *The Atomic Bomb and the Origins of the Cold War*. New Haven: Yale University Press, 2008.

———. "MAD, Not Marx: Khrushchev and the Nuclear Revolution." *Journal of Strategic Studies* 41, no. 1–2 (2018): 208–33.

Daitoku, Takaaki. "Resorting to Latency: Japan's Accommodation with Nuclear Realities." In *Uncovering the Sources of Nuclear Behavior: Historical Dimensions of Nuclear Proliferation*, edited by Andreas Wenger and Roland Popp. Washington, DC: Georgetown University Press, forthcoming.

Davenport, Kelsey. "The Joint Comprehensive Plan of Action at a Glance." Arms Control Association Fact Sheet, May 2018. https://www.armscontrol.org/factsheets/JCPOA-at-a-glance.

Dawson, Chester. "In Japan, Provocative Case for Staying Nuclear." *Wall Street Journal*, October 28, 2011. http://www.wsj.com/articles/SB1000142405297020365880457663839253743 0156.

Debs, Alexandre, and Nuno P. Monteiro. *Nuclear Politics: The Strategic Causes of Proliferation.* New York: Cambridge University Press, 2017.

———. "The Strategic Logic of Nuclear Proliferation." *International Security* 39, no. 2 (Fall 2014): 7–51.

Desai, Morarji. "Rajya Sabha Q&A on the Nuclear Explosion at Pokhran in 1974." December 21, 1978. History and Public Policy Program Digital Archive, Institute for Defence Studies and Analyses (ISDA), Rajya Sabha Q&A Documents. http://digitalarchive.wilsoncenter.org/document/119759.

Deshmukh, Bhalchandra Gopal. *A Cabinet Secretary Looks Back.* New York: HarperCollins Publishers India, 2004.

Doyle, James E. "Argentina and Brazil." In *Nuclear Safeguards, Security, and Nonproliferation: Achieving Security with Technology and Policy,* edited by James E. Doyle, 307–30. Oxford: Elsevier/Butterworth-Heinemann, 2008.

Duelfer, Charles. "Comprehensive Report of the Special Advisor to the DCI on Iraq's WMD." September 30, 2004. https://www.govinfo.gov/app/details/GPO-DUELFERREPORT.

"Extract from Speech by the South African Prime Minister at Congress of the National Party of Cape Province." August 24, 1977. History and Public Policy Program Digital Archive, UK National Archives, FCO45-2131. Obtained and contributed by Anna-Mart van Wyk. http://digitalarchive.wilsoncenter.org/document/116617.

Fitzpatrick, Mark. *Asia's Latent Nuclear Powers: Japan, South Korea, and Taiwan.* London: Routledge, 2016.

———. "How Japan Could Go Nuclear." *Foreign Affairs,* October 3, 2019. https://www.foreignaffairs.com/articles/asia/2019-10-03/how-japan-could-go-nuclear.

Fravel, M. Taylor. *Active Defense: China's Military Strategy since 1949.* Princeton: Princeton University Press, 2019.

Fuhrmann, Matthew. *Atomic Assistance: How "Atoms for Peace" Programs Cause Nuclear Insecurity.* Ithaca: Cornell University Press, 2012.

Fuhrmann, Matthew, and Sarah Kreps. "Targeting Nuclear Programs in War and Peace: A Quantitative Empirical Analysis, 1941–2000." *Journal of Conflict Resolution* 54, no. 6 (December 2010): 831–59.

Fuhrmann, Matthew, and Benjamin Tkach. "Almost Nuclear: Introducing the Nuclear Latency Dataset." *Conflict Management and Peace Science* 32, no. 4 (September 2015): 443–61.

Fukushima, Mayumi. "Japanese Nuclear Ambition: An Important Decision Yet to Be Made?" Unpublished manuscript, May 26, 2015.

Ganguly, Sumit. "India's Pathway to Pokhran II: The Prospects and Sources of New Delhi's Nuclear Weapons Program." *International Security* 23, no. 4 (Spring 1999): 148–77.

Gardner, Timothy. "U.S. Should Keep Congress Informed about Nuclear Talks with Saudi: GAO." Reuters, May 4, 2020. https://www.reuters.com/article/us-usa-saudi-nuclearpower/u-s-should-keep-congress-informed-about-nuclear-talks-with-saudis-gao-idUSKBN22G2XV.

Gates, Robert M. *Duty: Memoirs of a Secretary at War.* New York: Knopf, 2014.

Gavin, Francis J. *Nuclear Weapons and American Grand Strategy.* Washington, DC: Brookings Institution Press, 2020.

———. "Strategies of Inhibition: U.S. Grand Strategy, the Nuclear Revolution, and Nonproliferation." *International Security* 40, no. 1 (Summer 2015): 9–46.

Geddes, Barbara, Joseph Wright, and Erica Frantz. "Autocratic Breakdown and Regime Transition: A New Data Set," *Perspectives on Politics* 12, no. 2 (June 2014): 313–31.

Gerzhoy, Gene. "Alliance Coercion and Nuclear Restraint: How the United States Thwarted West Germany's Nuclear Ambitions." *International Security* 39, no. 4 (Spring 2015): 91–129.

Goldstein, Avery. *Deterrence and Security in the 21st Century: China, Britain, France, and the Enduring Legacy of the Nuclear Revolution.* Stanford: Stanford University Press, 2000.

Gordon, Michael R., and Gordon Lubold. "Trump Administration Weighs Troop Cut in South Korea." *Wall Street Journal*, July 17, 2020. https://www.wsj.com/articles/trump-administration-weighs-troop-cut-in-south-korea-11595005050.

Gordon, Philip. *A Certain Idea of France: French Security Policy and the Gaullist Legacy*. Princeton: Princeton University Press, 1993.

Gourevitch, Peter A. "The Second-Image Reversed: The International Sources of Domestic Politics." *International Organization* 32, no. 4 (Autumn 1978): 881–912.

Green, Michael J., and Katsuhisa Furukawa. "Japan: New Nuclear Realism." In *The Long Shadow: Nuclear Weapons and Security in 21st Century Asia*, edited by Muthiah Alagappa, 347–72. Stanford: Stanford University Press, 2008.

Gupta, Shekhar. "How We Built the Bomb." *Indian Express*, August 19, 2006. http://archive.indianexpress.com/news/how-we-built-the-bomb/10875/0.

Haass, Richard N., and Morton Halperin. *After the Tests: U.S. Policy toward India and Pakistan*. New York: Council on Foreign Relations Task Report, 1998. https://www.cfr.org/sites/default/files/pdf/1998/11/India_Pakistan.pdf.

Harel, Amos, and Aluf Benn. "No Longer a Secret: How Israel Destroyed Syria's Nuclear Reactor." *Haaretz*, March 23, 2018. https://www.haaretz.com/world-news/MAGAZINE-no-longer-a-secret-how-israel-destroyed-syria-s-nuclear-reactor-1.5914407.

Harris, Verne, Sello Hatang, and Peter Liberman. "Unveiling South Africa's Nuclear Past." *Journal of Southern African Studies* 30, no. 3 (September 2004): 457–75.

Hecht, Gabrielle. *The Radiance of France: Nuclear Power and National Identity after World War II*. Cambridge, MA: MIT Press, 2009.

Hedges, Chris. "Iran May Be Able to Build an Atomic Bomb in 5 Years, U.S. and Israeli Officials Fear." *New York Times*, January 5, 1995. https://www.nytimes.com/1995/01/05/world/iran-may-be-able-build-atomic-bomb-5-years-us-israeli-officials-fear.html.

Herring, George C., and Richard H. Immerman. "Eisenhower, Dulles, and Dienbienphu: 'The Day We Didn't Go to War' Revisited." *Journal of American History* 71, no. 2 (September 1984): 343–63.

Heuser, Beatrice. *Nuclear Mentalities? Strategies and Beliefs in Britain, France, and the FRG*. London: Palgrave Macmillan, 1998.

"History of the Custody and Deployment of Nuclear Weapons, July 1945–September 1947." Office of the Assistant to the Secretary of Defense (Atomic Energy), February 1978. https://nsarchive2.gwu.edu/nukevault/ebb442/docs/doc%201A%20custody%20and%20deployment%20history%2078.pdf.

Holloway, David. *Stalin and the Bomb: The Soviet Union and Atomic Energy, 1939–1956*. New Haven: Yale University Press, 1994.

Hook, Glenn D. "The Nuclearization of Language: Nuclear Allergy as Political Metaphor." *Journal of Peace Research* 21, no. 3 (September 1984): 259–75.

Hosokawa, Morihiro. "Are U.S. Troops in Japan Needed? Reforming the Alliance." *Foreign Affairs*, July/August 1998. https://www.foreignaffairs.com/articles/asia/1998-07-01/are-us-troops-japan-needed-reforming-alliance.

Houghton, Vince. *The Nuclear Spies: America's Intelligence Operation against Hitler and Stalin*. Ithaca: Cornell University Press, 2019.

Hughes, Llewelyn. "Why Japan Will Not Go Nuclear (Yet): International and Domestic Constraints on the Nuclearization of Japan." *International Security* 31, no. 4 (Spring 2007): 67–96.

Hussein, Saddam. "Meeting between Saddam Hussein and His Senior Advisors Following the Israeli Attack on Osirak." Washington, DC: Conflict Records Research Center, circa 1981. https://conflictrecords.files.wordpress.com/2013/06/sh-shtp-a-001-480.pdf.

———. "Transcript of a Speech Given by Saddam Hussein on 'The Role of the Iraqi Armed Forces in the Arab-Zionist Conflict' at Al-Bakr University." Washington, DC: Conflict Records

Research Center, June 3, 1978. https://conflictrecords.files.wordpress.com/2013/06/sh-pdwn-d-000-341.pdf.

Hymans, Jacques E. C. *Achieving Nuclear Ambitions: Scientists, Politicians, and Proliferation.* Cambridge: Cambridge University Press, 2012.

———. "Of Gauchos and Gringos: Why Argentina Never Wanted the Bomb, and Why the United States Thought It Did." *Security Studies* 10, no. 3 (Spring 2001): 153–85.

———. *The Psychology of Nuclear Proliferation: Identity, Emotions, and Foreign Policy.* Cambridge: Cambridge University Press, 2006.

———. "The Study of Nuclear Proliferation and Nonproliferation: Toward a New Consensus?" In *Forecasting Nuclear Proliferation in the 21st Century, Volume 1: The Role of Theory*, edited by William C. Potter and Gaukhar Mukhatzhanova. Stanford: Stanford University Press, 2010.

———. "Veto Players, Nuclear Energy, and Nonproliferation: Domestic Institutional Barriers to a Japanese Bomb." *International Security* 36, no. 2 (Fall 2011): 154–89.

———. "When Does a State Become a 'Nuclear Weapon State.'" *Nonproliferation Review* 17, no. 1 (2010): 161–80.

International Atomic Energy Agency (IAEA). "Fourth Consolidated Report of the Director General of the International Atomic Energy Agency." October 8, 1997. https://nsarchive2.gwu.edu/NSAEBB/NSAEBB80/wmd07.pdf.

Jackson, Galen. "The United States, the Israeli Nuclear Program, and Nonproliferation, 1961–69." *Security Studies* 28, no. 2 (March 15, 2019): 360–93.

Jafar, Jafar Dhia, and Numan Saadaldin al-Niaimi. *Al-I'tiraf al-Akhir: Haqiqat al-Barnamaj al-Nawawi al-Iraqi* (The Last Confession: The Truth about the Iraqi Nuclear Program). Unpublished English translation (2004). Beirut: Markaz Dirasat Al-Wahdah Al-Arabiya, 2005.

Jafar, Jafar Dhia, Numan Saadaldin al-Niaimi, and Lars Sigurd Sunnanå. *Oppdraget: Innsidehistorien om Saddams Atomvåpen.* Oslo: Spartacus Books, 2005.

"Japan Discussed Acquisition of 'Defensive' Nuclear Weapons in 1958." *Japan Times*, March 17, 2013. http://www.japantimes.co.jp/news/2013/03/17/national/history/japan-discussed-acquisition-of-defensive-nuclear-weapons-in-1958/#.VeBpyZd3AlM.

Jervis, Robert. *Why Intelligence Fails: Lessons from the Iranian Revolution and the Iraq War.* Ithaca: Cornell University Press, 2010.

"Joint Comprehensive Plan of Action." July 14, 2015. https://2009-2017.state.gov/e/eb/tfs/spi/iran/jcpoa/index.htm.

Jones, Matthew. *The Official History of the UK Strategic Nuclear Deterrent, Volume 1: From the V-Bomber Era to the Arrival of Polaris, 1945–1964.* London: Routledge, 2017.

Jonter, Thomas. *The Key to Nuclear Restraint: The Swedish Plans to Acquire Nuclear Weapons during the Cold War.* London: Palgrave Macmillan, 2016.

———. "Sweden and the Bomb: The Swedish Plans to Acquire Nuclear Weapons, 1945–1972." Swedish Nuclear Power Inspectorate (SKI) Report, 01:33, September 2001. https://www.stralsakerhetsmyndigheten.se/contentassets/bda8f1ac1d914cd9a27c846c8b524fb1/200133-sweden-and-the-bomb.-the-swedish-plans-to-acquire-nuclear-weapons-19451972.

———. "The Swedish Plans to Acquire Nuclear Weapons, 1945–1968: An Analysis of the Technical Preparations." *Science & Global Security* 18 (2010): 61–86.

Joshi, Yogesh. "How Technology Shaped India's Nuclear Submarine Program." Working paper, 2016.

Kamel, Hussein. "Meeting between Saddam and His Security Council Regarding Iraqi Biological and Nuclear Weapons Program." Conflict Records Research Center. Washington, DC, February 5, 1995.

Kampani, Gaurav. "New Delhi's Long Nuclear Journey: How Secrecy and Institutional Roadblocks Delayed India's Weaponization." *International Security* 38, no. 4 (Spring 2014): 79–114.

Kargil Review Committee. *From Surprise to Reckoning: The Kargil Review Committee Report.* New Delhi: Sage Publications, 2000.

Karnad, Bharat. *Nuclear Weapons and Indian Security: The Realist Foundations of Strategy.* Delhi: Macmillan, 2002.

Kase, Yuri. "The Costs and Benefits of Japan's Nuclearization: An Insight into the *1968/70 Internal Report.*" *Nonproliferation Review* 8, no. 2 (Summer 2001): 55–68.

Kelley, Robert E. "The Iraqi and South African Nuclear Weapons Program: The Importance of Management." *Security Dialogue* 27, no. 1 (1996): 27–38.

Kellher, Catherine McArdle. *Germany and the Politics of Nuclear Weapons.* New York: Columbia University Press, 1975.

Kemp, R. Scott. "The Nonproliferation Emperor Has No Clothes: The Gas Centrifuge, Supply-Side Controls, and the Future of Nuclear Proliferation." *International Security* 38, no. 4 (Spring 2014): 39–78.

Kennedy, Andrew B. "India's Nuclear Odyssey: Implicit Umbrellas, Diplomatic Disappointments, and the Bomb." *International Security* 36, no. 2 (Fall 2011): 120–53.

Khadduri, Imad. *Iraq's Nuclear Mirage: Memoirs and Delusions.* Richmond Hill, Ontario: Springhead Publishers, 2003.

Khan, Feroz Hassan. *Eating Grass: The Making of the Pakistani Bomb.* Stanford: Stanford University Press, 2012.

Koch, Susan J. "Extended Deterrence and the Future of the Nonproliferation Treaty." *Comparative Strategy* 39, no. 3 (April 2020): 239–49.

Kohl, Wilfred L. *French Nuclear Diplomacy.* Princeton: Princeton University Press, 1971.

Krepon, Michael. "Mao on the Bomb." *ArmsControlWonk,* February 9, 2014. https://www.armscontrolwonk.com/archive/404038/mao-on-the-bomb/.

Kroenig, Matthew. *Exporting the Bomb: Technology Transfer and the Spread of Nuclear Weapons.* Ithaca: Cornell University Press, 2010.

Kubo, Takuya. "A Point of View Regarding Japan's Defense Capabilities." Translated by Mayumi Fukushima. World and Japan Database: University of Tokyo Institute of Oriental Culture, February 20, 1971. http://www.ioc.u-tokyo.ac.jp/~worldjpn/documents/texts/JPSC/19710220.O1J.html.

Kuhn, Ulrich, Tristan Volpe, and Bert Thompson. "Tracking the German Nuclear Debate." Carnegie Endowment for International Peace, March 5, 2020. https://carnegieendowment.org/2017/09/07/tracking-german-nuclear-debate-pub-72884.

Küntzel, Matthias. *Bonn & the Bomb: German Politics and the Nuclear Option.* Boulder, CO: Pluto Press, 1995.

Kusunoki, Ayako. "The Sato Cabinet and the Making of Japan's Non-Nuclear Policy." *Journal of American-East Asian Relations* 15, no. 1 (2008): 25–50.

Kux, Dennis. *The United States and Pakistan, 1947–2000: Disenchanted Allies.* Baltimore: Johns Hopkins University Press, 2001.

Landler, Mark. "Trump Orders Pentagon to Consider Reducing U.S. Forces in South Korea." *New York Times,* May 4, 2018, p. A1. https://www.nytimes.com/2018/05/03/world/asia/trump-troops-south-korea.html.

Lee, Byong-Chul. "Don't Be Surprised When South Korea Wants Nuclear Weapons." *Bulletin of the Atomic Scientists,* October 23, 2019. https://thebulletin.org/2019/10/dont-be-surprised-when-south-korea-wants-nuclear-weapons/.

Lee, Gary. "Sweden Admits Nuclear Tests, Says It Will Not Build Bomb." *Washington Post,* April 27, 1985. https://www.washingtonpost.com/archive/politics/1985/04/27/sweden-admits-nuclear-test-says-it-will-not-build-bomb/29ecd3bc-80fe-4786-848c-c995ad6192c5/.

Levite, Ariel E. "Never Say Never Again: Nuclear Reversal Revisited." *International Security* 27, no. 3 (Winter 2002–2003): 59–88.

Levs, Josh. "Who's Killing Iranian Nuclear Scientists?" CNN, January 11, 2012. https://www.cnn.com/2012/01/11/world/meast/iran-who-kills-scientists/index.html.

Levy, Adrian, and Catherine Scott-Clark. *Deception: Pakistan, the United States, and the Secret Trade in Nuclear Weapons*. New York: Walker and Company, 2007.

Lewis, John W., and Xue Litai. *China Builds the Bomb*. Stanford: Stanford University Press, 1988.

———. *China's Strategic Seapower: The Politics of Force Modernization in the Nuclear Age*. Stanford: Stanford University Press, 1994.

Liberman, Peter. "Israel and the South African Bomb." *Nonproliferation Review* 11, no. 2 (Summer 2004): 46–80.

———. "The Rise and Fall of the South African Bomb." *International Security* 26, no. 2 (Fall 2001): 45–86.

"The Likelihood of Further Nuclear Proliferation." National Intelligence Estimate, NIE 4-66, January 20, 1966. http://nsarchive.gwu.edu/nukevault/ebb401/docs/doc%203.pdf.

Long, Austin G., and Joshua R. Shifrinson. "How Long until Midnight? Intelligence-Policy Relations and the United States Response to the Israeli Nuclear Program, 1959–1985." *Journal of Strategic Studies* 42, no. 1 (January 2, 2019): 55–90.

Mackby, Jenifer, and Walter B. Slocombe. "Germany: The Model Case, a Historical Imperative." In *The Nuclear Tipping Point: Why States Reconsider Their Nuclear Choices*, edited by Kurt Campbell, Robert J. Einhorn, and Mitchell Reiss, 175–217. Washington, DC: Brookings Institution Press, 2004.

Makovsky, David. "The Silent Strike: How Israel Bombed a Syrian Nuclear Installation and Kept It Secret." *New Yorker*, September 17, 2012.

Mallea, Rodrigo, Matias Spektor, and Nicholas J. Wheeler, eds. *The Origins of Nuclear Cooperation: A Critical Oral History between Brazil and Argentina*. Washington, DC: Wilson Center, 2015.

"Mattis Says Iran 'Fundamentally' in Compliance with Iran Deal." Reuters, October 3, 2017. https://www.reuters.com/article/us-usa-iran-nuclear/mattis-says-iran-fundamentally-in-compliance-with-nuclear-deal-idUSKCN1C82GK.

Mazzetti, Mark, David E. Sanger, and William J. Broad. "U.S. Examines Whether Saudi Nuclear Program Could Lead to Bomb Effort." *New York Times*, August 5, 2020. https://www.nytimes.com/2020/08/05/us/politics/us-examines-saudi-nuclear-program.html.

McNamee, Terence. "The Afrikaner Bomb: Nuclear Proliferation and Rollback in South Africa." In *Why Do States Want Nuclear Weapons? The Cases of Israel and South Africa*, by Avner Cohen and Terence McNamee, 13–23. Oslo: Norwegian Institute for Defence Studies, 2005.

Mearsheimer, John J. "Back to the Future: Instability in Europe after the Cold War." *International Security* 15, no. 1 (Summer 1990): 5–56.

———. *The Tragedy of Great Power Politics*. New York: W. W. Norton, 2001.

"Meeting between Saddam Hussein and the Revolutionary Council Regarding the Sanctions Placed on Iraq and Tariq Aziz's Trip to the UN Security Council." Conflict Records Research Center. Washington, DC, November 8, 1995. https://conflictrecords.files.wordpress.com/2013/06/sh-shtp-a-000-789.pdf.

Mehta, Rupal N. *Delaying Doomsday: The Politics of Nuclear Reversal*. New York: Oxford University Press, 2020.

Mendl, Wolf. *Deterrence and Persuasion: French Nuclear Armament in the Context of National Policy, 1945–1969*. London: Faber and Faber, 1970.

Meyer, Stephen M. *The Dynamics of Nuclear Proliferation*. Chicago: University of Chicago Press, 1984.

Miller, Nicholas L. "Nuclear Dominoes: A Self-Defeating Prophecy?" *Security Studies* 23, no. 1 (2014): 33–73.

———. "The Secret Success of Nonproliferation Sanctions." *International Organization* 68, no. 4 (Fall 2014): 913–44.

———. *Stopping the Bomb: The Sources and Effectiveness of U.S. Nonproliferation Policy*. Ithaca: Cornell University Press, 2018.

Miller, Nicholas L., and Vipin Narang. "North Korea Defied the Theoretical Odds: What Can We Learn from Its Successful Nuclearization." *Texas National Security Review* 1, no. 2 (March 2018): 59–74.

Mitchell, Derek J. "Taiwan's Hsin Chu Program: Deterrence, Abandonment, and Honor." In *The Nuclear Tipping Point: Why States Reconsider Their Nuclear Choices*, edited by Kurt Campbell, Robert J. Einhorn, and Mitchell B. Reiss, 293–316. Washington, DC: Brookings Institution Press, 2004.

Mochizuki, Mike M. "Japan Tests the Nuclear Taboo." *Nonproliferation Review* 14, no. 2 (July 2007): 303–28.

"Nakasone Proposes Japan Consider Nuclear Weapons." *Japan Times*, September 6, 2006.

Nanto, Dick N., and Mark E. Manyin. "China-North Korea Relations." Congressional Research Service, December 28, 2010. https://fas.org/sgp/crs/row/R41043.pdf.

Narang, Vipin. *Nuclear Strategy in the Modern Era: Regional Powers and International Conflict*. Princeton: Princeton University Press, 2014.

———. "Pride and Prejudice and Prithvis: Strategic Weapons Behavior in South Asia." In *Inside Nuclear South Asia*, edited by Scott D. Sagan. Stanford: Stanford University Press, 2009.

———. "Strategies of Nuclear Proliferation: How States Pursue the Bomb." *International Security* 41, no. 3 (Winter 2016/17): 110–50.

———. "The Use and Abuse of Large-n Methods in Nuclear Security." In "What We Talk about When We Talk about Nuclear Weapons," edited by James McAllister and Diane Labrosse, 91–97. H-Diplo ISSF Forum, No. 2, 2014. http://issforum.org/ISSF/PDF/ISSF-Forum-2.pdf.

———. "What Does It Take to Deter?: Regional Power Nuclear Postures and International Conflict." *Journal of Conflict Resolution* 57, no. 3 (June 2013): 478–508.

Narang, Vipin, and Scott D. Sagan, eds. *The Fragile Balance of Terror: Deterrence in the New Nuclear Age*, Ithaca, NY: Cornell University Press, forthcoming.

Narang, Vipin, and Paul Staniland. "Democratic Accountability and Foreign Security Policy: Theory and Evidence from India." *Security Studies* 27, no. 3 (2018): 410–47.

Nehru, Jawaharlal. *Constituent Assembly of India (Legislative Debates)*. Book I, Vol. 5, April 6, 1948. New Delhi: Lok Sabha Secretariat, 2014. https://eparlib.nic.in/bitstream/123456789/760449/1/CA_Debate_Eng_Vol_01.pdf.

———. *Lok Sabha Debates*. Series 2, Vol. 3, July 24, 1957. New Delhi: Lok Sabha Secretariat, 1957. https://eparlib.nic.in/bitstream/123456789/1489/1/lsd_02_02_24-07-1957.pdf.

Nephew, Richard. "What the Nuclear Deal Means for Moderates in Iranian Politics." *Markaz*. Brookings Institution, February 16, 2016. https://www.brookings.edu/blog/markaz/2016/02/16/what-the-nuclear-deal-means-for-moderates-in-iranian-politics/.

Norman, Laurence, and Michael R. Gordon. "Iran's Stockpile of Enriched Uranium Has Jumped, U.N. Atomic Agency Says." *Wall Street Journal*, March 3, 2020. https://www.wsj.com/articles/irans-stockpile-of-enriched-uranium-has-jumped-u-n-atomic-agency-says-11583243861.

Norris, Robert S., William M. Arkin, and William Burr. "Where They Were." *Bulletin of the Atomic Scientists* 55, no. 6 (December 1999): 26–35.

"Note for [Name Excised] from [Name Excised], 'State/INR Request for Update of Pak SNIE, and Assessment of Argentine Nuclear Program.'" June 4, 1982. In *New Documents Spotlight Reagan-Era Tensions over Pakistani Nuclear Program*, edited by William Burr, Document 11. National Security Archive Electronic Briefing Book, no. 377. 2012. https://www.documentcloud.org/documents/347024-doc-11-6-4-82.html.

Nuclear Threat Initiative Country Profile. "Libya." January 2015. https://www.nti.org/learn/countries/libya/nuclear/.

Nutt, Cullen G. "Proof of the Bomb: The Influence of Previous Failure on Intelligence Judgments of Nuclear Programs." *Security Studies* 28, no. 2 (2019): 321–59.

Obama, Barack. "Statement by the President on the Framework to Prevent Iran from Acquiring a Nuclear Weapon." The White House, Office of the Press Secretary, April 2, 2015. https://obamawhitehouse.archives.gov/the-press-office/2015/04/02/statement-president-framework-prevent-iran-obtaining-nuclear-weapon.

———. "Transcript: President Obama's Full NPR Interview on Iran Nuclear Deal." National Public Radio, April 7, 2015. https://www.npr.org/2015/04/07/397933577/transcript-president-obamas-full-npr-interview-on-iran-nuclear-deal.

Obeidi, Mahdi, and Kurt Pitzer. *The Bomb in My Garden: The Secrets of Saddam's Nuclear Mastermind.* Hoboken, NJ: Wiley and Sons, 2004.

Obergfaell, Kim. "U.S.-Saudi Nuclear Cooperation under Scrutiny." International Institute for Strategic Studies, March 4, 2019. https://www.iiss.org/blogs/analysis/2019/03/us-saudi-nuclear-cooperation.

"The Outlook for Israel." National Intelligence Estimate, No. 35–61, October 5, 1961.

"Pakistan's Nuclear Programme." Ministry of External Affairs, National Archives, New Delhi, August 19, 1981.

Pant, K. C. "Rajya Sabha Extensive Debate on India's Peaceful Nuclear Explosion." August 21, 1974. History and Public Policy Program Digital Archive, Institute for Defence Studies and Analyses (ISDA), Rajya Sabha Q&A Documents, pp. 251–53. http://digitalarchive.wilsoncenter.org/document/119760.

Paul, T. V. *Power versus Prudence: Why Nations Forgo Nuclear Weapons.* Montreal: McGill-Queen's University Press, 2000.

Pauly, Reid B. C. "'Stop or I'll Shoot, Comply and I Won't': Coercive Assurance in International Politics." PhD diss., Massachusetts Institute of Technology, 2019.

Péan, Pierre. *Les Deux Bombes, ou, Comment la guerre du Golfe a commencé le 18 novembre 1975.* Paris: Fayard, 1982.

Peres, Shimon. *Battling for Peace: A Memoir.* Edited by David Landau. New York: Random House, 1995.

Perkovich, George. "Could Anything Be Done to Stop Them? Lessons from Pakistan's Proliferating Past." In *Pakistan's Nuclear Future: Worries Beyond War*, edited by Henry D. Sokolski, 59–84. Carlisle, PA: Strategic Studies Institute, U.S. Army War College, 2008.

———. *India's Nuclear Bomb: The Impact on Global Proliferation.* Berkeley: University of California Press, 1999.

Polakow-Suransky, Sasha. *The Unspoken Alliance: Israel's Secret Relationship with Apartheid South Africa.* New York: Pantheon Books, 2010.

Pollack, Jonathan D. *No Exit: North Korea, Nuclear Weapons and International Security.* New York: Routledge, 2011.

Prawitz, Jan. *From Nuclear Option to Non-Nuclear Promotion: The Sweden Case.* Stockholm: Swedish Institute for International Affairs, 1995.

"President Kennedy, Memorandum of Conversation." December 27, 1962. In *Foreign Relations of the United States, 1961–1963, Volume XVIII, Near East, 1962–1963*, edited by Nina J. Noring, Document 121. Washington, DC: U.S. GPO, 1995. https://history.state.gov/historicaldocuments/frus1961-63v18/d121.

"Presidential Determination No. 88–5 of January 15, 1988." January 5, 1988. History and Public Policy Program Digital Archive, Federal Register, Vol. 83, No. 24. Obtained and contributed by William Burr for NPIHP Research Update No. 24. http://digitalarchive.wilsoncenter.org/document/118596.

"The Proliferation of Missile Delivery Systems for Nuclear Weapons." National Intelligence Estimate, NIE 4–67, January 26, 1967. http://nsarchive.gwu.edu/NSAEBB/NSAEBB155/prolif-14b.pdf.

"Prospects for a Proliferation of Nuclear Weapons over the Next Decade." National Intelligence Estimate, October 21, 1964. NIE 4-2-64. In *Foreign Relations of the United States, 1964–1968, Volume X, National Security Policy*, Document 57. Washington, DC: U.S. GPO, 2001. https://history.state.gov/historicaldocuments/frus1964-68v10/d57.

"Prospects for Further Proliferation of Nuclear Weapons." Atomic Energy Commission, October 2, 1974. https://nsarchive2.gwu.edu//NSAEBB/NSAEBB181/sa08.pdf.

Purkitt, Helen E., and Stephen F. Burgess. *South Africa's Weapons of Mass Destruction*. Bloomington: University of Indiana Press, 2005.

Rabinowitz, Or. *Bargaining on Nuclear Tests: Washington and Its Cold War Deals*. Oxford: Oxford University Press, 2014.

Rabinowitz, Or, and Nicholas L. Miller. "Keeping the Bombs in the Basement: U.S. Nonproliferation Policy toward Israel, South Africa, and Pakistan." *International Security* 40, no. 1 (Summer 2015): 47–86.

Reif, Kingston, Thomas Countryman, and Daryl Kimball. "Iran Takes Another Step Away from Compliance with JCPOA." *Arms Control Association*, September 15, 2019. https://www.armscontrol.org/pressroom/2019-09/iran-takes-another-step-away-compliance-jcpoa-experts-available.

Reiss, Mitchell. *Bridled Ambition: Why Countries Constrain Their Nuclear Capabilities*. Washington, DC: Woodrow Wilson Press, 1995.

Reiter, Dan. "Preventive Attacks against Nuclear Programs and the 'Success' at Osiraq." *Nonproliferation Review* 12, no. 2 (July 2005): 355–71.

"Report by the Committee on Nuclear Proliferation." January 21, 1965. In *Foreign Relations of the United States, 1964–1968, Volume XI, Arms Control and Disarmament*, edited by Evans Gerakas, David S. Patterson, and Carolyn B. Yee, Document 64. Washington, DC: U.S. GPO, 1997. https://history.state.gov/historicaldocuments/frus1964-68v11/d64.

"Report, Director General of the International Atomic Energy Agency, 'The Agency's Verification Activities in South Africa.'" September 23, 1993. History and Public Policy Program Digital Archive, IAEA Archives. Contributed by Sasha Polakow-Suransky. http://digitalarchive.wilsoncenter.org/document/116790.

"The Report of the Iraq Inquiry: Executive Summary." Report of the Privy Counsellors. London: Crown Copyright, 2016. https://capstone.ndu.edu/Portals/83/Documents/Capstone/the-report-of-the-iraq-inquiry_executive-summary.pdf?ver=2018-11-16-092328-023.

Rhodes, Richard. *The Making of the Atomic Bomb*. New York: Simon and Schuster, 1986.

Richelson, Jeffrey T. *Spying on the Bomb: American Nuclear Intelligence from Nazi Germany to North Korea*. New York: W. W. Norton, 2007.

Rose, Gideon. "Neoclassical Realism and Theories of Foreign Policy." *World Politics* 51, no. 1 (October 1998): 144–72.

Ross, Dennis. *Doomed to Succeed: The U.S.-Israel Relationship from Truman to Obama*. New York: Farrar, Straus and Giroux, 2015.

Rostow, Walt, and Rainer Barzel. "Memorandum of Conversation, February 23, 1968." In *Foreign Relations of the United States, 1964–1968, Volume XV, Germany and Berlin*, edited by James E. Miller, Document 248. Washington, DC: U.S. GPO, 1999. https://history.state.gov/historicaldocuments/frus1964-68v15/d248.

Rublee, Maria Rost. *Nonproliferation Norms: Why States Choose Nuclear Restraint*. Athens: University of Georgia Press, 2009.

Rusk, Dean, and Tom Rusk. *As I Saw It*. New York: Penguin Books, 1991.

Sagan, Scott D. "The Causes of Nuclear Weapons Proliferation." *Annual Review of Political Science* 14, no. 1 (June 2011): 225–44.

———. *Moving Targets: Nuclear Strategy and National Security*. Princeton: Princeton University Press, 1989.

———. "Nuclear Latency and Nuclear Proliferation." In *Forecasting Nuclear Proliferation in the 21st Century: The Role of Theory, Volume 1,* edited by William C. Potter and Gaukhar Mukhatzhanova. Stanford: Stanford University Press, 2010.

———. "Why Do States Build Nuclear Weapons? Three Models in Search of the Bomb." *International Security* 21, no. 3 (Winter 1996–97): 54–86.

Samore, Gary, ed. *Iran's Strategic Weapons Systems: A Net Assessment.* London: IISS, 2005.

Samuels, Richard J. *Securing Japan: Tokyo's Grand Strategy and the Future of East Asia.* Ithaca: Cornell University Press, 2007.

Samuels, Richard J., and James L. Schoff. "Japan's Nuclear Hedge: Beyond 'Allergy' and Breakout." In *Strategic Asia, 2013–2014: Asia in the Second Nuclear Age,* edited by Ashley J. Tellis, Abraham M. Denmark, and Travis Tanner, 233–66. Seattle: National Bureau of Asian Research, 2013.

Sanger, David E. "Obama Order Sped up Wave of Cyberattacks on Iran." *New York Times,* June 1, 2012. https://www.nytimes.com/2012/06/01/world/middleeast/obama-ordered-wave-of-cyberattacks-against-iran.html.

———. *The Perfect Weapon: War, Sabotage, and Fear in the Cyber Age.* New York: Crown, 2018.

Sanger, David E., and William J. Broad. "U.S. Revives Secret Program to Sabotage Iranian Missiles and Rockets." *New York Times,* February 13, 2019. https://www.nytimes.com/2019/02/13/us/politics/iran-missile-launch-failures.html.

———. "U.S. Sees an Opportunity to Press Iran on Nuclear Fuel." *New York Times,* January 2, 2010. https://www.nytimes.com/2010/01/03/world/middleeast/03iran.html.

———. "U.S. Strategy to Hobble North Korea Was Hidden in Plain Sight." *New York Times,* March 4, 2017. https://www.nytimes.com/2017/03/04/world/asia/left-of-launch-missile-defense.html.

"Saudi Crown Prince: If Iran Develops Nuclear Bomb, So Will We." *60 Minutes.* CBS News, March 15, 2018. https://www.cbsnews.com/news/saudi-crown-prince-mohammed-bin-salman-iran-nuclear-bomb-saudi-arabia/.

Saunders, Elizabeth N. "The Domestic Politics of Nuclear Choices—A Review Essay." *International Security* 44, no. 2 (Fall 2019): 146–84.

Scheinman, Lawrence. *Atomic Energy Policy in France under the Fourth Republic.* Princeton: Princeton University Press, 1965.

Schwarz, Hans-Peter. *Konrad Adenauer: A German Politician and Statesman in a Period of War, Revolution and Reconstruction.* Vol. 2. Translated by Geoffrey Penny. Providence, RI: Berghahn Books, 1997.

Schweller, Randall L. *Deadly Imbalances: Tripolarity and Hitler's Strategy of World Conquest.* New York: Columbia University Press, 1998.

Selbi, Dhafir, Zuhair al-Chalabi, and Imad Khadduri. *Unrevealed Milestones in the Iraqi National Nuclear Program, 1981–1991.* Edited by Imad Khadduri. CreateSpace Independent Publishing Platform, 2011.

"Shades of Red: China's Debate over North Korea." Asia Report No. 179. International Crisis Group, November 2, 2009. https://d2071andvip0wj.cloudfront.net/179-shades-of-red-china-s-debate-over-north-korea.pdf.

Shen, Zhihua, and Yafeng Xia. "Between Aid and Restriction: The Soviet Union's Changing Policies on China's Nuclear Weapons Program, 1954–1960." *Asian Perspective* 36, no. 1 (2012): 95–122.

Shichor, Yitzhak. "The Importance of Being Ernst: Ernst David Bergmann and Israel's Role in Taiwan's Defense." *Asia Paper 2* (2016).

"Shinzo Abe Quoted In." *Asahi Shimbun,* June 8, 2002. Translated by Mayumi Fukushima, August 28, 2015 edition.

Shulong, Chu, and Lin Xinzhu. "The Six Party Talks: A Chinese Perspective." *Asian Perspective* 32, no. 4 (2008): 29–43.

Shuster, Mike. "Inside the United States' Secret Sabotage of Iran." National Public Radio (NPR), May 9, 2011. https://www.npr.org/2011/05/09/135854490/inside-the-united-states-secret-sabotage-of-iran.

Sieg, Linda. "Japan Atomic Power Defenders: Keep Ability to Build Nuclear Weapons." Reuters, February 13, 2012. http://www.reuters.com/article/2012/02/13/japan-nuclear-arms-idUSL4E8DA2ZK20120213.

Singh, Sonali, and Christopher R. Way. "The Correlates of Nuclear Proliferation: A Quantitative Test." *Journal of Conflict Resolution* 47, no. 6 (2004): 859–85.

Sitapati, Vinay. *Half Lion: How P. V. Narasimha Rao Transformed India*. Delhi: Penguin India, 2016.

Smith, Hedrick. "A Bomb Ticks in Pakistan." *New York Times*, March 6, 1988. http://www.nytimes.com/1988/03/06/magazine/a-bomb-ticks-in-pakistan.html.

Sobek, David, Dennis M. Foster, and Samuel B. Robison. "Conventional Wisdom? The Effect of Nuclear Proliferation on Armed Conflict, 1945–2001." *International Studies Quarterly* 56, no. 1 (March 2012): 149–62.

Solingen, Etel. *Nuclear Logics: Contrasting Paths in East Asia and the Middle East*. Princeton: Princeton University Press, 2007.

"Speech by South African President F. W. De Klerk to a Joint Session of Parliament on Accession to the Non-Proliferation Treaty." March 24, 1993. History and Public Policy Program Digital Archive, Archives.un.org. Contributed by Jo-Ansie van Wyk. Obtained and contributed by Jo-Ansie van Wyk. http://digitalarchive.wilsoncenter.org/document/116789.

Stahel, David. *Operation Barbarossa and Germany's Defeat in the East*. Cambridge: Cambridge University Press, 2009.

Steyn, Hannes, Richardt van der Walt, and Jan van Loggerenberg. *Nuclear Armament and Disarmament: South Africa's Nuclear Experience*. Lincoln, NE: iUniverse, 2007.

Strobel, Warren P., Michael R. Gordon, and Felicia Schwartz. "Saudi Arabia, with China's Help, Expands Its Nuclear Program." *Wall Street Journal*, August 4, 2020. https://www.wsj.com/articles/saudi-arabia-with-chinas-help-expands-its-nuclear-program-11596575671.

———. "South Africa's Nuclear Weapons Program: From Deterrence to Dismantlement." *Arms Control Today* 25, no. 10 (December 1995): 3–8.

———. "South Africa's Nuclear Weapons Programme." In *Weapons of Mass Destruction: Costs versus Benefits*, edited by Kathleen C. Bailey, 63–81. Delhi: Manohar, 1994.

Stüssi-Lauterberg, Jürg. "Historical Outline on the Question of Swiss Nuclear Armament." Report prepared for the Swiss Federal Council. Federal Administration: Bern. Translated by United States Department of State. December 31, 1995. http://www.alexandria.admin.ch/bv001147186.pdf.

Subrahmanyam, K. "India's Nuclear Policy 1964–98 (A Personal Recollection)." In *Nuclear India*, edited by Jasjit Singh, 26–53. Delhi: Knowledge World, 1998.

Tabatabai, Ariane. "Negotiating the 'Iran Talks' in Tehran: The Iranian Drivers That Shaped the Joint Comprehensive Plan of Action." *Nonproliferation Review* 24, no. 3–4 (2017): 225–42.

———. "Nuclear Decisionmaking in Iran: Implications for U.S. Nonproliferation Efforts." Columbia University: Center on Global Energy Policy, August 2020. https://www.energypolicy.columbia.edu/sites/default/files/file-uploads/IranNuclear_CGEP-Report_080520.pdf.

Tertrais, Bruno. "'Destruction Assurée': The Origins and Development of French Nuclear Strategy, 1945–1981." In *Getting MAD: Nuclear Mutual Assured Destruction, Its Origins and Practice*, edited by Henry Sokolski, 51–122. Carlisle, PA: U.S. Army War College, 2004.

Tobey, William. "Cooperation in the Libya WMD Disarmament Case." *Studies in Intelligence* 61, no. 4 (December 2017): 31–42. https://www.cia.gov/static/c134fac60c8d3634a28629e6082d19eb/Cooperation-in-Libya-WMD.pdf.

Trachtenberg, Marc. *A Constructed Peace: The Making of the European Settlement, 1945–1963*. Princeton: Princeton University Press, 1999.

Truman, Harry S. *Memoirs by Harry Truman, Volume 1: Year of Decisions.* New York: Doubleday, 1955.

Trump, Donald. "Remarks by President Trump on the Joint Comprehensive Plan of Action." White House, Office of the Press Secretary, May 8, 2018. https://trumpwhitehouse.archives.gov/briefings-statements/remarks-president-trump-joint-comprehensive-plan-action/.

Villiers, J. W. de, Roger Jardine, and Mitchell Reiss. "Why South Africa Gave Up the Bomb." *Foreign Affairs* 72, no. 5 (November/December 1993): 98–109.

Volpe, Tristan A. "Atomic Leverage: Compellence with Nuclear Latency." *Security Studies* 26, no. 3 (July 2017): 517–44.

———. "Bargaining in the Sweet Spot: Coercive Diplomacy with Latency." Working paper, n.d.

Volpe, Tristan, and Ulrich Kühn. "Uninsured Allies: When Do States Divest from Nuclear Latency?" Working paper, n.d.

Walker, Mark. *Nazi Science: Myth, Truth, and the German Atomic Bomb.* New York: Springer Books, 1995.

"Warning Report—Nuclear Proliferation." Memorandum from Special Assistant for Nuclear Proliferation Intelligence to Director of Central Intelligence, April 30, 1980. http://nsarchive.gwu.edu/nukevault/ebb333/doc47.PDF.

Way, Christopher. "Nuclear Proliferation Dates." Working paper, June 12, 2012. http://falcon.arts.cornell.edu/crw12/documents/Nuclear%20Proliferation%20Dates.pdf.

Weiss, Leonard. "Flash from the Past: Why an Apparent Israeli Nuclear Test in 1979 Matters Today." *Bulletin of the Atomic Scientists*, September 8, 2015. http://thebulletin.org/flash-past-why-apparent-israeli-nuclear-test-1979-matters-today8734.

Wielligh, Nic von, and Lydia von Wielligh-Steyn. *The Bomb: South Africa's Nuclear Weapons Programme.* Pretoria: Litera Publications, 2015.

Wit, Joel S., Daniel B. Poneman, and Robert L. Gallucci. *Going Critical: The First North Korean Nuclear Crisis.* Washington, DC: Brookings Institution Press, 2004.

Wohlforth, William Curti. *The Elusive Balance: Power and Perceptions during the Cold War.* Ithaca: Cornell University Press, 1993.

Woods, Kevin M., David D. Palkki, and Mark E. Stout. *The Saddam Tapes: The Inner Workings of a Tyrant's Regime, 1978–2001.* Cambridge: Cambridge University Press, 2011.

Yanqiong, Liu, and Liu Jifeng. "Analysis of Soviet Technology Transfer in the Development of China's Nuclear Weapons." *Comparative Technology Transfer and Society* 7, no. 1 (April 2009): 66–112.

Zegart, Amy. "Understanding Nuclear Threats: The Past and Future of American Intelligence." In *The Fragile Balance of Terror: Deterrence in the New Nuclear Age*, edited by Vipin Narang and Scott D. Sagan. Draft manuscript.

Zetter, Kim. *Countdown to Zero: Stuxnet and the Launch of the World's First Digital Weapon.* New York: Crown, 2014.

Zhang, Hui. "The History of Fissile-Material Production in China." *Nonproliferation Review* 25, no. 5–6 (2018): 477–99.

Zimmerman, Peter D. "Iraq's Nuclear Achievements: Components, Sources, and Stature." Congressional Research Service Report, February 18, 1993.

INDEX

Page numbers in *italics* indicate figures and tables.

A NOTE ON THE TYPE

This book has been composed in Adobe Text and Gotham. Adobe Text, designed by Robert Slimbach for Adobe, bridges the gap between fifteenth- and sixteenth-century calligraphic and eighteenth-century Modern styles. Gotham, inspired by New York street signs, was designed by Tobias Frere-Jones for Hoefler & Co.

Printed in the USA
CPSIA information can be obtained
at www.ICGtesting.com
JSHW021803160724
66513JS00005B/53

9 780691 172620